The ARRL
General Class License Manual For Ham Radio

Cover photo:

Rhonda Leonard, KC1KYN, and Alex Norstrom, KC1RMO operating W1HQ in Newington, CT.

This book may be used for General class license exams given beginning July 1, 2023 and ending June 30, 2027. The ARRL website (**arrl.org**) will have news about any rules changes affecting the General class license or any of the material in this book.

We strive to produce books without errors. Sometimes mistakes do occur, however. When we become aware of problems in our books (other than obvious typographical errors), we post corrections on the ARRL website. If you think you have found an error, please check **arrl.org/general-class-license-manual** for corrections. If you don't find a correction there, please let us know by sending an e-mail to **pubsfdbk@arrl.org**.

The ARRL General Class License Manual ON THE WEB

arrl.org/general-class-license-manual

Visit *The ARRL General Class License Manual* home on the web for additional resources.

Contents

About ARRL

We're the American Radio Relay League, Inc. — better known as ARRL. We're the largest membership association for the amateur radio hobby and service in the US. For over 100 years, we have been the primary source of information about amateur radio, offering a variety of benefits and services to our members, as well as the larger amateur radio community. We publish books on amateur radio, as well as four magazines covering a variety of radio communication interests. In addition, we provide technical advice and assistance to amateur radio enthusiasts, support several education programs, and sponsor a variety of operating events.

One of the primary benefits we offer to the ham radio community is in representing the interests of amateur radio operators before federal regulatory bodies advocating for meaningful access to the radio spectrum. ARRL also serves as the international secretariat of the International Amateur Radio Union, which performs a similar role internationally, advocating for amateur radio interests before the International Telecommunication Union and the World Radiocommunication Conference.

Today, we proudly serve nearly 150,000 members, both in the US and internationally, through our national headquarters and flagship amateur radio station, W1AW, in Newington, Connecticut. Every year we welcome thousands of new licensees to our membership, and we hope you will join us. Let us be a part of your amateur radio journey. Visit www.arrl.org/join for more information.

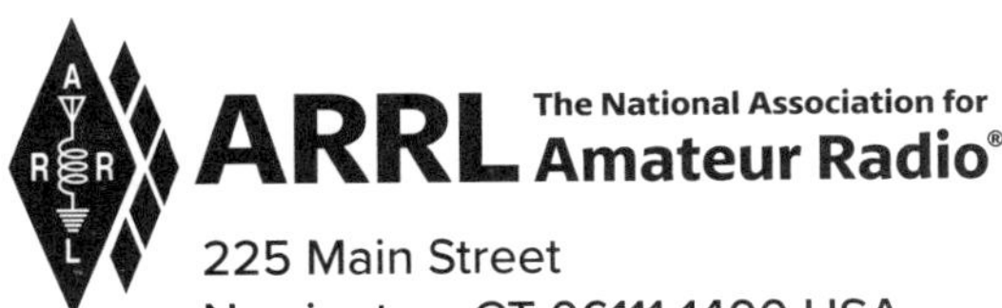

225 Main Street
Newington, CT 06111-1400 USA
Tel: 860-594-0200
FAX: 860-594-0259
Email: membership@arrl.org

arrl.org

Get more from your General Class License with ARRL Membership

Membership in ARRL offers unique opportunities to advance and share your knowledge of amateur radio. For over 100 years, advancing the art, science, and enjoyment of amateur radio has been our mission. Your membership helps to ensure that new generations of hams continue to reap the benefits of the amateur radio community.

Here are just a few of the benefits you will receive with your annual membership. For a complete list visit, arrl.org/membership.

KNOWLEDGE

ARRL offers you a wealth of knowledge to advance your skills with lifelong learning courses, local clubs where you can meet and share ideas, and publications to help you keep up with the latest information from the world of ham radio.

ADVOCACY

ARRL is a strong national voice for preserving and protecting access to Amateur Radio Service frequencies.

SERVICES

From free FCC license renewals, to our Technical Information Service that answers calls and emails about your operating and technical concerns, ARRL offers a range of member services.

RESOURCES

Digital resources including email forwarding, product review archives, e-newsletters, and more.

PUBLICATIONS

Members receive digital access to all four ARRL monthly and bimonthly publications – *QST*, the membership journal of ARRL; *On the Air*, an introduction to the world of amateur radio; *QEX*, which covers topics related to amateur radio and radio communications experimentation, and *National Contest Journal* (*NCJ*), covering radio contesting.

Two Easy Ways to Join

CALL
Member Services toll free at 1-888-277-5289

ONLINE
Go to our secure website at arrl.org/join

How to Use This Book

In each section of this book, the exam questions and correct answer are included for easy reference. The material most directly answering the question is followed by the question's ID in bold text, such as **[G1A01]**. These are the identifying numbers for each question in the exam's question pool. The question pool in chapter 10 also includes a page reference for each question.

Self Study and Classroom Tips

For self-study students, the book's material is designed to be studied in order from beginning to end. Read the material and then test your understanding by answering the questions, flash-card style, within each section. (To quiz yourself, cover up the answers with one hand.) If you find you are having trouble with a question, locate the question references in the text for explanatory information.

If you are taking a licensing class, the instructors will guide you through the material. Help your instructors by letting them know where you need more assistance. They want you to learn as thoroughly and quickly as possible, so don't hold back your questions. Similarly, if you find their explanations clear or helpful, tell them, so they can use the same explanation in their next class.

The ARRL web page **arrl.org/new-ham-resources**, features an extensive list of materials, videos, and links to help you navigate your amateur radio interests and study for the exam. Further, our new ham desk is available to answer specific questions via email at **newham@arrl.org**. For a focused discussion of each exam question, pick up a copy of *ARRL's General Q&A*. Every question is included along with with the correct answer and a short explanation.

When to Expect New Books

A Question Pool Committee (QPC) consisting of representatives from the various Volunteer Examiner Coordinators (VECs) prepares the license question pools. The QPC establishes a schedule for revising and implementing new Question Pools. The current Question Pool revision schedule is as follows:

Question Pool	*Current Study Guides*	*Valid Through*
Technician (Element 2)	*The ARRL Ham Radio License Manual, 5th Edition* *ARRL's Tech Q&A, 8th Edition*	June 30, 2026
General (Element 3)	*The ARRL General Class License Manual, 10th edition* *ARRL's General Q&A, 7th Edition*	June 30, 2027
Amateur Extra (Element 4)	*The ARRL Extra Class License Manual, 11th Edition* *ARRL's Extra Q&A, 4th Edition*	June 30, 2028

As new question pools are released, ARRL will produce new study materials before their effective dates. As the new Question Pool schedules are confirmed, the information will be published on the ARRL website at **arrl.org**.

Online Review and Practice Exams

Use this book with the ARRL Exam Review for Ham Radio to review material you are learning chapter-by-chapter. Take randomly generated practice exams using questions from the actual examination question pool. You won't have any surprises on exam day! Go to **arrl.org/examreview**.

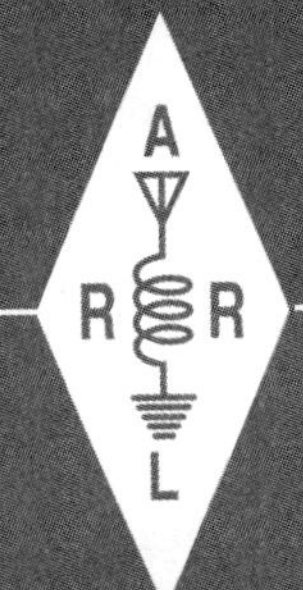

Chapter 1

Introduction

In this chapter, you'll learn about:
- **Expanded privileges enjoyed by Generals**
- **Reasons to upgrade from Technician**
- **Requirements and study materials for the General exam**
- **How to prepare for your exam**
- **How to find an exam session**
- **Where to find more resources**

Welcome to *The ARRL General Class License Manual*! Earning your General class license opens up the full amateur radio experience — the excitement and challenge of traditional shortwave operation along with the VHF+ and limited HF privileges enjoyed by Technician class licensees. You'll gain access to the broadest and most capable set of communication privileges available to private citizens. Only Amateur Extra licensees have more.

This study guide will not only teach you the answers to the General class exam questions, but will also provide explanations and supporting information. That way, you'll find it easier to learn the basic principles involved. That knowledge helps you remember what you've learned. The book is full of useful facts and figures, so you'll want to keep it handy after you pass the test and are using your new privileges.

1.1 The General Class License and Amateur Radio

Most of this book's readers will have already earned their Technician class license. Some may have been a ham for quite a while and others may be new to the hobby. In either case, you're to be commended for making the effort to upgrade. We'll try to make it easy to pass your exam by teaching you the fundamentals and rationale behind each question and answer.

REASONS TO UPGRADE

If you're browsing through this book, trying to decide whether to upgrade, here are a few good reasons:

• *More frequencies.* The General class licensee has access to lot more space in which to enjoy amateur radio! See **Figure 3.4** in chapter 3 for details of all of the frequencies available to General licensees.

• *More communications options.* Those new frequencies give you many more ways to make contacts on new modes and with new groups of hams. Your new skills are also valuable to your club or public service team.

Rusty Epps, W6OAT, mentors Rodna Presley, KJ6GVQ, at the Palo Alto Amateur Radio Association, W6ARA, Field Day operation. ARRL Field Day is the largest event in amateur radio as thousands of North American hams practice the skill of operating from portable stations. [James W. Brown, K9YC, photo]

• *New technical opportunities*. With your new privileges come new ways of assembling and operating a station. The effects of the ionosphere and solar conditions will become second nature to you. Your improved technical understanding of how radio works will make you a more knowledgeable and skilled operator.

• *More fun*. Take part in ragchewing (conversational contacts) with new acquaintances worldwide. Join the chase of DXing (searching for distant stations) and contesting or *radiosport* (on-the-air competitions) which attract more hams every year. Explore popular digital modes such as FT8.

Not only does upgrading grant you more privileges, but your experiences will be much broader. You'll enjoy the hobby in ways that give you a whole new view of ham radio. The extra privileges are well worth your effort!

GENERAL CLASS OVERVIEW

There are three classes of license being granted today: Technician, General, and Amateur Extra. Each grants the licensee more and more privileges, meaning access to frequencies and modes. **Table 1.1** shows the elements for each of the amateur licenses as of early 2019.

As shown in **Table 1.2**, to qualify for a General class license, you must have passed Elements 2 (Technician) and 3 (General). If you hold a Technician license, you are credited with Element 2, so you don't have to take it again. If you currently hold a Technician license issued before March 21, 1987, you can upgrade to General simply by going to a test session with proof of being licensed before that date.

Anne, KD9LRB, enjoys getting on the HF bands to make contacts that count for her Worked All States (WAS) award. [Anne Frank, KD9LRB, photo]

Table 1.1
Amateur License Class Examinations

License Class	Element Required	Number of Questions
Technician	2 (Written)	35 (passing is 26 correct)
General	3 (Written)	35 (passing is 26 correct)
Amateur Extra	4 (Written)	50 (passing is 38 correct)

Table 1.2
Exam Elements Needed to Qualify for a General Class License

Current License*	Exam Requirements	Study Materials
None or Novice	Technician (Element 2)	*The ARRL Ham Radio License Manual* and/or *ARRL's Tech Q&A*
	General (Element 3)	The *ARRL General Class License Manual* and/or *ARRL's General Q&A*
Technician (issued on or after March 21, 1987)**	General (Element 3)	The *ARRL General Class License Manual* and/or *ARRL's General Q&A*

*Individuals who were previously licensed as a General, Advanced, or Extra class may receive credit for those exam elements by presenting documentation of having been licensed and then passing Element 2 (Technician).

**Individuals who qualified for the Technician license before March 21, 1987, will be able to upgrade to General class by providing documentary proof to a Volunteer Examiner Coordinator, paying an application fee and completing NCVEC Quick Form 605. No additional exam is required.

Mobile operation provides an opportunity for combining travel adventures with some ham radio fun. Gene Chapline, K5YFL, participates in the FJ Summit annual backcountry off-road event, shown here on a road through Corkscrew Gulch in the San Juan Mountains. [Josie Chapline, K5JTC, photo]

If you were previously licensed as a General, Advanced, or Extra but your license expired and you're past the grace period for renewal, you can still receive credits for those elements you passed before. Present documentation of your previous license (a copy of the license or a *Callbook* copy, for example) and pass the Element 2 exam (Technician) to receive the necessary credits. Welcome back!

The 35 question multiple-choice test for Element 3 is more comprehensive than the Element 2 Technician exam because you'll be granted wider privileges. As we mentioned before, the General class licensee gains access to nearly all amateur frequencies. There are no bands on which a General class ham can't transmit! As a more experienced ham, your wider knowledge will allow you to experiment with, modify, and build equipment and antennas to improve your communications abilities.

MORSE CODE

Although you no longer need to learn Morse code for any license exam, Morse code, or "CW," has been part of the rich amateur tradition for 100 years, and many hams still use it extensively. If

Morse code operating is alive and well on the amateur bands. Combining skill and efficiency, Morse or "CW" is a favorite mode for many hams. The WB9Z multioperator team (L-R) of Jerry, KE9I; Don, K9NR; Val, NV9L; Mike, K9XZ; and Carl, K9CS, enjoys entering the ARRL 160 Meter Contest, an all-Morse event. [Jerry Rosalius, WB9Z, photo]

you are interested in learning Morse code, ARRL has a complete set of resources listed on its web page at **arrl.org/learning-morse-code**.

Computer software and on-the-air *code practice* sessions are available for personal training and practice. Organizations such as CWops (**cwops.org**) and FISTS (**fists.org**) — an operator's style of sending is referred to as his or her "fist" — help hams learn Morse code.

1.2 How to Use this Book

To earn a General class amateur radio license, you must pass (or receive credit for) FCC Elements 2 (Technician class) and 3 (General class). This book is designed to help you prepare for and pass the Element 3 written exam. If you do not already have a Technician license, you will need some additional study materials for the Element 2 (Technician) exam.

The Element 3 exam consists of 35 questions about amateur radio rules, theory and practice, as well as some basic electronics. A passing grade is 74%, so you must answer 26 of the 35 questions correctly.

The General Class License Manual begins with chapters on the operating practices you'll encounter on the HF bands and the applicable rules and regulations. The following chapters delve into radio technology — Circuits and Components, Radio Signals and Equipment, Digital Modes, Antennas and Feed Lines, and Propagation. Radio and electrical safety is covered in its own chapter. It is followed by the Question Pool, which includes the complete set of exam questions and answers.

Each section may begin with a short review of related material from the Technician exam and has practical examples and information you can use for reference later. The set of exam questions covered in that section, along with the correct answer, is listed so that you can immediately review what you learned. After you've read the section, turn to the Question Pool and confirm that you can answer those questions before moving on. If you have trouble answering the questions, you can drill yourself using the Question Pool or the questions and answers at the beginning of each section. And if you're having trouble understanding why an answer is what it is, you can make sure you understand the answer's rationale by finding the bold question references (**[G1A01]**, etc.) in each section.

ARRL also maintains a web page for General class students at **arrl.org/general-class-license-manual**. Organized in the same manner as this text, you can go to the web page and find helpful supplements and clarifications to the material in the book. The online references listed there put you one click away from related and useful information.

If you are taking a licensing class, help your instructors by letting them know about areas in which you need help. They want you to learn as thoroughly and quickly as possible, so don't hold back with your questions. Similarly, if you find the material particularly clear or helpful, tell them that, too, so it can be used in the next class!

WHAT WE ASSUME ABOUT YOU

You don't have to be a technical guru or an expert operator to upgrade to General class! As you progress through the material, you'll build on the basic science of radio and electricity that you mastered for the Technician exam. No advanced mathematics is introduced, and for help with math, an online tutorial information is available at **arrl.org/general-class-license-manual**. As with the Technician license, mastering rules and regulations will require learning some new words and remembering a few numbers. You should have a basic calculator, which you'll also be allowed to use during the license exam.

Advanced Students

If you have some background in radio, perhaps as an electronics technician or trained operator, you may be able to short-circuit some of the sections. Review the list of exam questions and answers in the text before each group of topics. Turn to the Question Pool to view the distractors and if you are confident you understand the "why" behind the answers without looking at the text, move to the next topic group. It's common for technically minded students to focus on the rules and regulations, while students with an operating background tend to need the technical material more. Whichever description fits you, be sure that you can answer the questions because any question could be on the test!

Self-Study or Classroom Students

The ARRL General Class License Manual can be used either by an individual student studying on his or her own, or as part of a licensing class taught by an instructor. If you're part of a class, the instructor will guide you through the book, section by section. The solo student can move at any pace and in any convenient order. You'll find that studying with a friend makes learning the material more fun as you help each other over the rough spots.

Don't hesitate to ask for help! Your instructor can provide information on anything you find difficult. Classroom students may find asking their fellow students to be helpful. If you're studying on your own, there are resources for you, too! If you can't find the answer in the book or at the website, email your question to ARRL's New Ham Desk, **newham@arrl.org**. ARRL's experts will answer directly or connect you with another ham who can answer your questions.

USING THE QUESTION POOL

As you complete each topic, be sure to review each of the exam questions highlighted in the text. This will tell you which areas need a little more study time. When you understand the answer to each of the questions, move on. Resist the temptation to just memorize the answers. Doing so leaves you without the real understanding that will make your new General class privileges enjoyable and useful. *The General Class License Manual* covers every one of the exam

Rita Haberman, NH6RH, operated from Nairobi, Kenya (5Z4) with Peter Vekinis, KH6VP, on a vacation-style all-solar QRP (low-power) expedition. They used a simple wire antenna and a 20 W solar panel to power the station. [Peter Vekinis, KH6VP, photo]

The 2018 World Radiosport Team Championships in Wittenberg, Germany featured several youth teams. The teams included (left to right) Y83Z: Bryant KG5HVO, and Matthias, CE2LR; Y82D: Philipp, DK6SP, and Tomas, HA8RT; and Y87Z: Leonid, UT5GW, and Alexandru, YO8TTT. [Nodir Tursun-Zade, EY8MM, ey8mm.com, photo]

questions, so you can be sure you're ready at exam time.

When using the Question Pool, cover or fold over the answers at the edge of the page to be sure you really do understand the question. Each question also includes a cross-reference back to the section of the book that covers that topic. If you don't completely understand the question or answer, please go back and review that section. ARRL's condensed study guide, *ARRL's General Q&A*, also provides short explanations for each exam question.

ONLINE PRACTICE EXAMS

When you feel like you're nearly ready for the actual exam, see if you are prepared by using ARRL's online General class practice exams. This web-based service uses the question pool to construct an exam with the same number and variety of questions that you'll encounter on exam day. You can practice taking the test over and over again in complete privacy.

These exams are quite realistic and you get quick feedback about the questions you missed. When you find yourself passing the online exams by a comfortable margin, you'll be ready for the real thing!

To find out more about ARRL's online practice exams, visit the *ARRL Exam Review for Ham Radio* web page (**arrl.org/examreview**). If you choose to use third-party software or websites to practice for the exam, be sure that the questions are from the correct question pool. This book is intended for the question pool that is in effect from July 1, 2023 through June 30, 2027.

FOR INSTRUCTORS

ARRL has created supporting material for instructors such as graphics files and handouts. Check **arrl.org/resources-for-license-instruction** for support materials.

CONVENTIONS AND RESOURCES

Throughout your studies, keep a sharp eye out for words in *italics*. These words are important, so be sure you understand them. Another thing to look for are the addresses or URLs for web resources in **bold**, such as **arrl.org/general-class-license-manual**. By browsing these web pages while you're studying, you will accelerate and broaden your understanding.

Throughout the book, there are sidebars and "For More Information" sections that extend and support the text material. These may tell an interesting story or supplement the explanations for a particular exam topic.

1.3 The Upgrade Trail

As you begin your studies remember that you've already overcome the biggest hurdle of all — taking and passing your first license exam! The questions may be more challenging for the General class exam, but you already know all about the testing procedure and the basics of ham radio. You can approach the process of upgrading with confidence!

FOCUS ON HF AND ADVANCED MODES

The General class exam mostly deals with the new types of operating you'll encounter on the HF bands. You'll also be expected to understand more about the modes you're already familiar with from operating as a Technician. We'll cover more advanced modes and signals, too. The goal is to help you "fill in the blanks" in your ham radio knowledge. Here are some examples of topics that you'll be studying:

- Operating effectively on HF
- Digital modes such as FT8, PSK31, PACTOR, and VARA
- Solar effects on HF propagation
- Test instruments such as the oscilloscope
- Practical electronic circuits
- Common antennas used on HF

Not every ham uses every mode and frequency, of course. Learning about this range of ideas helps hams make better choices while operating. You will become aware of just how wide and deep ham radio really is. Better yet, the introduction of these new ideas may just get you interested in giving them a try!

TESTING PROCESS

When you're ready, you'll need to find a test session. If you're in a licensing class, the

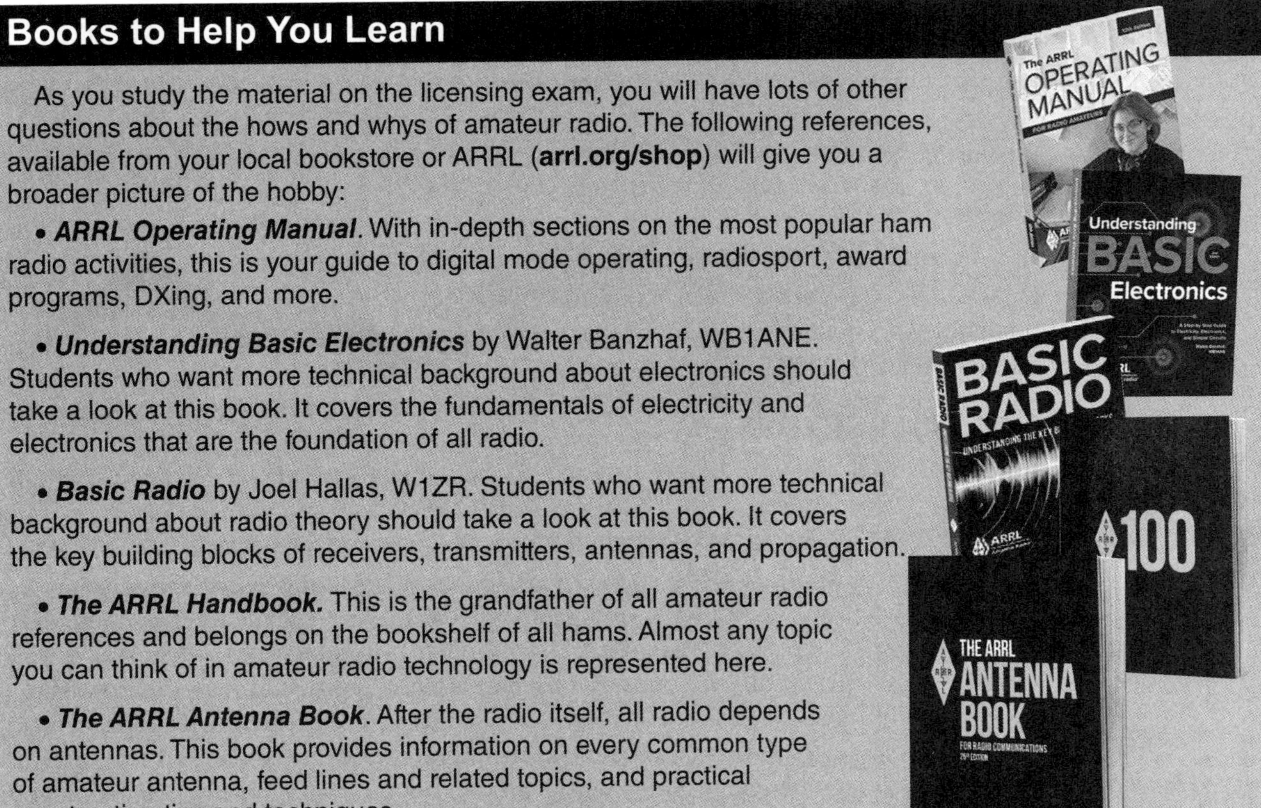

Books to Help You Learn

As you study the material on the licensing exam, you will have lots of other questions about the hows and whys of amateur radio. The following references, available from your local bookstore or ARRL (**arrl.org/shop**) will give you a broader picture of the hobby:

- *ARRL Operating Manual.* With in-depth sections on the most popular ham radio activities, this is your guide to digital mode operating, radiosport, award programs, DXing, and more.

- *Understanding Basic Electronics* by Walter Banzhaf, WB1ANE. Students who want more technical background about electronics should take a look at this book. It covers the fundamentals of electricity and electronics that are the foundation of all radio.

- *Basic Radio* by Joel Hallas, W1ZR. Students who want more technical background about radio theory should take a look at this book. It covers the key building blocks of receivers, transmitters, antennas, and propagation.

- *The ARRL Handbook.* This is the grandfather of all amateur radio references and belongs on the bookshelf of all hams. Almost any topic you can think of in amateur radio technology is represented here.

- *The ARRL Antenna Book.* After the radio itself, all radio depends on antennas. This book provides information on every common type of amateur antenna, feed lines and related topics, and practical construction tips and techniques.

instructor will help you find and register for a session. Otherwise, you can find a test session by using ARRL's web page for finding exams, **arrl.org/exam**. If you can register for the test session in advance, do so. Other sessions, such as those at hamfests or conventions, are available to anyone who shows up or to walk-ins. You may have to wait for an available space though, so go early! Online courses and test sessions are increasingly popular too. If you prefer to take the exam using your computer, you can find a list of VEs that offer online sessions at **arrl.org/online-exam-session**.

As for all amateur exams, the General class exam is administered by Volunteer Examiners (VEs). All VEs are certified by a Volunteer Examiner Coordinator (VEC) such as the ARRL VEC. This organization trains and certifies VEs and processes the FCC paperwork for their test sessions.

Bring a printed copy of either your official amateur radio license, or a reference copy available from the FCC website (**fcc.gov**). You'll need two forms of identification, including at least one photo ID, such as a driver's license, passport, or employer's identity card. Know your FCC Registration Number (FRN). You can bring pencils or pens, blank scratch paper, and a calculator, but any kind of computer or online device is prohibited for in-person exams. Online exam sessions will specify which programs may be open on your computer while taking the exam.

Once you're signed in, you'll need to fill out a copy of the National Conference of Volunteer Examiner Coordinator's (NCVEC) Quick Form 605 (see **Figure 3.3**). This is an application for a new or upgraded license. It is used only at test sessions and for a VEC to process a license renewal or a license change. *Do not* use an NCVEC Quick Form 605 for any kind of application directly to the FCC — it will be rejected. After filling out the form, pay the current test fee and get ready. Most online sessions will require you to provide an FRN, your current call sign, and your driver's license or equivalent photo ID.

THE EXAM

The General test takes from 30 minutes to an hour. You will be given a question booklet and an answer sheet. Be sure to read the instructions, fill in all the necessary information and sign your name wherever it's required. Check to be sure your booklet has all the questions and be sure to mark the answer in the correct space for each question. If taking the exam online, be sure to read any directions for the exam software in advance. Frequently, test sessions will use online conferencing software (like Zoom) and/or a cell phone as well as the testing software itself. Make sure your computer and Internet connection meet all of the stated requirements.

You don't have to answer the questions in order — skip the hard ones and go back to them. If you read the answers carefully, you'll probably find that you can eliminate one or more "distractors." Of the remaining answers, only one will be the best. If you can't decide which is the correct answer, go ahead and make your best guess. There is no additional penalty for an incorrect guess. When you're done, go back and check your

Special Testing Procedures

The FCC allows Volunteer Examiners (VEs) to use a range of procedures to accommodate applicants with various disabilities. If this applies to you, you'll still have to pass the test, but special exam procedures can be applied. Contact your local VE or the Volunteer Examiner Coordinator (VEC) responsible for the test session you'll be attending. Contact the ARRL VEC Office at 225 Main St., Newington CT 06111, by phone at 860-594-0200, or via email to **vec@arrl.org**. Ask for more information about special examination procedures

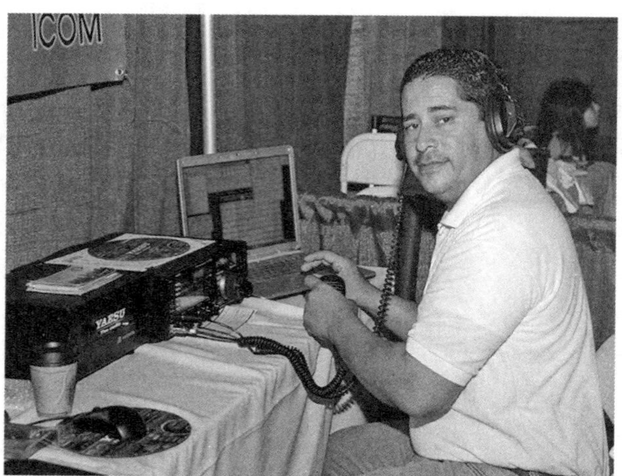

Special event stations attract a lot of attention on the air. For example, Edgardo Garcia, NP4EG, manager of the 2014 Puerto Rico Section Convention, activated KP4PR from the convention floor.

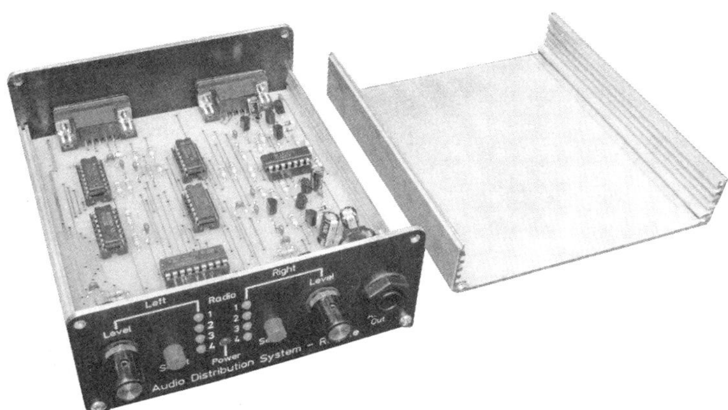

Hams design many types of equipment, including this professional-quality audio distribution system designed and built by William Ellis, KF7PB.

If you like to build electronic kits, there are plenty of kits available such as this 50 W amplifier that covers the 160 through 6 meter bands. [Phil Salas, AD5X, photo]

Hams can use online systems such as ARRL's Logbook of The World (arrl.org/lotw) to confirm contacts, but they also enjoy exchanging colorful and informative QSL cards. QSL cards can also be used to apply for operating achievement awards such as ARRL's Worked All States (WAS) or DX Century Club (DXCC).

answers and double-check your arithmetic — there's no rush!

Once you've answered all 35 questions, the Volunteer Examiners (VEs) will grade and verify your test results. Assuming you've passed (congratulations!) you'll fill out a *Certificate of Successful Completion of Examination* (CSCE). The exam organizers will submit your results to the FCC while you keep the CSCE as evidence that you've passed your General test.

If you are licensed and already have a call sign, you can begin using your new privileges im-mediately. When you give your call sign, append "/AG" (on CW or digital modes) or "slash AG" (on phone). As soon as your name and call sign appear in the FCC's database of licensees, typically a week to 10 days later (or faster if you completed an online exam),you can stop adding the suffix. The CSCE is good for 365 days in case there's a delay or problem with license processing or you decide to upgrade to Amateur Extra before your General license appears in the database.

If you don't pass, don't be discouraged! You might be able to take another version of the test right then and there if the session organizers can accommodate you. Even if you decide to try again later, you now know just how the test session feels — you'll be more relaxed and ready next time. The bands are full of hams who took their General test more than once before passing. You'll be in good company!

FCC AND ARRL VEC LICENSING RESOURCES

After you pass your exam, the examiners will file all of the necessary paperwork so that your license will be granted by the Federal Communications Commission (FCC). Soon you will be able see your new call sign in the FCC's database via the ARRL's website.

When you passed your Technician exam, you may have applied for your FCC Federal Registration Number (FRN). This allows you to access the information for any FCC licenses you may have and to request modifications to them. These functions are available via the FCC's Universal Licensing System website (**fcc.gov/wireless/systems-utilities/universal-licensing-system**) and complete instructions for using the site are available at **arrl.org/universal-licensing-system**.

The ARRL VEC can also process license renewals and modifications for you as described at **arrl.org/call-sign-renewals-or-changes**.

TIME TO GET STARTED

By following these instructions and carefully studying the material in this book, soon you'll be joining the rest of the General and Amateur Extra licensees on the HF bands. Each of us at ARRL Headquarters and every ARRL member look forward to the day when you join the fun. 73 (best regards) and good luck!

Table 1.3
General Class (Element 3) Syllabus
Effective July 1, 2023 to June 30, 2027

SUBELEMENT G1 — COMMISSION'S RULES
[5 Exam Questions — 5 Groups] 57 Questions
G1A — General class control operator frequency privileges; primary and secondary allocations
G1B — Antenna structure limitations; good engineering and good amateur practice; beacon operation; prohibited transmissions; retransmitting radio signals
G1C — Transmitter power regulations; data emission standards; 60-meter operation requirements
G1D — Volunteer Examiners and Volunteer Examiner Coordinators; temporary identification; element credit; remote operation
G1E — Control categories; repeater regulations; third-party rules; ITU regions; automatically controlled digital station

SUBELEMENT G2 — OPERATING PROCEDURES
[5 Exam Questions — 5 Groups] 60 Questions
G2A — Phone operating procedures; USB/LSB conventions; breaking into a contact; transmitter setup for voice operation; answering DX stations
G2B — Operating effectively; band plans; drills and emergencies; RACES operation
G2C — CW operating procedures and procedural signals; Q signals; full break-in
G2D — Volunteer Monitor Program; HF operations
G2E — Digital mode operating procedures

SUBELEMENT G3 — RADIO WAVE PROPAGATION
[3 Exam Questions — 3 Groups] 37 Questions
G3A — Sunspots and solar radiation; geomagnetic field and stability indices
G3B — Maximum Usable Frequency; Lowest Usable Frequency; short path and long path propagation;
determining propagation conditions; ionospheric refraction
G3C — Ionospheric regions; critical angle and frequency; HF scatter; near vertical incidence skywave (NVIS)

SUBELEMENT G4 — AMATEUR RADIO PRACTICES
[5 Exam Questions — 5 groups] 67 Questions
G4A — Station configuration and operation
G4B — Tests and test equipment
G4C — Interference to consumer electronics; grounding and bonding
G4D — Speech processors; S meters; sideband operation near band edges
G4E — Mobile and portable HF stations; alternative energy source operation

SUBELEMENT G5 — ELECTRICAL PRINCIPLES
[3 Exam Questions — 3 Groups] 40 Questions
G5A — Reactance; inductance; capacitance; impedance; impedance transformation; resonance
G5B — The decibel; current and voltage dividers; electrical power calculations; sine wave root-mean-
square (RMS) values; PEP calculations
G5C — Resistors, capacitors, and inductors in series and parallel; transformers

SUBELEMENT G6 — CIRCUIT COMPONENTS
[2 Exam Questions — 2 Groups] 24 Questions
G6A — Resistors; capacitors; inductors; rectifiers; solid-state diodes and transistors; vacuum tubes;
batteries
G6B — Analog and digital integrated circuits (ICs); microwave ICs (MMICs); display devices; RF connectors;
ferrite cores

SUBELEMENT G7 — PRACTICAL CIRCUITS
[3 Exam Questions — 3 Groups] 38 Questions
G7A — Power supplies; schematic symbols
G7B — Digital circuits; amplifiers and oscillators
G7C — Transceiver design; filters; oscillators; digital signal processing (DSP)

SUBELEMENT G8 — SIGNALS AND EMISSIONS
[3 Exam Questions — 3 Groups] 43 Questions
G8A — Carriers and modulation: AM, FM, and single sideband; modulation envelope; digital modulation;
overmodulation; link budgets and link margins
G8B — Frequency changing; bandwidths of various modes; deviation; intermodulation
G8C — Digital emission modes

SUBELEMENT G9 — ANTENNAS AND FEED LINES
[4 Exam Questions — 4 Groups] 46 Questions
G9A — Feed lines: characteristic impedance and attenuation; standing wave ratio (SWR) calculation,
measurement, and effects; antenna feed point matching
G9B — Basic dipole and monopole antennas
G9C — Directional antennas
G9D — Specialized antenna types and applications

SUBELEMENT G0 — ELECTRICAL AND RF SAFETY
[2 Exam Questions — 2 Groups] 25 Questions
G0A — RF safety principles, rules, and guidelines; routine station evaluation
G0B — Station safety: electrical shock, grounding, fusing, interlocks, and wiring; antenna and tower safety

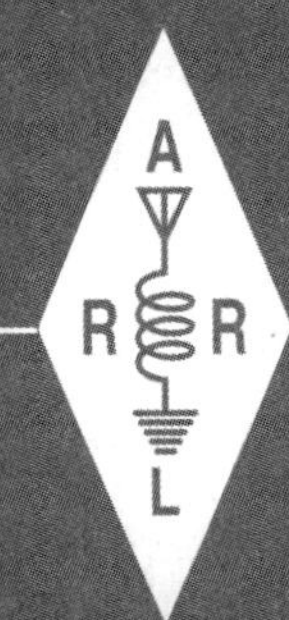

Chapter 2
Procedures and Practices

In this chapter, you'll learn about:
- **Basic HF operating procedures**
- **Common HF practices and modes**
- **Receiving and transmitting on HF**
- **Digital operating on HF**
- **Emergency communications**
- **ARES and RACES organizations**
- **Distress calls**

Technician licensees focus their studies and develop operating skills for techniques used on the VHF and higher bands. The most popular mode of operation on these bands is FM voice repeaters with evenly spaced channels and local or regional contacts. You'll find operating on HF is a bit different from what you're used to on VHF and UHF FM but it is easy to learn.

Before proceeding, don't forget to add **arrl.org/general-class-license-manual** to your internet browser's list of bookmarked web pages for easy reference. That page contains supplemental information and online resources you may find helpful during your studies.

2.1 HF Operating Techniques

GOOD PRACTICES

G2B01 — Which of the following is true concerning access to frequencies?

Except during emergencies, no amateur station has priority access to any frequency .

G2B03 — What is good amateur practice if propagation changes during a contact creating interference from other stations using the frequency?

Attempt to resolve the interference problem with the other stations in a mutually acceptable manner

G2B04 — When selecting a CW transmitting frequency, what minimum separation from other stations should be used to minimize interference to stations on adjacent frequencies?

150 Hz to 500 Hz

G2B05 — When selecting an SSB transmitting frequency, what minimum separation should be used to minimize interference to stations on adjacent frequencies?

2 kHz to 3 kHz

G2B06 — How can you avoid harmful interference on an apparently clear frequency before calling CQ on CW or phone?

Send "QRL?" on CW, followed by your call sign; or, if using phone, ask if the frequency is in use, followed by your call sign

G2B07 — Which of the following complies with commonly accepted amateur practice when choosing a frequency on which to initiate a call?

Follow the voluntary band plan

G2C04 — What does the Q signal "QRL?" mean?

"Are you busy?" or "Is this frequency in use?"

G2D07 — Which of the following are examples of the NATO Phonetic Alphabet?

Alpha, Bravo, Charlie, Delta

G4A12 — Which of the following is a common use of the dual-VFO feature on a transceiver?

To transmit on one frequency and listen on another

Almost everything you know about operating courtesy and good practices from VHF and UHF operating can be applied to HF operating. There are some differences in terminology, of course.

HF operating is similar to that of the so-called "weak signal" modes on the lower portions of the VHF and UHF bands. Simplex SSB, CW, and digital modes are by far the most commonly used. As a Technician, you may have some HF experience on 10 meters or maybe CW on the 80, 40, and 15-meter bands. The General license opens up many more frequencies, modes, and activities.

One thing you will find familiar is the use of phonetics for HF phone contacts just as they are on repeaters. The NATO phonetics (Alfa, Bravo, Charlie, Delta, and so on) are recommended and the most commonly used. **[G2D07]** Standard phonetics are listed on the *General Class License Manual* web page, **arrl.org/general-class-license-manual**.

SELECTING A FREQUENCY

Choosing a frequency to use is an important first step. You can tune around the band and find some other station calling CQ or engaged in a QSO. You can answer or break in as described in the next section. If you're unsure of yourself, listen for other stations and emulate their successful practices. You can also call CQ yourself following the procedure given later in this chapter. Listen to other stations to learn how others call and answer.

As a General, check the FCC Part 97 frequency and mode restrictions to be sure you're within the privileges allocated to Generals. Charts showing frequency privileges for the various license classes can be downloaded from **arrl.org/graphical-frequency-allocations** or found in Chapter 1. You should also be aware of the *band plan* for normal circumstances on that band. By following the band plan, you'll operate according to the usual practices for that band and mode. The HF band plans are available in the sidebar, "Band Plans — Band-by-Band Frequency Guide." **[G2B07]**

Within the appropriate frequency limits, tune to find a clear frequency. On a repeater or simplex channel, you simply have to wait until any ongoing QSOs are over before making your call. On HF, however, a perfectly clear channel is a rarity. There will always be some noise present and the signals of other stations may occasionally be heard. Your goal is to find a frequency on which your transmissions minimize interference to adjacent stations and vice versa. **Table 2.1** shows the recommended station-to-station spacings for different modes under normal conditions. **[G2B04, G2B05]**

After finding an apparently clear frequency, check to see if any other station is using it. Just as with a VHF simplex contact, you might not be able to hear both stations taking part in a QSO. Start by listening for 10 or 20 seconds. On phone, you can then ask "Is the frequency in use? This is [your call]"

Table 2.1

Recommended Signal Separation

CW	150 – 500 Hz
SSB	2 – 3 kHz
RTTY	250 – 500 Hz
PSK31	150 – 500 Hz

The FCC's regulations dividing the amateur bands help stations using compatible modes stay together. In addition, there are voluntary operating guidelines created by amateurs themselves. These are called *band plans*. ARRL maintains a set of band plans for 160-meters through the microwave bands at **arrl.org/band-plan**. Band plans for HF are found in the table below. (All frequencies are in MHz.)

Band plans go beyond what the FCC requires and were created in the interests of efficient operating. Many features of band plans just evolved on their own while others were created to address a particular need. In either case, the FCC considers the band plans "good practice" and expects amateurs to follow them voluntarily when possible and practical. For example, the international beacon frequency of 14.100 MHz is in the band plan to help stations avoid unintentionally interfere with stations that use the beacons to assess long-distance propagation. That's what band plans are for — education and guidance.

The band plans often list frequencies associated with the mode or style of operating you intend to use. Sometimes a range of frequencies is listed or a single *calling frequency* is shown. Other stations using that mode are much more likely to be operating near that frequency. Nothing in the band plan establishes a net's, group's, or any individual's special right to use any specific frequency. No one "owns" a frequency.

Band plans are not regulations; they are guidelines. Like special events in your town, there will be circumstances in which conditions or the number of stations on the band overwhelm the usual customs. For example, a major contest or DXpedition can result in thousands of stations on a band at once, making it very difficult to follow a plan describing normal conditions. These situations are just temporary, however, and operating returns to normal in a short time.

It's good practice — and plain old common sense — for any operator, regardless of mode, to check to see if the frequency is in use prior to engaging operation. If you are there first, other operators should make an effort to protect you from interference to the extent possible, given that 100% interference-free operation is an unrealistic expectation in today's congested bands.

Frequencies	Modes/Activities
1.800-2.000	CW
1.800-1.810	Digital Modes
1.810	QRP CW calling frequency
1.843-2.000	SSB, SSTV and other wideband modes
1.910	SSB QRP calling frequency
1.995-2.000	Experimental
1.999-2.000	Beacons
3.500-3.510	CW DX window
3.560	QRP CW calling frequency
3.570-3.600	RTTY/Data
3.585-3.600	Automatically controlled data stations
3.590	RTTY/Data DX
3.790-3.800	DX window
3.845	SSTV
3.885	AM calling frequency
3.985	QRP SSB calling frequency
7.030	QRP CW calling frequency
7.040	RTTY/Data DX
7.070-7.125	RTTY/Data
7.100-7.105	Automatically controlled data stations
7.171	SSTV
7.173	D-SSTV
7.285	QRP SSB calling frequency
7.290	AM calling frequency
10.130-10.140	RTTY/Data
10.140-10.150	Automatically controlled data stations
14.060	QRP CW calling frequency
14.070-14.095	RTTY/Data
14.095-14.0995	Automatically controlled data stations
14.100	IBP/NCDXF beacons
14.1005-14.112	Automatically controlled data stations
14.230	SSTV
14.233	D-SSTV

Frequencies	Modes/Activities
14.236	Digital Voice
14.285	QRP SSB calling frequency
14.286	AM calling frequency
18.100-18.105	RTTY/Data
18.105-18.110	Automatically controlled data stations
18.110	IBP/NCDXF beacons
18.162.5	Digital Voice
21.060	QRP CW calling frequency
21.070-21.110	RTTY/Data
21.090-21.100	Automatically controlled data stations
21.150	IBP/NCDXF beacons
21.340	SSTV
21.385	QRP SSB calling frequency
24.920-24.925	RTTY/Data
24.925-24.930	Automatically controlled data stations
24.930	IBP/NCDXF beacons
28.060	QRP CW calling frequency
28.070-28.120	RTTY/Data
28.120-28.189	Automatically controlled data stations
28.190-28.225	Beacons
28.200	IBP/NCDXF beacons
28.385	QRP SSB calling frequency
28.680	SSTV
29.000-29.200	AM
29.300-29.510	Satellite downlinks
29.520-29.580	Repeater inputs
29.600	FM simplex
29.620-29.680	Repeater outputs

ARRL band plans for frequencies above 28.300 MHz are shown in *The ARRL Repeater Directory* and on **arrl.org.**

once or twice before starting your CQ. On CW and the digital modes, "QRL? DE [your call]" does the trick. QRL is a *Q signal* hams use to mean "Is this frequency in use?" **[G2B06, G2C04]** If a station is listening, they'll usually say, "Yes, it is" or send "C" or "R" or make some other transmission that lets you know the frequency is occupied. Move to a new frequency and try again.

If you're engaged in a QSO and a station calls to request the use of a frequency for a scheduled activity, try to accommodate their need by changing to a new frequency. After all, we are a variable frequency service! All parties must remember that no group or amateur has priority access to any frequency except in the case of emergency communications. **[G2B01]** Be flexible, taking advantage of amateur radio's unique ability to use any frequency within its allocations.

In summary, choosing a frequency is very simple:
- Be sure the frequency is authorized for your license's privileges
- Follow the band plan under normal circumstances
- Listen on the frequency to avoid interfering with ongoing communications

It's just that easy! It is also normal for propagation to change during a contact and you may start to experience interference. Perhaps moving your beam or switching to another antenna will help you avoid it while continuing your contact. You could also change frequencies if that is practical. Whatever the circumstances, you should attempt to resolve the interference problem with the other stations in a mutually acceptable manner. **[G2B03]**

Split- or Dual-Frequency Operation

When a rare or interesting station is on the air with many calling stations, it's common for the station to operate "split." That means setting a transceiver to listen on one frequency and transmit on another. By transmitting on one frequency and having callers transmit on another frequency, callers can hear the station and keep "in sync" for more orderly, effective operating.

Many transceivers can listen to a second frequency, independently of the main receive frequency. **[G4A12]** If you are trying to contact a DX station, this allows you to listen to both the DX station and the pileup at the same time. As a result, you can quickly find the right transmit frequency.

For More Information

The main difference from VHF/UHF FM is that HF operation is not channelized at all except for the small 60-meter band that consists of five specific channels for operation with USB (upper sideband voice), CW, and certain digital modes. Channel designations are not used, although *calling frequencies* are common along with regular meeting frequencies for nets and special operations. On the HF amateur bands, "channel" only means "current frequency," not "assigned frequency."

HF equipment is designed for continuous tuning. The control used for continuous frequency adjustment is called a *VFO* for *variable frequency oscillator*. This is usually the largest knob on an HF transceiver (**Figure 2.1**), replacing the channel select control on a VHF/UHF FM rig. The VFO tunes the radio (both receiver and transmitter) in small steps, usually less than 100 Hz. The minimum frequency change is called *step size* or *step rate*. (Memory channels are also

Figure 2.1 — The VFO control is usually front-and-center on a transceiver. It allows continuous frequency adjustments in small steps for smoothly tuning in signals.

used on HF, but they are not the primary way frequencies are selected.)

If you're interested in short-range, regional contacts, maybe 80 or 40 meters would be a good choice. Longer range contacts are easiest on the higher-frequency bands of 30 through 10 meters. Don't use a long-distance band for short-range contacts since your signal will be heard over a much wider range than you are using. This needlessly occupies precious radio spectrum space.

MAKING CONTACTS

G1C04 — Which of the following is required by the FCC rules when operating in the 60-meter band?

If you are using an antenna other than a dipole, you must keep a record of the gain of your antenna

G2A08 — What is the recommended way to break into a phone contact?

Say your call sign once

G2A11 — Generally, who should respond to a station in the contiguous 48 states who calls "CQ DX"?

Any stations outside the lower 48 states

G2B08 — What is the voluntary band plan restriction for U.S. stations transmitting within the 48 contiguous states in the 50.1 to 50.125 MHz band segment?

Only contacts with stations not within the 48 contiguous states

G2B10 — Which of the following is good amateur practice for net management?

Have a backup frequency in case of interference or poor conditions

G2D05 — Which of the following indicates that you are looking for an HF contact with any station?

Repeat "CQ" a few times, followed by "this is," then your call sign a few times, then pause to listen, repeat as necessary

G2D08 — Why do many amateurs keep a station log?

To help with a reply if the FCC requests information about your station

G2D09 — Which of the following is required when participating in a contest on HF frequencies?

Identify your station according to normal FCC regulations

Although calling CQ is rare on VHF/UHF FM channels, that is how many contacts are initiated on HF. Hams tune across the bands and respond to stations calling CQ or who are carrying on an interesting QSO.

To call CQ on phone, you say "CQ CQ CQ, this is [your call repeated a few times using phonetics]." Then pause to listen for a station responding to your CQ. If no one answers, repeat your CQ as conditions require. **[G2D05]** On CW, replace "this is" with the abbreviation "DE" and of course no phonetics are used. Many stations say "from" rather than "this is" on phone. "DE" is usually used on digital modes too, although some stations may spell out "from."

CQ variations include:

• CQ DX with DX meaning "distant stations" — If you hear "CQ DX" from a station on the US mainland, for example, it means the CQer is looking for stations outside the lower 48 states. **[G2A11]** On HF, "DX" generally refers to any station outside the caller's country.

• CQ for stations operating in a contest or from a special event station — They will say something like "CQ contest" or "CQ test" or "CQ from special event station…"

• CQ for stations from a certain area — such as "CQ North America" or "CQ California"

Joining an ongoing QSO or *breaking in* is also common. On phone the customary procedure is to say just your call sign during a pause in the conversation. **[G2A08]** On CW or digital modes, send "BK" (break) followed by your call sign.

You will find the fast-paced style of contest operating to be quite popular on HF. The rules such as identifying your station still apply during these competitive events. **[G2D09]** Because contest contacts are very short, the identification rules are satisfied if you give your call sign just once at the beginning of a contact.

The band plans may reference a *DX window* a few kilohertz (kHz) wide on some of the bands. These were originally devised to give amateurs from countries with restricted privileges a bit of band space to make DX contacts outside their own country or region. As world-wide frequency allocations become more common, the DX windows are less needed but are still part of operating on some bands. For example, if you live in the US, the DX window of 50.1 to 50.125 MHz is where you listen for and make long-distance contacts with stations outside the contiguous 48 states. **[G2B08]**

Logging Your Contacts

Part of keeping an orderly and efficient station is maintaining a *log*, a record of your station's activities. While traditional paper logbooks are still common, most amateurs are converting to computer-based logging programs. Software-based logs are very flexible and can easily interface directly with your transceiver and with online contact confirmation services that help you obtain operating awards.

A typical log contains the time, date, frequency or band, and mode of each contact; the

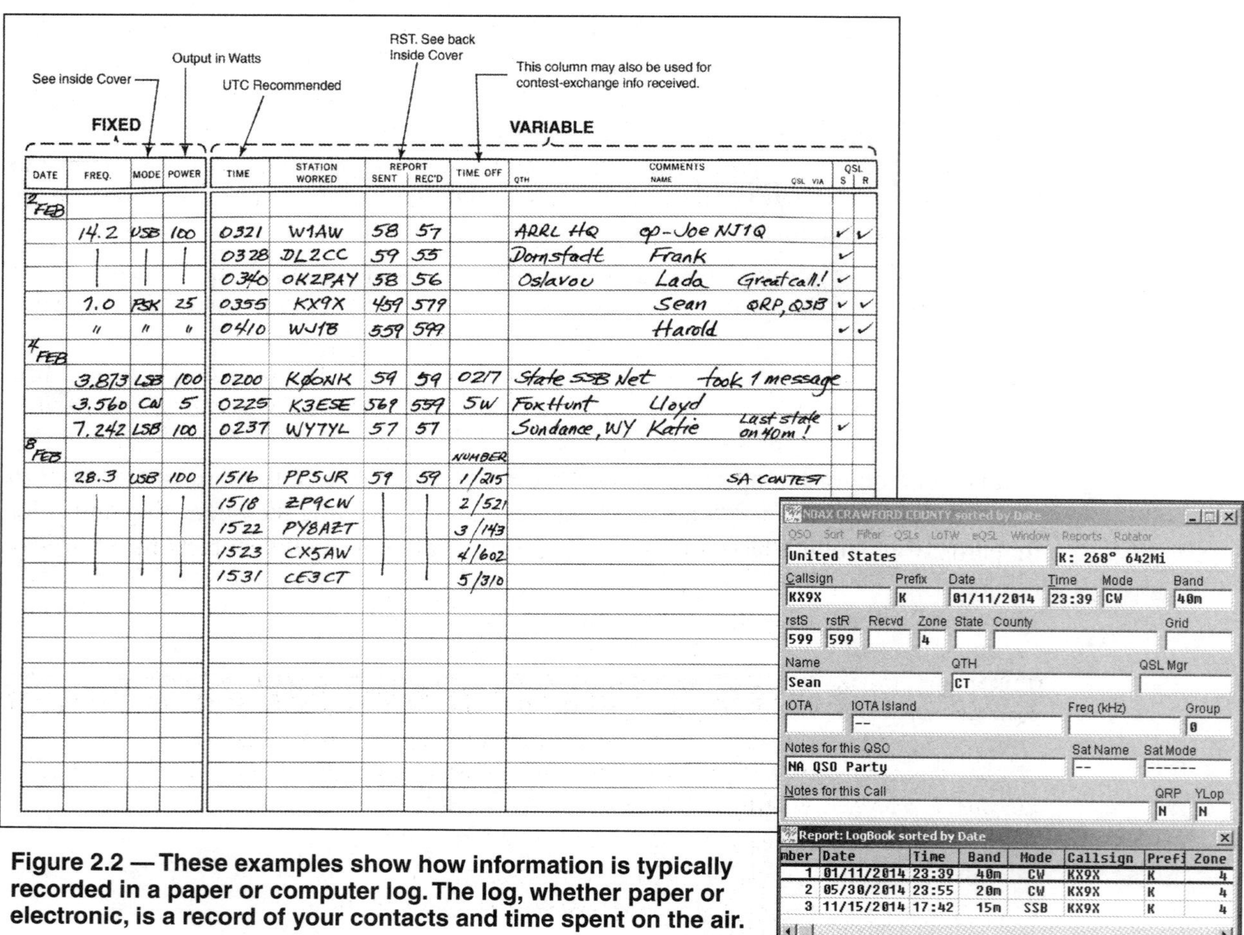

Figure 2.2 — **These examples show how information is typically recorded in a paper or computer log. The log, whether paper or electronic, is a record of your contacts and time spent on the air.**

Many on-the-air activities are scheduled in advance, such as person-to-person contacts between friends or family members ("skeds") and regularly scheduled nets. For scheduled contacts and nets to run smoothly, flexibility is required from everyone.

If you're the one making the schedule, avoid calling frequencies and popular band areas. Use contest calendars and the ARRL Net Search to avoid congestion (see the sidebar, "Radio Calendars"). Always have a "Plan B," such as an alternate time or frequency for your activity. For example, if you are a net control station and find the net's chosen frequency to be occupied, find a clear frequency nearby and run the net there or change to your backup frequency. **[G2B10]**

contacted station's call sign; and information about the contact such as signal reports, names, and equipment used. Most amateurs keep a log to verify contacts for awards, and to record items of interest, such as personal, technical, and operating information. **Figure 2.2** shows typical log entries.

A log also establishes the identity of the control operator at any date and time as well as helping provide any other information requested by the FCC. **[G2D08]** If you operate on 60 meters with any antenna other than a dipole, the FCC also requires you to keep a record of the antenna gain calculations or manufacturer's data. **[G1C04]** This ensures that your station meets the 100 W ERP restrictions.

For More Information

When breaking in, your transmission must be short to be received as stations switch from receive to transmit, called "turning it over." Saying or sending your call sign is all that's needed. If you are heard and the stations in the ongoing QSO want to accept stations breaking in, they will stand by and ask "the breaking station" to go ahead or some similar remark. Identify yourself with your call sign and ask if you may join the contact. If you are already in a contact, leave a little time between starting your transmission in case another station is trying to get your attention.

Contests, also known as "radiosport," take place mostly on the weekends and involve making as many contacts as you can within the contest period. Listen for stations calling "CQ contest" or CQ followed by the name of a contest. Contests avoid 60, 30, 17, and 12 meters entirely and most only take place on one mode so you can avoid them if you prefer.

Nearly all contests allow any station to participate in one way or another. You can use an online contest calendar to find out what information is being exchanged. One of the best is provided by WA7BNM at **contestcalendar.com** which provides all the information you need, including how to submit your contest log.

Operating in a contest is a great way to practice your operating skill, learn about propagation, build up contacts to qualify for awards, and learn how to use your station more effectively. To learn more about contesting, try the *ARRL Operating Manual* section on radiosport. There are a number of clubs that specialize in contest operating. You can find them by using the ARRL website's affiliated club search service at **arrl.org/find-a-club**, entering "contest" as the keyword to look for.

It is common for HF operators to exchange *QSL cards* or electronic records to confirm a contact. (QSL stands for "I acknowledge receipt.") Collecting the interesting and colorful cards from around the world is very popular, whether to verify contacts for awards or as a personal memento. Computer logging makes it easy to find and sort QSO information as well as tracking whether you've sent or received a QSL.

Managing Interference

Amateur radio's HF frequencies are not channelized and there are very many amateurs. *Voila!* Interference! Interference occurs not only from crowding, but also from propagation and personal choice. Regardless of its source, every amateur needs to be skilled at dealing with interference. This sidebar will help you deal with interference from other amateur signals. (Interference from signals generated by consumer electronics or atmospheric noise is covered elsewhere.)

If the bands are very busy, such as on the weekends when many more hams may be active in contests, chasing DX, or just making QSOs, you will find fewer unoccupied or clear frequencies and experience more incidental interference. Learning how to make contacts under these circumstances is part of becoming a good operator!

Types of Interference

Most interference caused by signals from other hams is incidental and not terribly disruptive. Once you've gained some experience, it's easy to copy a desired signal through a little bit of QRM (interference) from a nearby signal. You may experience (or even cause!) accidental interference when another station begins transmitting on or very near a frequency that you're using. Like collisions between shopping carts at the store, these incidents are easily managed.

There are two types of interference, however, that are not so easily managed. The first is *harmful interference*, defined by the FCC in §97.3(a)(23) as "Interference which…seriously degrades, obstructs or repeatedly interrupts a radiocommunication service operating in accordance with the Radio Regulations." Harmful interference is not always illegal, but needs to be resolved to keep communicating. The second and more pernicious type of interference is *malicious, deliberate* or *willful interference* and it is specifically forbidden by the FCC rules [§97.101(d)]. Sad to say, it does happen on the amateur bands, but it is uncommon.

Avoiding Interference

The best way to avoid interference is to be smart and use your knowledge of the amateur service, starting with reasonable expectations. Learn what bands are crowded and when. Learn the characteristics of each band with respect to propagation and noise. Know how to use your equipment and understand its weaknesses and strengths. Check published calendars so that you are not surprised by major operating events. Armed with this information, you'll have a much better idea of what to expect and a much higher chance of having a good experience on the air.

Next, hone your frequency selection skills. There are many sources of good propagation predictions to help you choose an optimum band or time for operating. Band plans and calling frequencies are widely published online and in print. Net frequencies are available online and in directories. With a few minutes of research, you can avoid many sources of interference and operate on a frequency well-suited for your intended purpose.

While on the air, operate so as to maximize the enjoyment of other operators. Use an appropriate power level to the job at hand. Avoid long-distance bands for short-distance contacts. Especially, make sure your transmitted signal is "clean," meaning free of excessive spurious signals that cause interference.

Reacting to Interference

Sooner or later, you will experience interference. What is the appropriate way to react? Start by keeping your options open and being flexible. No one has a claim to any frequency — it's often simplest to change frequency to avoid an interfering signal. Know how to operate your receiver to reject interference from nearby and strong signals.

Plan ahead by always having a backup or alternate operating plan in place. This is particularly important for scheduled contacts and nets. Everyone involved should know what to do in case the primary frequency is occupied or propagation is poor. The time to create these procedures is in advance, not at contact time!

Above all, keep a cool head! Sometimes harmful interference leads to deliberate interference when emotions get the better of us. Don't let a sore-head get into your head! Even though it may be vexing, don't react to a jammer or someone creating deliberate interference as that just encourages them. Sometimes it's just best to turn the power switch OFF and find something else to do. Encourage your fellow amateurs to follow these simple guidelines and everyone will benefit.

MODES

G2A01 — Which mode is most commonly used for voice communications on frequencies of 14 MHz or higher?
Upper sideband

G2A02 — Which mode is most commonly used for voice communications on the 160-, 75-, and 40-meter bands?
Lower sideband

G2A03 — Which mode is most commonly used for SSB voice communications in the VHF and UHF bands?
Upper sideband

G2A04 — Which mode is most commonly used for voice communications on the 17-meter and 12-meter bands?
Upper sideband

G2A05 — Which mode of voice communication is most commonly used on the HF amateur bands?
Single sideband

G2A06 — Which of the following is an advantage of using single sideband, as compared to other analog voice modes on the HF amateur bands?
Less bandwidth used and greater power efficiency

G2A07 — Which of the following statements is true of single sideband (SSB)?
Only one sideband is transmitted; the other sideband and carrier are suppressed

G2A09 — Why do most amateur stations use lower sideband on the 160-, 75-, and 40-meter bands?
It is commonly accepted amateur practice

Amateurs use many different modes of communication — more than any other service, licensed or unlicensed. The invention, use, and management of different modes are good examples of amateur radio fulfilling its mission to "contribute to the state of the radio art." (Part 97.1b) This section presents some of the conventions associated with each mode and compares them.

CW

Morse code, called "CW" for *continuous wave*, is found in the lower ranges of each HF band because FCC rules prohibit phone and data signals there. It's often forgotten that CW can be transmitted anywhere on the HF bands, (including on the five 60-meter channels), including the portion allocated to phone operation! Nevertheless, most CW operators tend to operate in the segments of the band reserved for CW and data.

AM and SSB Phone

On the HF bands, single sideband (SSB) is by far the most common voice mode or phone signal. **[G2A05]** First introduced in the 1950s, SSB displaced AM as the preferred HF voice modulation method. SSB uses less spectrum space than AM — a properly-adjusted SSB signal occupies about 3 kHz and an AM signal 6 kHz. The AM signal carrier and "extra" sideband are suppressed when creating an SSB signal so all of the power is allocated to the speech information. This increases efficiency. **[G2A06, G2A07]** The result is that under equal conditions an SSB signal will have a greater range than an AM signal. Amateur use of AM remains common with a number of groups on the bands every day.

Which of the two sidebands is used? Because of technical considerations in early SSB radio design, good amateur practice is to use upper sideband (USB) on frequencies above 9 MHz (20 through 10-meter bands) and lower sideband (LSB) elsewhere except on 60-meters. On VHF and UHF, the upper sideband is used. **[G2A01 to G2A04, G2A09]**

FM, in general, is not used on HF because the higher noise level hurts intelligibility. But FM repeaters can be found on the higher frequencies of 10-meters (above 29 MHz) where cross-continent and DX contacts can be made when the band is open!

Digital Voice

A new type of voice signal is appearing on the HF bands — digital voice! The operator's voice is converted to and from a stream of digital information by a modem or sound card, just like computer-generated digital signals. The modem or sound card then connects to a regular SSB transceiver's microphone input and speaker or headphone output.

Digital voice transmissions have fidelity comparable to regular SSB signals but are less affected by fading and there is less noise in the recovered signal. This type of voice transmission is likely to become more popular as the technique is refined. The two most common digital voice modes are FreeDV (**freedv.org**) and a protocol developed by G4GUO that is supported by AOR equipment.

Digital Modes

You may have used packet radio on VHF or UHF to exchange digital data. There are plenty of digital signals on HF, as well. The most popular today is FT8, which is one of several modes in the *WSJT-X* software package. Effective at low power levels, PSK31, PSK63, and FT8 are widely used. The oldest, and still common, is *radioteletype* or *RTTY*. (Most hams pronounce it as "ritty.") PACTOR is used for semi-automatic and automatic message and transferring small files. On HF, SSB radios are used to send and receive the digital signals, which are transmitted as audio tones. There are many more digital modes used on HF than on VHF. (Chapter 6 explores digital modes, protocols, and operating practices in detail.)

Image Modes

Image mode transmissions on HF encode the photos and graphics as tones. The received tones are reconstructed as an image on a display. Image modes are permitted wherever phone transmissions are allowed, except on 60 meters. The most common HF image mode is *slow-scan television* (SSTV). Each image takes several seconds, thus the name "slow scan." Computers and sound cards have greatly simplified the use of image modes and software for SSTV operation is readily available.

Fast-scan amateur television (ATV), which allows full motion video, is restricted to the 432 MHz and higher frequency bands due to its wide bandwidth.

Mode Comparison

Table 2.2 lists common modes and compares their basic characteristics. You'll learn about the details of these modes in Chapters 5 and 6. This table is intended to summarize the overview you've just read.

Table 2.2

Mode Comparison

Mode	Bandwidth	Examples	Data Rate	Notes
CW	Up to 150 Hz		Up to 60 WPM	
AM	6 kHz			Can be higher fidelity than SSB
SSB	3 kHz			
Narrow Bandwidth HF Digital	Up to 500 Hz	RTTY, PSK31 JT65 or FT8	Up to 100 WPM	Keyboard-to-keyboard
Wide Bandwidth HF Digital	Up to 2.3 kHz	PACTOR	Up to 5,200 bit/s	Keyboard-to-keyboard and file transfer
VHF/UHF Digital	Up to 100 kHz	Packet, D-STAR SystemFusion, Digital Mobile Radio (DMR)		Max bandwidth varies by band
Narrow Bandwidth Image	3 kHz max on HF	SSTV		
Video (full motion)	6 MHz max	NTSC, HDTV		UHF and microwave only

Figure 2.3 — HF transceivers have a variety of controls to help minimize interference on crowded bands. These may include notch filters, passband filters, audio peak filters and similar features.

HF RECEIVING

G2C07 — When sending CW, what does a "C" mean when added to the RST report?

Chirpy or unstable signal

G2C10 — What does the Q signal "QRN" mean?

I am troubled by static

G2D11 — Why are signal reports typically exchanged at the beginning of an HF contact?

To allow each station to operate according to conditions

On VHF, FM receivers have three basic controls: frequency (or channel), squelch, and volume. SSB/CW receivers have many more adjustments such as those shown in **Figure 2.3** because they are designed for non-channelized, continuous-tuning operation. They must be able to receive desired signals in the presence of noise and interference from adjacent channels.

Selectivity, the ability to discriminate between closely-spaced signals, is more important on HF than *sensitivity*, the ability to detect a signal. This is because atmospheric noise, referred to as *QRN*, is much higher on the HF bands than on VHF and UHF. QRN is caused by storms or other natural atmospheric processes, and by man-made sources such as sparks generated by motors and power lines. **[G2C10]** *Preamplifiers* are rarely required except on higher HF bands such as 15 through 10-meters.

Signal Reporting

One of the first items of information exchanged between stations at the beginning of a contact is the signal report. This lets each station know how well their signal is being received so that they can adjust procedures according to conditions. **[G2D11]**

The most common signal reporting system is the RST (Readability, Strength, Tone) numeric system. Readability is reported on a scale of 1 to 5 with 5 being the best. Strength and Tone are both reported on a 1 to 9 scale. A strength of 9 roughly corresponds to an S9 reading on a receiver. Tone indicates signal purity and values of less than 9 indicate some kind of transmitter problem. (Tone is only exchanged for CW and digital mode contacts.) C added after an RST indicates an unstable signal or "chirp" — a short change in frequency at the beginning of each dot or dash. **[G2C07]** On phone, many stations use the Quality system of reporting with numbers 1 to 5 indicating signal clarity and intelligibility. See **Table 2.3** for more information about the RST system.

For More Information

HF receivers use sharp filters to reject unwanted signals. Analog receivers use filter modules based on quartz crystals or mechanical assemblies. Digital signal processing (DSP) software is also used to perform the filtering and some radios use a combination of discrete and DSP filters. A typical receiver has at least one filter configuration for SSB reception, another for CW, and a third for AM or FM.

Because HF operation is not channelized, you'll also encounter signals close enough in frequency to be audible as low- or high-pitched speech fragments or CW tones. This is the interference referred to as *QRM*. Along with the main VFO tuning control, HF receivers offer the ability to shift the receive frequency without changing the transmit frequency to fine-tune desired signals and avoid or minimize QRM. This is called *receiver incremental tuning* or *RIT*. Some transceivers also offer the ability to shift the *transmit* frequency without changing the receiver — *transmitter incremental tuning* or *XIT*. A steady tone from a station tuning up or a broadcast carrier can be rejected by a *notch filter* that removes a narrow range of signal frequencies from the channel.

To avoid interference-like effects from *overload* or *intermodulation* (signals mixing together and creating unwanted by-products), a receiver's gain should be set so that it is just sensitive enough for the job. Features such as noise blankers and preamplifiers can make a receiver easy to overload and should only be used when necessary. Receiver technology is discussed in more detail in Chapter 5.

Table 2.3
The RST System

The RST reporting system is used on both CW and voice; leave out the "tone" report on voice.

Readability
1 — Unreadable
2 — Barely readable, occasional words distinguishable
3 — Readable with considerable difficulty
4 — Readable with practically no difficulty
5 — Perfectly readable

Signal Strength
1 — Faint signals, barely perceptible
2 — Very weak signals
3 — Weak signals
4 — Fair signals
5 — Fairly good signals
6 — Good signals
7 — Moderately strong signals
8 — Strong signals
9 — Extremely strong signals

Tone
1 — Sixty-cycle ac or less, very rough and broad
2 — Very rough ac, very harsh and broad
3 — Rough ac tone, rectified but not filtered
4 — Rough note, some trace of filtering
5 — Filtered rectified ac but strongly ripple-modulated
6 — Filtered tone, definite trace of ripple modulation
7 — Near pure tone, trace of ripple modulation
8 — Near perfect tone, slight trace of ripple modulation
9 — Perfect tone, no trace of ripple or modulation of any kind
On CW, if the signal has chirp, add the letter C. Similarly for a key click, add K.

HF TRANSMITTING

G2A10 — Which of the following statements is true of VOX operation versus PTT operation?

It allows "hands free" operation

G2B11 — How often may RACES training drills and tests be routinely conducted without special authorization?

No more than 1 hour per week

G2C01 — Which of the following describes full break-in CW operaton (QSK)?

Transmitting stations can receive between code characters and elements

G2C02 — What should you do if a CW station sends "QRS?"

Send slower

G2C03 — What does it mean when a CW operator sends "KN" at the end of a transmission?

Listening only for a specific station or stations

G2C05 — What is the best speed to use when answering a CQ in Morse code?

The fastest speed at which you are comfortable copying, but no faster than the CQ

G2C06 — What does the term "zero beat" mean in CW operation?

Matching the transmit frequency to the frequency of a received signal

G2C08 — What prosign is sent to indicate the end of a formal message when using CW?

AR

G2C09 — What does the Q signal "QSL" mean?

I have received and understood

G2C11 — What does the Q signal "QRV" mean?

I am ready to receive

G4A10 — What is the function of an electronic keyer?

Automatic generation of dots and dashes for CW operation

This section discusses methods of using an HF transmitter. The details of adjusting a transmitter are covered in Chapter 5.

Phone

On HF phone, there are several ways to put your transceiver into transmit mode (called "keying" the transmitter) when you want to talk. If you're used to an FM mobile or hand-held radio, you'll find *push-to-talk* (*PTT*) works just the same as on FM. PTT is best when operating in noisy environments. HF operators sometimes use a footswitch rather than the PTT button on a microphone to key the transmitter during busy operating periods.

HF operators also frequently use *voice-operated transmit*, most often referred to as simply *VOX*. A special circuit in the transmitter uses audio from the microphone input to turn on the transmitter when the operator is speaking. VOX allows "hands-free" operation, which is more convenient for long periods of operation. **[G2A10]** Mobile operators use VOX to keep both hands on the steering wheel! (Note: It is unsafe to wear headphones while driving and illegal in many areas.)

CW

Morse contacts are far more common on HF than above 30 MHz. The code segments

Figure 2.4 — An electronic keyer generates precisely formed and spaced dits and dahs under the control of a paddle. This combination makes it easy to send code at speeds over 15 words per minute (WPM) with much less effort.

of open bands are busy with signals and sometimes filled to overflowing! Morse is alive and well on the ham bands. If you decide to learn "the code," you will add a powerful radio tool to your rapidly growing collection.

Most CW operators begin by using a *straight key* but most graduate to an *electronic keyer* such as shown in **Figure 2.4**. The keyer is operated by a *paddle* to automatically generate the strings of Morse code elements — dots and dashes. **[G4A10]** Using a keyer and paddle makes it a lot easier to send at higher speeds than with a key. Some radios have keyers built-in.

There are two choices as to how to set up a transceiver to switch between sending and receiving when using Morse. If you use the VOX circuit as described in the previous section on phone operating, the rig will switch back to receive after the VOX delay period expires. This is *semi break-in* operation. VOX delay can be set to a very short time to drop out between words or long enough that the transmitter stays on the whole time you're sending.

Under some circumstances, it is more convenient to be able to hear what is going on between the Morse characters and elements. You might want to do this when the station you're in contact with has to interrupt your transmissions or if interference is present. Most modern radios include a *full break-in* option in which the radio switches between transmit and receive in just a few milliseconds. When using full break-in, the operator can hear incoming signals between all transmitted code characters and elements. **[G2C01]** Full break-in is also referred to as *QSK*, the Q-signal for break-in operation.

CW Prosigns

Just as with text messaging, it is a lot of work to spell out the full text of all words and phrases, so telegraphers developed an extensive set of abbreviations and procedural signals called *prosigns*. Prosigns are two letters sent together as a single character as indicated by an overbar. For example, the prosign $\overline{AR}$ (didahdidahdit) is used to indicate "End of Message." **[G2C08]**

Respond to a CQ at the fastest speed you are comfortable copying up to the speed of the sending station. **[G2C05]** If you are uncomfortable receiving at the station's sending speed, send the Q-signal "QRS" ("send slower") before the final K. If you want to go faster, "QRQ" means "send faster." **[G2C02]**

Remember to match your transmitting frequency with the received signal. That is called "zero beat" because the two signals produce the same audio tone in a receiver. Check your radio's operating manual for instructions on how to zero beat another signal. **[G2C06]**

Once you are in contact with another station, the prosign KN is used instead of K to prevent other stations from breaking in during the contact. It means, "Only the specific station or stations I am contacting should respond." **[G2C03]** When asked if you are ready to receive information, "QRV" means "I am ready to receive messages." After you have copied the message, "QSL" means "I acknowledge receipt" or "I have received and understood." **[G2C09, G2C11]**

When it's time to end the QSO, the prosign SK is used to let any listener know that the contact is completed:

WB8IMY DE W1AW SK

Finally, be sure to give your call sign every 10 minutes and at the end of the contact.

For More Information

There are three basic controls for a transceiver's VOX system:
- VOX Gain — sets the sensitivity of the VOX circuit to your speech
- VOX Delay — sets the length of time the transmitter remains keyed after you stop speaking
- Anti-VOX — prevents speaker or headphone audio from activating the VOX circuit

Each of these will be thoroughly described by your radio's operating manual and a typical set of manual VOX adjustments is shown in **Figure 2.5**. (Many transceivers use software menus to adjust VOX operation.) Get to know the individual controls so that you can adjust the VOX circuit properly at any time.

VOX can also be used for CW and digital transmissions. For CW, closing the external key activates the VOX circuit as for voice. VOX Gain and Anti-VOX have no effect when using CW. For digital transmissions, the audio output from a modem or sound card activates the VOX system just as a voice does. All three VOX controls have the same function in digital and voice operation.

Figure 2.5 — VOX controls — Gain, Anti-VOX (called Anti-Trip on this transceiver) and Delay. Because they aren't often adjusted, many rigs place manual Gain and Anti-VOX controls out of the way. They are menu items if controlled by software. Delay is adjusted most often and is usually made the easiest to access by a front-panel control. Some radios even have separate Delay controls for CW and phone.

Phone Procedures and Abbreviations

You've already learned about the procedural signals "CQ" and "Break." From operating on FM, you know when to use "Over" and "Clear." HF phone operation uses all of those signals and a few more. Don't forget to give your call sign every 10 minutes and at the end of the contact.

You will also hear many operators using Q-signals on phone, even though they were really intended for use on CW. Their meaning is so widely understood, for example QRM and QRN that you met in the previous section, that it is hard to resist using them. A good reason to use Q-signals on phone is when you are in contact with an operator who does not speak the same language. That is why Q-signals were developed so many years ago.

In any case, avoid the use of "10 codes" such as "10-4" since those are long obsolete and no longer used even by most police and fire departments. Professional radio users have decided it's better to use plain speech for clarity and understanding. If you're going to change frequency or close down the station, say just so.

CW Procedures

Morse speed for on-air contacts ranges from 5 to 10 WPM to the majority of day-to-day contacts at speeds between 15 and 30 WPM. Contest signals are faster but contesters will slow down if asked when there aren't faster operators calling. Slower signals tend to be found at the high end of the CW and data band segments. To get started with Morse, try the FISTS (**fists.org**) and CWOps (**cwops.org**) organizations. Both have training and operating programs for beginning CW operators.

Calling CQ on CW follows the same form as on phone. "DE" is an abbreviation used in place of "from" and the procedural signal K replaces "over":

CQ CQ CQ DE W1AW W1AW W1AW K

A response to a CQ looks like this:

W1AW DE WB8IMY WB8IMY K

There's no need to send the CQing station's call more than once unless there is interfer-

§97.401 Operation during a disaster.
A station in, or within 92.6 km (50 nautical miles) of, Alaska may transmit emissions J3E and R3E on the channel at 5.1675 MHz (assigned frequency 5.1689 MHz) for emergency communications. The channel must be shared with stations licensed in the Alaska-Private Fixed Service. The transmitter power must not exceed 150 W PEP. A station in, or within 92.6 km of, Alaska may transmit communications for tests and training drills necessary to ensure the establishment, operation, and maintenance of emergency communication systems.

§97.403 Safety of life and protection of property.
No provision of these rules prevents the use by an amateur station of any means of radiocommunication at its disposal to provide essential communication needs in connection with the immediate safety of human life and immediate protection of property when normal communication systems are not available.

§97.405 Station in distress.
(a) No provision of these rules prevents the use by an amateur station in distress of any means at its disposal to attract attention, make known its condition and location, and obtain assistance.
(b) No provision of these rules prevents the use by a station, in the exceptional circumstances described in paragraph (a), of any means of radiocommunications at its disposal to assist a station in distress.

§97.407 Radio amateur civil emergency service.
(a) No station may transmit in RACES unless it is an FCC-licensed primary, club, or military recreation station and it is certified by a civil defense organization as registered with that organization, or it is an FCC-licensed RACES station. No person may be the control operator of a RACES station, or may be the control operator of an amateur station transmitting in RACES unless that person holds a FCC-issued amateur operator license and is certified by a civil defense organization as enrolled in that organization.
(b) The frequency bands and segments and emissions authorized to the control operator are available to stations transmitting communications in RACES on a shared basis with the amateur service. In the event of an emergency which necessitates invoking the President's War Emergency Powers under the provisions of section 706 of the Communications Act of 1934, as amended, 47 U.S.C. 606, RACES stations and amateur stations participating in RACES may only transmit on the frequency segments authorized pursuant to part 214 of this chapter.
(c) A RACES station may only communicate with:
  (1) Another RACES station;

ence or the signal is weak. When signals are strong and clear, operators responding to a CQ may send their own call only once or twice.

Abbreviations are used to shorten common words, for example "AND" becomes "ES," "GOING" becomes "GG" and "WEATHER" becomes "WX" in Morse code. This saves a lot of time and energy! Long lists of abbreviations and prosigns are available online at **arrl.org/general-class-license-manual**. Digital operation follows many of the same conventions, using the same prosigns and abbreviations.

2.2 Emergency Operation

G2B02 — What is the first thing you should do if you are communicating with another amateur station and hear a station in distress break in?
Acknowledge the station in distress and determine what assistance may be needed

G2B09 — Who may be the control operator of an amateur station transmitting in RACES to assist relief operations during a disaster?
Only a person holding an FCC-issued amateur operator license

(2) An amateur station registered with a civil defense organization;

(3) A United States Government station authorized by the responsible agency to communicate with RACES stations;

(4) A station in a service regulated by the FCC whenever such communication is authorized by the FCC.

(d) An amateur station registered with a civil defense organization may only communicate with:

(1) A RACES station licensed to the civil defense organization with which the amateur station is registered;

(2) The following stations upon authorization of the responsible civil defense official for the organization with which the amateur station is registered:

(i) A RACES station licensed to another civil defense organization;

(ii) An amateur station registered with the same or another civil defense organization;

(iii) A United States Government station authorized by the responsible agency to communicate with RACES stations; and

(iv) A station in a service regulated by the FCC whenever such communication is authorized by the FCC.

(e) All communications transmitted in RACES must be specifically authorized by the civil defense organization for the area served. Only civil defense communications of the following types may be transmitted:

(1) Messages concerning impending or actual conditions jeopardizing the public safety, or affecting the national defense or security during periods of local, regional, or national civil emergencies;

(2) Messages directly concerning the immediate safety of life of individuals, the immediate protection of property, maintenance of law and order, alleviation of human suffering and need, and the combating of armed attack or sabotage;

(3) Messages directly concerning the accumulation and dissemination of public information or instructions to the civilian population essential to the activities of the civil defense organization or other authorized governmental or relief agencies; and

(4) Communications for RACES training drills and tests necessary to ensure the establishment and maintenance of orderly and efficient operation of the RACES as ordered by the responsible civil defense organizations served. Such drills and tests may not exceed a total time of 1 hour per week. With the approval of the chief officer for emergency planning the applicable State, Commonwealth, District or territory, however, such tests and drills may be conducted for a period not to exceed 72 hours no more than twice in any calendar year. **[G2B11]**

Providing service to your community is a significant factor in the decision of many people to become hams and more importantly, to stay hams. Recent events around the world clearly demonstrate that amateur radio is needed and emergency communications is an important part of our operation, just as much as technical experimentation and operator knowledge.

Amateurs should be familiar with emergency rules and procedures so that they can contribute effectively when normal communications are unavailable. **Table 2.4** lists the FCC rules pertaining to emergency communications. Even if you are not affected by the emergency or disaster directly, you may receive emergency communications from an amateur who is. Emergency communications in any form take priority over *all* other types of amateur communication. Regardless of what else is happening on a frequency, all other operators must stand by and wait for the emergency communications to occur. You should be prepared to respond effectively.

ARES and RACES

Amateurs have organized themselves in order to respond effectively to emergencies. There are two primary organizations for this purpose: The *Amateur Radio Emergency Service* (ARES®) and the *Radio Amateur Civil Emergency Service* (RACES). ARES is

Figure 2.6 — In time of emergency, when normal communications are disrupted, ARRL Amateur Radio Emergency Service (ARES) volunteers set up portable stations to assist emergency management agencies and relief organizations.

sponsored by the ARRL and RACES is sponsored by government agencies. The missions of ARES and RACES are similar and may overlap in many areas, but RACES has different rules from ordinary amateur operation.

ARES is organized and managed by members of the ARRL's Field Organization (**arrl.org/field-organization**). The mission of ARES is to provide communications assistance to local and regional government and relief agencies. Served agencies include organizations such as the American Red Cross, Salvation Army and National Weather Service. ARES may also assist local and regional emergency management agencies or even the Federal Emergency Management Agency (FEMA) if normal communications systems fail. Membership in ARES is open to any licensed amateur, whether an ARRL member or not, although ARRL membership is required to hold an official appointment.

RACES is a specific part of the Amateur Service governed by FCC rule §97.407 to provide communications for civil defense purposes during local, regional, or national civil emergencies (**arrl.org/ares-races-faq**). Although RACES is sponsored by the Federal Emergency Management Agency (FEMA), it is usually administered by local, county, and state emergency management agencies. You must register with a local civil defense organization to participate in RACES. Only an FCC-licensed amateur may be the control operator of a RACES station. **[G2B09]**

Distress Calls

Because amateurs operate from so many locations and on so many frequencies, distress calls are sometimes received by amateurs. It's important that each amateur know what to do if a distress call is received or how to make a distress call.

What would you do if you heard a call for help? Your responsibility is to react to the call for help and do your best to obtain assistance for the station in distress. First, immediately suspend your existing contact, if any. Then:

1) Immediately acknowledge to the station calling for help that you hear them.

2) Stand by to receive the location of the emergency and the nature of the assistance required. **[G2B02]**

3) Relay the information to the proper authorities and stay on frequency for further information or until help arrives.

If you are the station making the distress call:

1) On a voice mode, say "Mayday Mayday Mayday" or on CW or a digital mode send "SOS SOS SOS" followed by "any station come in please." (Mayday should not be confused with the Pan-Pan urgency call.)

2) Identify the transmission with your call sign.

3) State your location with enough detail to be located and the nature of the situation.

4) Describe the type of assistance required and give any other pertinent information.

FCC rule §97.405 allows a station in distress and requesting emergency help to use *any* means of radio communication at their disposal to attract attention and request help. *Any* frequency on which you think you will be heard, any mode, any power level necessary — even those outside your normal privileges — may be used as long as the emergency exists. Even unidentified transmissions outside of amateur bands, such as to allow direction finding, are permitted if required to provide the necessary communications. Similarly, if you hear a distress call, the same permission to respond by any means necessary applies to you.

Chapter 3
Rules and Regulations

In this chapter, you'll learn about:
- **International operating rules**
- **The ITU, FCC and FAA**
- **Rules for exams and examiners**
- **Frequency privileges**
- **Primary and secondary allocations**
- **Third-party rules**
- **Technical rules and standards**

As a General class licensee, you'll be operating on a new set of HF bands and modes. Along with different propagation and procedures, there are also new regulations and frequency limits that apply. We'll build on the rules and regulations you learned to pass your Technician exam.

You can quickly access the exact wording of any FCC Part 97 rule through ARRL's website (**arrl.org**) by entering the rule number, such as "97.301" in the search function window. For a complete copy of Part 97, see **arrl.org/part-97-amateur-radio**. In references to specific rules, the symbol § is used as an abbreviation for "part."

Reading the text of rules that apply to each question will help you remember and interpret them. This will help when you refer to the rules after you've received your General class license. More information on rules and regulations can be found through the resources at **arrl.org/general-class-license-manual**.

3.1 Regulatory Agencies

G1B01 — What is the maximum height above ground for an antenna structure not near a public use airport without requiring notification to the FAA and registration with the FCC?
200 feet

G1B06 — Under what conditions are state and local governments permitted to regulate Amateur Radio antenna structures?
Amateur Service communications must be reasonably accommodated, and regulations must constitute the minimum practical to accommodate a legitimate purpose of the state or local entity

G1D05 — When operating a US station by remote control from outside the country, what license is required of the control operator?
A US operator/primary station license

G1D12 — When operating a station in South America by remote control over the internet from the US, what regulations apply?
Only those of the remote station's country

G1E06 — The frequency allocations of which ITU region apply to radio amateurs operating in North and South America?
Region 2

G2D01 — What is the Volunteer Monitor Program?
>Amateur volunteers who are formally enlisted to monitor the airwaves for rules violations

G2D02 — Which of the following are objectives of the Volunteer Monitor Program?
>To encourage amateur radio operators to self-regulate and comply with the rules

G2D03 — What procedure may be used by Volunteer Monitors to localize a station whose continuous carrier is holding a repeater on in their area?
>Compare beam headings on the repeater input from their home locations with that of other Volunteer Monitors

On the HF bands, signals travel long distances and cross international borders with ease. That makes the international rules and regulations much more than an academic exercise! The rules for the amateur service vary around the world, sometimes dramatically. Let's start by asking the question, who's in charge here?

INTERNATIONAL TELECOMMUNICATION UNION (ITU)

The ITU is the organization responsible for all international radio regulations. Individual nations agree by treaty to abide by those regulations. Each country decides how to administer and implement those regulations and may even impose additional regulations, as long as they do not conflict with the ITU regulations.

The ITU has created three administrative areas, called *regions*. Each region has its own set of frequency *allocations* or divisions of the radio spectrum. **Figure 3.1** shows the three ITU regions. North and South America, Alaska, Hawaii, and most US territories and pos-

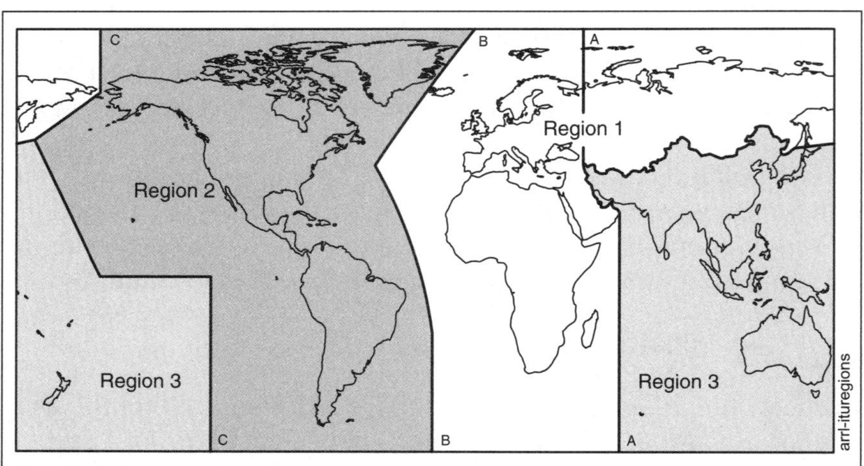

Figure 3.1 — This map shows the world divided into the three ITU regions.

sessions are in Region 2. **[G1E06]** ITU regions have their greatest effect on amateurs in frequency allocations around the world. For example, the 75-meter allocation varies from 50 kHz in Region 1 to 250 kHz in Region 2. Individual country allocations can also vary within a region, such as the difference between Canadian and US phone bands.

Section 97.301 contains a complete listing of frequency allocations by region. Parts (a) and (d) of that section contain the Region 2 frequency allocations that apply to General class amateurs operating from the US.

FEDERAL COMMUNICATIONS COMMISSION (FCC)

The FCC is the agency in the United States charged with writing and administering the rules for US amateurs. FCC regulations apply to any amateur (US or foreign) who is operating where the FCC has jurisdiction. That includes all US states, possessions, and territories, as well as operation from US-flagged vessels operating in international waters, and remote operation of stations located within the US. **[G1D05]**

There are some areas outside ITU Region 2 where the FCC has jurisdiction. For example, some US-administered Pacific islands (American Samoa, the Northern Mariana Islands, Guam and Wake Island) are in Region 3. For US amateurs operating in these areas, frequency allocations may be different from those here in Region 2.

Frequency sharing arrangements on the different bands are controlled by §97.303. Rule 97.307(f)(11) applies to US amateurs using phone in the Pacific and Caribbean. US amateurs operating abroad are required to abide by the appropriate regional frequency limits, subject to their host government's regulations. Similarly, US amateurs operating foreign stations remotely must abide by the rules of the remote station's country. **[G1D12]**

Volunteer Monitoring Program

The Amateur Service prides itself on being largely *self-policing* so that amateurs follow FCC regulations with little government oversight. ARRL created the Amateur Auxiliary (**arrl.org/amateur-auxiliary**) in 1982 so that amateurs could assist the FCC with enforcement (Official Observers) as well as interference issues (Local Interference Committees). In 2018, the Official Observer program was changed to the Volunteer Monitoring Program (VMP). The VMP's goal is to encourage self-regulation and compliance with the rules by amateurs. **[G2D02]** The VMP is made up of amateur volunteers who are formally enlisted to monitor the airwaves for rules violations. **[G2D01]**

Amateurs who participate in the Volunteer Monitoring Program can have fun training through the popular *foxhunting* or *radio direction-finding* (RDF) activities. These events combine radio skills with outdoor orienteering (and exercise!) to quickly locate a hidden transmitter (the fox). The resulting direction-finding skills learned can be used, for example, to locate stations violating FCC rules, intentionally or not. To do so, Volunteer Monitors can compare beam headings on the repeater input from their home locations with that of other Volunteer Monitors to triangulate the location of violating stations, just like during a foxhunt. **[G2D03]** The hunt can be a friendly local competition for practice or a large-scale event attended by hams from around the world. More information about foxhunting and direction-finding is available at **homingin.com**.

FEDERAL AVIATION ADMINISTRATION (FAA)

Along with the FCC, the FAA is the other federal agency that has jurisdiction over amateur affairs. Amateurs who want to construct an antenna structure more than 200 feet high must notify the FAA and register the tower with the FCC to avoid unknowingly creating hazards to aircraft. Additional restrictions apply if the antenna is within about 4 miles of a public use airport or heliport. **[G1B01]**

LOCAL BUILDING AUTHORITIES

Local building rules and codes may also affect your ability to put up towers and antennas. In the FCC rule known as PRB-1, the FCC requires that Amateur Service communications must be reasonably accommodated. Any regulations must be the minimum practical and have a legitimate purpose. **[G1B06]**

3.2 Amateur Licensing Rules

G1D01 — Who may receive partial credit for the elements represented by an expired amateur radio license?

Any person who can demonstrate that they once held an FCC-issued General, Advanced, or Amateur Extra class license that was not revoked by the FCC

G1D02 — What license examinations may you administer as an accredited Volunteer Examiner holding a General class license?

Technician only

G1D03 — On which of the following band segments may you operate if you are a Technician class operator and have an unexpired Certificate of Successful Completion of Examination (CSCE) for General class privileges?
On any General or Technician class band segment

G1D04 — Who must observe the administration of a Technician class license examination?
At least three Volunteer Examiners of General class or higher

G1D06 — Until an upgrade to General class is shown in the FCC database, when must a Technician licensee identify with "AG" after their call sign?
Whenever they operate using General class frequency privileges

G1D07 — Volunteer Examiners are accredited by what organization?
A Volunteer Examiner Coordinator

G1D08 — Which of the following criteria must be met for a non-US citizen to be an accredited Volunteer Examiner?
The person must hold an FCC granted amateur radio license of General class or above

G1D09 — How long is a Certificate of Successful Completion of Examination (CSCE) valid for exam element credit?
365 days

G1D10 — What is the minimum age that one must be to qualify as an accredited Volunteer Examiner?
18 years

G1D11 — What action is required to obtain a new General class license after a previously held license has expired and the two-year grace period has passed?
The applicant must show proof of the appropriate expired license grant and pass the current Element 2 exam

VOLUNTEER EXAMINER RULES

As a Technician class licensee, you've already experienced a unique aspect of the Amateur Service — the volunteer-administered licensing program. Along with being largely self-policing, amateurs and amateur organizations make licensing and examination services widely available. After you receive your General class license, you'll be able to fully participate in this program.

The volunteer licensing program is administered by *Volunteer Examiner Coordinators* (VECs). VECs are organizations that have entered into an agreement with the FCC to coordinate amateur license examinations. ARRL is the largest VEC (**arrl.org/volunteer-examiners**). You can find the other 13 VECs on the National Conference of Volunteer Examiner Coordinators' website (**ncvec.org**).

To become *accredited* by a VEC, you must meet the FCC's requirements in §97.509(b): **[G1D07, G1D08, G1D10]**
- Be accredited by a VEC
- Be at least 18 years of age
- Hold a General class or higher license (must be listed in the FCC database)
- Have never had your amateur license suspended or revoked

You must also pass a short multiple-choice test based on the *Volunteer Examiner's Manual*. Becoming accredited costs nothing and you can then administer amateur license exams.

American Radio Relay League VEC
Certificate of Successful Completion of Examination

ARRL — The National Association for Amateur Radio®

NOTE TO VE TEAM:
COMPLETELY CROSS OUT ALL BOXES BELOW THAT DO NOT APPLY TO THIS CANDIDATE.

The applicant named herein has presented valid proof for the exam element credits indicated below
Element 3 credit
Element 4 credit

Test Site (City/State): Newington, CT   Test Date: 03/13/2023

CREDIT FOR ELEMENTS PASSED VALID FOR 365 DAYS
You have passed the written element(s) indicated at right. You will be given credit for the appropriate examination element(s), for up to 365 days from the date shown at the top of this certificate.

EXAM ELEMENTS EARNED
Passed written Element 2
Passed written Element 3
Passed written Element 4

LICENSE UPGRADE NOTICE
If you hold a valid FCC-issued Amateur Radio license and call sign, this certificate validates temporary operation with the operating privileges of your new operator class (see Section 97.9[b] of the FCC Rules) until you are granted the license for your new operator class, or for a period of 365 days from the test date stated above on this certificate, whichever comes first. See the back of the certificate for temporary operating instructions.

NEW LICENSE CLASS EARNED

APPLICATION STATUS AND FEES
Visit **www.arrl.org/FCC-Application-Fee** for the instructions on how to pay the FCC application fee. You can find out if a new license or upgrade has been issued by the FCC by visiting the FCC website at **http://www.fcc.gov/wireless/systems-utilities/universal-licensing-system** (Click on License Search); or by calling the FCC at 1-888-225-5322 or the ARRL at 1-860-594-0300 during business hours (8am-5pm).

TECHNICIAN
GENERAL
EXTRA
NONE

THIS CERTIFICATE IS NOT A LICENSE, PERMIT, OR ANY OTHER KIND OF OPERATING AUTHORITY IN AND OF ITSELF. THE ELEMENT CREDITS AND/OR OPERATING PRIVILEGES THAT MAY BE INDICATED IN THE LICENSE UPGRADE NOTICE ARE VALID FOR 365 DAYS FROM THE TEST DATE. THE HOLDER NAMED HEREIN MUST ALSO HAVE BEEN GRANTED AN AMATEUR RADIO LICENSE ISSUED BY THE FCC TO OPERATE ON THE AIR.

Candidate's Signature: *Maria Somma*   Call Sign: KB1KJC (If none, write none)
Candidate's Name: Maria Somma
Address: 225 Main Street
City: Newington   State: CT   ZIP: 06111

VE #1: *Ronney Hartes*   N1NAG   Signature / Call Sign
VE #2: *Rose-Ann Lawrence*   KB1DMW   Signature / Call Sign
VE #3: *Perry Green*   WY1O   Signature / Call Sign

COPIES: **WHITE**–Candidate, **YELLOW**–VE Team, **PINK**–ARRL VEC
MVE 1/2022

Figure 3.2 — The CSCE (Certificate of Successful Completion of Examination) is your test session receipt that serves as proof that you have completed one or more exam elements. It can be used at other test sessions for 365 days.

Table 3.1
Allowed License Exams by VE License Class

VE License Class	Allowed Examinations
General	Technician (Element 2)
Advanced	General (Element 3) Technician (Element 2)
Amateur Extra	Amateur Extra (Element 4) General (Element 3) Technician (Element 2)

EXAMINATION RULES

No matter what licensing elements are available in the exam session, the rules are the same, all spelled out in §97.509. Every exam session must be coordinated by one of the VECs and administered under the observation of three primary VEs accredited by that VEC. (Other VEs may assist, but at least three VEs from the coordinating VEC must be present.) The three primary VEs must hold the necessary license class shown in **Table 3.1** to give the exam elements. For example, at least three General class or above, VEs must observe the test session to administer Technician class exams. **[G1D04]**

As a General class licensee, you are only allowed to administer the Element 2 Technician class exam. Table 3.1 shows which exams can be administered by VEs holding the various license classes. **[G1D02]**

Once the exams are completed, the VEs must create the necessary documents. Each successful applicant is given a *Certificate of Successful Completion of Examination* (CSCE) showing what elements the examinee has passed. (**Figure 3.2** shows a filled out CSCE.) The CSCE is good for 365 days and can be presented at any other exam session

NCVEC QUICK-FORM 605 APPLICATION
AMATEUR OPERATOR/PRIMARY STATION LICENSE

SECTION 1 - TO BE COMPLETED BY APPLICANT   PLEASE PRINT LEGIBLY!

PRINT LAST NAME	SUFFIX (Jr., Sr.)	FIRST NAME	M.I.	AMATEUR RADIO CALL SIGN (IF LICENSED)

MAILING ADDRESS (Number and Street or P.O. Box)	FCC REGISTRATION NUMBER (FRN) (MANDATORY)
225 Main St	0009876543

CITY	STATE CODE	ZIP CODE	DAYTIME TELEPHONE NUMBER (Including Area Code)
Newington		06111	860-594-0200

EMAIL ADDRESS (MANDATORY)
KB1KJC@arrl.org

Basic Qualification Question -- *Answer Required in Order to Process Your Application*

Has the Applicant or any party to this application, or any party directly or indirectly controlling the Applicant, ever been convicted

of a felony by any state or federal court? ☐ YES ☐ NO

If "YES", see "FCC BASIC QUALIFICATION QUESTION INSTRUCTIONS AND PROCEDURES" on the back of this form.

I HEREBY APPLY FOR [Make an X in the appropriate box(es)]:

☐ **EXAMINATION** for a new license grant   ☐ **CHANGE** my mailing address to **above** address

☐ **EXAMINATION** for **upgrade** of my license class   ☐ **CHANGE** my station **call sign** systematically

☐ **CHANGE** my **name** on my license to my new name   Applicant's Initials To Confirm __________

Former Name: ___________________________   ☐ **RENEWAL** of my license grant
         (Last name) (Suffix)   (First name)   (MI)

Exp. Date:___________________________

I certify that:
- I waive any claim to the use of any particular frequency regardless of prior use by license or otherwise;
- All statements and attachments are true, complete, and correct to the best of my knowledge and belief and are made in good faith;
- I am not a representative of a foreign government;
- I am not subject to a denial of Federal benefits pursuant to Section 5301of the Anti-Drug Abuse Act of 1988, 21 U.S.C. § 862;
- The construction of my station will NOT be an action which is likely to have a significant environmental effect [See 47 CFR Sections 1.1301-1.1319 and Section 97.13(a)];
- I have read and WILL COMPLY with Section 97.13(c) of the Commission's Rules regarding RADIO FREQUENCY (RF) RADIATION SAFETY and the amateur service section of OST/OET Bulletin Number 65.

Signature of Applicant:

X   *Maria Somma*   Date Signed: ___________________________

SECTION 2 - TO BE COMPLETED BY ALL ADMINISTERING VEs

Applicant is qualified for operator license class:

☐ **NO NEW LICENSE OR UPGRADE WAS EARNED**

☐ **TECHNICIAN**   Element 2

☐ **GENERAL**   Elements 2 and 3

☐ **AMATEUR EXTRA**   Elements 2, 3, and 4

DATE OF EXAMINATION SESSION
EXAMINATION SESSION LOCATION
VEC ORGANIZATION   ARRL VEC
VEC RECEIPT DATE

I CERTIFY THAT I HAVE COMPLIED WITH THE ADMINISTERING VE REQUIREMENTS IN PART 97 OF THE COMMISSION'S RULES AND WITH THE INSTRUCTIONS PROVIDED BY THE COORDINATING VEC AND THE FCC.

1st VE's NAME (Print First, MI, Last, Suffix)	VE's STATION CALL SIGN	VE's SIGNATURE (Must match name)	DATE SIGNED
		Rommey Harter	
2nd VE's NAME (Print First, MI, Last, Suffix)	VE's STATION CALL SIGN	VE's SIGNATURE (Must match name)	DATE SIGNED
		Rose-Ann Lawrence	
3rd VE's NAME (Print First, MI, Last, Suffix)	VE's STATION CALL SIGN	VE's SIGNATURE (Must match name)	DATE SIGNED
		Perry Green	

DO NOT SEND THIS FORM TO FCC — THIS IS NOT AN FCC FORM.   NCVEC FORM 605 - July 2022

IF THIS FORM IS SENT TO FCC, FCC WILL RETURN IT TO YOU WITHOUT ACTION.   FOR VE/VEC USE ONLY - Page 1

Figure 3.3 — This sample NCVEC Quick Form 605 shows how your form will look after you have completed your upgrade to General.

as evidence of having obtained credit for specific elements. **[G1D09]** Use the CSCE until your new license arrives from the FCC. An NCVEC Quick-Form 605 (shown in **Figure 3.3**) must also be filled out for each candidate who successfully acquires or upgrades their amateur license class.

IDENTIFICATION REQUIREMENTS

As soon as you receive a CSCE showing that you've achieved General class, you can start using *all* of your new General class privileges along with those of the Technician class. **[G1D03]** As long as you already have a call sign in the FCC database, you don't have to wait for the FCC to update your license class! You must, however, add an *indicator* to your call sign whenever you operate outside Technician privileges. This tells a listener that you are operating legally. On phone, say your call sign followed by "temporary AG" or "slash AG." On CW or digital modes, add "/AG" to your call sign. **[G1D06]** (If you pass the General class exam before your initial call sign is added to the FCC database, congratulations on the quick work but you'll have to wait for your call sign to be assigned before you can operate.) As soon as your license class is updated in the FCC database, you can stop adding the indicator.

CREDIT FOR PREVIOUS LICENSES

As of 2019, amateurs who were previously licensed but let their licenses expire may receive credit for exam elements they passed. While you still must pass the current Element 2 exam, if you can provide documentation that you had a General, Advanced, or Amateur Extra license that was not revoked, you will be credited with having passed those written exam elements. Welcome back! **[G1D01, G1D11]**

3.3 Control Operator Privileges and Rules

G1A01 — On which HF and/or MF amateur bands are there portions where General class licensees cannot transmit?

80 meters, 40 meters, 20 meters, and 15 meters

G1A02 — On which of the following bands is phone operation prohibited?

30 meters

G1A03 — On which of the following bands is image transmission prohibited?

30 meters

G1A04 — Which of the following amateur bands is restricted to communication only on specific channels, rather than frequency ranges?

60 meters

G1A05 — On which of the following frequencies are General class licensees prohibited from operating as control operator?

7.125 MHz to 7.175 MHz

G1A06 — Which of the following applies when the FCC rules designate the amateur service as a secondary user on a band?

Amateur stations must not cause harmful interference to primary users and must accept interference from primary users

G1A07 — On which amateur frequencies in the 10-meter band may stations with a General class control operator transmit CW emissions?

The entire band

G1A08 — Which HF bands have segments exclusively allocated to Amateur Extra licensees?
80 meters, 40 meters, 20 meters, and 15 meters

G1A09 — Which of the following frequencies is within the General Class portion of the 15-meter band?
21300 kHz

G1A10 — What portion of the 10-meter band is available for repeater use?
The portion above 29.5 MHz

G1A11 — When General class licensees are not permitted to use the entire voice portion of a band, which portion of the voice segment is available to them?
The upper frequency portion

G1B02 — With which of the following conditions must beacon stations comply?
No more than one beacon station may transmit in the same band from the same station location

G1B03 — Which of the following is a purpose of a beacon station as identified in the FCC rules?
Observation of propagation and reception

G1B09 — On what HF frequencies are automatically controlled beacons permitted?
28.20 MHz to 28.30 MHz

G1B10 — What is the power limit for beacon stations?
100 watts PEP output

G1E04 — Which of the following conditions require a licensed amateur radio operator to take specific steps to avoid harmful interference to other users or facilities?
All these choices are correct

G1E07 — In what part of the 2.4 GHz band may an amateur station communicate with non-licensed Wi-Fi stations?
No part

G1E10 — Why should an amateur operator normally avoid transmitting on 14.100, 18.110, 21.150, 24.930 and 28.200 MHz?
A system of propagation beacon stations operates on those frequencies

G8C01 — On what band do amateurs share channels with the unlicensed Wi-Fi service?
2.4 GHz

This section covers the basic requirements that a General class licensee must satisfy on the air. Some, such as the prohibition against broadcasting, you'll find familiar from your Technician class studies. Others, such as third-party rules, are new and may take a little study to understand clearly. Nevertheless, since you have already passed the Technician exam, you already know how radio "works" — that will make understanding easier!

FREQUENCY PRIVILEGES

While General class licensees gain access to all those new frequencies on HF, you are also expected to know what those frequencies are. Relax — it's not necessary to have every individual band segment memorized! The way most General licensees operate is to have a frequency chart at the operating position, such as the one shown in **Figure 3.4**. (For reference and study, download your own copy of the chart from

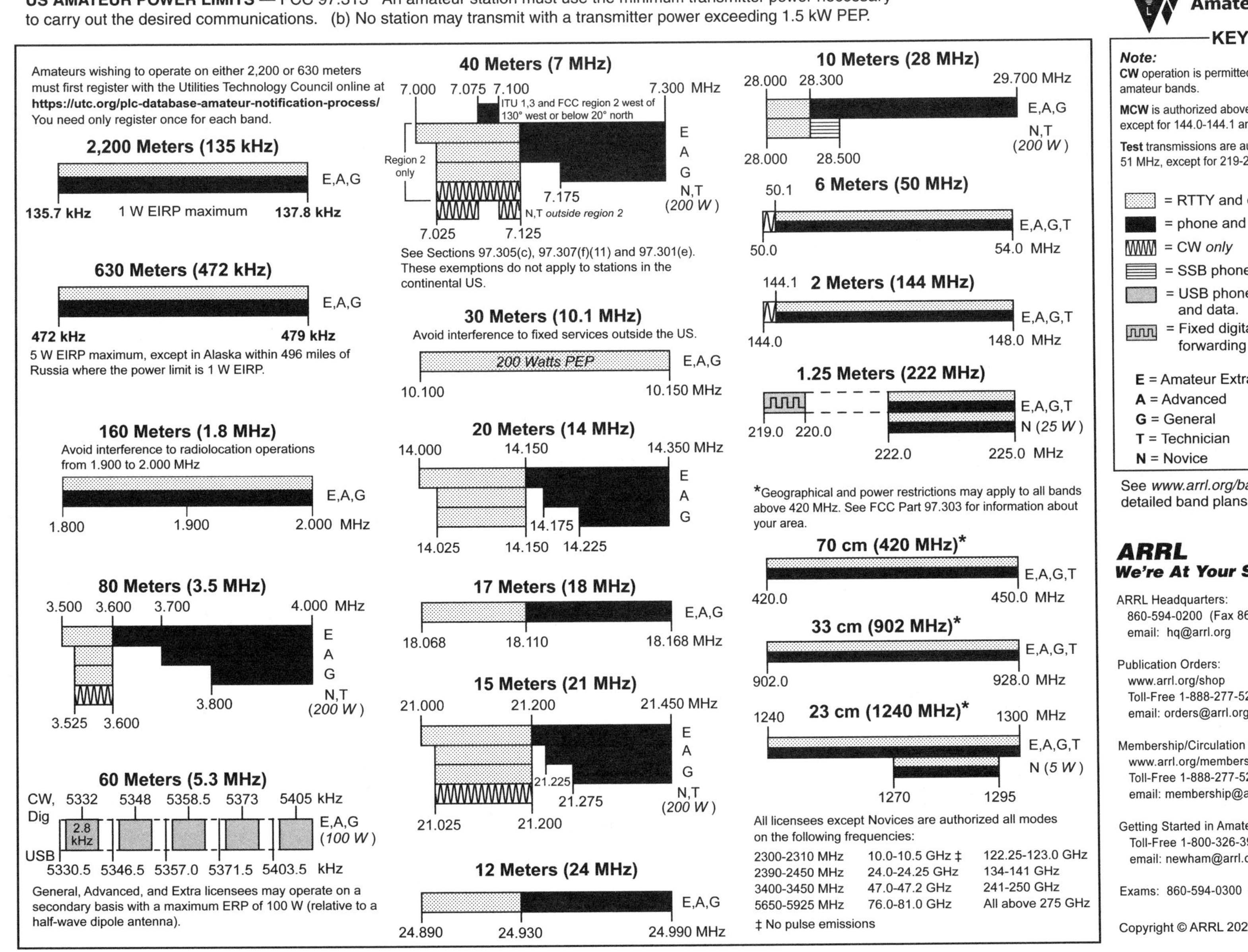

Figure 3.4 — Current Amateur Allocations Guide.

arrl.org/graphical-frequency-allocations.) When you tune the bands, check the chart to be sure you're within the proper band segment before transmitting. **[G1A05, G1A07 through G1A09]**

As the frequency chart shows, on all of the bands where Generals have access to part of the band, their privileges for each mode are located at the top of the band segment in which that mode is permitted. **[G1A11]** For example, on 40 meters Generals are only restricted from using CW, RTTY, and data at the lowest frequencies of 7000 – 7025 kHz. On 40-meter phone, General privileges begin at 7175 kHz and extend to the top of the band at 7300 kHz. On 75 meters, it's 3800 – 4000 kHz.

Generals have all amateur privileges on the 160, 60, 30, 17, 12, and 10-meter bands. **[G1A01]** Repeater operation on HF is limited to the 10-meter band from 29.5 to 29.7 MHz. **[G1A10]**

Two HF bands have special regulations. The 60-meter band privileges only permit channelized operation on USB, CW and certain digital modes with a power limit of 100 W ERP (see the Technical Rules and Standards section later in this chapter for details). This is the only channelized amateur band. **[G1A04]** The 30-meter band privileges permit only CW, RTTY, and data signals with a power limit of 200 W PEP. **[G1A02, G1A03]**

In some bands, amateur share access with other services. These are *secondary amateur allocations*, meaning that stations in the *primary services* have priority. Amateur stations in secondary or *shared* allocations must not cause harmful interference to stations in the primary service. If you are operating in a secondary amateur allocation and a station in the primary service begins transmitting, you must move to a clear frequency or stop transmitting. **[G1A06]** Even if the station in primary service is using the same type of signal, amateurs in the secondary service may not contact them. For example, hams share some spectrum in the 13-centimeter (2.4 GHz) band with Wi-Fi channels and may even use some of the Wi-Fi protocols but amateurs may not communicate with unlicensed Wi-Fi stations. **[G1E07, G8C01]**

Special Circumstances

Amateurs are required to take special steps to mitigate interference in the following circumstances **[G1E04]**:

- When operating within one mile of an FCC Monitoring Station
- When transmitting spread spectrum (SS) emissions
- When using a band where the Amateur Service is secondary

FCC Monitoring Stations require an environment free of strong or spurious signals that can interfere with their receivers. The location of monitoring stations can be determined from a regional FCC office. Because of their nature, SS signals have the potential to interfere with fixed frequency stations, so SS users should be sure their transmissions will not cause interference. And remember that amateur radio is not the primary service on 60 and 30-meters. On those bands, we are a secondary service and must not interfere with primary users.

Beacons

Beacon transmissions are very useful on the HF bands, just as they are on VHF and UHF. Beacons are used for observation of propagation and reception, as well as for other related activities. **[G1B03]** The *General Class License Manual* website provides links to beacon directories in the Propagation section.

Perhaps you would like to put up your own beacon station. The rules, contained in §97.203, are quite simple. The most important are that there must be no more than one beacon signal in the same band from a single location and beacons are limited to 100 W PEP output. **[G1B02, G1B10]** The FCC rule also lists the frequency ranges in which beacons are permitted to operate. 28.2 to 28.3 MHz is the only HF band segment where automatically controlled beacons may operate. **[G1B09]** In addition, amateurs should avoid transmitting on the frequencies of the system of international beacons operated by the Northern California DX Foundation. (See the sidebar "A System of DX Beacons") **[G1E10]**

For More Information

You should learn the basic frequency limits of each band as shown in **Table 3.2**. This is easier than you might think because most of the amateur HF bands are harmonically related. For example, it's easy to remember the sequence "1.8 - 3.5 - 7 - 14 - 21 - 28 MHz" because the frequencies are close to being multiples of each other. These are the "traditional" HF amateur bands. You can convert the frequencies to wavelength as 300 / f (frequency in MHz) to get "160 - 80 - 40 - 20 - 15 - 10." (For example, 300 / 21 = 14.3. The conversion isn't exact — it's just a handy approximation.) Practice those two sequences and you're more than halfway home!

Other HF bands have been made available to amateurs since 1980: the "WARC" bands and 60 meters. (WARC stands for World Administrative Radio Conference.) At the 1979 WARC, amateurs were granted allocations at 30, 17, and 12 meters (10, 18, and 24 MHz). Amateurs also gained access to five fixed-frequency channels on 60 meters (5 MHz) in 2003.

Table 3.2

Summary of Amateur HF Bands

Wavelength (meters)	Frequency (MHz)
160	1.800 – 2.00
80 and 75	3.500 – 3.600 and 3.600 – 4.000
60	5.3305, 5.3465, 5.3570, 5.3715, and 5.4035 (USB carrier frequency – see note)
40	7.000 – 7.300
30	10.100 – 10.150
20	14.000 – 14.350
17	18.068 – 18.168
15	21.000 – 21.450
12	24.890 – 24.990
10	28.000 – 29.700

Note – on 60 meters, CW and digital emissions must be centered 1.5 kHz above the carrier frequencies indicated above. Only one signal at a time is permitted on any channel.

Table 3.3
Third-Party Traffic Agreements List

Occasionally, DX stations may ask you to pass a third-party message to a friend or relative in the States. This is all right as long as the US has signed an official third-party traffic agreement with that particular country, or the third party is a licensed amateur. The traffic must be noncommercial and of a personal, unimportant nature. During an emergency, the US State Department will often work out a special temporary agreement with the country involved. But in normal times, never handle traffic without first making sure it is legally permitted.

US amateurs may handle third-party traffic with:

V2	Antigua/Barbuda	C5	Gambia, The	OA-OC	Peru
LO-LW	Argentina	9G	Ghana	DU-DZ	Philippines
VK	Australia	J3	Grenada	VR6	Pitcairn Island*
V3	Belize	TG	Guatemala	V4	St. Kitts/Nevis
CP	Bolivia	8R	Guyana	J6	St. Lucia
E7	Bosnia-Herzegovina	HH	Haiti	J8	St. Vincent and
PP-PY	Brazil	HQ-HR	Honduras		the Grenadines
VE, VO, VY	Canada	4X, 4Z	Israel	9L	Sierra Leone
CA-CE	Chile	6Y	Jamaica	ZR-ZU	South Africa
HJ-HK	Colombia	JY	Jordan	3DA	Swaziland
D6	Comoros (Federal	EL	Liberia	9Y-9Z	Trinidad/Tobago
	Islamic Republic of)	V7	Marshall Islands	TA-TC	Turkey
TI, TE	Costa Rica	XA-XI	Mexico	GB	United Kingdom
CM, CO	Cuba	V6	Micronesia,	CV-CX	Uruguay
HI	Dominican Republic		Federated States of	YV-YY	Venezuela
J7	Dominica	YN	Nicaragua	4U1ITU	ITU - Geneva
HC-HD	Ecuador	HO-HP	Panama	4U1VIC	VIC - Vienna
YS	El Salvador	ZP	Paraguay		

Notes:
Since 1970, there has been an informal agreement between the United Kingdom and the US, permitting Pitcairn and US amateurs to exchange messages concerning medical emergencies, urgent need for equipment or supplies, and private or personal matters of island residents.

Please note that Region 2 of the International Amateur Radio Union (IARU) has recommended that international traffic on the 20 and 15 meter bands be conducted on 14.100 – 14.150, 14.250 – 14.350, 21.150 – 21.200, and 21.300 – 21.450 MHz. The IARU is the alliance of Amateur Radio societies from around the world; Region 2 comprises member-societies in North, South, and Central America and the Caribbean.

At the end of an exchange of third-party traffic with a station located in a foreign country, an FCC-licensed amateur must transmit the call sign of the foreign station as well as his own call sign.

Current as of February 2023; see **arrl.org/third-party-operating-agreements** for the latest information.

When Morse code testing was eliminated from amateur exams, Novice and Technician licensees were allowed the same 80, 40, and 15-meter CW frequency privileges as General class licensees. On 10 meters, Novices and Techs are allowed the same CW, RTTY, and data privileges as other operators in the 28.0 to 28.3 MHz segment, plus SSB phone and CW operation from 28.3 to 28.5 MHz.

THIRD-PARTY TRAFFIC

G1E01 — Which of the following would disqualify a third party from participating in sending a message via an amateur station?

The third party's amateur license has been revoked and not reinstated

G1E05 — What are the restrictions on messages sent to a third party in a country with which there is a Third-Party Agreement?

They must relate to amateur radio, or remarks of a personal character, or messages relating to emergencies or disaster relief

G1E12 — When may third-party messages be transmitted via remote control?

Under any circumstances in which third party messages are permitted by FCC rules

Amateur radio is often used to send messages on behalf of someone who is not an amateur. This is called *third-party communication*. Because amateur radio can bypass the normal Internet, telephone, and postal systems, particularly over the long-distance HF bands, many foreign governments have a legitimate interest in limiting this loss of revenue.

Table 3.3 shows which countries have third-party agreements with the United States. If the other country isn't on this list, third-party communication to or from that country is not permitted. This is important to remember because hams like to be helpful and can inadvertently violate third-party rules if not careful.

The FCC recognizes that third-party communication is part of the ham radio mission, specifically to train operators and to provide an effective emergency communications resource. Handling messages, also called "passing traffic," is part of both normal and emergency communications. As a result, third-party communications may be exchanged between any two amateur stations operating under FCC rules with the constraint that the communications must be noncommercial and of a personal, unimportant nature or be messages relating to emergencies or disaster relief. **[G1E05, G1E12]** Third-party traffic may never be exchanged on behalf of someone whose amateur license has been suspended or revoked and not reinstated. **[G1E01]**

For More Information

Any time that you send or receive information via ham radio on behalf of any unlicensed person or organization, even if the person is right there in the station with you — that's third-party communications. Here are some clarifying points:

• The entity on whose behalf the message is sent is the "third party" and the control operators who make the radio contact are the first and second parties.

• A licensed ham generates third-party traffic by communicating a message to or from someone who is not a licensed amateur. If you contact a DX station who then asks you to pass a message to his family, doing so would be third-party communications. Check to be sure the DX station's country has a third-party agreement with the US before accepting the message.

• A licensed amateur capable of being a control operator at either station is not considered a third party regardless of whether he or she is at the station. A message from one ham to another ham is not third-party communications, whether directly transmitted or relayed by other stations. Making a contact to allow a visiting student to talk to his family in South America is third-party communications even if both the student and the family are present at the stations involved. Be sure there is a third-party agreement in place.

• The third party need not be present in either station. A message can be taken to a ham station or a ham can transmit speech from a third-party's telephone call over ham radio (this is called a *phone patch*).

• The communications transmitted on behalf of the third party need not be written. Spoken words, data or images can all be third-party communications, as can messages or files transmitted via digital modes.

• The third party may participate in transmitting or receiving the message at either station. An unlicensed person in your station engages in third-party communications when they speak into the microphone, send Morse code, or type on a keyboard. Letting someone who is not licensed make contacts under your supervision is third-party communications, even if the contact is short and for demonstration or training purposes, such as during a contest or special event.

- An organization, such as a church or school, can also be a third party.

PROHIBITED AND RESTRICTED COMMUNICATIONS

G1B04 — Which of the following transmissions is permitted for all amateur stations?

Occasional retransmission of weather and propagation forecast information from US government stations

G1B05 — Which of the following one-way transmissions are permitted?

Transmissions to assist with learning the International Morse code

G1B07 — What are the restrictions on the use of abbreviations or procedural signals in the amateur service?

They may be used if they do not obscure the meaning of a message

G1B08 — When is it permissible to communicate with amateur stations in countries outside the areas administered by the Federal Communications Commission?

When the contact is with amateurs in any country except those whose administrations have notified the ITU that they object to such communications

G1E02 — When may a 10-meter repeater retransmit the 2-meter signal from a station that has a Technician class control operator?

Only if the 10-meter repeater control operator holds at least a General class license

The FCC has allowed amateurs a lot of room to operate, so to speak, giving hams a free hand to transmit what they like. There are a few general prohibitions. For example, transmitting a false distress signal is absolutely prohibited under all circumstances. Some other prohibitions have special exceptions, however.

Generally, one-way transmissions are not permitted but there is an exception for "code practice." **[G1B05]** This traditional method of hams-training-hams has helped thousands to learn the International Morse code by listening to text sent over the air. W1AW also transmits code practice every day and conducts regular "runs" for you to qualify for a Code Proficiency Certificate. (See **arrl.org/code-transmissions**.)

In general, you can't retransmit a broadcast but there are exceptions. Broadcasts of weather or propagation predictions from a US government station may be retransmitted, as long as you only do it occasionally. **[G1B04]**

It is also permitted for US amateurs to communicate with amateur stations in countries outside the areas administered by the Federal Communications Commission *unless* the country's administration has notified the ITU that it objects to such communications. **[G1B08]**

Codes that are intended to obscure the meaning of the message are prohibited. **[G1B07]** What about Q-signals and prosigns? Those are well-known abbreviations intended to make normal communications more efficient and not more obscure, so they're perfectly acceptable.

Some satellites have uplinks or downlinks in the 10-meter amateur band. If the downlink is on 10 meters, is it okay for a Technician licensee to transmit on the VHF or UHF uplink and have the satellite retransmit their signals on the 10-meter band? The satellites are acting as repeater stations that simultaneously retransmit the signals of other stations on another frequency. The same question applies to terrestrial *cross-band repeaters* that receive signals on one frequency band and retransmit them on another frequency band. Such transmissions are permitted if the control operator of the repeater transmitter that operates on the HF band has a General class license or higher. **[G1E02]**

3.4 Technical Rules and Standards

G1B11 — Who or what determines "good engineering and good amateur practice" as applied to the operation of an amateur station in all respects not covered by the Part 97 rules?

The FCC

G1C01 — What is the maximum transmitter power an amateur station may use on 10.140 MHz?

200 watts PEP output

G1C02 — What is the maximum transmitter power an amateur station may use on the 12-meter band?

1500 watts PEP output

G1C03 — What is the maximum bandwidth permitted by FCC rules for Amateur Radio stations transmitting on USB frequencies in the 60-meter band?

2.8 kHz

G1C05 — What is the limit for transmitter power on the 28 MHz band for a General Class control operator?

1500 watts PEP output

G1C06 — What is the limit for transmitter power on the 1.8 MHz band?

1500 watts PEP output

G1C09 — What is the maximum power limit on the 60-meter band?

ERP of 100 watts PEP with respect to a dipole

G1C11 — What measurement is specified by FCC rules that regulate maximum power output?

PEP output from the transmitter

G1E08 — What is the maximum PEP output allowed for spread spectrum transmissions?

10 watts

G2D10 — What is QRP operation?

Low-power transmit operation

GOOD AMATEUR PRACTICES

There are many operating procedures and technical areas not covered by the exam or even by the FCC Part 97 rules. Setting exact rules for every type of operating would work against one of the basic tenets of the Amateur Service — technical experimentation and innovation. What has worked well for amateurs is to operate in conformance with good engineering and good amateur practice. Amateurs themselves set the day-to-day operating standards, although the FCC reserves the right to rule on what is and isn't "good engineering and good amateur practice." **[G1B11]**

How can you find out what those standards are? Amateurs are expected to educate themselves and assist others in doing so. ARRL publishes a number of respected references, such as *The ARRL Handbook* and *the ARRL Antenna Book*. (The complete set of

ARRL publications is available at **arrl.org/shop**.) Other publishers offer their own materials and there are ham websites for every technical topic you can think of. The *General Class License Manual* website (**arrl.org/general-class-license-manual**) lists several sources for technical reference information.

OUTPUT POWER

General, Advanced, and Amateur Extra licensees are limited to a maximum transmitter output power of 1500 W *peak envelope power* or *PEP* on the HF bands. **[G1C02, G1C06, G1C11]** Maximum legal power is sometimes called a "full gallon," while operating without an amplifier is called "barefoot." Two Q-signals are used to indicate power level: QRP means "reduce power" or "I am using low power" (usually 5 W or less). QRO means "increase power" or "I am using high power." **[G2D10]** PEP is the standard power measurement specified in the FCC rules for maximum power.

There are two restrictions that affect the maximum power for Generals and Extras on the HF bands:

• Amateurs are restricted to 200 W PEP on the 30-meter band (10.1 MHz) **[G1C01]**

• Amateurs are restricted to 100 W ERP with respect to a half-wave dipole on the 60-meter band (5 MHz) with a maximum signal bandwidth of 2.8 kHz. **[G1C03, G1C09]**

Novice and Technician licensees operating on HF are limited to 200 W PEP output. General, Advanced, and Extra licensees may use full 1500 W PEP output in the former Novice segments on 80, 40, and 15 meters. **[G1C05]**

Amateurs have also begun using spread spectrum (SS) technology on the higher UHF and microwave bands. Since spread spectrum creates a noise-like signal that can affect other users, the output power limit for amateurs for SS signals is 10 watts. **[G1E08]** Because high-gain antennas are available for these bands, the focused beam can be an RF exposure risk. Be careful when using significant power on microwave frequencies!

The FCC also requires amateurs to use the *minimum* power necessary to carry out the desired communication. That doesn't require you to reduce output power until your signal is just barely audible. What that means is to use the minimum power necessary for the desired signal quality and coverage. This allows other amateurs that are out of range of your signal to share the frequency, reducing congestion. Experience will allow you to judge propagation and band conditions so as to make the appropriate choice.

For More Information

Many HF operators use an amplifier to increase the transmitter output power and their signal's readability at the receiving end. Because SSB and AM operation requires amplifiers to operate linearly to avoid distorting the input signal, RF power amplifiers are *linear amplifiers*, often just referred to as "linears."

The station's output power measurement must be made at the output of the transmitter or amplifier, whichever is the final piece of equipment that generates RF power before the connection to the antenna system. The antenna system includes feed lines and any impedance matching devices.

To determine your ERP (effective radiated power), multiply your transmitter output power by the gain of your antenna. Unless stated otherwise, assume that gain is referenced to a half-wave dipole (dBd). For example, assume your antenna has a gain of 3 dBd. Your transmitter output power is 100 watts and 3 dB is a factor of 2, so your ERP is $100 \times 2 = 200$ watts. To use this antenna on the 60-meter band, your transmitter output power should be no more than 50 watts because $50 \times 2 = 100$ watts ERP. (For simplicity, this calculation did not include feed line loss.)

DIGITAL TRANSMISSIONS

G1C07 — What must be done before using a new digital protocol on the air?
Publicly document the technical characteristics of the protocol

G1C08 — What is the maximum symbol rate permitted for RTTY or data emission transmitted at frequencies below 28 MHz?
300 baud

G1C10 — What is the maximum symbol rate permitted for RTTY or data emission transmissions on the 10-meter band?
1200 baud

Technical standards for digital transmissions (referred to in the FCC rules as RTTY or data) are primarily concerned with the bandwidth of the transmitted signal. (The **Digital Modes** chapter covers digital signals in detail.) The transmitted signal bandwidth is closely tied to its *symbol rate* which is a measure of how many signaling events take place every second (see the sidebar "Bits or Bauds" in the **Radio Signals and Equipment** chapter). In general, the higher the symbol rate, the wider the bandwidth required to transmit the signal.

FCC rules §97.305(c) and §97.307(f) restrict the symbol rate of transmitted signals to make sure that digital signals do not consume too much bandwidth at the expense of other modes. **Table 3.4** shows the limits by band. On the HF bands, symbol rate and bandwidth are restricted because those bands are relatively narrow and a wide bandwidth signal would cause a lot of interference. As the size of the amateur bands increases with frequency, faster (wider) signals are allowed. At 33 cm (902 MHz) and above, there is no limit except for the band edges themselves, creating the "autobahn" of amateur digital signaling. **[G1C08 through G1C10]**

Amateurs are actively experimenting and innovating with digital modes. There are new protocols being introduced all the time. The FCC recognizes the need for amateurs to receive and understand signals must be balanced with the benefits of innovation. That is why the FCC requires the technical characteristics of the protocol be publicly documented before using it on the air. That can be as simple as posting the protocol's rules on a web page or in a magazine. **[G1C07]**

Table 3.4
Maximum Symbol Rates and Bandwidth

Band	Symbol Rate (baud)	Bandwidth (kHz)
160 through 12 m	300	1
10 m	1200	1
6 m, 2 m	19.6k	20
1.25 m, 70 cm	56k	100
33 cm and above	no limit	no limit

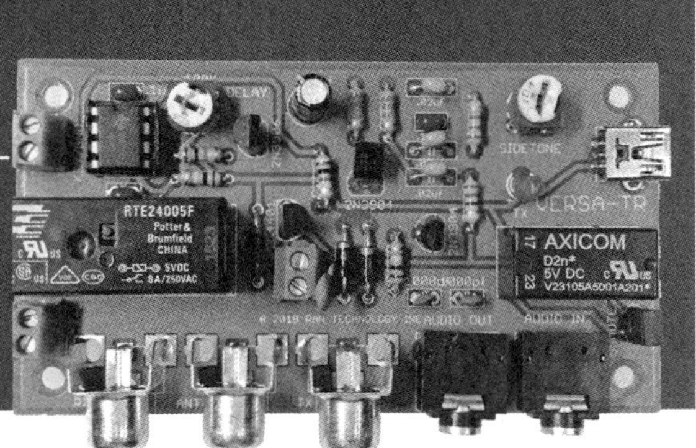

Chapter 4

Components and Circuits

In this chapter, you'll learn about:
- Basic electrical concepts — a review
- Decibels, RMS and PEP
- Resistors, capacitors and inductors
- Series and parallel circuits
- Transformers and vacuum tubes
- Reactance, impedance and resonance
- Semiconductors and ICs
- Basic test equipment

Get ready to "lift the hood" and learn more about electronics, the heart and soul of what makes a radio go! As a General, you'll understand the basic mechanics of how simple circuits work and how the components work together. That understanding enables to you to adjust your equipment and maintain your station knowledgeably. Even more importantly, you'll be able to respond effectively when things aren't working exactly right or when you need to operate under field or emergency conditions.

You've already learned the fundamentals of electricity and radio to pass the Technician exam and we'll dive one layer deeper for the General. A section of review material is provided to get you back up to speed, if necessary.

4.1 Power and Decibels

G5B01 — What dB change represents a factor of two increase or decrease in power?
Approximately 3 dB

G5B03 — How many watts of electrical power are consumed if 400 VDC is supplied to an 800-ohm load?
200 watts

G5B04 — How many watts of electrical power are consumed by a 12 VDC light bulb that draws 0.2 amperes?
2.4 watts

G5B05 — How many watts are consumed when a current of 7.0 milliamperes flows through a 1,250-ohm resistance?
Approximately 61 milliwatts

G5B10 — What percentage of power loss is equivalent to a loss of 1 dB?
20.6 percent

Substituting the Ohm's Law equivalents for voltage ($E = I \times R$) and current ($I = E / R$) allows power to be calculated using resistance:

$$P = I^2 \times R \text{ and } P = \frac{E^2}{R}$$

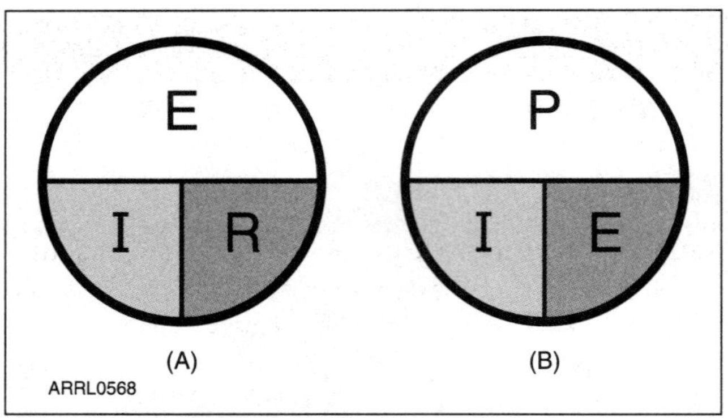

Figure 4.1 — These simple diagrams will help you remember the Ohm's Law relationships and power equations. If you know any two of the quantities, you can find the third by covering up the unknown quantity. The positions of the remaining two symbols show if you have to multiply (side-by-side) or divide (one above the other).

The drawings in **Figure 4.1** are aids to remembering Ohm's Law and the power equations in any of their forms. Here are a few examples:

To find out how many watts of electrical power are used if 400 V dc is supplied to an 800 Ω resistor:

$$P = \frac{E^2}{R} = \frac{400 \times 400}{800} = \frac{160,000}{800} = 200 \text{ W}$$

[G5B03]

To find out how many watts of electrical power are used by a 12 V dc light bulb that draws 0.2 A:

$$P = E \times I = 12 \times 0.2 = 2.4 \text{ W} \quad \textbf{[G5B04]}$$

To find out how many watts are being dissipated when a current of 7.0 mA of current flows through a 1.25 kΩ resistor:

$$P = I^2 \times R = 0.007 \times 0.007 \times 1250 = 0.06125 \text{ W} = 61.25 \text{ mW} \quad \textbf{[G5B05]}$$

Remember that 7 mA (milliamperes) is equal to 0.007 A, 1.25 kΩ (kilohms) is equal to 1250 Ω and 0.06125 W is equal to approximately 61 mW milliwatts).

Calculating a Power or Voltage Ratio from dB

You already know how to turn power and voltage ratios into decibels. What if you are given a ratio in dB and asked to calculate the power or voltage ratio? Here are the formulas:

$$\text{power ratio} = \log^{-1}\left(\frac{dB}{10}\right) \text{ and}$$

$$\text{voltage ratio} = \log^{-1}\left(\frac{dB}{20}\right)$$

Note that the inverse log (written as $\log_{10}^{-1}$ or just $\log^{-1}$) is sometimes referred to as antilog. Most calculators use the inverse log notation. On scientific calculators the inverse log key may be labeled LOG^{-1}, ALOG, or 10^X, which means "raise 10 to the power of this value." Some calculators require a two-button sequence such as INV then LOG.

Example 1: A power ratio of 9 dB = $\log^{-1} (9 / 10) = \log^{-1} (0.9) = 8$

Example 2: A voltage ratio of 32 dB = $\log^{-1} (32 / 20) = \log^{-1} (1.6) = 40$

A very useful value to remember is that any time you double the power (or cut it in half), there is a 3 dB change. **[G5B01]** A two-times increase (or decrease) in power results in a gain (or loss) of:

$$dB = 10 \log_{10}\left(\frac{2}{1}\right) = 10 \log_{10} (2) = 10 \times (0.3) = 3 \text{ dB}$$

Converting dB to Percentage and Vice Versa

$$dB = 10 \log \left(\frac{\text{Percentage Power}}{100\%} \right)$$

$$dB = 20 \log \left(\frac{\text{Percentage Voltage}}{100\%} \right)$$

$$\text{Percentage Power} = 100\% \times \log^{-1} \left(\frac{dB}{10} \right)$$

$$\text{Percentage Voltage} = 100\% \times \log^{-1} \left(\frac{dB}{20} \right)$$

Here's a practical application. Suppose you are using an antenna feed line that has a loss of 1 dB. You can calculate the amount of transmitter power that's actually reaching your antenna and how much is lost in the feed line.

$$\text{Percentage Power} = 100\% \times \log^{-1} \left(\frac{-1}{10} \right) = 100\% \times \log^{-1}(-0.1) = 79.4\% \quad \textbf{[G5B10]}$$

79.4% of your power is reaching the antenna and 20.6% is lost in the feed line.

Example 3: A power ratio of 20% = 10 log (20% / 100%) = 10 log (0.2) = –7 dB
Example 4: A voltage ratio of 150% = 20 log (150% / 100%) = 20 log (1.5) = 3.52 dB
Example 5: –3 dB represents a percentage power = 100% × log^{-1} (–3 / 10) = 50%
Example 6: 4 dB represents a percentage voltage = 100% × log^{-1} (4 / 20) = 158%

For More Information — Electrical Review

This section reviews topics that were introduced in study material for the Technician exam.

Current, Voltage, and Power

Electronic current (represented by the letter I) is the flow of electrons, atomic particles with one unit of negative electric charge. Current is measured in *amperes* (A or amps) with an *ammeter*. *Voltage* (E) is the force that makes electrons move and is measured in *volts* (V) with a *voltmeter*. The *polarity* of a voltage refers to the direction from positive to negative. *Power* (P), measured in *watts* (W), is the product of voltage and current, P = E × I.

Discussions of electronic circuits should be assumed to use *conventional current* in which positive charge flows in the direction of positive to negative voltage. This is the exact opposite of *electronic current* in which electrons move in the direction of negative to positive voltage. Although it results in confusion, this convention was assigned before the true nature of electricity was understood. Unless texts and references specifically refer to the flow of electrons, assume that conventional current is used.

Resistance and Ohm's Law

The opposition of a material to current flow is called *resistance* (R) and is measured in *ohms* (Ω) with an *ohmmeter*. Georg Ohm discovered that voltage, current and resistance are proportional.

Ohm's Law states that R = E / I. If you know any two of I, E or R, you can determine the missing quantity:

$$R = \frac{E}{I} \text{ and } I = \frac{E}{R} \text{ and } E = I \times R$$

The voltage caused by current flowing through a resistance (E = I × R) is called a *voltage drop*.

AC and DC Waveforms

Current that flows in one direction all the time is called *direct current*, abbreviated dc or DC. Current that reverses direction is called *alternating current*, abbreviated ac or AC. A voltage that has the same polarity all the time is a *dc voltage*. A voltage that reverses polarity is an *ac voltage*.

Frequency

A complete sequence of ac current flowing, stopping, reversing and stopping again is called a *cycle*. The number of cycles per second is the current's *frequency* (f) measured in *hertz* (Hz). A *harmonic* is a frequency at some integer multiple (2, 3, 4 and so on) of a lowest or *fundamental* frequency. The harmonic at twice the fundamental frequency is called the *second harmonic*, at three times the fundamental frequency the *third harmonic*, and so forth. There is no "first harmonic."

Wavelength

The speed of light in space and air is approximately 300 million (3×10^8) meters per second and somewhat slower in wires and cables. The *wavelength* (λ) of a radio wave is the distance it travels during one complete cycle.

$$\lambda = \frac{c}{f} \text{ and } f = \frac{c}{\lambda}$$

A radio wave can be referred to by wavelength or frequency because the speed of light is constant. As frequency increases wavelength decreases and vice-versa.

Series and Parallel Circuits

A *circuit* is any complete path through which current can flow. If two or more components are connected in a circuit so that the same current flows through all of the components, that is a *series circuit*. If two or more components are connected so that the same voltage is applied to all of the components, that is a *parallel circuit*.

Decibels

You were introduced to the decibel (dB) in your studies for the Technician class exam. As you become more and more experienced in ham radio, you'll notice the "deebee" everywhere — it's the standard way of referring to power or voltage ratios.

The formula for computing decibels is:

$$dB = 10 \log_{10} (\text{power ratio}) = 20 \log_{10} (\text{voltage ratio})$$

If you are comparing a measured power or voltage (P_{MEAS} or V_{MEAS}) to some reference power (P_{REF} or V_{REF}) the formulas are:

$$dB = 10 \log_{10} \left(\frac{P_M}{P_{REF}} \right) = 20 \log_{10} \left(\frac{V_M}{V_{REF}} \right)$$

Positive values of dB mean the ratio is greater than 1 and negative values of dB indicate a ratio of less than 1. Ratios greater than 1 can be referred to as *gain*, while ratios less than 1 can be called a *loss* or *attenuation*. Note that loss and attenuation are often given as positive values of dB (for example, "a loss of 10 dB" or "a 6 dB attenuator") with the understanding that the ratio is less than one and the calculated value of change in dB will be negative.

For example, if an amplifier turns a 5 W signal into a 25 W signal, that's a gain of:

$$dB = 10 \log_{10} \left(\frac{25}{5} \right) = 10 \log_{10} (5) = 10 \times (0.7) = 7 \text{ dB}$$

On the other hand, if by adjusting a receiver's volume control the audio output signal voltage is reduced from 2 volts to 0.1 volt, that's a change of:

$$dB = 20 \log_{10} \left(\frac{0.1}{2} \right) = 20 \log_{10} (0.05) = 20 \times (-1.3) = -26 \text{ dB}$$

4.2 AC Power

G5B06 — What is the PEP produced by 200 volts peak-to-peak across a 50-ohm dummy load?
100 watts

G5B07 — What value of an AC signal produces the same power dissipation in a resistor as a DC voltage of the same value?
The RMS value

G5B08 — What is the peak-to-peak voltage of a sine wave with an RMS voltage of 120 volts?
339.4 volts

G5B09 — What is the RMS voltage of a sine wave with a value of 17 volts peak?
12 volts

G5B11 — What is the ratio of PEP to average power for an unmodulated carrier?
1.00

G5B12 — What is the RMS voltage across a 50-ohm dummy load dissipating 1,200 watts?
245 volts

G5B13 — What is the output PEP of an unmodulated carrier if the average power is 1,060 watts?

1060 watts

G5B14 — What is the output PEP of 500 volts peak-to-peak across a 50-ohm load?

625 watts

RMS: DEFINITION AND MEASUREMENT

As ac electrical power became common, it was important to know how much ac voltage delivered the same average power compared to a dc voltage. The power equation is quite clear for dc: $P = E^2 / R$. But what value for E is used for ac power? The peak voltage, an average…or what? The answer turns out to be the *root mean square (RMS)* voltage (often abbreviated V_{RMS}). If RMS voltage is used in the equations shown above for calculating power, the result for the ac signal is the same as for an unvarying dc voltage. **[G5B07]**

"Root mean square" refers to the method used to calculate the RMS voltage — it is the square *root* of the average (*mean*) of the *squares* of the values of the signal voltages that are present.

The RMS value for a sine wave is simply 0.707 times the sine wave's peak voltage, V_{PK}, as shown in **Figure 4.2**.

$$V_{RMS} = 0.707 \times V_{PK} = 0.707 \times \frac{V_{P-P}}{2}$$

$$V_{PK} = 1.414 \times V_{RMS}$$

$$V_{P-P} = 2 \times 1.414 \times V_{RMS} = 2.828 \times V_{RMS}$$

Do not use these formulas for waveforms that are not sine waves, such as speech, square waves or dc voltages combined with ac voltages!

Example 7: A sine wave with a peak voltage of 17 V has an RMS value of $V_{RMS} = 0.707 \times 17 = 12$ V **[G5B09]**

Example 8: A sine wave with a peak-to-peak voltage of 100 V has an RMS value of $V_{RMS} = 0.707 \times (100 / 2) = 35.4$ V

Example 9: A sine wave with an RMS voltage of 120.0 V has a peak-to-peak voltage of $V_{P-P} = 2 \times 1.414 \times 120 = 2.828 \times 120 = 339.4$ V **[G5B08]**

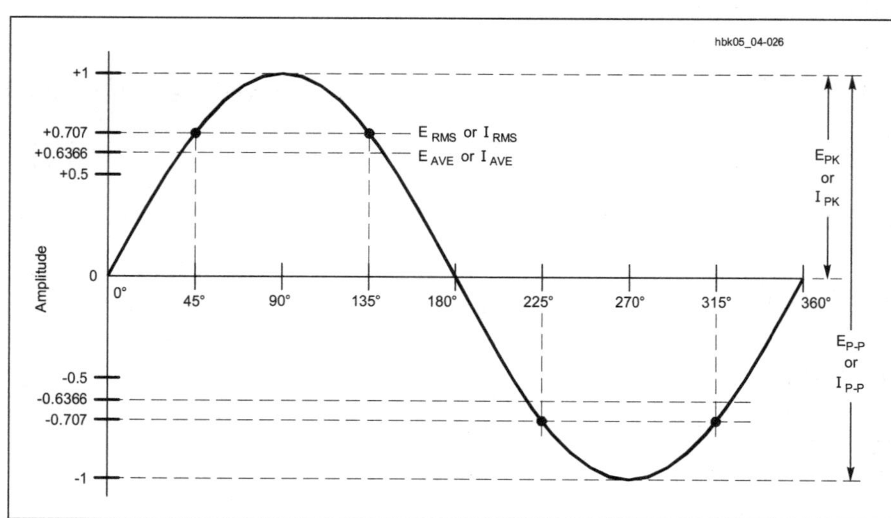

Figure 4.2 — The relationships between RMS, average, peak and peak-to-peak values of ac voltage and current for a sine wave.

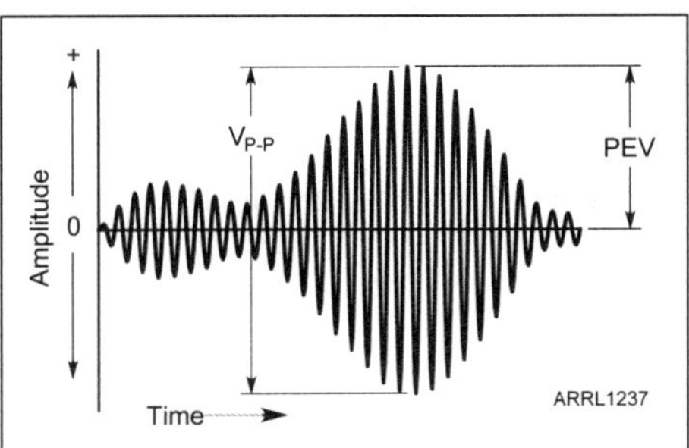

Figure 4.3 — The peak envelope voltage (PEV) for a composite waveform.

It is particularly important to know the relationship between RMS and peak voltages to choose components that have sufficient voltage ratings. Capacitors are often connected across the ac power line to perform RF filtering. The capacitor must be rated to withstand the ac peak voltage. For example, a capacitor placed across a 120 V ac power line will experience a peak voltage of $120 \times 1.414 = 169.7$ V. A capacitor with a 200 V rating or higher should be used.

PEP: DEFINITION AND MEASUREMENT

PEP (or *peak envelope power*) is the average power of one complete RF cycle at the peak of the signal's envelope. (It is *not* the instantaneous power at the peak of an RF cycle during a peak of the signal's envelope.) PEP is used because it is a convenient way to measure or specify the maximum power of amplitude-modulated signals.

To calculate average ac power, you need to know the load impedance and the RMS voltage. Measure the RF voltage at the very peak of the modulated signal's envelope — this is the *peak envelope voltage* (*PEV*) as shown in **Figure 4.3**. PEV is equal to one-half of the waveform's peak-to-peak voltage, V_{P-P}.

PEP is then calculated as follows:

$$PEP = \frac{\left[\dfrac{V_{P-P}}{2} \times 0.707\right]^2}{R} = \frac{\left(PEV \times 0.707\right)^2}{R} = \frac{V_{RMS}^{\;2}}{R}$$

Example 10: If PEV is 50 V across a 50 Ω load, the PEP power is

$$PEP = \frac{\left(50 \times 0.707\right)^2}{50} = 25 \text{ W}$$

Example 11: If a 50-Ω load is dissipating 1200 W PEP, the RMS voltage is

$$V_{RMS} = \sqrt{PEP \times R} = \sqrt{1200 \times 50} = 245 \text{ V} \;\; \textbf{[G5B12]}$$

Example 12: In Example 11, the peak voltage is

$$V_{PK} = 245 \text{ V} \times 1.414 = 346 \text{ V}$$

Example 13: If an oscilloscope measures 200 V_{P-P} across a 50 Ω load, the PEP power is

$$PEP = \frac{\left[\dfrac{0.707 \times 200}{2}\right]^2}{50} = \frac{4999}{50} = 100 \text{ W} \;\; \textbf{[G5B06]}$$

For 500 V_{P-P}, the PEP power is

$$PEP = \frac{\left[\dfrac{0.707 \times 500}{2}\right]^2}{50} = \frac{31241}{50} = 625 \text{ W} \;\; \textbf{[G5B14]}$$

PEP is equal to the average power if an amplitude-modulated signal is not modulated. **[G5B11]** This is the case when modulation is removed from an AM signal (leaving only the steady carrier) or when a CW transmitter is keyed. Likewise, an FM signal is a constant-power signal, so PEP is always equal to average power for FM signals. If an average-reading wattmeter connected to your transmitter reads 1060 W when you close the key on CW, your PEP output is also 1060 W. **[G5B13]**

4.3 Basic Components

G7A09 — Which symbol in Figure G7-1 represents a field effect transistor?
  Symbol 1

G7A10 — Which symbol in Figure G7-1 represents a Zener diode?
  Symbol 5

G7A11 — Which symbol in Figure G7-1 represents an NPN junction transistor?
  Symbol 2

G7A12 — Which symbol in Figure G7-1 represents a solid core transformer?
  Symbol 6

G7A13 — Which symbol in Figure G7-1 represents a tapped inductor?
  Symbol 7

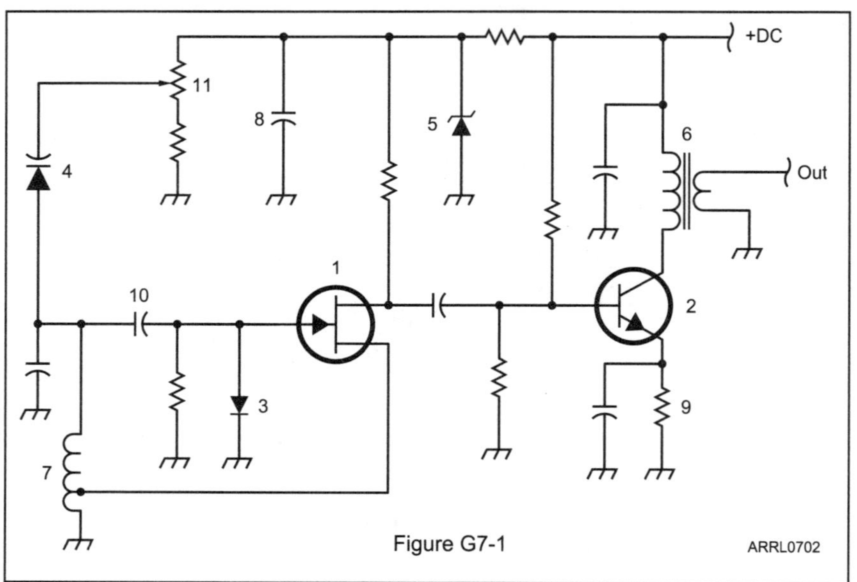

In this section, you'll learn some basic characteristics of resistors, capacitors, inductors, and transformers. The symbols that represent each type of component on electronic schematics are presented in **Figure 4.4** for reference. Refer to this figure as you read this section. **[G7A09 to G7A13]**

Use the following conversion factors to convert units with one metric prefix to another:

• Divide by 1,000 to convert: pico to nano, nano to micro, micro to milli, kilo to mega, and mega to giga.

• Multiply by 1,000 to convert: nano to pico, micro to nano, milli to micro, mega to kilo, and giga to mega.

Examples of component value conversions are given below.

Common Schematic Symbols Used in Circuit Diagrams

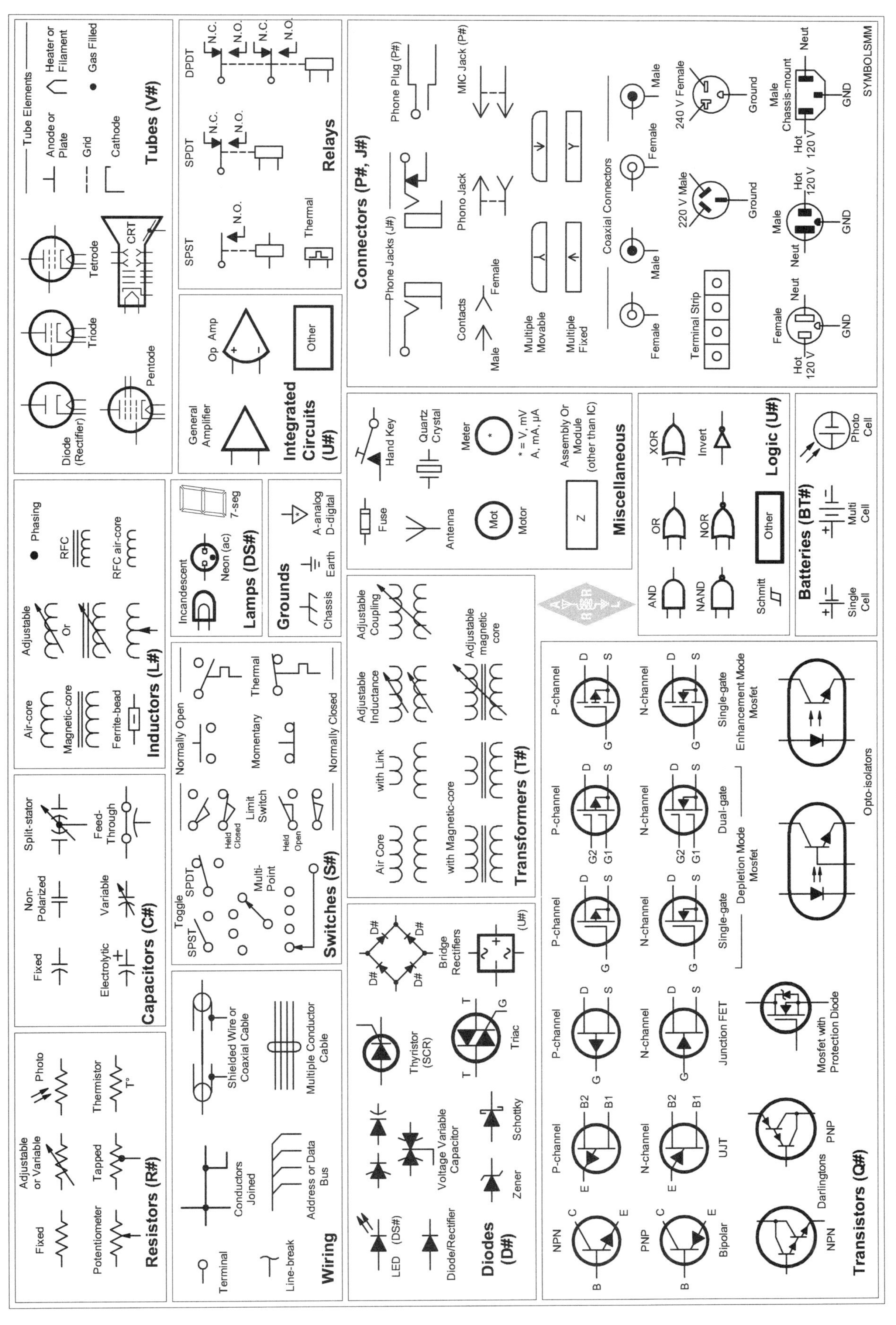

Figure 4.4 — These are the standard symbols used by the ARRL on schematic diagrams.

The three most basic types of electronic components are resistors, capacitors and inductors (coils). Resistors, designated with an R, have a resistance specified in ohms (Ω), kilohms (kΩ) or megohms (MΩ). Capacitors, designated with a C, store electric energy and have values measured in picofarads (pF), nanofarads (nF) and microfarads (μF). Inductors, designated L, store magnetic energy and have values measured in nanohenrys (nH), microhenrys (μH), millihenrys (mH) and henrys (H).

The following terms apply to all components and may be important when selecting a component for a design or for repair.

• *Nominal value* — the quantity of a specific characteristic that the component is manufactured to exhibit, such as a 10 Ω resistor.

• *Tolerance* — the amount by which the actual value is allowed to vary from the nominal value, usually expressed in percent, such as a 5% tolerance resistor.

• *Temperature coefficient* — the variation of the component's actual value with temperature, such as 10 mΩ per degree Centigrade. Temperature coefficients (or "tempco") may be either positive (increasing value with temperature) or negative. For a positive temperature coefficient, as temperature increases so does resistance. Most components are available with several different values of tempco.

• *Power (or voltage or current) rating* — the rated ability of the component to withstand heat or dissipate power, such as a ¼ W resistor.

A more complete description of electronic components can be found in *The ARRL Handbook,* and the website for this book contains links to more information.

RESISTORS AND RESISTANCE

A selection of resistors is shown in **Figure 4.5** ranging from subminiature *surface-mount technology (SMT)* packages to a *power resistor* that can dissipate several watts of power. There are several common types of resistors. **Table 4.1** illustrates how their characteristics differ and in what applications they are most commonly used.

Resistors of all types are available with nominal values from 1 Ω or less to more than 1 MΩ. The nominal value is printed directly on the body of the resistor as text or by using colored bands of paint. (This book's website, **arrl.org/general-class-license-manual**, has links to more information on component marking.) Several tolerances are available, from precision resistors with tolerances of 1% or less, to general-purpose resistors with tolerances of 5% or 10%.

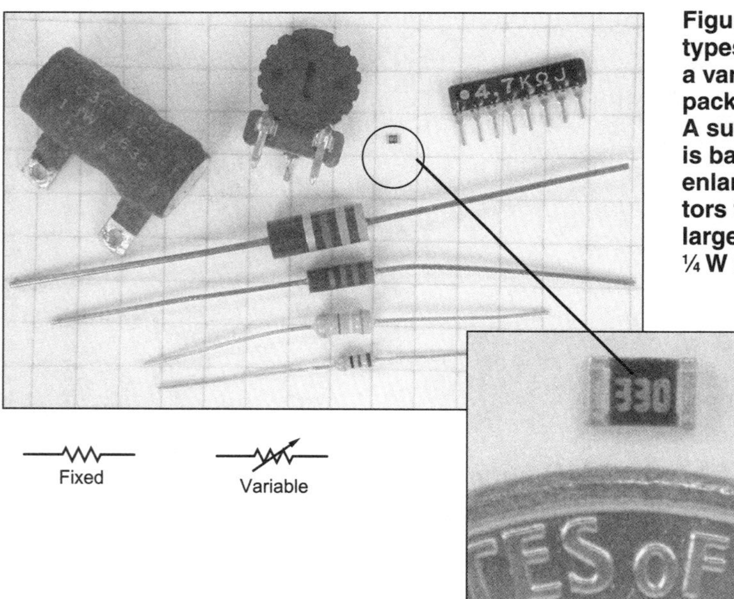

Figure 4.5 — These examples of common resistor types include a 10 W power resistor at the upper left, a variable resistor at top center, and a single in-line package (SIP) of several resistors at the upper right. A surface-mount technology (SMT) resistor package is barely visible next to the variable resistor but is enlarged in the inset photo. Several low-power resistors fill the bottom half of the photograph, from the large 1 W carbon composition resistor to the small ¼ W resistor at the bottom.

Table 4.1

Characteristics of Resistor Types

Resistor Type	Power Ratings	Applications
Carbon composition	⅛ – 2 W	General use, wire leads
Carbon film	⅒ – ½ W	General use, wire leads and SMT package
Metal film	⅒ – ½ W	Low-noise, wire leads and SMT package
Wirewound	1 W – 100 W or more	Power circuits
Metal oxide	½ – 10 W	Noninductive for RF applications

The most common units for resistors are ohms (Ω), kiloohms (kΩ), and megohms (MΩ). To convert between these units use the following conversions:

From ohms	To kiloohms divide by 1,000	To megohms divide by 1,000,000
From kilohms	To ohms multiply by 1,000	To megohms divide by 1,000
From megohms	To ohms multiply by 1,000,000	To kiloohms multiply by 1,000

Example 14: 150 Ω = 150 / 1,000 = 0.15 kΩ and 150 Ω = 150 / 1,000,000 = 0.00015 MΩ

Example 15: 4.7 kΩ = 4.7 × 1,000 = 4,700 Ω and 4.7 kΩ = 4.7 / 1,000 = 0.0047 MΩ

Example 16: 2.2 MΩ = 2.2 × 1,000,000 = 2,200,000 Ω and 2.2 MΩ = 2.2 × 1,000 = 2,200 kΩ

INDUCTORS AND INDUCTANCE

G6B01 — What determines the performance of a ferrite core at different frequencies?

The composition, or "mix," of materials used

G6B05 — What is an advantage of using a ferrite core toroidal inductor?

All these choices are correct

Figure 4.6 shows several common types of inductors and their corresponding schematic symbols. Double solid lines next to the inductor symbol indicate the presence of a solid magnetic core. Air cores are represented by dashed lines or no lines at all. The variable inductor in the middle also has a magnetic core — showing the double lines in the variable inductor symbol is optional. Miniature inductors (not shown in the figure) have the

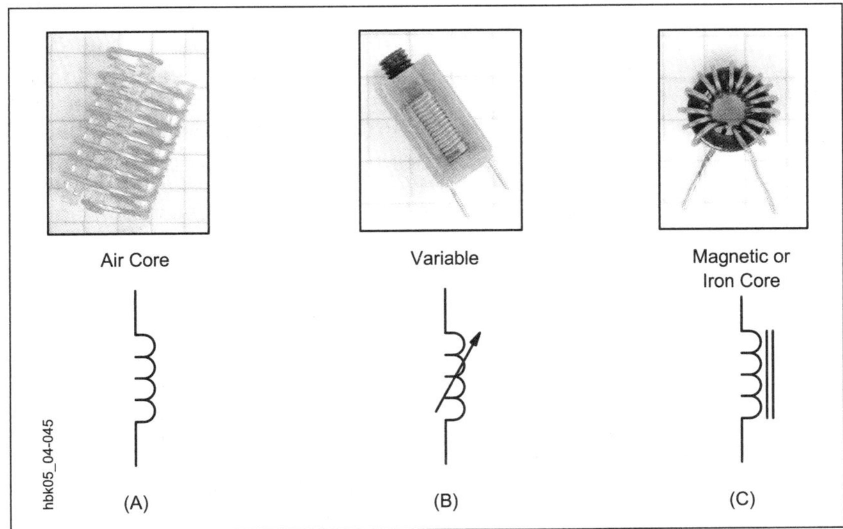

Figure 4.6 — Photos and schematic symbols for common inductors.

same style of package and are easily confused with resistors. (This book's web page has links to more information on component marking and will take you to more information how these inductors are identified.)

Inductance, the measure of an inductor's ability to store magnetic energy, is directly proportional to the square of the number of turns and the area enclosed by each turn. Making an inductor longer without changing the number of turns or diameter reduces inductance. The higher the inductance, the greater the amount of magnetic energy is stored for a given amount of current. Increasing the core's ability to store magnetic energy, called its *permeability*, also increases its inductance.

The type of core and winding of an inductor are important to the type of circuit in which it is to be used. Here is a list of several common types of inductors you'll encounter:

- *Laminated iron core* — dc and ac power and filtering
- *Powdered iron solenoid* — power supplies, RF chokes, audio, and low-frequency radio circuits
- *Powdered iron* and *ferrite toroid*s — audio and radio circuits
- *Air core* — RF transmitting

Variable inductors are encountered in low-power receiving and transmitting applications. Low-power variable inductors are adjusted by moving a magnetic core in and out of the inductor. The core is threaded and moves when turned. In a transmitter or impedance matching circuit, high-power variable inductors are adjusted by moving a sliding contact along the inductor.

The most common units for inductors are millihenries (mH), microhenries (μH), and nanohenries (nH). To convert between these units use the following conversions:

Conversions for Nano-, Micro-, and Millihenries

From	To	Action
Nanohenries	Microhenries	÷ 1,000
	Millihenries	÷ 1,000,000
Microhenries	Nanohenries	x 1,000
	Millihenries	÷ 1,000
Millihenries	Nanohenries	x 1,000,000
	Microhenries	x 1,000

Example 17: 330 nH = 330 / 1,000 = 0.33 μH and 330 nH = 330 / 1,000,000 = 0.00033 mH

Example 18: 6.8 μH = 6.8 × 1,000 = 6,800 nH and 6.8 μH = 6.8 / 1,000 = 0.0068 mH

Example 19: 88 mH = 88 × 1,000,000 = 88,000,000 nH and 88 mH = 88 × 1,000 = 8,800 μH

While resistors dissipate energy entirely within their bodies, the stored energy of an inductor is not so well-behaved. As **Figure 4.7** shows, when two inductors are placed close together with their axes aligned, the magnetic field from one inductor can also pass through the second inductor, sharing some of its energy. This is called *coupling*. The ability of inductors to share or transfer magnetic energy is called *mutual inductance*.

For a *toroidal winding* (shown at the right in Figure 4.6) the ring-shaped core contains nearly all of the inductor's magnetic field. Since very little of the field extends outside of the core, toroidal inductors (or "toroids") can be placed next to each other in nearly any orientation with minimal mutual inductance. This property makes them ideal for use in RF circuits, where you do not want interaction between nearby inductors.

Toroids may be wound on ferrite or powdered iron cores. (Ferrite is a ceramic containing iron, zinc, and manganese compounds.) These cores make it possible to obtain large values of inductance in a relatively small package compared to using an air core. The combination of materials (or "mix") used to make the core is selected so the inductor performs best over a specific range of frequencies. **[G6B01, G6B05]**

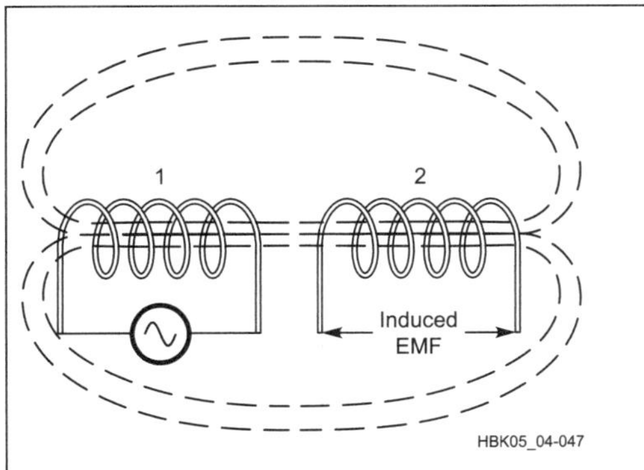

Figure 4.7 — When ac voltage is applied, current flows through coil number 1, setting up a shared magnetic field that causes a voltage to be induced in the turns of coil number 2.

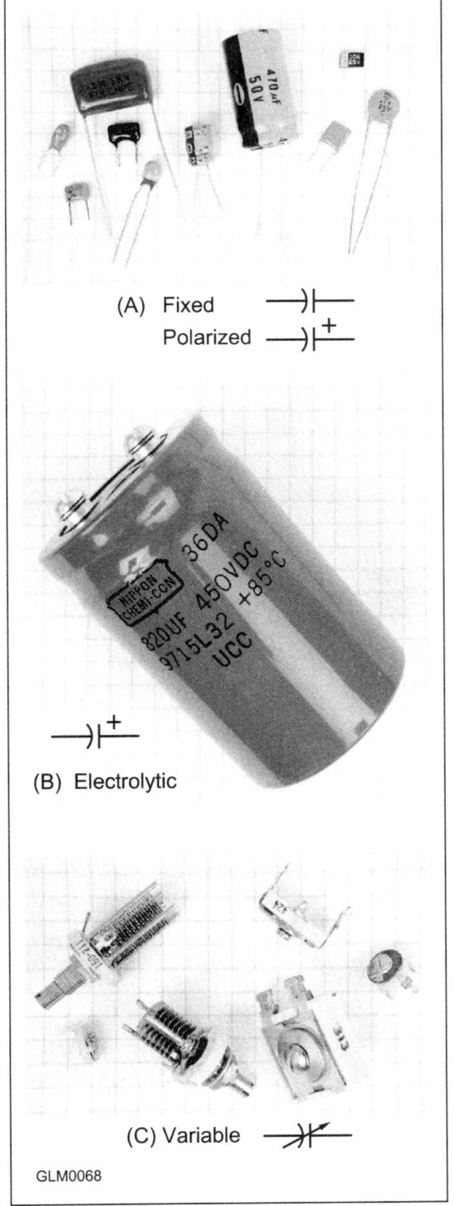

CAPACITORS AND CAPACITANCE

G6A04 — Which of the following is characteristic of an electrolytic capacitor?

High capacitance for a given volume

G6A08 — Which of the following is characteristic of low voltage ceramic capacitors?

Comparatively low cost

Several types of capacitors or "caps" used in radio electronics are shown in **Figure 4.8** and additional symbols for capacitors in Figure 4.4. All capacitors have the same basic structure — two conducting surfaces (called *electrodes*) separated by a *dielectric* that stores electrical energy while preventing dc current flow between the surfaces. Capacitance is increased by larger surface areas, bringing the surfaces closer together, or using a dielectric material that can store more energy.

The simplest capacitor is a pair of metal plates separated by air. You can see examples of this type of capacitor in Figure 4.8C. These variable capacitors have two sets of plates, one fixed and the other moveable, so that as the moveable plates are rotated between the fixed plates, the changing area of overlap varies the capacitance as well.

Two popular styles of capacitors are designed to optimize their energy storage capabilities: aluminum and tantalum electrolytic capacitors. Aluminum electrolytic capacitors use metal foil for the conducting surfaces and the dielectric is an insulating layer on the foil created by a wet paste or gel of chemicals (the *electrolyte*). Tantalum capacitors are similar in that a porous mass of tantalum is immersed in an electrolyte. The electrolyte and the large surface area of these capacitors create large capacitances in comparatively small volumes. **[G6A04]** Electrolytic capacitors can be seen near the center of Figure 4.8A and in Figure 4.8B. The small "gumdrop" shaped capacitor toward the lower left of Figure 4.8A is a tantalum capacitor. Tantalum and electrolytic capacitors are also *polarized*, meaning that a dc voltage may only be applied in one direction without damaging the electrolyte in the capacitor. If the applied voltage is reversed, the capacitor may be damaged or destroyed. Look for the polarity markings on the capacitor to install it correctly.

Another important rating for capacitors is their *voltage rating*. Above the voltage limit the dielectric material's insulating ability breaks down and an arc occurs between the capacitors' conducting surfaces. Except for air-dielectric capacitors, arcing usually destroys the capacitor.

There are many uses of capacitors in radio circuits. Each requires different characteristics that are satisfied by the various

Figure 4.8 — Photo A shows fixed value capacitors, including aluminum electrolytic capacitors near the center. Film and mica capacitors are shown on the left and ceramic units on the right. Photo B shows a large "computer grade" electrolytic capacitor used in power supply filters. Photo C shows several small adjustable or "trimmer" capacitors.

styles of capacitor construction. Here are some examples of common capacitor types and their uses:

• *Ceramic* — RF filtering and bypassing at high frequencies, comparatively low cost [G6A08]

• *Plastic film* — circuits operating at audio and lower radio frequencies
• *Silvered-mica* — highly stable, low-loss, used in RF circuits
• *Electrolytic and tantalum* —power supply filter circuits
• *Air and vacuum dielectric* — transmitting and RF circuits

Capacitors have many uses, but several are common enough to have a special name. *Blocking* capacitors pass ac signals while blocking dc signals. *Bypass* capacitors provide a low impedance path for ac signals around a higher-impedance component or circuit. *Filter* capacitors smooth out the voltage pulses of rectified ac to an even dc voltage. *Suppressor* capacitors absorb the energy of voltage transients or "spikes." *Tuning* capacitors vary the frequency of resonant circuits or filters or adjust impedance matching circuits.

The most common units for capacitors are microfarads (µF), nanofarads (nF), and picofarads (pF). To convert between these units use the following conversions:

Conversions for Pico-, Nano-, and Microfarads

From	To	Action
Picofarads	Nanofarads	÷ 1,000
	Microfarads	÷ 1,000,000
Nanofarads	Picofarads	x 1,000
	Microfarads	÷ 1,000
Microfarads	Picofarads	x 1,000,000
	Nanofarads	x 1,000

Example 20: 820 pF = 820 / 1,000 = 0.82 nF and 820 pF = 820 / 1,000,000 = 0.00082 µF

Example 21: 22 nF = 22 × 1,000 = 22,000 pF and 22 nF = 22 / 1,000 = 0.022 µF

Example 22: 4.7 µF = 4.7 × 1,000,000 = 4,700,000 pF and 4.7 µF = 4.7 × 1,000 = 4,700 nF

TRANSFORMERS

G5C01 — What causes a voltage to appear across the secondary winding of a transformer when an AC voltage source is connected across its primary winding?

Mutual inductance

G5C02 — What is the output voltage if an input signal is applied to the secondary winding of a 4:1 voltage step-down transformer instead of the primary winding?

The input voltage is multiplied by 4

G5C05 — Why is the primary winding wire of a voltage step-up transformer usually a larger size than that of the secondary winding?

To accommodate the higher current of the primary

G5C06 — What is the voltage output of a transformer with a 500-turn primary and a 1500-turn secondary when 120 VAC is applied to the primary?

360 volts

In the previous discussion on inductors, mutual inductance was introduced. Mutual inductance is put to good use in the *transformer*. Transformers transfer ac power between two or more inductors sharing a common core (see Figure 4.4 for schematic symbols). The inductors are called *windings*. The winding to which power is applied is called the *primary winding* and the winding from which power is supplied is called the *secondary winding*. When voltage is applied to the primary winding, mutual inductance causes voltage to appear across the secondary winding. **[G5C01]** Transformers work equally well "in both directions," so the primary and secondary winding assignments are made based on construction and safety considerations.

Transformers can change power from one combination of ac voltage and current to another by using windings with different numbers of turns. This transformation occurs because all windings share the same magnetic field by virtue of being wound on the same core. If the energy in all windings is the same but the windings have different numbers of turns, then the current in each winding must change so that the total power into and out of the transformer is the same, regardless of what load is attached to the secondary windings. A significant change between primary and secondary voltage usually requires a change in the size of wire between windings. For example, in a step-up transformer, the primary winding carries higher current and is wound with larger-diameter wire than the secondary. **[G5C05]**

The ratio of the number of turns in the primary winding, N_P, to the number of turns in the secondary winding, N_S, determines how current and voltage are changed by the transformer. Most electronic circuits are primarily concerned with voltage, so the most common transformer equations are those that relate transformer input (or primary) voltage, E_P, to output (or secondary) voltage, E_S:

$$\frac{E_S}{E_P} = \frac{N_S}{N_P}$$

or

$$E_S = E_P \times \frac{N_S}{N_P}$$

Example 23: What is the voltage across a 1,500-turn secondary winding if 120 V ac is applied across the 500-turn primary winding?

$$E_S = 120 \times \frac{1500}{500} = 360 \text{ Vac} \quad \textbf{[G5C06]}$$

Example 24: What would be the secondary-to-primary turns ratio to change 115 V ac to 500 V ac?

$$\frac{N_S}{N_P} = \frac{E_S}{E_P} = \frac{500}{115} = 4.35$$

Example 25: What happens if a signal is applied to the secondary winding of a 4:1 transformer instead of the primary? In the equation above for primary and secondary voltages, reverse E_P and E_S. The resulting output voltage of the transformer is 4 times the input voltage. **[G5C02]**

COMPONENTS IN SERIES AND PARALLEL CIRCUITS

G5B02 — How does the total current relate to the individual currents in a circuit of parallel resistors?

It equals the sum of the currents through each branch

G5C03 — What is the total resistance of a 10-, a 20-, and a 50-ohm resistor connected in parallel?

5.9 ohms

G5C04 — What is the approximate total resistance of a 100- and a 200-ohm resistor in parallel?
> 67 ohms

G5C08 — What is the equivalent capacitance of two 5.0-nanofarad capacitors and one 750-picofarad capacitor connected in parallel?
> 10.750 nanofarads

G5C09 — What is the capacitance of three 100-microfarad capacitors connected in series?
> 33.3 microfarads

G5C10 — What is the inductance of three 10-millihenry inductors connected in parallel?
> 3.3 millihenries

G5C11 — What is the inductance of a circuit with a 20-millihenry inductor connected in series with a 50-millihenry inductor?
> 70 millihenries

G5C12 — What is the capacitance of a 20-microfarad capacitor connected in series with a 50-microfarad capacitor?
> 14.3 microfarads

G5C13 — Which of the following components should be added to a capacitor to increase the capacitance?
> A capacitor in parallel

G5C14 — Which of the following components should be added to an inductor to increase the inductance?
> An inductor in series

Now that you know about the basic electronic components, the next step is to learn how to combine them! First, let's review the two fundamental circuit rules illustrated in **Figure 4.9**:

- Voltages add in a series circuit, and
- Currents add in a parallel circuit.

Using an analogy between electricity and water pressure and flow, if a pump supplies pressure to a closed water system, the pressure drops around the system must add up to equal the pressure supplied by the pump. There can be no "spare" or "leftover" pressure. Whether voltage is applied by a battery, power supply or ac outlet, around a series circuit

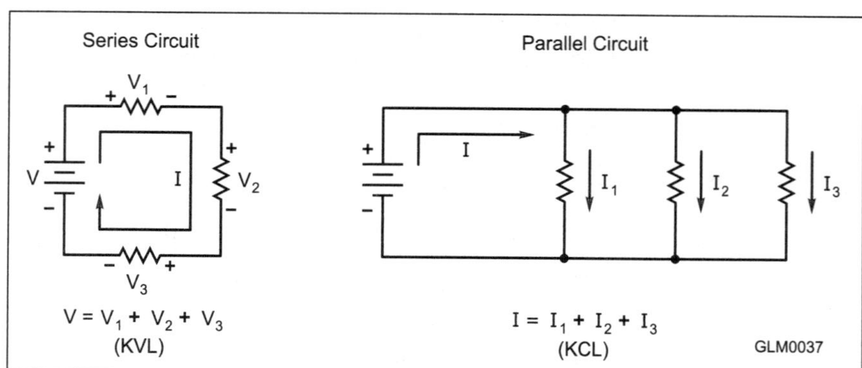

Figure 4.9 — In series circuits, the current is the same in all components and voltages are summed. In parallel circuits, voltage across all components is the same and the sum of currents into and out of circuit junctions must be equal.

the voltages across the various components must add up to be equal to the voltage applied to the circuit. This is *Kirchoff's Voltage Law (KVL)*.

Parallel circuits also have a water analogy. Where several pipes come together, the sum of water flows entering the junction must be equal to the sum of water flows leaving the junction. Stated in a different way, the sum of water flows entering and leaving the junction must equal zero. Water in must equal water out. Electrical current works in just the same way: the total current entering a circuit junction must equal the sum of currents leaving the junction. This is *Kirchoff's Current Law (KCL)*. **[G5B02]**

Components connected in series or parallel can be replaced with a single *equivalent* component. The rules for determining the equivalent component's value are summarized in **Table 4.2** and **Table 4.3**, and shown graphically in **Figure 4.10**. **[G5C13, G5C14]** There are really only two formulas to remember — a simple sum (add the values) and the "reciprocal of reciprocals" as shown in Table 4.2.

When there are only two components, the reciprocal of reciprocals equation simplifies quite a bit, shown here for resistors:

$$R_{EQU} = \frac{R1 \times R2}{R1 + R2}$$

Example 26: What is the total resistance of three 100 Ω resistors in series?

$$R_{EQU} = 100 + 100 + 100 = 300 \ \Omega$$

What is the approximate total resistance of a 100- and a 200-ohm resistor in parallel?

$$R_{EQU} = \frac{100 \times 200}{100 + 200} = \frac{20,000}{300} = 66.67 \ \Omega \quad \text{[G5C04]}$$

Table 4.2

Calculating Series and Parallel Equivalent Values

Component	In Series
Resistor	Add values, R1 + R2 + R3 +…
Inductor	Add values, L1 + L2 + L3 +…
Capacitor	Reciprocal of reciprocals, 1/(1/C1 + 1/C2 + 1/C3 +…)

Component	In Parallel
Resistor	Reciprocal of reciprocals, 1/(1/R1 + 1/R2 + 1/R3 +…)
Inductor	Reciprocal of reciprocals, 1/(1/L1 + 1/L2 + 1/L3 +…)
Capacitor	Add values, C1+C2+C3+…

Table 4.3

Effect on Total Value of Adding Components in Series and Parallel

Component	Adding In Series	Adding In Parallel
Resistor	Increase	Decrease
Inductor	Increase	Decrease
Capacitor	Decrease	Increase

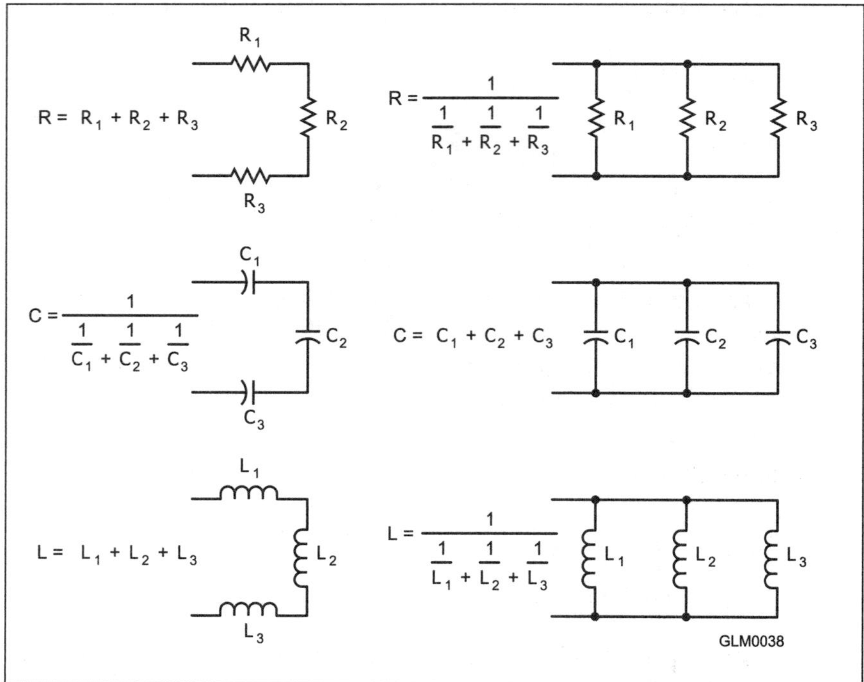

Figure 4.10 — This drawing illustrates how components in series and parallel can be combined into a single equivalent component value.

Example 27: What is the total capacitance of three 100 µF capacitors in series?

$$C_{EQU} = \cfrac{1}{\cfrac{1}{100} + \cfrac{1}{100} + \cfrac{1}{100}} = \cfrac{1}{\cfrac{3}{100}} = \frac{100}{3} = 33.3 \,\mu F \ \ \textbf{[G5C09]}$$

In parallel?

$$C_{EQU} = 100 + 100 + 100 = 300 \,\mu F$$

Example 28: What is the total inductance of three 10 mH inductors in parallel?

$$L_{EQU} = \cfrac{1}{\cfrac{1}{10} + \cfrac{1}{10} + \cfrac{1}{10}} = \frac{10}{3} = 3.3 \,mH \ \ \textbf{[G5C10]}$$

In series?

$$L_{EQU} = 10 + 10 + 10 = 30 \,mH$$

Example 29: What is the total inductance of a 20 mH and 50 mH inductor in series?

$$L_{EQU} = 20 + 50 = 70 \,mH \ \ \textbf{[G5C11]}$$

In parallel?

$$L_{EQU} = \frac{L1 \times L2}{L1 + L2} = \frac{20 \times 50}{20 + 50} = 14.29 \,mH$$

Example 30: What is the total capacitance of a 20 μF and 50 μF capacitor in parallel?

$$C_{EQU} = 20 + 50 = 70 \ \mu F$$

In series?

$$C_{EQU} = \frac{C1 \times C2}{C1 + C2} = \frac{20 \times 50}{20 + 50} = 14.29 \ \mu F \ \textbf{[G5C12]}$$

Example 31: What is the total resistance of a 10 Ω, a 20 Ω and a 50 Ω resistor in series?

$$R_{EQU} = 10 + 20 + 50 = 80 \ \Omega$$

In parallel?

$$R_{EQU} = \frac{1}{\dfrac{1}{10} + \dfrac{1}{20} + \dfrac{1}{50}} = 5.9 \ \Omega \quad \textbf{[G5C03]}$$

Example 32: What is the total capacitance of two 5 nF and one 750 pF capacitors in series?

First, convert 5 nF to pF: 5 nF × 1,000 = 5,000 pF.

$$C_{EQU} = \frac{1}{\dfrac{1}{5,000} + \dfrac{1}{5,000} + \dfrac{1}{750}} = 577 \ pF$$

In parallel?

$$C_{EQU} = 5,000 + 5,000 + 750 = 10,750 \ pF = 10.75 \ nF \quad \textbf{[G5C08]}$$

Knowing these equations for combinations of components can be used to create a specific equivalent value.

Example 33: What three equal-value resistors can be combined in series to create an equivalent value of 450 Ω? If R is the unknown value:

$$R_{EQU} = R + R + R = 3R = 450 \ \Omega$$

so

$$R = \frac{450}{3} = 150 \ \Omega$$

4.4 Reactance, Impedance, and Resonance

REACTANCE

G5A02 — What is reactance?

Opposition to the flow of alternating current caused by capacitance or inducTANCE

G5A03 — Which of the following is opposition to the flow of alternating current in an inductor?

Reactance

G5A04 — Which of the following is opposition to the flow of alternating current in a capacitor?

Reactance

G5A05 — How does an inductor react to AC?

As the frequency of the applied AC increases, the reactance increases

G5A06 — How does a capacitor react to AC?

As the frequency of the applied AC increases, the reactance decreases

G5A09 — What unit is used to measure reactance?

Ohm

G6A06 — Why should wire-wound resistors not be used in RF circuits?

The resistor's inductance could make circuit performance unpredictable

Capacitors and inductors resist the flow of ac differently than they do dc. The resistance to ac current flow caused by capacitance or inductance is called *reactance* (symbolized by X) and is measured in ohms, like resistance. **[G5A02, G5A03, G5A04, G5A09]** Reactance occurs because capacitors and inductors store energy. Let's find out how by starting with the capacitor.

Capacitive Reactance

If a dc voltage is applied to a capacitor that is fully discharged (that is, there is no stored energy and the voltage across the capacitor is zero), at first the current rushes in and the capacitor begins to store energy in its internal electric field. This causes the voltage across the capacitor to rise, opposing the voltage causing current to flow into the capacitor. This reduces the amount of current flowing into the capacitor. As shown in **Figure 4.11**, the more energy is stored and the higher the voltage across the capacitor, the smaller the current that flows. Eventually the capacitor charges to the same voltage as the source of the current and current flow stops. When voltage is initially applied, the capacitor looks like a short circuit to dc signals. After the capacitor is charged, it looks like an open circuit to dc signals and that is how a capacitor blocks dc current.

For ac current, the situation is different. If the ac voltage is at

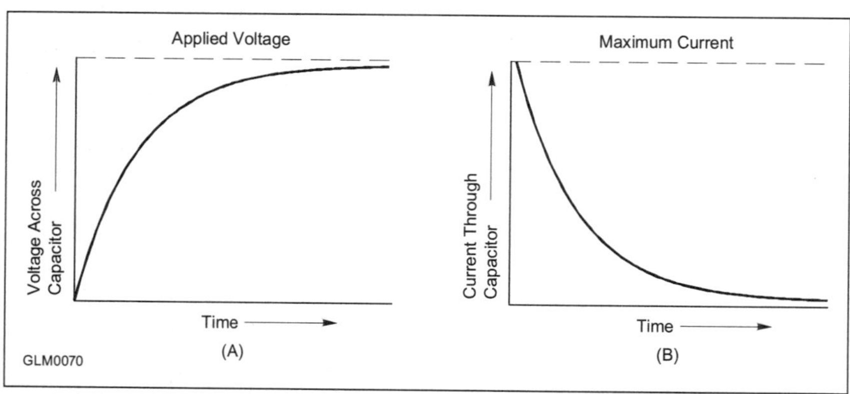

Figure 4.11 — When a circuit containing a capacitor is first energized, the voltage across the capacitor is zero and the current is very large. As time passes, the voltage across the capacitor increases, as shown at A, and the current drops toward zero, as shown at B.

a low enough frequency, it acts like a slowly varying dc voltage and the capacitor can stay charged enough to reduce current to a small value. If the ac voltage is at a higher frequency, however, the capacitor never gets sufficiently charged to reduce current very much. So a capacitor blocks dc current, resists low-frequency ac current and passes high-frequency ac current.

The opposition to ac current flow from the stored energy in a capacitor is called *capacitive reactance* and is denoted with a subscript, X_C. Its behavior with frequency is described by the following equation:

$$X_C = \left(\frac{1}{2\pi f C} \right)$$

where f is the frequency in Hz and C is the capacitance in farads. As the frequency of the applied signal increases, capacitive reactance decreases and vice-versa. **[G5A06]** Be sure to account for the units of frequency (such as kHz and MHz) and capacitance (such as pF, nF and μF).

Example 34: What is the reactance of a 1 nF capacitor at 2 MHz?

$$X_C = \left(\frac{1}{2 \times 3.14 \times (2 \times 10^6) \times (1 \times 10^{-9})} \right) = 79\,\Omega$$

Inductive Reactance

Inductors also resist ac current but in a complementary way. If a dc voltage is applied to an inductor with no stored energy, the resulting current creates a changing magnetic field that opposes the incoming current. Initially, the current flow in the inductor is very small, but gradually builds up, storing more and more energy until opposition to the current disappears and the inductor is "fully charged" with magnetic energy. This is illustrated in **Figure 4.12**. When voltage is originally applied, the inductor looks like an open circuit to dc voltage. After the magnetic field is at full strength, the inductor looks like a short circuit to dc voltage.

This behavior is the opposite of a capacitor that blocks dc currents. If an ac voltage with a high frequency is applied to an inductor, the resulting magnetic field is always changing and so the current is always opposed. If the frequency of the ac voltage is low, the inductor's magnetic

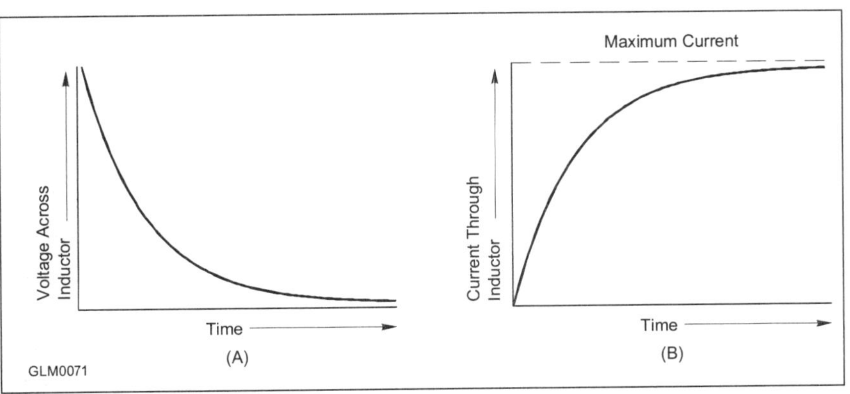

Figure 4.12 — When a circuit containing an inductor is first energized the initial current is zero and the full applied voltage appears across the inductor. As time passes, the voltage drops toward zero as shown at A, and the current increases, as shown at B.

field can be established and the opposition to current is low. So an inductor blocks high-frequency and passes low-frequency ac currents while acting like a short circuit to dc currents.

The opposition to ac current flow from the stored energy in a inductor is called *inductive reactance* and is denoted with a subscript, X_L. Its behavior with frequency is described by the following equation:

$$X_L = 2 \pi f L$$

where f is the frequency in Hz and L is the inductance in henrys. As the frequency of the applied signal increases, inductive reactance increases and vice-versa. **[G5A05]** As with the formula for capacitive reactance, be sure to account for the units of frequency and inductance.

Example 35: What is the reactance of a 10 µH inductor at 5 MHz?

$$X_L = 2 \times 3.14 \times (5 \times 10^6) \times (1 \times 10^{-5}) = 314 \ \Omega$$

Here's another way to look at the effect of the stored energy in capacitors and inductors: Capacitors oppose changes in voltage, while inductors oppose changes in current. Both oppose the flow of ac current, but in complementary ways.

Parasitic Inductance and Capacitance

"Parasitic" means "an unwanted characteristic resulting from the component's physical construction." In radio electronics uses, the *parasitic inductance* of a component is important. For example, wire-wound power resistors are made by winding resistive wire on a ceramic form, making a small coil. This type of construction results in significant amounts of parasitic inductance. The wire leads of a component also create parasitic inductance. In an inductor, each pair of turns also creates as small amount of *parasitic capacitance* in series with the inductance.

If a wire-wound resistor is used in a radio frequency circuit, the resulting inductive reactance is often enough to disrupt the circuit's operation or affect the tuning. **[G6A06]** Non-inductive resistor types such as carbon composition, carbon film, or metal oxide are used in circuits operating at radio frequencies.

Some types of capacitors are made of thin foils separated by a plastic film and rolled up. The "rolled up" aspect of their construction creates a significant amount of parasitic inductance. Electrolytic capacitors use the "rolled up" method of construction and have a high parasitic inductance. The inductive reactance limits electrolytic capacitors to use at relatively low frequencies for audio circuits and power supplies. Tantalum capacitors have relatively little parasitic inductance compared to electrolytics and can be used at higher frequencies.

A ceramic capacitor is made from thin plates of ceramic with one side coated with a metal film and many such layers stacked together. As a result of this construction, ceramic capacitors have relatively little parasitic inductance and can be used through microwave frequencies.

IMPEDANCE AND RESONANCE

G5A01 — What happens when inductive and capacitive reactance are equal in a series LC circuit?
>Resonance causes impedance to be very low

G5A07 — What is the term for the inverse of impedance?
>Admittance

G5A08 — What is impedance?
>The ratio of voltage to current

G5A10 — Which of the following devices can be used for impedance matching at radio frequencies?
>All these choices are correct

G5A11 — What letter is used to represent reactance?
>X

G5A12 — What occurs in an LC circuit at resonance?
>Inductive reactance and capacitive reactance cancel

G5C07 — What transformer turns ratio matches an antenna's 600-ohm feed point impedance to a 50-ohm coaxial cable?
>3.5 to 1

G6A11 — What happens when an inductor is operated above its self-resonant frequency?
>It becomes capacitive

G7C03 — What is one reason to use an impedance matching transformer at a transmitter output?
>To present the desired impedance to the transmitter and feed line

Impedance is a general term for the opposition to current flow in an ac circuit caused by resistance (Z), reactance (X), or any combination of the two. **[G5A11]** Impedance is symbolized by the letter Z and measured in ohms. In a series LC circuit, when inductive and capacitative reactance are equal, resonance causes the impedance to be very low. **[G5A01]** The inverse of impedance is called admittance. **[G5A07]** If impedance is the opposition to ac current flow, then admittance measures the ease with which ac current flows. When you know the impedance, it is straightforward to calculate admittance. The formula is simply

$$Y = 1/Z$$

where
Y is admittance, and Z is impedance.

Like resistance, impedance is the ratio of voltage to current. **[G5A08]** For example, in **Figure 4.13**, the impedance of whatever is in the "black box" is computed as the applied voltage of 250 V ac divided by the measured current of 2 A. The result is 125 Ω, regardless of whether the impedance is the result of a 125 Ω resistor or an inductor or a capacitor with a reactance of 125 Ω at the frequency of the ac voltage or even a combination of resistance and reactance that limited current to 2 A. How could you tell what was inside the box? Changing frequency and re-measuring current would be useful, since resistance does not change with frequency, while reactances do!

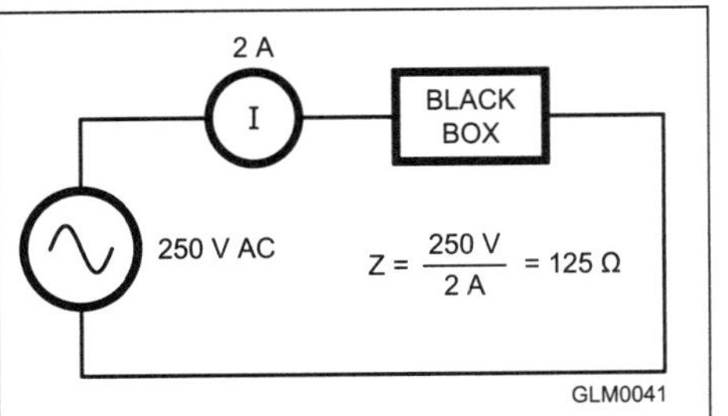

Figure 4.13 — In this circuit we know that the box presents 125 Ω of impedance (opposition to ac current), but we don't know what's in the box.

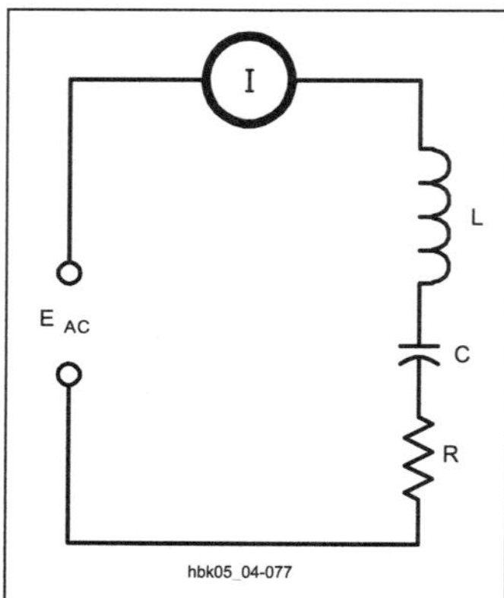

Figure 4.14 — This series circuit is resonant when the capacitive reactance of C equals the inductive reactance of L. At resonance the reactances cancel, leaving R as the only impedance in the circuit.

RESONANCE

Resonance is the condition in which there is a match between the frequency at which a circuit or antenna naturally responds and the frequency of an applied signal. Resonance in a circuit or antenna occurs when the capacitive and inductive reactances present are equal.

In the series circuit shown in **Figure 4.14**, at resonance the reactances of L and C cancel to make a short circuit. **[G5A12]** This leaves the resistance, R, as the circuit's impedance. In a resonant parallel circuit of L, C and R the reactances cancel, but this time L and C form an open circuit and again only R is left as the circuit impedance. Resonance is put to good use in filters and tuning circuits to select or reject specific frequencies at which resonance occurs.

Resonance can also occur when a component's expected reactance is equal to the reactance of its parasitic reactance. This is called *self-resonance*. The result is a component that appears to be a short- or open-circuit at the self-resonant frequency. Above the self-resonant frequency, the component's reactance switches type, making an inductor capacitive and a capacitor inductive. **[G6A11]** This can cause significant problems in a radio-frequency circuit!

IMPEDANCE TRANSFORMATION

A transformer can change the combination of voltage and current while transferring energy. Impedance is the ratio of voltage to current in an ac circuit, so the transformer also changes or transforms impedance between the primary and secondary circuits. In this way, the transformer acts similarly to an automobile's transmission, transferring mechanical power while changing one combination of torque and rotating speed at the engine's drive shaft to a different combination at the wheels.

Electrically, the transformer changes the impedance connected to the secondary winding, Z_S, to a different impedance when measured through the primary winding, Z_P. The turns ratio controls the transformation in the same way as the ratio of gear teeth in a mechanical transmission.

$$Z_P = Z_S \left[\frac{N_P}{N_S} \right]^2 \text{ or } \sqrt{\frac{Z_P}{Z_S}} = \frac{N_P}{N_S}$$

Example 36: What is the primary impedance if a 200 Ω load is connected to the secondary of a transformer with a 5:1 secondary-to-primary turns ratio?

$$Z_P = 200 \left[\frac{1}{5} \right]^2 = 8 \, \Omega$$

Example 37: What turns ratio is required to change a 600 Ω impedance to a 50 Ω impedance? In this case, take the square root of the impedance ratio:

$$\text{Turns ratio} = \frac{N_P}{N_S} = \sqrt{\frac{Z_P}{Z_S}} = \sqrt{\frac{600}{50}} = \sqrt{12} = 3.46$$

Note that the impedance to be changed (in this case 600 Ω) can be connected to the primary or secondary but turns ratios are always stated with the larger number first. In this example, it is stated as 3.46:1 not 1:3.46 (which rounds to 3.5:1). **[G5C07]**

IMPEDANCE MATCHING

An energy source's ability to deliver power to a load is limited by its *internal impedance*. For example, a battery's internal resistance limits how much current it can

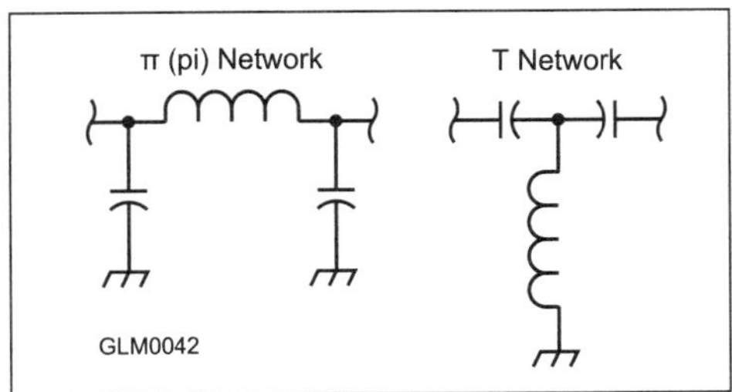

Figure 4.15 — The pi (π) and T networks are named for the letters that they resemble. The pi network is often used to transform the impedances between transistors or tubes in amplifiers and feed lines. The T network is common in stand-alone "antenna tuners" or "transmatches."

deliver. The same is true for sources of RF power, such as circuits and transmitting equipment. An RF source can deliver the maximum amount of power when its internal impedance and the load impedance are the same or *matched*. Both the source and load impedances must also be purely resistive — that is, have no reactance.

Amateur transmitting equipment is designed so that the internal impedance of its output circuits is 50 Ω. If the difference between the antenna system impedance and the transmitter's output impedance is great enough, the transmitter may reduce its output power to avoid damage. The solution is an *impedance-matching circuit* that transforms the undesired impedance to the desired value.

Most impedance-matching circuits are *LC circuits* made of inductors and capacitors. **Figure 4.15** shows two popular LC circuits used for impedance matching: the pi network (a *network* is a formal name for circuit) and the T network. The names are derived from the letters π and T, which the circuit schematics resemble. These can be made entirely of fixed-value components for loads such as a single-band antenna. Adjustable components can also be used, allowing the circuit to be used for different frequencies or loads.

Another popular method of performing impedance matching was introduced in the section on transformers. Special RF *impedance transformers* are often employed in this role, equalizing impedances of source and load to maximize the transfer of power. This is a reason to use an impedance matching transformer at the transmitter's output. Impedance-matching can also be performed by special lengths and connections of transmission line. [G5A10, G7C03]

4.5 Active Components

In order to amplify, switch, shape, or otherwise process a signal, it is necessary to use *active* components. These usually require a source of power and may include passive components, such as resistors or capacitors, as elements of a more complex device.

SEMICONDUCTOR COMPONENTS

G6A03 — What is the approximate forward threshold voltage of a germanium diode?
0.3 volts

G6A05 — What is the approximate forward threshold voltage of a silicon junction diode?
0.7 volts

G6A07 — What are the operating points for a bipolar transistor used as a switch?
Saturation and cutoff

G6A09 — Which of the following describes the MOSFET construction?
The gate is separated from the channel by a thin insulating layer

The most common active components are made of semiconductors. Semiconductors are materials that conduct electricity better than an insulator but not as well as a metal. Silicon (chemical symbol Si) and germanium (Ge) are examples of semiconductors used in radio electronics. The electrical properties of semiconductors can be controlled by the addition of small amounts of other materials such as indium (In) or phosphorus (P). These impurities are called *dopants* and adding them to the base material is called *doping*. If the

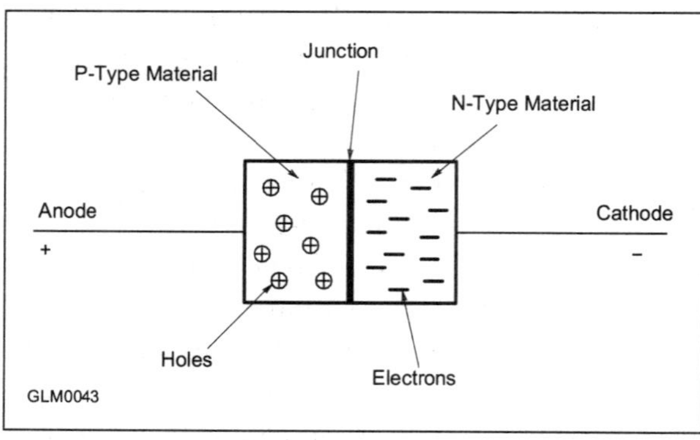

Figure 4.16 — A PN-junction consists of P-type (not enough electrons) and N-type (too many electrons) material in direct contact. The junction is formed at the boundary between the layers of material.

impurity's presence creates an excess of electrons to conduct electricity, the result is N-type material. Otherwise, the impurity creates P-type material which has *holes* or a deficit of the electrons that conduct electricity. All semiconductors are created from combinations of N-type and P-type material. Where the two types of material are in contact is a *PN junction*.

Diodes and Rectifiers

A semiconductor *junction diode* uses a PN junction to block current flow in one direction as shown in **Figure 4.16**. Wire leads are attached to each layer. Current flows when positive voltage is applied from the P-type to the N-type material, called *forward bias*, forcing electrons across the junction. Voltage applied in the reverse direction from N-type to P-type, called *reverse bias*, pulls electrons away from the junction so that no current flows. The voltage required to force electrons across the junction is the diode's *forward voltage* or *junction threshold voltage* and is abbreviated V_F. For silicon diodes, V_F is approximately 0.7 V and for germanium 0.3 V. **[G6A03, G6A05]** Typical diode packages are shown in **Figure 4.17**. (For more information about semiconductors, follow the links on the *General Class License Manual's* web page.)

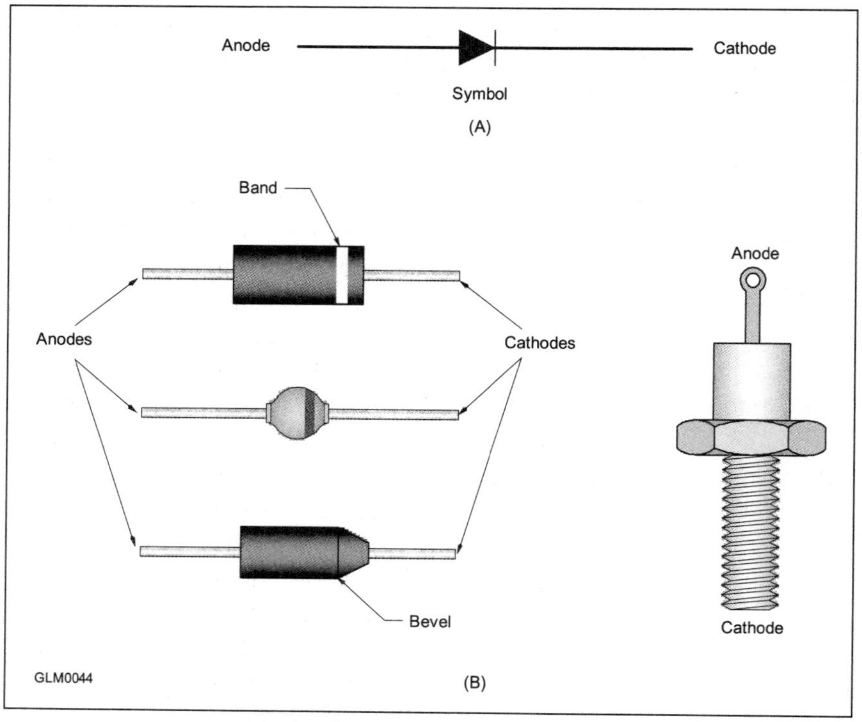

Bipolar and Field-Effect Transistors

The back-to-back layers of P- and N-type material cause the diode's unidirectional current flow. Adding another layer of semiconductor material, however, creates a device capable of amplifying a signal — the transistor. **Figure 4.18** illustrates the basic structure of a *bipolar junction transistor* or *BJT*. Bipolar transistors are made from P- and N-type material and use current to control their operation. Unlike the diode the transistor requires power to function.

Bipolar junction transistors have three electrodes — the *collector (C)*, *emitter (E)* and *base (B)*. The collector and emitter leads carry the current controlled by the transistor. Transistor operation is controlled by current flowing between the base and emitter. The thin base layer of material creates a pair of back-to-back PN junctions that would seem to prevent current flow through the transistor no matter which way voltage is applied because one junction is always reverse-biased. When current flows between the base and

Figure 4.17 — The schematic symbol for a diode is shown at A. Several common diode and rectifier package styles are shown at B.

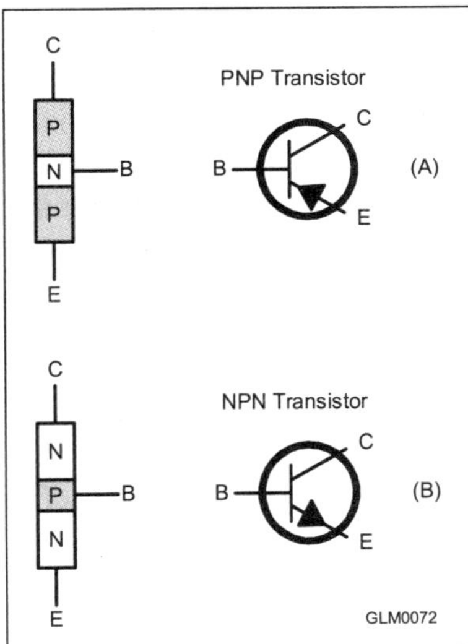

Figure 4.18 — Bipolar transistors are made from three layers of P- and N-type material. At A, a thin layer of N-type material is sandwiched between two layers of P-type material, forming a PNP transistor. The schematic symbol has three leads: collector (C), base (B) and emitter (E), with the arrow pointing in toward the base. At B, the opposite construction creates an NPN transistor, with the emitter arrow pointing out away from the base.

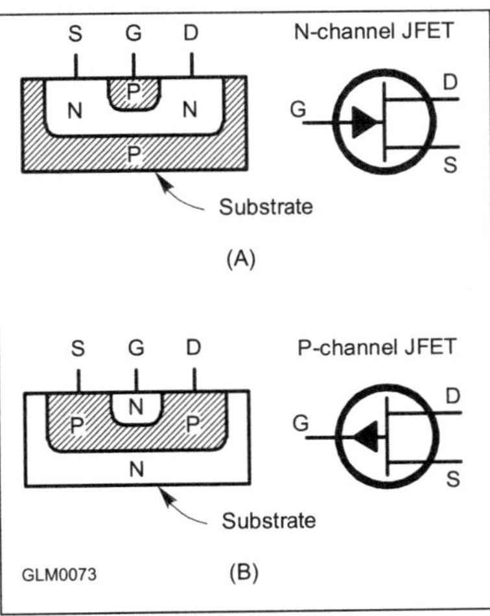

Figure 4.19 — JFET devices are made from P- and N-type material like bipolar transistors, but use a gate embedded in a channel to control electron flow. An N-channel JFET is shown at A and a P-channel JFET at B.

emitter, however, the base is so thin that the current causes both junctions to break down, allowing current flow between collector and emitter.

The amount of base-emitter current required for collector-emitter current to flow is quite small. The control of a large current by a smaller current is *amplification* and the ratio of the collector-emitter current to base-emitter current is called *current gain*. Current gain for dc signals is represented by the symbol β (*beta*). Current gain for ac signals is represented by the symbol h_{fe}.

Another type of transistor, shown in **Figure 4.19** is the *field effect transistor* (FET). The FET has three electrodes like the bipolar transistor — the *drain (D), source (S)* and *gate (G)*. Instead of controlling drain-source current with gate-source current, the voltage between the gate and source is used. Instead of current gain, the FET has *transconductance* (g_m) — the ratio of source-drain current to gate-source voltage. A *junction FET* or *JFET* is constructed with the gate material in direct contact with the material that connects the source and drain electrodes. The *metal-oxide-semiconductor FET* or *MOSFET* and a related device, the *insulated-gate FET* or *IGFET*, have an insulating layer of oxide between the gate and the rest of the transistor. **[G6A09]** Both JFETs and MOSFETs are very sensitive, with small amounts of voltage able to control the source-drain current.

The high amplification of transistors also makes them ideal for use as switches for both voltage and current. By applying enough base-emitter current or gate-source voltage, the transistor can be driven into *saturation* where further increases in input result in no output change. Similarly, the input signal can reduce output current to zero — the condition of *cutoff*. These two states make an excellent representation of digital ON/OFF signals in logic circuits. **[G6A07]**

VACUUM TUBES

G6A10 — Which element of a vacuum tube regulates the flow of electrons between cathode and plate?

Control grid

G6A12 — What is the primary purpose of a screen grid in a vacuum tube?

To reduce grid-to-plate capacitance

The vacuum tube, the oldest device capable of amplification, still makes a valuable contribution in high-power amplifiers. In addition to amplifiers, many amateurs enjoy using antique "tube gear," just as audiophiles do. As a General class licensee, you're likely to encounter vacuum tubes, so you'll need to know how they operate.

A vacuum tube has three basic parts: a source of electrons, an electrode to collect the

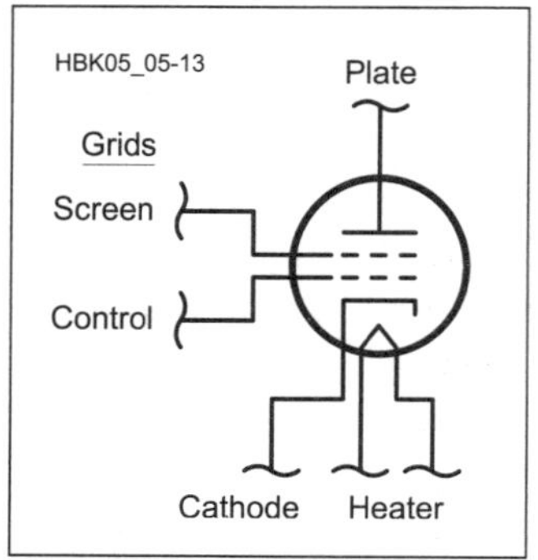

Figure 4.20 — The schematic symbol of a vacuum tube tetrode includes a heater, cathode, the control and screen grids and the anode or plate. The heavy circle represents the tube's enclosing envelope.

electrons, and intervening electrodes that control the electrons traveling from source to collector. Each electrode of the tube is called an *element*. **Figure 4.20** shows the schematic symbol for a tube and the tube's elements.

A tube with two elements is a *diode*, three elements a *triode*, four elements a *tetrode*, and so forth. The most common tubes in amateur service today are triodes and tetrodes.

Some tube terminology:

- *Filament* or *heater* — heats the cathode, causing it to emit electrons
- *Cathode* — the source of electrons
- *Control grid* — the grid closest to the cathode, used to regulate electron travel between the cathode and plate **[G6A10]**
- *Screen grid* — an electrode that reduces grid-to-plate capacitance that diminishes the tube's ability to amplify at high frequencies **[G6A12]**
- *Suppressor grid* — an electrode that prevents electrons from traveling from the plate to the control or screen grid
- *Plate* — the electrode that collects electrons, called *plate current*

All amplifying tubes have at least three electrodes — a cathode (and a filament to heat it), a grid and a plate. Heated to a high temperature by a heater or filament, the cathode emits electrons into the vacuum of the tube. The plate is placed at a positive voltage with respect to the cathode (plate-to-cathode voltage) to attract the electrons. The electrons travel toward the plate through holes in the control grid. If the control grid is at a negative voltage with respect to the cathode (grid-to-cathode voltage), the electrons are repelled and are either slowed down, decreasing plate current, or stopped altogether, called *cutoff*. Conversely, a positive grid-to-cathode voltage accelerates the electrons toward the plate, increasing plate current. Varying the control grid's voltage therefore varies plate current, amplifying the input signal.

For More Information

A semiconductor diode has several ratings that place limits on how it may be used. These are the two most important ratings:

- *Peak inverse (or reverse) voltage (PIV)* — the maximum reverse voltage (voltage in the non-conducting direction) that may be applied before *reverse breakdown* occurs, allowing current to flow in the reverse direction
- *Average forward current (I_F)* — because of the forward voltage, current through the diode dissipates a power of $I_F \times V_F$ in the form of heat. Exceeding this rating will destroy the diode's internal structure.

Another parameter that affects how a diode works at high frequencies is its *junction capacitance (C_J)*. When reverse-biased, the layers of P- and N-type material act like the plates of a small capacitor. The larger C_J becomes, the longer it takes the diode to switch from being reverse-biased to conducting forward current.

Different methods of construction create diodes with a different set of characteristics useful for certain types of circuits.

- *PIN diode* — conducts ac signals with low forward voltage drop, used for RF switching and control
- *Schottky diode* — low junction capacitance allows operation at high frequencies
- *Varactor* — the reverse-biased junction acts like a capacitor and can be used as a small variable capacitor
- *Zener diode* — extra levels of doping allow Zener diodes to be used as voltage regulators while in reverse breakdown

Diodes that are designed for circuits with low-power signals are called *signal* or *switching diodes*. Heavy-duty diodes for use in high-power circuits must carry high currents,

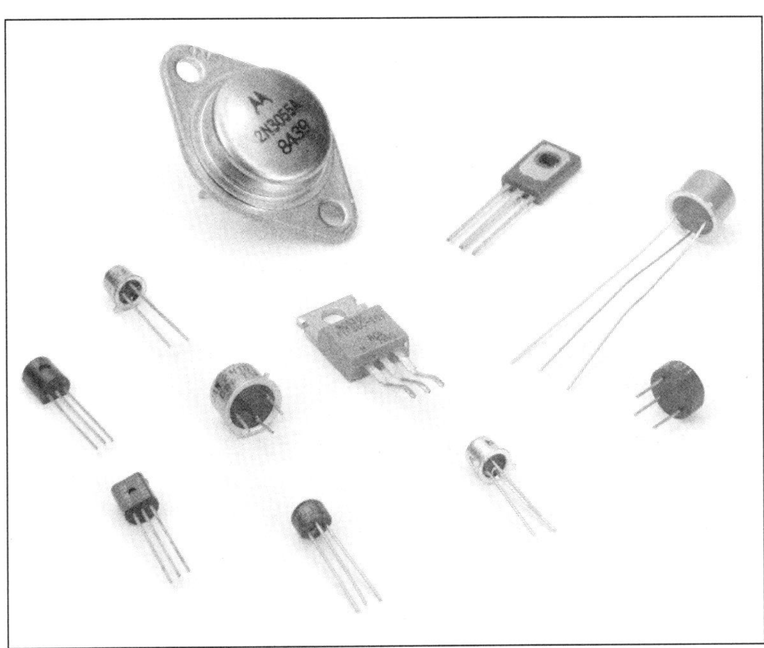

Figure 4.21 — Transistors come in a variety of package styles. The smaller packages are used in low-power circuits for small signals. The larger packages are used in power-control and transmitter circuits.

withstand high voltages or dissipate a lot of power. These diodes are called *rectifiers* and may have PIV and I_F ratings as high as 1,000 V or 100 A!

Transistors come in many types of packages. The different styles are often identified with package numbers beginning with "TO" (for Transistor Outline), such as the TO-3, TO-92 and TO-220 packages shown in **Figure 4.21**. Low-power transistors usually have insulated, plastic packages. Plastic packaging is unsuitable for transistors that must dissipate larger amounts of power. Their packages have metal surfaces through which excess heat can be easily removed. The metal surface is often connected internally to the collector or source of the transistor so a direct connection to a metal heat sink or equipment chassis would short that electrode to ground. Some sort of insulation is often required between the case and heat sink. Be cautious when installing or replacing high-power transistors to avoid short circuits.

Vacuum tubes typically operate at hazardous voltages — as high as two or three thousand volts in power amplifiers. Equipment that uses high-voltage has numerous safety features to prevent electrical shock. Lower-voltage tube equipment relies on the operator or technician to exercise the proper procedures. Take extra safety precautions when servicing or maintaining tube equipment.

ANALOG AND DIGITAL INTEGRATED CIRCUITS

G6B02 — What is meant by the term MMIC?
    Monolithic Microwave Integrated Circuit

G6B03 — Which of the following is an advantage of CMOS integrated circuits compared to TTL integrated circuits?
    Low power consumption

G6B06 — What kind of device is an integrated circuit operational amplifier?
    Analog

G7B03 — Which of the following describes the function of a two-input AND gate?
    Output is high only when both inputs are high

G7B05 — How many states does a 3-bit binary counter have?
    8

G7B06 — What is a shift register?
    A clocked array of circuits that passes data in steps along the array

If one transistor is good, more must be better! The processes that make transistors on thin wafers of silicon can just as easily create many diodes, transistors, resistors, capaci-

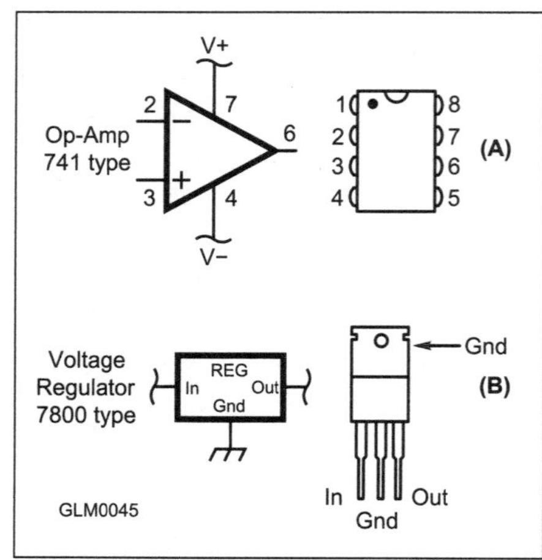

Figure 4.22 — The popular 741 op-amp symbol and dual in-line package (DIP) connections are shown at A. A common three-terminal voltage regulator, the 7800-series, is shown in the TO-220 package at B.

tors and even tiny spiral inductors and connect them with wires made of thin plated-on metal. The result is an *integrated circuit* (IC) also known as a "chip." The two most common types of integrated circuits are *analog* (or *linear*) and *digital* (or *logic*).

Analog ICs operate over a continuous range of voltages and currents. **Figure 4.22** shows the schematic symbol and connection diagrams for two of the most common analog ICs, the operational amplifier and the linear voltage regulator. **[G6B06]** The operational amplifier or "op amp" is widely used for dc and audio circuits as an inexpensive source of gain. Linear voltage regulators are used to maintain a power supply output at a constant voltage over a wide range of currents.

Digital ICs operate with discrete values of voltage and current representing the *binary number system* values 0 and 1. There are several different types of digital circuits called *logic families* that use a specific style of circuit design to create different logic functions. Different families may use different power supply voltages or use different voltage and current levels to represent digital values. Complex digital circuits can be constructed by using ICs from the same family of circuits so that voltage and current levels are compatible for all of the individual circuits.

Characteristics of some common logic families are shown in **Table 4.4**. Although you may find transistor-transistor logic (TTL) logic devices in some equipment, the most popular logic family in use today is the *complementary metal-oxide*

Table 4.4

Logic Family Characteristics

Family Name	Maximum Frequency of Operation	Power Consumption	Power Supply
TTL	100 MHz	High	5 V
CMOS	1 GHz	Low	3 – 5 V
CMOS (CD4000)	1 MHz	Very Low	3 – 15 V

semiconductor (*CMOS*) logic family because of its high speed and low power consumption. **[G6B03]**

Digital Logic Basics

The basic building block of digital circuits are circuits called *gates* that perform *inversion* (changing a 1 to a 0 and vice versa) and the OR and AND functions. Because of the way digital circuits are designed, the most common gates in actual use are the inverter, NAND and NOR. All three of these functions and their schematic symbols are shown in **Figure 4.23**. **[G7B03]** More complex functions — all the way up to microprocessors and digital signal processors — are constructed from combinations of these three functions. Digital circuits that use gates to combine binary inputs to generate a binary output or combination of binary outputs are called *combinational logic*.

Another class of digital circuits combines binary signals in a way that depends on time and on the sequence of inputs to the circuits. These circuits are called *sequential logic*. The basic building block of sequential logic is the *flip-flop*, which has two stable states. The flip-flop responds to a *clock* signal that causes its outputs to change based on the input signals. The two outputs, Q and $\overline{Q}$ (the overbar indicates that the signal is inverted), are always in opposite states. There are several kinds of flip-flops and the most common, the D-type, is shown in Figure 4.23. When a digital signal, such as a pulse or square wave, is applied to the clock input, the rising edge (the edge that goes from low to high or from 0 to 1) causes the Q output to be 1 if the D input is 1 and vice versa. The Q and $\overline{Q}$ outputs stay in that state until the next rising edge is applied to the clock input.

By connecting flip-flops together so that one flip-flop's outputs feed the next flip-flop's

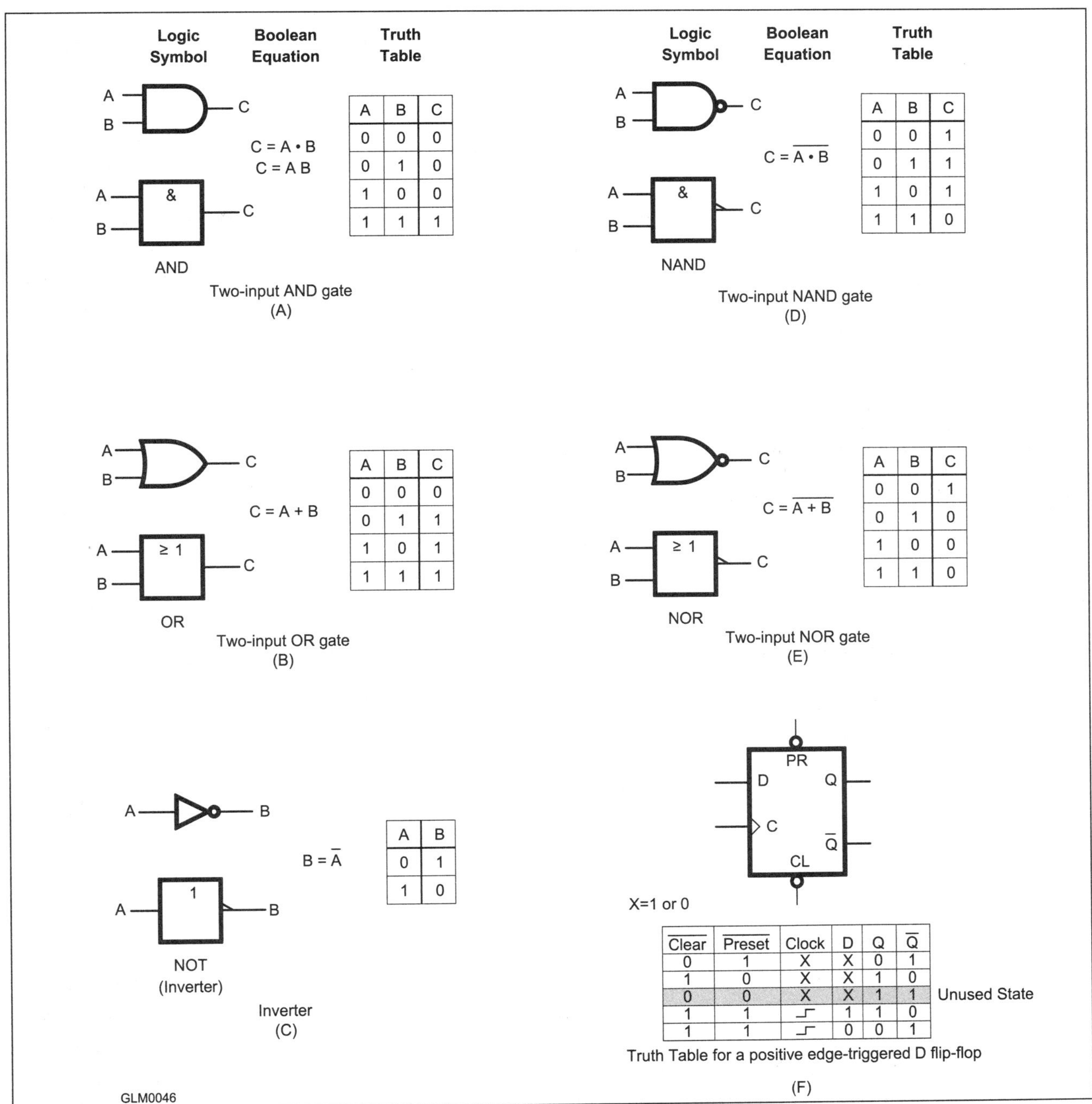

Figure 4.23 — Schematic symbols for the basic digital logic functions with the logic equations and truth tables that describe their operation. The two-input AND gate is shown at A, a two-input OR gate at B, an inverter at C, a two-input NAND gate at D and a two-input NOR gate at E. A D-type flip-flop is shown at F.

input, two important types of circuits are created: *counters* and *shift registers*. In a counter, the outputs of the chain of flip-flops make up a binary number or state representing the number of clock signals that have occurred. Each flip-flop stores one bit of the total count. The highest number that a counter can represent is 2^N, where N is the number of flip-flops that make up the counter. For example, a 3-bit counter (one with three flip-flops) can count $2^3 = 8$ different states, a 4-bit counter can count 16 states, and so on. **[G7B05]**

Connecting the array of flip-flops slightly differently results in a shift register. The shift register stores a sequence of 1s and 0s from its input as the flip-flop outputs. Each clock signal causes the value at the shift register's input to pass or shift to the next flip-flop in the string. **[G7B06]** Some shift-register circuits can be configured to shift up or down (forward or backward) along the array. Shift registers are a simple form of digital memory. (For more information on flip-flops and digital circuits in general, see the website for this book, **arrl.org/general-class-license-manual**.)

RF INTEGRATED CIRCUITS

RF ICs are specially designed for functions commonly required at radio frequencies, such as low-level high-gain amplifiers, mixers, modulators and demodulators, and even filters. RF ICs greatly reduce the number of discrete devices required to build radio circuits.

An MMIC (monolithic microwave integrated circuit) is a special type of RF IC that works through microwave frequencies. **[G6B02]** Taking advantage of integration to combine many RF devices into a single package, some MMICs perform several functions. The MMIC is what enables communications engineers to construct low-cost cell phones, GPS receivers and other sophisticated examples of wireless technology.

MICROPROCESSORS AND RELATED COMPONENTS

G6B08 — How is an LED biased when emitting light?
Forward biased

G6B09 — How does a liquid crystal display compare to an LED display?
Higher contrast in high ambient lighting

Microprocessor and microcontroller ICs are capable of performing millions of computing instructions per second and often include functions such as parallel and serial input-output ports, counters and timers right on the chip.

Memory

The program must be stored in some kind of memory devices so that a microprocessor can read the instructions. There are several kinds of memory. *Volatile* memory loses the data it stores when power is removed. *Nonvolatile* memory stores data permanently, even if the power is removed. *Random-access memory* (RAM) can be read from or written to in any order. *Read-only memory* (ROM) stores data permanently and cannot be changed. There are several common types of each as shown in **Table 4.5**. Memory devices or systems are connected to the microprocessor by a high-speed interface called a *memory bus* that can transfer data at high rates.

Data Interfaces

Microprocessors and computers communicate through data interfaces — special circuits, methods and connectors for data exchange. There are two types of interface, *serial* and *parallel*. *Serial interfaces* transfer one bit of data in each transfer operation. Some common computer serial interfaces are listed in **Table 4.6**. *Parallel interfaces* transfer multiple bits of data in each operation.

Table 4.5
Memory Types

Memory	Volatile/Nonvolatile
Static RAM (SRAM)	Volatile
Dynamic DRAM (DRAM)	Volatile, data must be continually refreshed
Programmable ROM (PROM)	Nonvolatile
EPROM (Erasable PROM)	Nonvolatile, can be erased by exposure to UV
EEPROM (Electrically-erasable PROM)	Nonvolatile, can be electrically erased, Flash EEPROM erased in sections
Mass storage	Nonvolatile, data stored on hard drive, CD-ROM or tape

---

Table 4.6

Common Computer Serial Interfaces

Interface	Typical Speed
RS-232	115 Kbits/sec
USB 1.1	1.5 Mbits/sec
USB 2.0	480 Mbits/sec
USB 3.0	5 Gbits/sec
Firewire	800 Mbits/sec

Visual Interfaces

Amateur equipment uses two types of devices to present information visually, the *indicator* and the *display*. An indicator is a device that presents on/off information visually by the presence, absence or color of light. Common indicators are the incandescent light bulb and the light-emitting diode (*LED*). A display is a device that is capable of presenting text or graphics information in visual form. One example is the display showing frequency and operating information on the front panel of most transceivers.

Incandescent light bulbs have been largely replaced by LEDs in most amateur equipment. LEDs last longer, can be turned on and off far quicker, use less power and generate less heat than light bulbs. Some indicators include LEDs of different colors, creating more than one color or even white light. An LED is a diode made from special types of semiconductor material that emit light when the PN junction is forward biased. **[G6B08]**

The most common type of display is the *LCD* (liquid crystal display) created by sandwiching liquid crystal material between transparent glass panels. A pattern of electrodes is printed in a thin, transparent film on the front glass panel with a single electrode covering the rear panel. As voltage is applied to the electrodes on the front panel, the liquid crystals twist into a configuration that blocks light. LCDs require ambient or *back lighting* (a light source behind the liquid crystal layer) since the liquid crystal layer does not generate light on its own. Compared to liquid crystal displays, LEDs have higher contrast when viewed in situations with high ambient light, such as outside on a sunny day. **[G6B09]**

4.6 Practical Circuits

RECTIFIERS AND POWER SUPPLIES

G7A01 — What is the function of a power supply bleeder resistor?
It discharges the filter capacitors when power is removed

G7A02 — Which of the following components are used in a power supply filter network?
Capacitors and inductors

G7A03 — Which type of rectifier circuit uses two diodes and a center-tapped transformer?
Full-wave

G7A04 — What is characteristic of a half-wave rectifier in a power supply?
Only one diode is required

G7A05 — What portion of the AC cycle is converted to DC by a half-wave rectifier?
180 degrees

G7A06 — What portion of the AC cycle is converted to DC by a full-wave rectifier?
360 degrees

G7A07 — What is the output waveform of an unfiltered full-wave rectifier connected to a resistive load?
A series of DC pulses at twice the frequency of the AC input

G7A08 — Which of the following is characteristic of a switchmode power supply as compared to a linear power supply?
High-frequency operation allows the use of smaller components

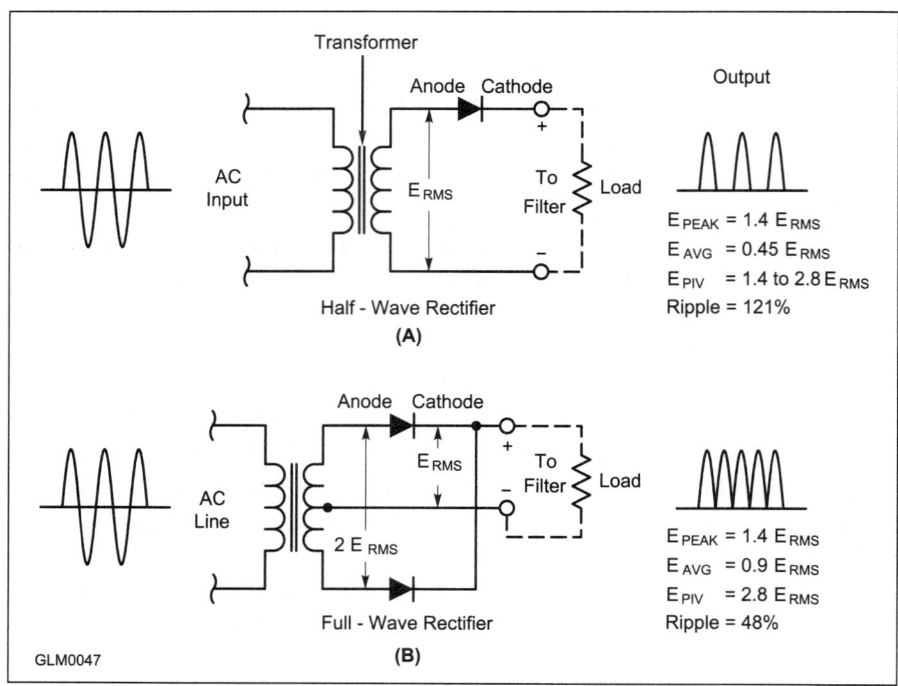

Figure 4.24 — Two basic rectifier circuits and their output waveforms. (A) Half-wave. (B) Full-wave center-tapped. The half-wave circuit converts only one-half of the input waveform (180°) while the full-wave circuit converts the entire input waveform (360°). In most power supplies, a capacitor is connected across the output of the rectifier and will charge to a voltage of E_{PEAK}, the normal peak output of the supply.

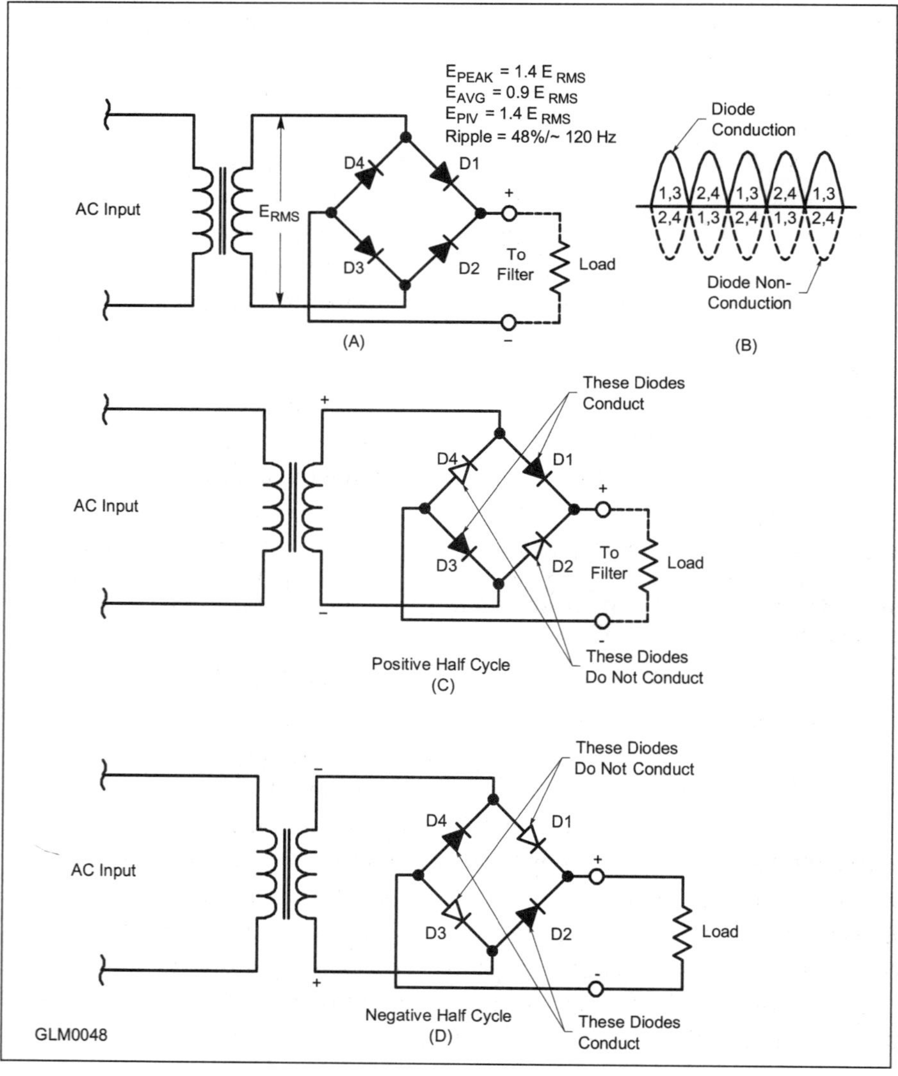

Figure 4.25 — The full-wave bridge rectifier has an equivalent output to the full-wave center-tapped rectifier without a center-tapped transformer winding, but requires twice as many rectifier diodes.

Almost every piece of amateur equipment requires power. Electronic equipment requires dc to operate, so a *power supply* (either built-in or external) is required to run equipment from household ac power. Most amateur equipment uses dc power at +13.8 V, a voltage chosen to be compatible with vehicle power systems for mobile operation.

A power supply has three basic parts — an input transformer, a rectifier and a filter-regulator output circuit. The input transformer converts the 120 V ac household power to a voltage closer to the desired 13.8 V. It also serves to isolate the power supply output from the ac power line. This is an important safety feature because the power supply's negative output is usually connected to the station's ground and metal equipment enclosures that are frequently in direct contact with the operator.

Rectifier Circuits

After the ac voltage has been reduced to a lower value by the input transformer, a rectifier circuit converts the bipolar ac waveform into dc pulses as shown in **Figure 4.24**. Don't confuse a single-diode rectifier with the rectifier circuit — they both have the same name but one is a component and the other a circuit. There are two basic rectifier circuits — the *half-wave* and the *full-wave*.

The half-wave rectifier shown in Figure 4.24A uses only one diode that permits current flow during one-half of the input ac waveform (180°) from the transformer. **[G7A04, G7A05]** That creates a series of pulses of current in the load at the same frequency as the input voltage. There is an equal duration between pulses when no current flows.

The full-wave rectifier shown in Figure 4.24B is really two half-wave rectifiers operating on alternate half-cycles. This rectifier requires that the transformer output winding be center-tapped to provide a return path for current that flows in the load. **[G7A03]** The advantage of the full-wave rectifier is that output is produced during the entire 360° of the ac cycle. **[G7A06]** The output from full-wave rectifiers is a series of pulses at twice the frequency of the input voltage. **[G7A07]**

A second type of full-wave rectifier called a *full-wave bridge* is shown in **Figure 4.25**. This circuit adds two diodes (a total of four), but eliminates the need for a center-tapped winding.

Power Supply Filter Circuits

A rectifier's output pulses of dc current are unsuitable for direct use by electronic circuits. The pulses must be smoothed out so that the output is a relatively steady voltage. This smoothing is performed by a *filter network* consisting of capacitors or capacitors and inductors. **[G7A02]**

The variation in output voltage caused by the current pulses is called *ripple,* and it is measured as the percentage of the peak-to-peak variation compared to average output voltage. The most common way of reducing ripple is to use a large *filter capacitor* at the output of the rectifier. Shown in **Figure 4.26**, this is called a *capacitor-input filter.* You may encounter older high voltage (HV) supplies for RF power amplifiers that include a *choke* inductor with a second filter capacitor. Simple supplies rarely include an inductor since the capacitor alone provides sufficient filtering in most cases.

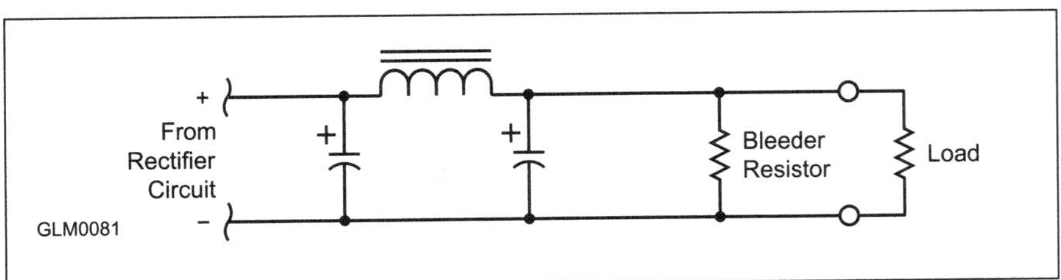

Figure 4.26 — A capacitor-input power supply filter circuit. The bleeder resistors slowly discharge stored energy from the capacitors when the power supply is turned off. A choke inductor and second capacitor are sometimes used in older high voltage (HV) supplies for RF power amplifiers.

Power Supply Safety

Safety is important in power supply design because of the connection to the ac power line and because a lot of energy is supplied by and stored in the supply. Fuses in the primary are used to protect against the hazard of excessive current loads or short circuits, and all power supplies should have an on/off switch to remove ac power when not in use.

Another hazard encountered in power supplies is the stored energy in filter capacitors. If the supply is simply turned off with no load connected, the energy stored in the capacitor has nowhere to go and a significant voltage will remain at the capacitor terminals. *Bleeder resistors* are used to discharge the stored energy when power is removed. **[G7A01]** Connected across the filter capacitors as shown in Figure 4.26, these resistors have a high enough value that they do not affect normal operation. When power is turned

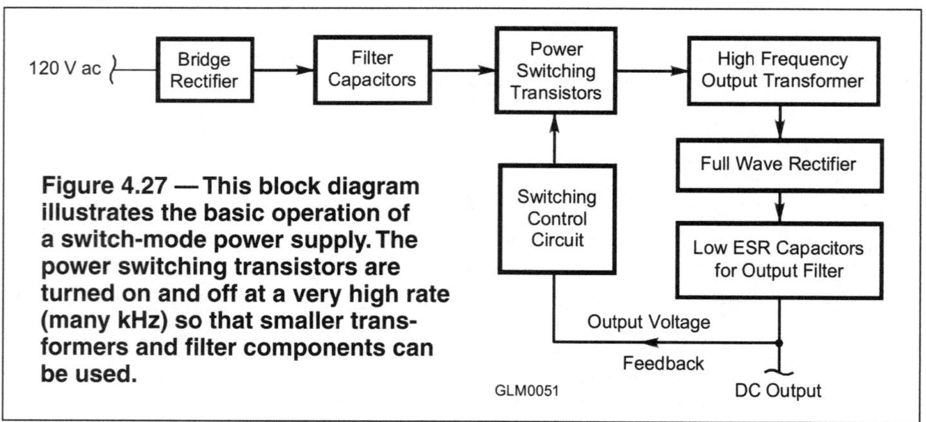

Figure 4.27 — This block diagram illustrates the basic operation of a switch-mode power supply. The power switching transistors are turned on and off at a very high rate (many kHz) so that smaller transformers and filter components can be used.

off, if there is no load, the resistors slowly dissipate the stored energy as heat, discharging the capacitor to a safe voltage within a few seconds. If you are working on a power supply, be sure to wait long enough for the bleeder resistors to do their work after turning power off.

Switchmode or Switching Supplies

Power supplies that use capacitor- or inductor-input filters and linear voltage regulators to provide filtering and regulation are called *linear supplies*. Another type of power supply filter and regulation circuit uses high-frequency pulses of current to control the output voltage. This is called a *switch-mode supply* or *switching supply*.

In the block diagram of a switching supply in **Figure 4.27**, the ac input is first rectified and filtered. A transistor switch then supplies current pulses to a small inductor or transformer at a very high frequency — 20 kHz or more compared to 60 Hz for a linear supply — which transfers the energy into another filter capacitor that smoothes the pulses for a steady output voltage. The high frequency of the pulses means that the supply can react quickly to changing current demands. The high frequency also means that small, lightweight inductors and capacitors can be used to smooth the pulses and filter the output. **[G7A08]**

For More Information

The half-wave rectifier output waveform's average voltage is 0.45 times the transformer winding's output voltage, or 0.45 E_{RMS}. There is also one diode forward voltage drop in series with the load current that reduces the peak output voltage by 0.6 V for regular silicon diodes.

The output voltage from the full-wave rectifier is 0.9 E_{RMS} (minus one diode forward voltage drop). Since the output winding is center-tapped, each half of the winding must be capable of generating the full output voltage, E_{RMS}, so the total winding must put out twice the full output voltage, 2 E_{RMS}.

Figure 4.25 shows how the full-wave bridge rectifier works. One pair of diodes conducts on alternate half-cycles. The pairs of diodes work like switches synchronized to the ac waveform, connecting the winding to the load first with one polarity, then the other. Output voltage is again 0.9 E_{RMS}, but less two forward voltage drops because there are two diodes in series with the current at all times.

If the usual capacitor-input filter (see Figure 4.26) is used to construct a power supply, there are key differences in the peak inverse voltage and forward currents experienced by the diodes in the three rectifier circuits:

• In the full-wave center-tapped rectifier circuit, when a rectifier diode is not conducting it must withstand not only the negative peak voltage from its own half of the winding

Table 4.7

Rectifier Diode Voltage and Current

Rectifier Type	Number of Diodes	PIV	Avg Forward Current
Half-wave	1	1.4 to 2.8 E_{RMS} (2 E_{PK})	I_{LOAD}
Full-wave	2	2.8 E_{RMS} (2 E_{PK})	0.5 I_{LOAD}
Full-wave bridge	4	1.4 E_{RMS} (E_{PK})	0.5 I_{LOAD}

but also the positive voltage from the other winding. Thus the peak inverse voltage applied to the diodes is twice the normal peak output voltage of the supply.

• The peak inverse voltage applied to the diode in a half-wave rectifier circuit is twice the supply's peak output voltage.

• In a full-wave bridge rectifier circuit each rectifier diode only has to withstand the supply's peak output voltage.

• In the half-wave rectifier circuit the entire load current goes through one diode and so it must be rated to carry the average load current.

• In both full-wave rectifiers the diodes each supply only one-half of the load current, halving their current rating requirement. **Table 4.7** summarizes the maximum reverse voltage and average forward current for the diodes in all three rectifier circuits.

At the output of the rectifier, the most common filter circuit uses a high-value capacitor to smooth the current pulses. The capacitance must be high enough to keep the power supply output voltage close to the average value of the rectifier output even for heavy load currents. (In practice, several capacitors in parallel may be used to increase the value of capacitance to the desired level.) The rectifier supplies current to the capacitor, charging it and raising its voltage whenever the rectifier output voltage is greater than the capacitor voltage. The capacitor then discharges the stored energy as current through the load until the rectifier can charge it up again. The percentage of variation in output voltage between no load and full load is called the supply's *regulation*. For a properly sized filter capacitor, the rectifier charges the capacitor in short pulses of high current while the load draws current from the capacitor more slowly.

The capacitor in a power supply output filter is continuously charging and discharging, with current flowing in and out of the capacitor. These currents can be quite high, so it is important to avoid losses caused by losses in the capacitor. There are several sources of capacitor losses such as the resistance of conducting surfaces and of the internal electrolyte. All of the losses are lumped together in a single parasitic resistance called the *equivalent series resistance* (ESR).

BATTERIES AND CHARGERS

G4E08 — In what configuration are the individual cells in a solar panel connected together?

Series-parallel

G4E09 — What is the approximate open-circuit voltage from a fully illuminated silicon photovoltaic cell?

0.5 VDC

G4E10 — Why should a series diode be connected between a solar panel and a storage battery that is being charged by the panel?

To prevent discharge of the battery through the panel during times of low or no illumination

G4E11 — What precaution should be taken when connecting a solar panel to a lithium iron phosphate battery?

The solar panel must have a charge controller

G6A01 — What is the minimum allowable discharge voltage for maximum life of a standard 12-volt lead-acid battery?
10.5 volts

G6A02 — What is an advantage of batteries with low internal resistance?
High discharge current

Battery power operation is important to amateurs. Everyday use of handheld and portable radios requires dependable, high-capacity batteries that can be easily recharged. Public service and portable operation depends on battery power. Because of these important roles for batteries, the General exam focuses on the different types of batteries and how to recharge them.

There are two basic types of batteries: *primary* and *secondary*. A primary, or disposable, battery is discarded after it is discharged. Examples of primary batteries include carbon-zinc, alkaline and silver-nickel. Each of these types describes the chemicals that store energy in the battery, called the *battery chemistry*. For emergency operation, disposable batteries are preferred because battery chargers may not function if ac power is unavailable. Never attempt to recharge a primary battery such as carbon-zinc or silver-nickel. The chemical reaction that produces energy is not intended to be reversed and often produces gasses and corrosive chemicals that can damage the charging equipment.

A secondary, or rechargeable, battery can be recharged and reused many times. Examples of secondary batteries include nickel-cadmium (NiCd), nickel-metal hydride (NiMH), lithium-ion (Li-ion) and lead-acid. **Table 4.8** lists several common types of batteries and their important characteristics. There is one schematic symbol for batteries with a single cell, and another for those with multiple cells. Note that these symbols are the same for all battery types (NiCd, NiMH, lead acid, and so on). There are battery chargers designed specifically for each type of rechargeable battery. Using the correct charger maximizes the life and usefulness of the battery. Heed any manufacturer's warnings about heating or venting of gasses during recharging which should always be performed in a well-ventilated area.

Larger secondary batteries are also known as *storage batteries*. Storage batteries, such as deep-cycle lead-acid marine or RV storage batteries are often used as a portable or emergency power source to replace a power supply operating from ac power. These batteries are available with liquid electrolyte for vehicle use or with the electrolyte in gel form ("gel-cells"). These batteries are rated as "12 V" batteries, but should actually be maintained at a voltage of 13.8 V. Lead-acid storage batteries can produce useful power

Table 4.8

Battery Types and Characteristics

Battery Style	Chemistry	Type	Full-Charge Voltage (V)	Energy Rating (average, mAh)
AAA	Alkaline	Disposable	1.5	1100
AA	Alkaline	Disposable	1.5	2600 – 3200
AA	Carbon-Zinc	Disposable	1.5	600
AA	Nickel-Cadmium (NiCd)	Rechargeable	1.2	700
AA	Nickel-Metal Hydride (NiMH)	Rechargeable	1.2	1500 – 2200
AA	Lithium	Disposable	1.7	2100 – 2400
C	Alkaline	Disposable	1.5	7500
D	Alkaline	Disposable	1.5	14,000
9 V	Alkaline	Disposable	9	580
9 V	Nickel-Cadmium (NiCd)	Rechargeable	9	110
9 V	Nickel-Metal Hydride (NiMH)	Rechargeable	9	150
Coin Cells	Lithium	Disposable	3 – 3.3	25 – 1000

Battery Schematic Symbols — Single Cell / Multi Cell

until their output voltage drops to approximately 10.5 V, after which the voltage will fall quickly and the battery should be recharged. Discharging these batteries past their minimum voltage will reduce the life of the battery. **[G6A01]**

To get the most energy from a battery, limit the amount of current drawn. A low discharge rate keeps the battery cool inside and minimizes losses from the battery's natural internal resistance. Some types of batteries, such as NiCds or "Nicads," are specially designed to have low internal resistance to supply high discharge currents. **[G6A02]** A battery will also slowly lose its charge when not in use, called *self-discharge*. The rate of self-discharge varies with battery type. In general, self-discharge can be minimized by keeping the battery cool and dry. Do not freeze batteries because expanding water inside might crack the case or damage the electrodes. If a battery is damp, the moisture on the outside of the battery will supply a path for leakage current to flow directly between the battery terminals, discharging it.

ALTERNATIVE POWER

What is most often meant by "solar power" is really *photovoltaic conversion* of sunlight directly to electricity. Solar panels and solar cells are made of silicon PN-junctions that are exposed to sunlight and arranged in a series-parallel configuration **[G4E08]**. As opposed to transistors and diodes that are quite small, solar cells can be inches across with the PN-junction sandwiched between layers of P- and N-type material. The photons of sunlight are absorbed by electrons that then have enough energy to travel across the PN-junction and create dc current flow. The forward voltage created as the electron crosses the junction is approximately 0.5 V and can be measured as the *open-circuit voltage* of the solar cell. **[G4E09]**

Systems that create energy from wind and solar power require one more component that adds to the cost of using them — a substantial energy storage system. When connecting a solar panel to a lithium iron phosphate battery (like a LiFePO4),you should use a charge controller to avoid overcharging the battery, which can be a safety concern and can also decrease the battery's usable lifespan. **[G4E11]** When the sun is down or the wind doesn't blow, no power is available. If excess energy has been stored during periods of peak generation, there can be enough power to supply the operating needs until the winds pick up or the sun rises again.

Storage batteries are the usual means of energy storage and most alternative energy systems are designed with battery backup capabilities. In solar power systems, the battery connection is made through a series-connected diode to prevent the battery from discharging back through the panel or panels during periods of low illumination when the voltage from the solar cells is reduced. **[G4E10]**

CONNECTORS

G6B04 — What is a typical upper frequency limit for low SWR operation of 50-ohm BNC connectors?
    4 GHz

G6B07 — Which of the following describes a type N connector?
    A moisture-resistant RF connector useful to 10 GHz

G6B11 — What is an SMA connector?
    A small threaded connector suitable for signals up to several GHz

G6B12 — Which of these connector types is commonly used for low frequency or dc signal connections to a transceiver?
    RCA Phono

Connectors are a convenient way to make an electrical connection by using mating electrical contacts. There are quite a few connector styles, but common terms apply to all of them. *Pins* are contacts that extend out of the connector body, and connectors in which pins make the electrical contact are called "male" connectors. *Sockets* are hollow, recessed contacts, and connectors with sockets are called "female." Connectors designed to attach to each other are called "mating connectors." *Keyed connectors* have specially shaped bodies or inserts that require a complementary shape on a mating connector to prevent damage from incorrect connections.

Plugs are connectors installed on the end of cables and *jacks* or *receptacles* are installed on equipment. *Adapters* make connections between two different styles of connector, such as between two different families of RF connectors. Other adapters join connectors of the same family, such as double-male, double-female and gender changers. *Splitters* divide a signal between two connectors.

Power Connectors

Amateur radio equipment uses a variety of power connectors. Some examples are shown in **Figure 4.28**. Most low power amateur equipment uses coaxial power connectors. These are the same type found on consumer electronic equipment that is supplied by a wall transformer or "wall wart" style of power supply. Transceivers and other equipment that requires high current in excess of a few amperes often use Molex connectors (**molex.com** — enter "MLX" in the search window) with a white, nylon body housing pins and sockets crimped onto the end of wires.

Another standard, particularly popular among ARRL Amateur Radio Emergency Service (ARES) and other emergency communication groups, is the use of Anderson Powerpole connectors (**andersonpower.com**). These connectors are "sexless" meaning that any two connectors of the same series can be mated — there are no male or female connectors. By standardizing on a single connector style, equipment can be shared and replaced easily in the field.

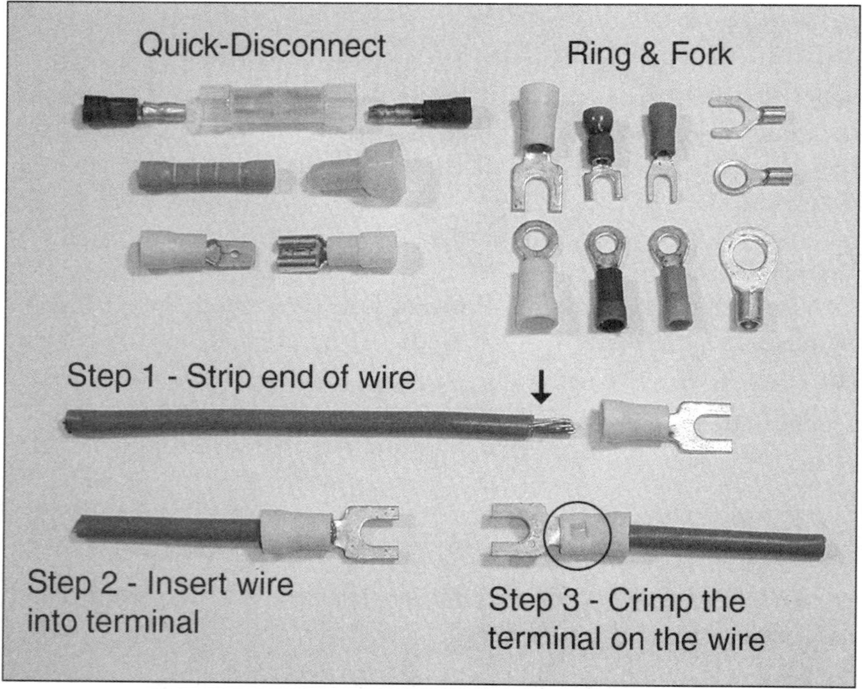

Figure 4.28 — These are the most common connectors used on amateur equipment to make power connections. (Courtesy of Wiley Publishing, *Ham Radio for Dummies*, or *Two-Way Radios & Scanners for Dummies*)

Figure 4.29 — Power connectors often use terminals that are crimped onto the end of wires with special crimping tools. (Courtesy of Wiley Publishing, *Ham Radio for Dummies*, or *Two-Way Radios & Scanners for Dummies*)

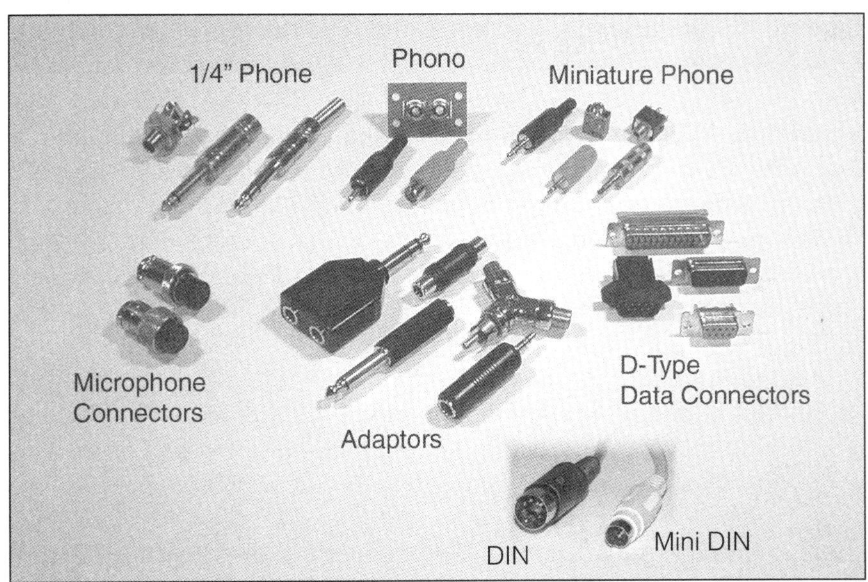

Figure 4.30 — Audio and data signals are carried by a variety of different connectors. Individual cable conductors are either crimped or soldered to the connector contacts. The popular DIN and Mini-DIN style of connectors are shown at the lower right.

Molex and Powerpole connectors use *crimp terminals* installed on the end of wires. A special *crimping tool* is used to attach the wire to the terminal and the terminal is then inserted into the body of the connector. Making a solid connection requires the use of an appropriate tool — do not use pliers or some other tool to make a crimp connection.

Some equipment uses terminal strips for direct connection to wires or crimp terminals, often with screws. Other equipment uses spring-loaded terminals or binding posts to connect to bare wire ends. **Figure 4.29** shows some common crimp terminals that are installed on the ends of wires using special tools.

Audio and Control Connectors

Consumer audio equipment and amateur radio equipment share many of the same connectors for the same uses. *Phone* plugs and jacks are used for mono and stereo audio circuits. These connectors, shown in **Figure 4.30** come in ¼-inch, ⅛-inch (miniature) and subminiature varieties. The contact at the end of the plug is called the *tip* and the connector at the base of the plug is the *sleeve*. If there is a third contact between the tip and sleeve, such as for a stereo audio plug, it is the *ring*. These are often referred to as "TRS" for tip-ring-sleeve. There are TS and TRRS varieties, as well.

Phono plugs and jacks (sometimes called "RCA connectors" since they were first used on RCA brand equipment) are used for audio, video and other low-level RF signals. They are also widely used for control signals. **[G6B12]**

The most common microphone connector on mobile and base station equipment is an 8-pin round connector, also called a "Foster connector." On older transceivers you may see 4-pin round connectors used for microphones. Eight-pin RJ-45 modular connectors are often used in mobile and smaller radios.

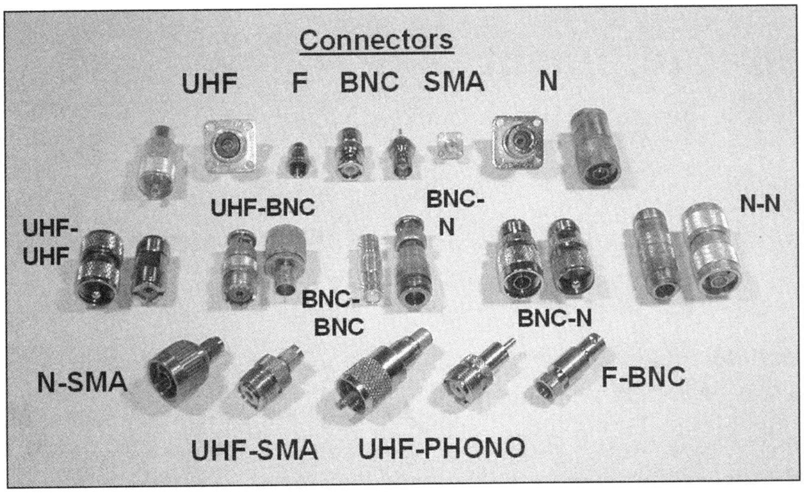

RF Connectors

Feed lines used for radio signals require special connectors for use at RF frequencies. The connectors must have approximately the same characteristic impedance as the feed line they are attached to or some of the RF signal will be reflected by the connector. Inexpensive audio and control connectors cannot meet that

Figure 4.31 — Each type of RF connector is specially made to carry RF signals and preserve the shielding of coaxial cable. Adapters are available to connect one style of connector to another.

requirement, nor can they handle the high power levels often encountered in RF equipment. Occasionally, phono connectors are used for HF receiving and low-power transmitting equipment.

By far, the most common connector for RF in amateur equipment is the UHF family shown in **Figure 4.31**. (The UHF designation does not refer to frequency in this case.) A PL-259 is the plug that goes on the end of feed lines, and the SO-239 is the jack mounted on equipment. A "barrel" (PL-258) is a double-female adapter that allows two feed lines to be connected together. UHF connectors are typically used up to 150 MHz and can handle legal-limit transmitter power at HF.

UHF connectors have several drawbacks including lack of weatherproofing, inconsistent performance above 150 MHz, and limited power handling at higher frequencies. The Type N series of RF connectors addresses all of those needs. Type N connectors are somewhat more expensive than UHF connectors, but they require less soldering and perform better in outdoor use since they are moisture resistant. Type N connectors can be used to 10 GHz. **[G6B07]**

For low power, BNC connectors are often used. BNC connectors are the standard for laboratory equipment, as well, and they are often used for dc and audio connections. BNC connectors are common on handheld radios for antenna connections. The typical upper frequency limit for low SWR operation is 4 GHz. **[G6B04]**

SMA connectors are small threaded connectors designed for miniature coaxial cable and are rated for use up to 18 GHz. Handheld transceivers often use SMA connectors for attaching antennas. **[G6B11]**

Data Connectors

Digital data is exchanged between computers and pieces of radio equipment more than ever before in the amateur station. The connector styles follow those found on computer equipment.

D-type connectors are used for RS-232 (COM port) interfaces. The model number of a typical D-type connector specifies number of individual circuits and a "P" or "S" depending on whether the connector uses pins or sockets. For example, D-type 9-pin connectors often referred to as "DB-9" or "DE-9" are used for COM ports on PCs.

USB connectors are becoming more popular in amateur equipment as the computer industry moves to eliminate the bulkier and slower RS-232 interface. A number of manufacturers make devices for converting USB ports to RS-232 interfaces.

4.7 Basic Test Equipment

G4B01 — What item of test equipment contains horizontal and vertical channel amplifiers?

An oscilloscope

G4B02 — Which of the following is an advantage of an oscilloscope versus a digital voltmeter?

Complex waveforms can be measured

G4B03 — Which of the following is the best instrument to use for checking the keying waveform of a CW transmitter?

An oscilloscope

G4B04 — What signal source is connected to the vertical input of an oscilloscope when checking the RF envelope pattern of a transmitted signal?

The attenuated RF output of the transmitter

G4B05 — Why do voltmeters have high input impedance?
> It decreases the loading on circuits being measured

G4B06 — What is an advantage of a digital multimeter as compared to an analog multimeter?
> Higher precision

G4B09 — When is an analog multimeter preferred to a digital multimeter?
> When adjusting circuits for maximum or minimum values

G4B10 — Which of the following can be determined with a directional wattmeter?
> Standing wave ratio

G4B11 — Which of the following must be connected to an antenna analyzer when it is being used for SWR measurements?
> Antenna and feed line

G4B12 — What effect can strong signals from nearby transmitters have on an antenna analyzer?
> Received power that interferes with SWR readings

G4B13 — Which of the following can be measured with an antenna analyzer?
> Impedance of coaxial cable

There's more to a radio than just operating it! As you gain experience with radios and accessories, you'll find yourself needing to make some simple checks and tests. You might try your hand at building some equipment and even repairing an ailing radio. To do so, you'll need some basic test equipment, and this section introduces you to some of the common items found on the radio workbench

ANALOG AND DIGITAL METERS

The *volt-ohm-meter* (VOM, also referred to as a *voltmeter*, *volt-ohm-milliammeter*, and *multimeter*) is the simplest piece of test equipment and amazingly versatile. A garden-variety meter purchased new for $20 or less can measure voltage, current and resistance, act as a continuity checker, and even test diodes and transistors! For a few more dollars, you can add frequency counting, capacitance and inductance measurement, and a data interface to your PC to record readings.

There are two types of VOMs: analog and digital, as shown in **Figure 4.32**. The analog meter has a moving needle with calibrated scales on the meter face. While this type of meter can't perform more advanced functions, it is perfectly okay for basic go/no-go testing, tuning and troubleshooting. In fact, experienced hams prefer analog meters for finding a peak or minimum reading, such as when adjusting a tuned circuit, since it's easier to just watch the meter needle move than a numeric display. **[G4B09]**

The digital meter or *DMM* (for *digital multimeter*) uses a microprocessor to take care of all the basic functions and adds the ability to count and perform calculations. The digital meter also offers significantly greater precision (ability to resolve small changes) than an analog meter. **[G4B06]** Many hams have both a digital and an analog meter for different uses.

For both meter types, the instrument should affect the circuit being measured to the smallest degree possible. When measuring voltage, the meter should have a high input impedance so that it places the minimum load on the circuit being measured. **[G4B05]** In a sensitive circuit, the small current required by a voltmeter can affect the circuit's operation. Other useful features include fused current inputs to prevent damage from a temporary overload, *peak hold* to capture a maximum value, and *autoranging* to automatically select the proper display range.

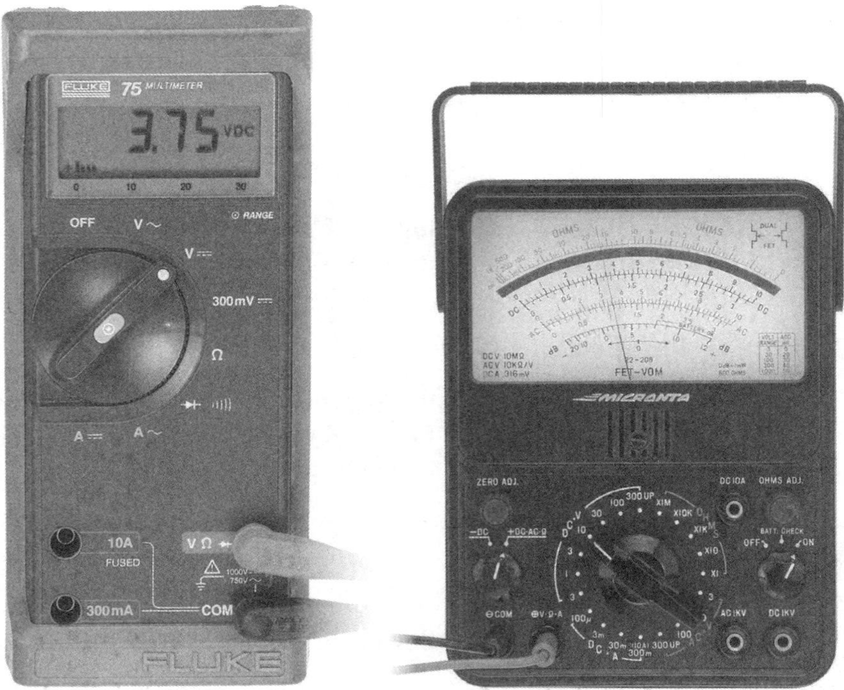

Figure 4.32 — A digital voltmeter (DVM) shown at the left provides precise measurements of voltage, current and resistance. Many models can also act as a frequency counter or component tester. Analog meters (right) are often preferable for tuning and adjustments since the needle's movement makes adjusting for a maximum or minimum quite easy.

OSCILLOSCOPE

For working with fast-changing audio, data and RF signals, no instrument is more versatile or useful than the *oscilloscope*, often called a "scope." The oscilloscope provides a visual display of voltage against time as shown in **Figure 4.33**. The display can be updated thousands or even millions of times per second, giving the operator a real-time view of a signal's characteristics. This allows you to measure complex, fast-changing waveforms that can't be measured by meters. **[G4B02]** (For an on-line tutorial about oscilloscopes, see the ARRL's Technical Information Service web page **arrl.org/servicing-equipment**.)

External signals from the circuits under test are connected to the scope through horizontal and vertical *channel amplifiers*. The gain of the amplifiers is variable to adjust the vertical sensitivity of the oscilloscope's display. **[G4B01]** An internal *time base* controls the duration represented by the display's horizontal divisions.

For a digital scope, signals are converted to digital data and manipulated by a microprocessor that controls how the signals are displayed. Some digital scopes use a USB connection to display the signals on a computer.

In the amateur station, a *monitoring oscilloscope* is very useful in monitoring transmitted signals by connecting the attenuated RF output of the transmitter to the vertical channel of the oscilloscope. **[G4B04]** Being able

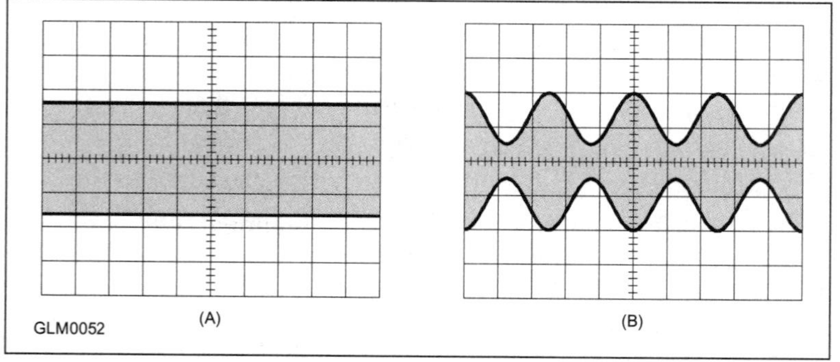

Figure 4.33 — Oscilloscope displays of RF signals. At A is an unmodulated carrier. The signal at B is from a full-carrier AM transmitter modulated with a single-frequency sine wave.

to monitor the transmitter output waveform in real time is of great assistance in adjusting keying waveforms, microphone gain and speech processing. Figure 4.33 shows an unmodulated carrier and an AM carrier modulated by a sine wave.

Figure 4.34 shows a typical keying waveform synchronized to the key closures that turn the transmitter on and off. The operator can clearly see the effects of any adjustments or conditions that might cause distortion or key clicks on the transmitted signal. **[G4B03]**

IMPEDANCE AND RESONANCE MEASUREMENTS

It is often necessary to measure impedance when building or testing a new antenna or when performing maintenance on an existing antenna. An incredibly useful instrument that has made antenna testing much easier is the *antenna analyzer* shown in **Figure 4.35**. The analyzer contains a CW signal generator, a frequency counter, an SWR bridge and an impedance meter. Different models of analyzers can display both resistive and reactance values of antenna impedance as well as the precise frequency at which the measurement is being made. By connecting the analyzer to the antenna and feed line, SWR can be checked without having to transmit a signal at high power. **[G4B11]** The analyzers are also capable of measuring feed line velocity factor, electrical length, characteristic impedance, and other parameters. **[G4B13]**

Battery-powered analyzers are also small enough to be part of a tool kit so that antennas can be tested at the point of adjustment without having to go back into the shack to make measurements. A point of caution: because analyzers use small signals to make measurements, its accuracy can be affected by strong signals from nearby transmitters. **[G4B12]**

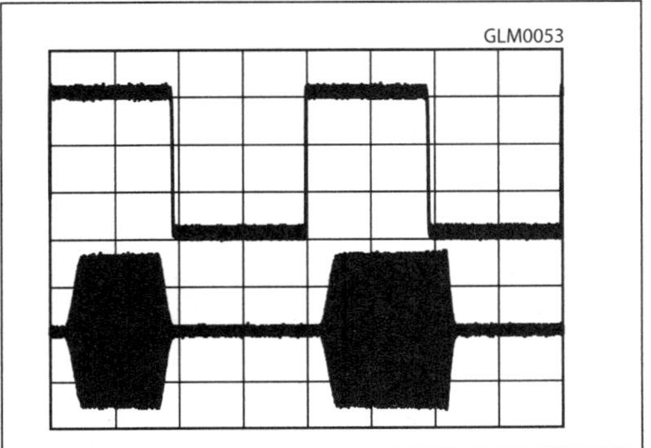

Figure 4.34 — It is easy to see the relationship between the key closure (top trace) and the transmitter output. If the transmitter turns on and off too abruptly or erratically, key clicks can result.

FIELD STRENGTH AND RF POWER METERS

Another useful set of tests measure the antenna's efficiency and radiation pattern. A receiver can make these measurements, but it is often inconvenient to take a receiver into the field. A *field strength meter* is the better choice for that job, making calibrated readings of electric field strength. **Figure 4.36** shows a typical unit. While signal strength levels can be inferred from measurements of power and SWR, a field strength meter actually measures the transmitted signal level. It is often used to compare relative levels of RF output during antenna and transmitter adjustments.

By placing the field strength meter in one location and rotating the antenna, the radiation pattern of the antenna can be measured. Conversely, the meter can be carried to different locations to determine the radiation pattern of a fixed antenna, such as a wire beam or array.

Another power measurement tool is the *directional wattmeter* shown in **Figure 4.37**. A directional wattmeter

Figure 4.35 — An antenna analyzer, such as the MFJ-269 shown here, is handy for testing transmission lines and antennas. It displays SWR and impedance at frequencies of 1.5 to 170 MHz and across the 70 cm band.

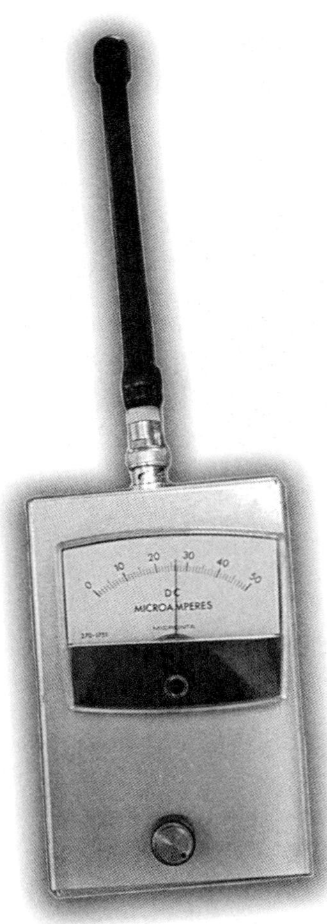

Figure 4.36 — A field strength meter is used to check relative performance of an antenna by measuring the electric field intensity.

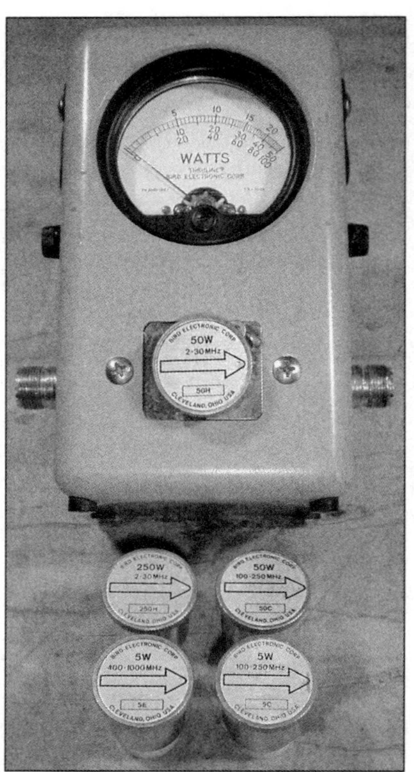

Figure 4.37 — The Bird Model 43 directional wattmeter uses sensing elements designed for a specific frequency range and power level. Forward and reflected power are read by rotating the sensing element. (One sensing element is plugged into the meter, and four other elements for different power levels and frequency ranges are shown below the meter.)

can measure both *forward* (P_F) and *reflected power* (P_R) in the line. Some meters can measure both simultaneously with independent meters or by turning a switch or power sensing element. Power meters are used to adjust transmitter and amplifier output circuits and drive levels.

Standing wave ratio (SWR) can be calculated from forward and reflected power measurements made using a directional wattmeter. **[G4B10]** SWR is then calculated using the following formula:

$$SWR = \frac{1 + \sqrt{P_R / P_F}}{1 - \sqrt{P_R / P_F}}$$

Chapter 5

Radio Signals and Equipment

In this chapter, you'll learn about:
- **Modes and bandwidth**
- **Filter types**
- **Oscillators**
- **Mixers, multipliers and modulators**
- **Transmitter and amplifier fundamentals**
- **Receiver fundamentals**
- **Installing an HF station**

After learning about the fundamentals of electronics and components, you're ready to build on that knowledge. In this section, we study real radios and investigate what's going on as adjustments are made. We'll start with the building blocks and then put them together into complete packages — transmitters, receivers, and amplifiers. You'll be getting deeper into circuits and the structure of radio equipment, so you may need to brush up on your understanding of schematics and block diagrams. A helpful tutorial is available on the *General Class License Manual* web page, **arrl.org/general-class-license-manual**. This chapter leads to the things you'll need to know about putting a station together and managing it. Set the power switch to ON and let's get busy!

5.1 Basic Modes and Bandwidth

G8A02 — What is the name of the process that changes the phase angle of an RF signal to convey information?
Phase modulation

G8A03 — What is the name of the process that changes the instantaneous frequency of an RF wave to convey information?
Frequency modulation

G8A05 — What type of modulation varies the instantaneous power level of the RF signal?
Amplitude modulation

G8A07 — Which of the following phone emissions uses the narrowest bandwidth?
Single sideband

G8A13 — What is a link budget?
The sum of transmit power and antenna gains minus system losses as seen at the receiver

G8A14 — What is a link margin?
The difference between received power level and minimum required signal level at the inputs to the receiver

The combination of modulation, the type of information carried, and the way in which the information is exchanged is the signal's *mode*. The simplest mode is a continuous wave turned on and off in a coded pattern, such as Morse code.

AMPLITUDE MODULATED MODES

Varying the power or amplitude of a signal to add speech or data information is called *amplitude modulation* or AM. The information is contained in the signal's *envelope* — the maximum values of the instantaneous power for each cycle. **[G8A05]** The process of recovering speech or music from the envelope of an AM signal is called *detection*. An AM signal is composed of a *carrier* and two *sidebands*. The total power of an AM signal is divided between the carrier and sidebands. The AM signal's carrier is a continuous wave with an amplitude that does not change and contains no information.

An AM signal modulated by a tone has two sidebands that are present as steady, unchanging signals as long as the tone is transmitted. The *upper sideband* (USB) is higher in frequency than the carrier by the frequency of the tone. The *lower sideband* (LSB) is lower in frequency than the carrier. The information to recover the tone is contained in the amplitude of the sidebands and their differences in frequency from that of the carrier. Each sideband contains an exact copy of the modulating signal.

An AM signal with the carrier and one sideband removed is called a *single sideband* signal (SSB). SSB transmissions have more range compared to AM because all of an SSB signal's power is contained in the remaining sideband. SSB's smaller bandwidth also makes it possible to fit more signals in a fixed range of frequencies. The wider AM signals tend to have a fuller frequency response that sounds "warmer" on the air.

FREQUENCY AND PHASE MODULATED MODES

Modes that vary the frequency of a signal to add speech or data information are called *frequency modulation* or FM. The frequency is varied in proportion to the instantaneous amplitude of the modulating signal. **[G8A03]** The amount that an FM signal's frequency varies when modulated is called *deviation*. *Phase modulation* (PM) is created by varying a signal's *phase angle*. **[G8A02]** Receivers can demodulate FM and PM with the same demodulator circuits.

FM and PM are types of *angle modulation* because both techniques modulate the signal by varying the signal's phase angle. FM changes the amount of time it takes for the signal to make a 360° cycle. PM varies the relative phase difference between the signal and some reference phase. FM and PM signals have one carrier and many sidebands. These signals have a *constant power*, whether modulated or not.

BANDWIDTH DEFINITION

Composite signals are groups of individual signals that combine to create a complex signal. Composite signals have *components* that may cover a range of frequencies. The difference in frequency between the lowest and highest component of a composite signal is the signal's *bandwidth*.

The FCC has a more specific definition of bandwidth in section §97.3(a)(8): "*Bandwidth*. The width of a frequency band outside of which the mean [average] power of the transmitted signal is attenuated at least 26 dB below the mean power within the band." **Figure 5.1** illustrates how this measurement is made.

The FCC limits signal bandwidth so that many stations and types of signals can share the limited amount of spectrum space. **Table 5.1** lists the bandwidth of the most common amateur signals. **[G8A07]**

Figure 5.1 — The FCC defines bandwidth as "the width of a frequency band outside of which the mean [average] power of the transmitted signal is attenuated at least 26 dB below the mean power."

Table 5.1

Amateur Signal Bandwidths

Type of Signal	Typical Bandwidth
AM voice	6 kHz
Amateur television	6 MHz
SSB voice	2 to 3 kHz
Digital using SSB	50 to 3000 Hz (0.05 to 3 kHz)
CW	100 to 300 Hz (0.1 to 0.3 kHz)
FM voice	5 to 16 kHz

LINK BUDGETS

A *link budget* is a telecommunications term that accounts for all the power gains and losses a signal experiences within a system. The system can be from your wi-fi router to your computer or from the cable company to your television or from an amateur radio transmitter to a receiver. In amateur radio, this generally boils down to the transmit power and antenna gains from the sending station minus any system losses the receiving station experiences. **[G8A13]** Losses can result from ionospheric refraction, attenuation, or a variety of other causes. Building on the idea of a link budget, a *link margin* (*LKM*) is the difference between the minimum power level needed to receive a signal and the actual power level of the received signal. **[G8A14]** LKM is measured in dB.

For More Information

A radio signal at one frequency whose strength never changes is called a *continuous wave*, abbreviated CW. Adding information to a signal by modifying it in some way, such as changing its frequency, phase angle, or amplitude, is called *modulation*.

Recovering the information from a modulated signal is called *demodulation*. A signal that doesn't carry any information is *unmodulated*. If speech is the information used to modulate a signal, the result is a *voice mode* or *phone* (short for *radiotelephone*) signal. If data is the information used to modulate a signal, the result is a *data mode* or *digital mode* signal. *Analog* modes carry information such as speech that can be understood directly by a human. Digital or data modes carry information as data characters between two computers.

Any characteristic of a signal can be varied to carry information if the variations are observable at the receiving end to recover the information. Three characteristics that can be modulated are the signal's amplitude or strength, its frequency, and its phase. The term *instantaneous* when applied to amplitude, frequency, or phase refers to the value of those characteristics at a specific instant in time.

5.2 Radio's Building Blocks

G7B07 — Which of the following are basic components of a sine wave oscillator?
    A filter and an amplifier operating in a feedback loop

G7B09 — What determines the frequency of an LC oscillator?
    The inductance and capacitance in the tank circuit

G7C05 — Which of the following is characteristic of a direct digital synthesizer (DDS)?
    Variable output frequency with the stability of a crystal oscillator

G7C07 — What term specifies a filter's attenuation inside its passband?
    Insertion loss

G7C09 — What is the phase difference between the I and Q RF signals that software-defined radio (SDR) equipment uses for modulation and demodulation?
    90 degrees

G7C10 — What is an advantage of using I-Q modulation with software-defined radios (SDRs)?
    All types of modulation can be created with appropriate processing

G7C11 — Which of these functions is performed by software in a software-defined radio (SDR)?
    All these choices are correct

G7C12 — What is the frequency above which a low-pass filter's output power is less than half the input power?
    Cutoff frequency

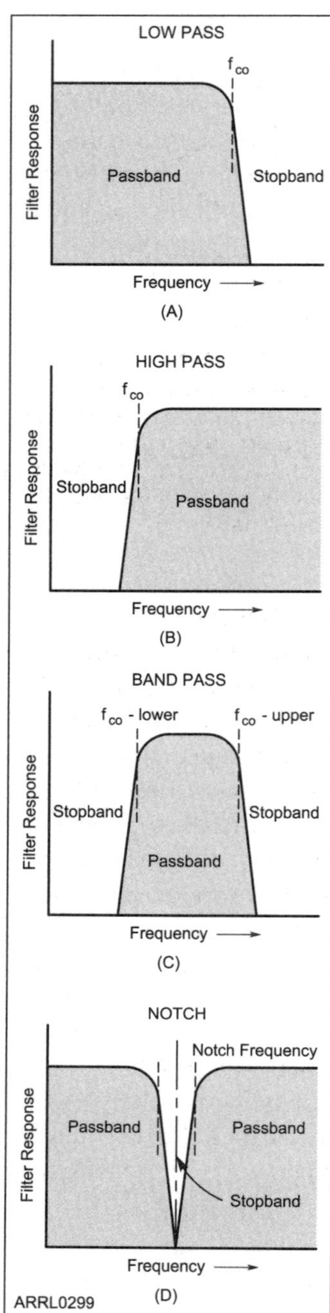

Figure 5.2 — Generic filter response curves showing how filters of different types affect signals. A larger filter response means less attenuation of the signal. Cutoff frequencies are shown as f_{co}.

G7C13 — What term specifies a filter's maximum ability to reject signals outside its passband?
Ultimate rejection

G7C14 — The bandwidth of a band-pass filter is measured between what two frequencies?
Upper and lower half-power

G8A04 — What emission is produced by a reactance modulator connected to a transmitter RF amplifier stage?
Phase modulation

G8B03 — What is another term for the mixing of two RF signals?
Heterodyning

G8B04 — What is the stage in a VHF FM transmitter that generates a harmonic of a lower frequency signal to reach the desired operating frequency?
Multiplier

G8B11 — What combination of a mixer's Local Oscillator (LO) and RF input frequencies is found in the output?
The sum and difference

Nearly all radios are made up of a few fundamental types of circuits. The way in which the circuit designers choose to build those circuits varies quite a bit, but the basic functions of the circuit are the same. In this section we cover four of those circuits: *oscillators, mixers, multipliers*, and *modulators*. You'll learn the functions and important characteristics of each.

Although this section is focused on the circuits that perform the signal generating and processing functions, the same functions can also be performed on digital data by software in a radio that uses *digital signal processing* or *DSP*. This is generally referred to as *software-defined radio* or *SDR*. **[G7C11]** Nevertheless, the functions are similar in both types of radio — analog and digital

FILTERS

Filters are used to *attenuate* (reduce in strength) or pass signals with some defined range of frequencies. Filters are classified by their *response* — how they act on signals as shown by the graphs in **Figure 5.2**. The range of signal frequencies that are passed is the *passband* and the range that are attenuated is the *stopband*. Attenuation is also referred to as *rejection*.

A *low-pass filter* (Figure 5.2A) is one in which all frequencies below the *cutoff frequency* are passed with little or no attenuation. The cutoff frequency (f_{co}) is the frequency at which the output signal power is reduced to one-half that of the input signal. **[G7C12]** Above a low-pass filter's cutoff frequency, the attenuation generally increases with frequency. A *high-pass filter* (Figure 5.2B) is just the opposite; signals are passed above the cutoff frequency and attenuated below.

A *band-pass filter* (Figure 5.2C) has both an upper and a lower cutoff frequency. Signals between the cutoff frequencies are passed while those outside the passband are attenuated. The frequency range between the upper and lower cutoff frequencies is the filter's bandwidth. **[G7C14]** The opposite of a band-pass filter is a *band-stop filter*. It attenuates signals at frequencies between the cutoff frequencies. If the stopband is very narrow, that is a *notch filter*. (Figure 5.2D)

Even though a filter passes a range of frequencies, it may still attenuate signals in its passband. This is called *insertion loss*. **[G7C07]** Outside the passband, attenuation may vary but the maximum attenuation is the filter's *ultimate rejection*. **[G7C13]**

OSCILLATORS

The function of most oscillators used in radio is to produce a pure sine wave with no noise or distortion — as close to a single-frequency signal as possible. The block diagram symbol for an oscillator (a circle with a sine wave inside) is shown in **Figure 5.3** along with the fundamental circuit that makes an oscillator work.

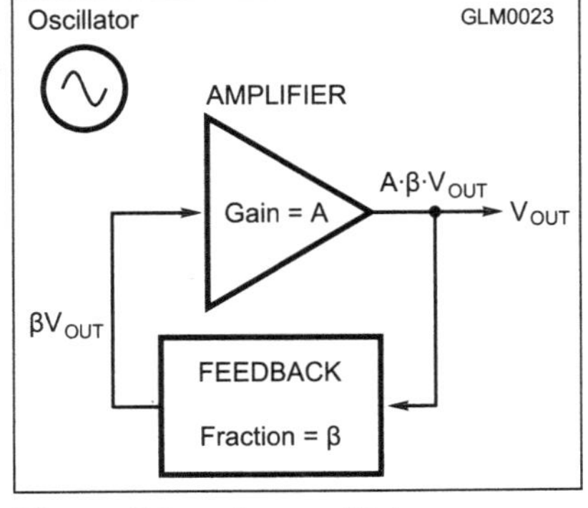

Figure 5.3 — An oscillator consists of an amplifier with feedback from the output to input. The product of the gain and feedback ratio must be equal to 1 at the frequency of oscillation.

An oscillator consists of an amplifier (the triangle is the amplifier's block diagram symbol) that increases signal amplitude (*gain*) and a *feedback* circuit to route some of the amplifier's output signal back to its input. At start-up, the circuit's loop gain through the amplifier and feedback path has to be greater than 1 so that circuit noise can be gradually built up into a single-frequency signal. Once the amplitude of the output has reached the desired level, gain is reduced (called compression) in order to maintain a stable, self-sustaining, sine-wave output. This is called *oscillation*. **[G7B07]** There are two basic types of fixed-frequency oscillators used in radio circuits: LC and crystal.

The LC oscillator's feedback circuit consists of an inductor (L) and capacitor (C) connected in parallel or series to form a resonant circuit, often called a *tank circuit* because it stores electrical energy like a flywheel stores mechanical energy. The resonant frequency of the LC circuit, determined by the values of L and C, is the frequency of the oscillator. **[G7B09]**

A quartz crystal is often substituted for the LC tank circuit, creating a *crystal oscillator*. The quartz crystal acts like a resonant LC circuit and is orders of magnitude more precise than an LC circuit. Crystal oscillators are used whenever an accurate, stable signal source is required.

A *variable-frequency oscillator* (VFO) whose output frequency can be adjusted is used to tune a radio to different frequencies. The frequency of an LC VFO is adjusted by varying the value of one or more of the LC components in the feedback circuit. Two other widely used VFO circuits are the *phase-locked loop* (PLL) and *direct digital synthesizer* (DDS). The DDS has the advantage of being controllable by software and has stability comparable to a crystal oscillator. **[G7C05]** DDS oscillators are used as the high-stability VFO in most current transceivers.

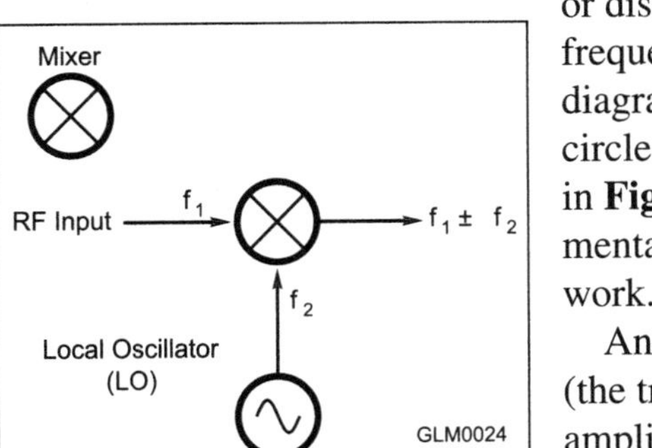

Figure 5.4 — The mixer combines signals of different frequencies, producing signals at the sum and difference frequency. Mixers are used to change or shift the frequency of signals.

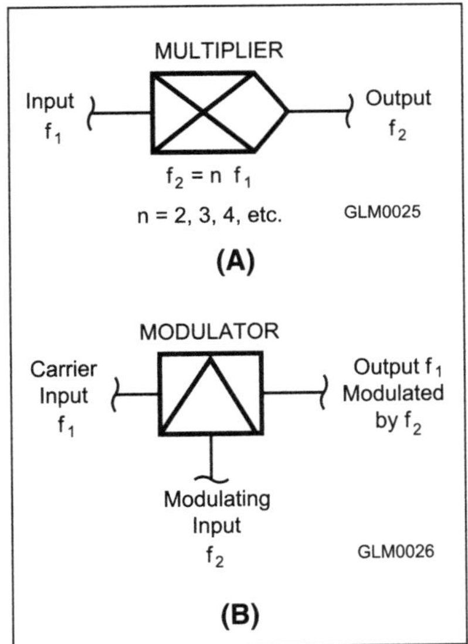

Figure 5.5 — A multiplier (A) is a special type of tuned amplifier that creates harmonics of an input signal and then selects the desired harmonic at its output. The output of low frequency oscillators or modulators can be multiplied to frequencies at which it is difficult to build and modulate oscillators. The general symbol (B) can be used for a modulator of any type — AM, FM, or SSB.

MIXERS

A key function in both receivers and transmitters is to be able to change the frequency of a signal. The circuit that performs this job is called a *mixer*. The block diagram symbol for a mixer is shown in **Figure 5.4**.

The two input frequencies, f_1 and f_2, are combined and the mixer produces signals with their sum ($f_1 + f_2$) and difference ($f_1 - f_2$) as its output. This process is called *heterodyning*. **[G8B03, G8B11]** For example, if f_1 = 14.050 MHz and f_2 = 3.35 MHz, the output of the mixer will contain signals at 17.4 MHz ($f_1 + f_2$) and 10.7 MHz ($f_1 - f_2$). A mixer can change a signal to any other frequency — the input and output frequencies do not have to be related.

In radio circuits, the input f_1 to the mixer is usually referred to as the RF input because that signal is usually associated with a received or transmitted signal. Input f_2 is usually labeled the *local oscillator* (LO) because it represents a reference signal produced locally by an oscillator within the equipment. All of the mixer outputs are called *mixing products*.

MULTIPLIERS

A circuit that acts similarly to a mixer is the *multiplier*. Instead of creating the sum and difference of two input frequencies, a multiplier creates a harmonic of an input frequency. **[G8B04]** The block diagram symbol for a multiplier circuit is shown in **Figure 5.5A**. Multipliers are often used when a stable VHF or UHF signal is required, but constructing an oscillator at that frequency would be difficult. A low-frequency oscillator supplies the multiplier input and the output is tuned to the desired harmonic of the input signal. Multipliers are also used in FM transmitters as you will see in a following section.

MODULATORS

Modulators are the circuits that add information to a *carrier* signal by varying the carrier's amplitude, frequency, or phase. The block diagram symbol for a modulator is shown in Figure 5.5B. The input signal on the left-hand side is usually the unmodulated input. The input from below is the signal containing information that is to be added to the unmodulated input, and the output is on the right. (You may have noticed that all four of the block diagram symbols support the left-to-right signal flow that is recommended for schematics and block diagrams.) The same symbol is used to represent demodulator circuits, as well.

Amplitude Modulation

AM was first generated by varying the power supply voltage to the output circuit of a CW transmitter. You can easily imagine this process: As the voltage is varied, the amplitude of the output signal's envelope follows along. This is called *plate* or *collector (or drain) modulation* because the voltage that is varied is connected to a vacuum tube plate or a transistor's collector or drain. A modulation transformer was used to add and subtract an amplified version of the operator's voice to the power supply voltage, creating the modulation.

An AM signal consists of a carrier signal and two sidebands; one higher in frequency than the carrier (the *upper sideband* or *USB*) and one below it (the *lower sideband* or *LSB*). This is illustrated in **Figure 5.6**. If the carrier signal is removed or *suppressed*, the result is a *double sideband* or *DSB* signal with only the USB and LSB signals. Finally, one of the sidebands can also be removed, leaving only the USB or LSB. By transmitting only one sideband, the available signal power can be used more effectively compared to AM.

DSB can also be produced by a *balanced modulator* — a special type of mixer where

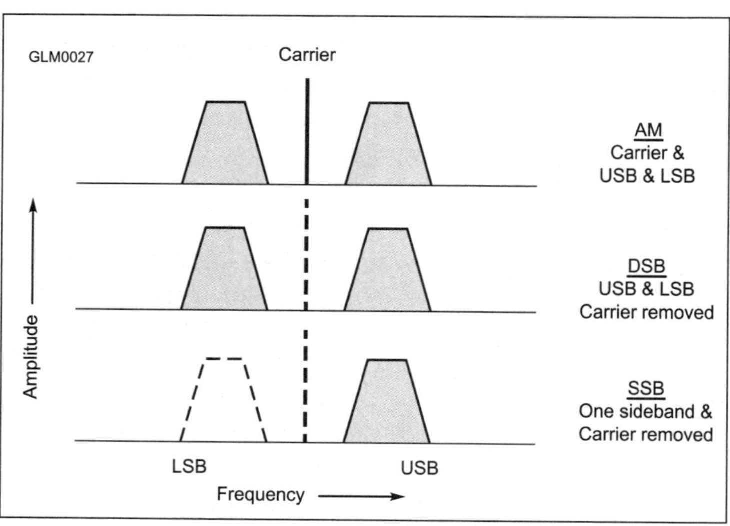

Figure 5.6 — The spectrum of three types of AM signals. Full AM has both sidebands and the carrier. The carrier is represented by the vertical line in the middle and the sidebands contain speech or data signals that have been used to modulate the carrier. DSB removes the carrier, but has the same bandwidth as AM. SSB removes one sideband and has the lowest bandwidth of the three.

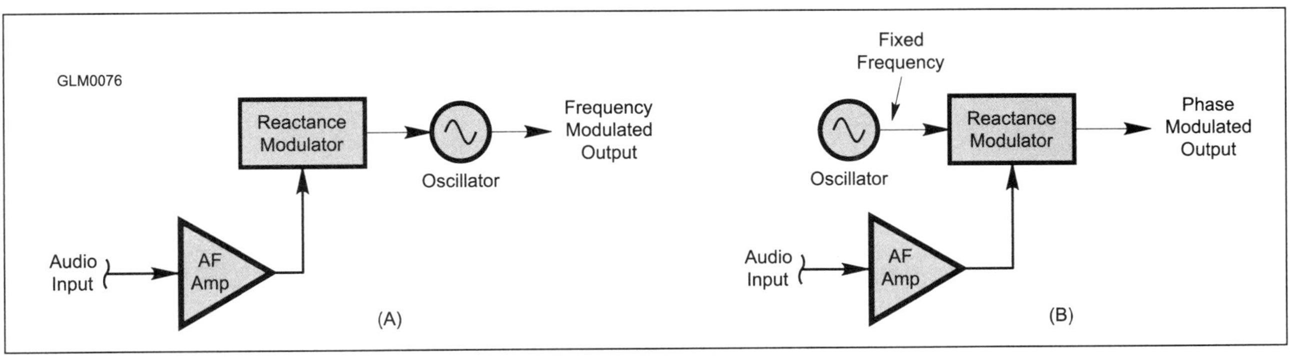

Figure 5.7 — Reactance modulators can be used to create frequency modulation (A) or phase modulation (B).

f_1 is the carrier signal and f_2 is the modulating signal. The balanced modulator produces DSB because it cancels the carrier signal internally.

Starting with a DSB signal, SSB results from filtering out the unwanted sideband. This is the *filter method* of generating SSB. The *phasing method* of generating SSB signals without filters uses a pair of balanced modulators fed by carrier and modulating signals that are 90° out of phase. The resulting DSB signals are then added together, with the result being an SSB signal.

Frequency and Phase Modulation

Frequency modulation (FM) is the result when only the frequency of the modulated signal change in proportion to the modulating signal's amplitude. This change in signal frequency is called *deviation*. *Phase modulation (PM)* occurs if the deviation is proportional to both the modulating signal's amplitude and frequency. The design of the modulator circuit determines whether the output signal is FM or PM. It is important to note that except for very specific circumstances, FM and PM sound identical on the air and can both be demodulated by the same circuits.

The most common method of performing angle modulation is a *reactance modulator*, shown in **Figure 5.7**. If the modulator is connected to the tuned circuit that controls the oscillator's frequency then the frequency will change when modulation is applied, creating frequency modulation. To create phase modulation, the reactance modulator is connected to a tuned RF amplifier following the oscillator. When modulation is applied, the phase of the carrier will be changed but the average frequency will not be changed. **[G8A04]**

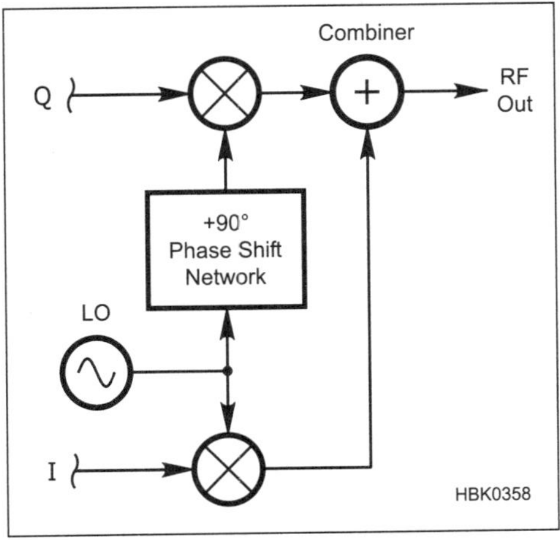

Figure 5.8 — Block diagram of an I/Q modulator. I and Q are input signals that can be analog signals or streams of digital data.

Quadrature Modulation

Quadrature modulation is also called *I/Q modulation* because of the I and Q signals that create the modulated output signal. This technique is primarily used to transmit digital data but different combinations of the I and Q signals can create signals with any form of modulation. **[G7C10]** The technique is particularly well-suited to DSP and is widely used with SDR radios.

I refers to *in-phase* and Q to *quadrature*. I and Q represent input signals. **Figure 5.8** shows how I/Q modulation works. An RF carrier from a local oscillator (LO) signal is split into two signals, one of which is phase-shifted by 90 degrees. (This is where the word "quadrature" comes from.) The LO signals are applied to a mixer along with the I or Q signal. The result is a pair of modulated signals that are then added together in the *combiner* stage. The RF output of the combiner consists of a pair of modulated signals that have carrier signals with a 90-degree difference in phase. **[G7C09]**

5.3 Transmitters

G2A12 — What control is typically adjusted for proper ALC setting on a single sideband transceiver?
Transmit audio or microphone gain

G4B07 — What signals are used to conduct a two-tone test?
Two non-harmonically related audio signals

G4B08 — What transmitter performance parameter does a two-tone test analyzer?
Linearity

G4D01 — What is the purpose of a speech processor in a transceiver?
Increase the apparent loudness of transmitted voice signals

G4D02 — How does a speech processor affect a single sideband phone signal?
It increases average power

G4D03 — What is the effect of an incorrectly adjusted speech processor?
All these choices are correct

G4D08 — What frequency range is occupied by a 3 kHz LSB signal when the displayed carrier frequency is set to 7.178 MHz?
7.175 MHz to 7.178 MHz

G4D09 — What frequency range is occupied by a 3 kHz USB signal with the displayed carrier frequency set to 14.347 MHz?
14.347 MHz to 14.350 MHz

G4D10 — How close to the lower edge of the phone segment should your displayed carrier frequency be when using 3 kHz wide LSB?
At least 3 kHz above the edge of the segment

G4D11 — How close to the upper edge of a band's phone segment should your displayed carrier frequency be when using 3 kHz wide USB?
At least 3 kHz below the edge of the band

G7B10 — Which of the following describes a linear amplifier?
An amplifier in which the output preserves the input waveform

G7C01 — What circuit is used to select one of the sidebands from a balanced modulator?
Filter

G7C02 — What output is produced by a balanced modulator?
Double-sideband modulated RF

G8A08 — Which of the following is an effect of overmodulation?
Excessive bandwidth

G8A10 — What is meant by the term "flat-topping," when referring to an amplitude-modulated phone signal?
Signal distortion caused by excessive drive or speech levels

G8A11 — What is the modulation envelope of an AM signal?
The waveform created by connecting the peak values of the modulated signal

G8B06 — What is the total bandwidth of an FM phone transmission having 5 kHz deviation and 3 kHz modulating frequency?
16 kHz

G8B07 — What is the frequency deviation for a 12.21 MHz reactance modulated oscillator in a 5 kHz deviation, 146.52 MHz FM phone transmitter?
416.7 Hz

From the building blocks are assembled the equipment of radio — transmitters and receivers. In this section, you'll learn how the components produce some of the signals you hear on the air — CW, SSB, and FM. As in the previous section, while the functions

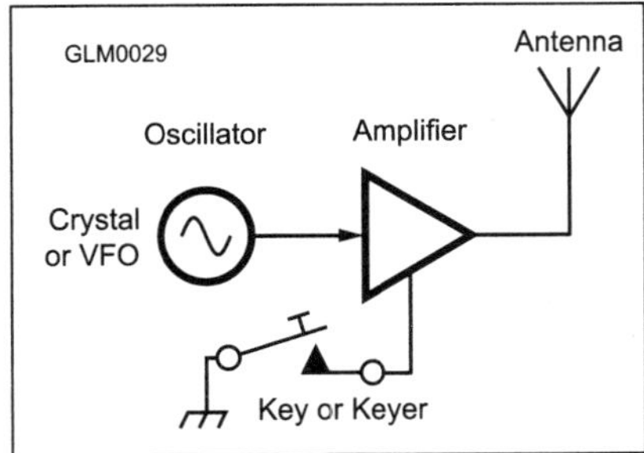

Figure 5.9 — The simplest transmitter consists of the oscillator and amplifier and a means of turning the output signal on and off — the key.

here are discussed as individual circuits or stages, the same functions are implemented by software in a DSP-based radio.

After you learn more about how transmitters work, you'll understand the effects of transmitter controls and how to keep your signal "clean." We'll also take a close look at amplifiers and how to use them properly. The goal is for you to transmit a signal you can be proud of every time.

CW TRANSMITTERS

The simplest transmitter has two stages for sending CW, shown in **Figure 5.9**. It has an oscillator and an amplifier, with the amplifier turned on and off by a key or keyer. A single-crystal oscillator can be replaced with a variable-frequency oscillator to allow the transmitter to be tuned to different frequencies.

In a VFO-controlled transmitter that operates on more than one band, mixers are used to change the transmitter output frequency band without changing the VFO frequency range. This keeps the VFO design simple and stable for good signal quality. **Figure 5.10** shows a simple scheme for a three-band, VFO-controlled transmitter. The mixer input from the VFO always covers the same frequency range. The local oscillator (LO) outputs a signal on one of three frequencies determined by which crystal is switched in. A filter tuned to one of the three bands follows the mixer to eliminate the undesired sum or difference frequency.

SSB PHONE TRANSMITTERS

Figure 5.11 shows how to change the CW transmitter to SSB phone. Starting with

Figure 5.10 — By changing the frequency of the local oscillator (LO), the VFO's output can be shifted from band to band, creating a multiband transmitter.

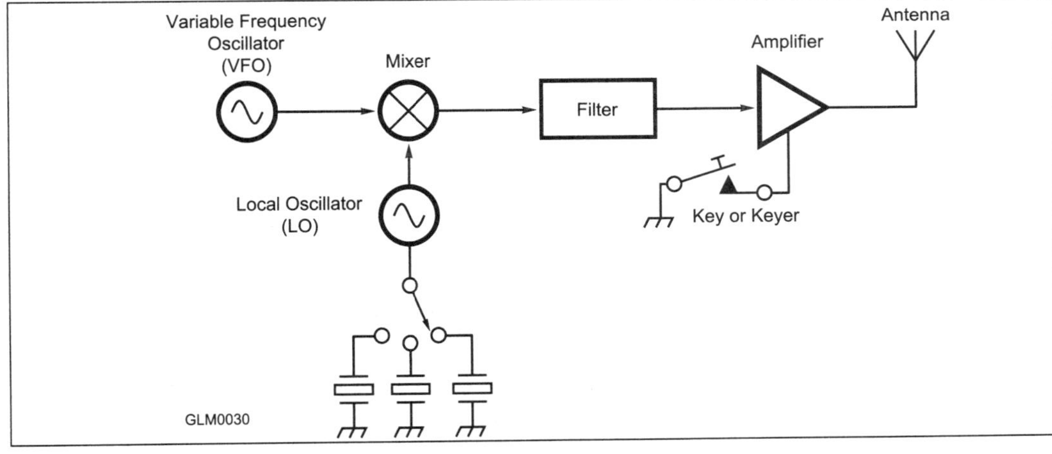

Figure 5.11 — Substituting the circuits to create an SSB signal for the VFO creates a multiband SSB transmitter.

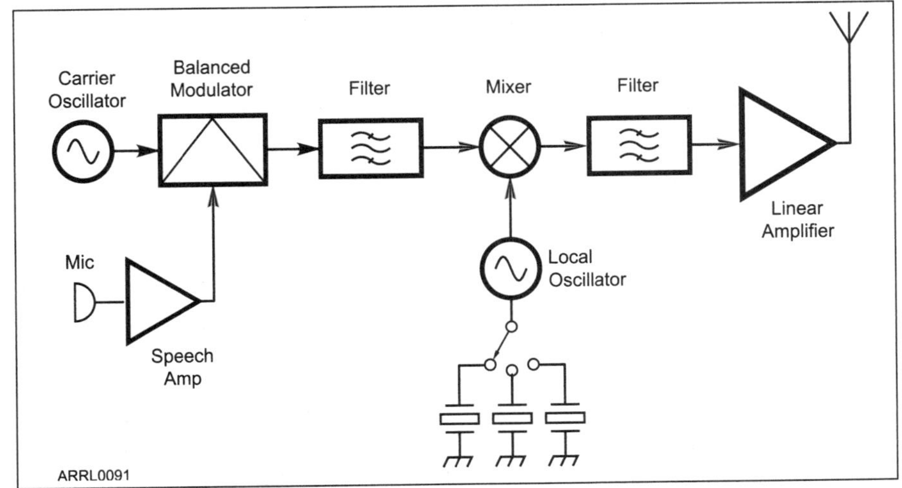

the three-band CW transmitter in Figure 5.10, a balanced modulator stage is added between the oscillator and mixer. Voice signals from a microphone (mic) are processed by a speech amplifier and input to the balanced modulator. The variable-frequency carrier oscillator is the other input to the balanced modulator. **[G7C02]** The output is a DSB signal, so a filter is used to remove the undesired sideband. **[G7C01]**

Note that the output amplifier is now labeled a "Linear Amplifier." That change is necessary because the transmitter must accurately reproduce the rapidly changing speech waveform. In a CW transmitter, it is only necessary to turn a sine wave on and off. In an AM or SSB transmitter, however, all of the stages must be designed to accurately reproduce the input signal, whether they amplify, mix, or filter it. Distortion anywhere in the *transmit chain* (meaning the sequence of circuits that produce the transmitted signal) will generate unwanted spurious signals such as harmonics, mixing products, or splatter. **[G7B10]**

FM TRANSMITTERS

Modulation and frequency changing are performed differently in FM transmitters. While it is possible to generate an FM signal and then use mixers, it is much less expensive and more practical to generate the FM signal at a low frequency and multiply it to reach the desired band. This technique is illustrated in **Figure 5.12**. In a 2 meter band FM transmitter, the modulated oscillator frequency is approximately 12 MHz and the multiplier selects the 12th harmonic for transmission. For example, for an output on 146.52 MHz, the oscillator must produce a 146.52 / 12 = 12.21 MHz signal.

It's important to realize that the frequency deviation of the modulated oscillator output is also multiplied, increasing with each harmonic. For example, if the 146.52 MHz signal is to have the standard deviation of 5 kHz, the deviation of the oscillator can be a maximum of 5 / 12 = 416.7 Hz. **[G8B07]**

Just as for AM signals, the FCC requires amateurs to limit the bandwidth (BW) of FM signals to that which represents good amateur practice. Any angle modulated signal has a theoretically infinite number of sidebands, so what is the bandwidth of an FM signal? *Carson's Rule* is a formula that gives a good approximation of an FM signal's bandwidth: BW = 2 × (peak deviation + highest modulating frequency).

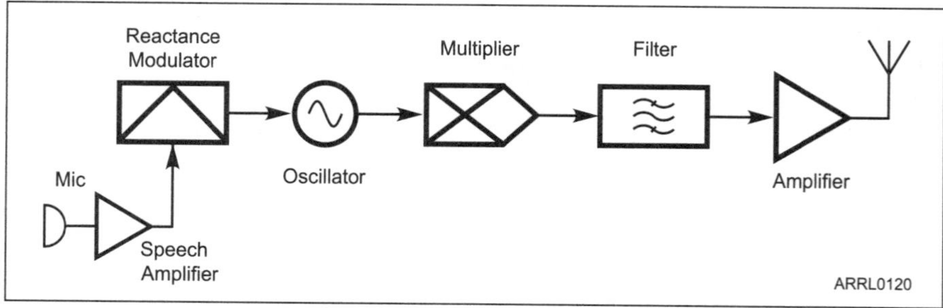

Figure 5.12 — The carrier and modulation are generated at relatively low frequencies in an FM transmitter. The modulated signal is then multiplied to the desired output frequency. The amount of signal deviation is also multiplied.

As an example, if an FM phone signal's peak deviation is limited to 5 kHz and the highest modulating frequency is 3 kHz, then BW = 2 × (5 + 3) = 16 kHz. **[G8B06]** This signal will stay safely within the standard 20 kHz channels specified by repeater coordinators. It is important to control both deviation and the frequency content of the modulating signal.

Something you might have noticed about Figure 5.12 is that the output amplifier is no longer required to be a linear amplifier. FM and PM signals have a constant power level, so it doesn't matter whether an amplifier can faithfully reproduce the input waveform or not. The only important characteristic of the FM signal is its frequency. Amplifiers in an FM transmitter can be highly nonlinear as long as harmonics and off-channel spurious signals are filtered out.

SIGNAL QUALITY

Operating a transmitter so that the on-the-air signal is intelligible and does not occupy excessive bandwidth is an important part of operating. The FCC does not specify bandwidth limits on any phone signal except to say that signals should not occupy more bandwidth than is dictated by "good amateur practice" [§97.307(a)]. Generally speaking, that means an SSB signal should have a bandwidth of no more than 3 kHz and an AM signal about 6 kHz. There is one exception. On 60 meters, the FCC specifies in §97.303(s) that the USB signals should occupy no more than 2.8 kHz of bandwidth as defined in §97.3(a)(8).

Overmodulation — AM Modes

If the amplitude of an AM or SSB signal is varied excessively in response to the modulating signal, this is called *overmodulation*. Overmodulation is caused by speaking too loudly or by setting the microphone or audio gain too high. Examples of properly modulated and *overmodulated* signals are shown in **Figure 5.13**. The figure shows the *modulation envelope* of an AM signal, the waveform created by connecting the peaks of the modulated signal. (The modulation envelope of an SSB signal is similar.) **[G8A11]**

Figure 5.13B shows an example of *cutoff* in which the transmitter output is turned off instead of following the modulating signal. *Flattopping* occurs when the transmitter output reaches a maximum limit and cannot increase further even though the modulating signal is still increasing. **[G8A10]** If the output signal is completely cut off between peaks, the result is *carrier cutoff*. Both types of overmodulation cause interference to nearby channels by generating spurious signals beyond the normal signal bandwidth. **[G8A08]** These spurious signals are *distortion products*,

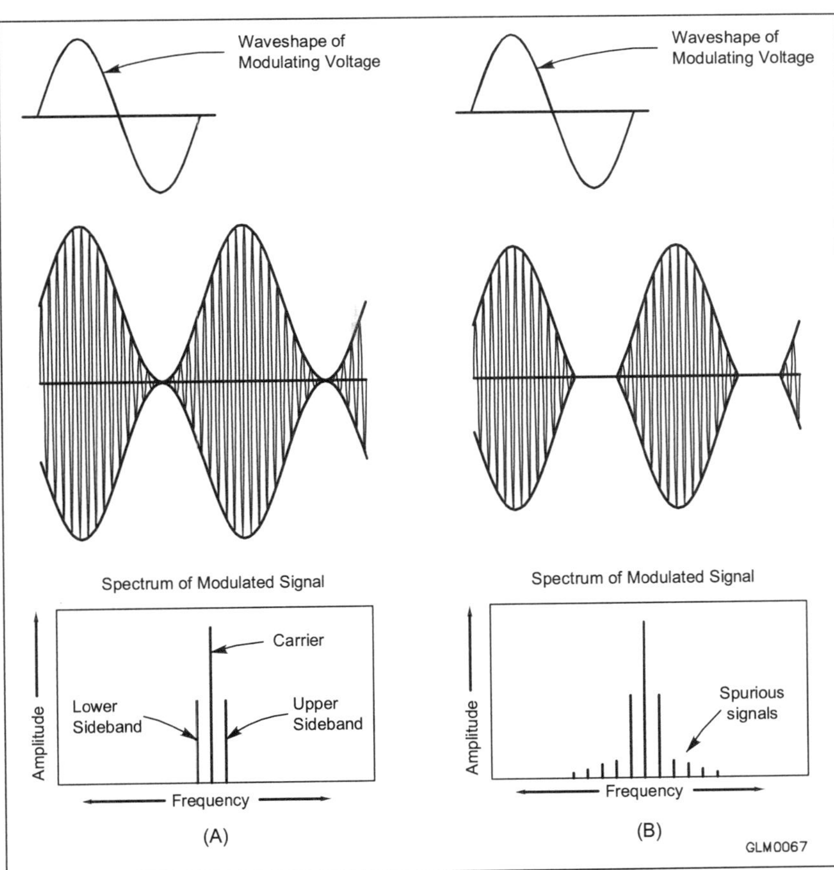

Figure 5.13 — A properly modulated signal at A. The results of overmodulation are visible at B. This distorted signal causes interference on nearby frequencies.

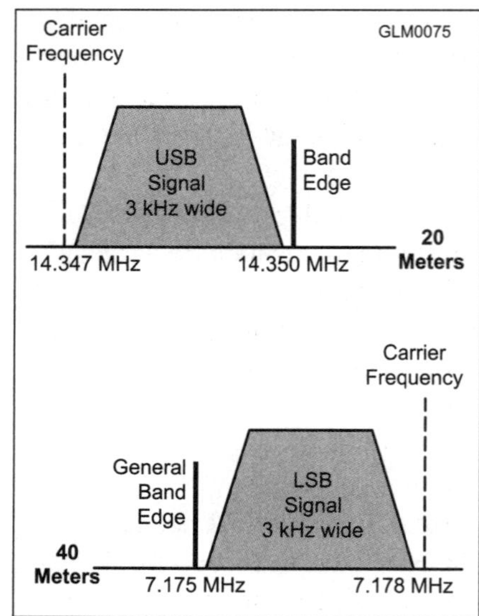

Figure 5.14 — When sidebands extend from the carrier toward a band edge or a band segment edge, operate with a displayed carrier frequency no closer than 3 kHz to the edge frequency and be sure your signal is "clean."

commonly referred to as *splatter* or *buckshot.*

The *automatic level control* (*ALC*) circuits of your transmitter also help prevent overmodulation. ALC reduces output power during voice peaks. Your radio's manual will have some instructions on how to use ALC to properly set your transmit audio or microphone gain. **[G2A12]** In general, the microphone gain should be adjusted to cause the ALC to activate only on voice peaks.

On AM or SSB, a *two-tone test* can be used to monitor transmitter linearity. This test consists of modulating your transmitter with a pair of audio tones that are not harmonically related (700 and 1900 Hz are typical frequencies) while watching the transmitted signal on a monitoring oscilloscope. The transmitter and any external amplifier are then adjusted for an output free of distortion. This test needs only to be performed occasionally to note the appropriate settings of gain and level adjustments. **[G4B07, G4B08]**

Controlling Sideband Frequency

When operating on SSB, it's important to know where your actual signals appear on the band. Nearly all radios display the carrier frequency of an SSB signal. That means your actual signal lies entirely above (USB) or below (LSB) the displayed frequency.

If the sidebands occupy 3 kHz of spectrum, you'll need to stay far enough from the edge of your frequency privileges to avoid transmitting a signal outside them. For example, Generals are permitted to use up to 14.350 MHz, so the displayed carrier frequency of a USB signal should be at least 3 kHz below the band edge — 14.347 MHz — so that the signal occupies 14.347 to 14.350 MHz. If your carrier frequency is higher than that, the sidebands begin to extend into the non-amateur frequencies above 14.350 MHz!

Similarly, using LSB on 40 meters, Generals should operate with the carrier frequency at least 3 kHz above the edge of their band segment — 7.178 MHz — thus occupying the range of 7.175 to 7.178 MHz. See **Figure 5.14**. **[G4D08** to **G4D11]**

Speech Processing

Compared to modes such as CW, the average power of an AM or SSB signal is quite low. Human speech spreads its energy out over a wide frequency range with only short periods of high sound levels. When transmitted over HF as an amplitude-modulated signal in the presence of noise, interference, or fading, the received signal can be difficult to understand. *Speech processing* addresses this problem by increasing the average power of the speech signal without excessively distorting the signal. The result is improved intelligibility of the received signal in poor conditions. **[G4D01, G4D02]** Speech processing requires careful adjustment of transmitter modulation to avoid causing splatter on adjacent channels. Speech processors can also amplify low-level background noise, reducing intelligibility. **[G4D03]** The proper use of speech processing balances the increase in average power against any reduction in intelligibility.

Watch the Noise!

A common downfall of speech processing is background noise, such as fans, wind or other conversations. Noise entering a microphone is indistinguishable from soft speech and can mask speech components, with the expected loss in signal quality. When using a processor, be sure to reduce room noise as much as possible.

For More Information

Microphone (or mic) gain is the control used to adjust the amount by which speech modulates the transmitter output signal. If you have a monitoring oscilloscope, you can watch the transmitter output on voice peaks to see if your signal appears "clean." It also helps to have a friend check your signal quality on the air. Once your transmitter is operating properly, take note of the transmitter settings, meter behavior and oscilloscope images so that you can keep your signal properly adjusted in the future.

Audio level adjustment is somewhat different for each radio and style of signal monitoring equipment. The basics are similar, however. First, use normal speech or audio levels during both testing and on the air contacts. It's natural under difficult conditions to raise your voice but that usually only reduces intelligibility. Next, make use of the transceiver's monitor function to listen to your own signal while you transmit. This is not an exact copy of your output signal, but is helpful in controlling your own speech volume and in catching distortion in the audio circuits of the transmitter.

A common way to make your speech audio stronger is *compression*, which increases gain at low input levels while holding gain constant for louder speech components. The amount of compression is measured in dB as the difference in gain for different levels of input. For example, if low-level input signals are amplified with 10 dB more gain than for high-level signals, it is referred to as "10 dB of compression." Modest amounts of compression make a voice "sound louder" because the low-level speech components are easier to hear in the received signal.

Any kind of speech processing is, by definition, distortion. Too much processing (called *overprocessing*) results in a signal with plenty of power, but is more distorted and harder to understand than the unprocessed signal!

Many digital modes generate the modulated output signal by routing low-level audio tones into the transmitter's microphone input. For these modes, compression should never be used because of the resulting distortion. Similarly, the ALC system should be disabled for these modes or audio levels adjusted so that the ALC system never activates.

Overdeviation

FM and PM signals can be overmodulated as well, but instead of distorting the signal envelope, the result is excessive deviation. This increases the strength of the extra FM signal sidebands that are usually too small to cause interference. The result of overdevia-

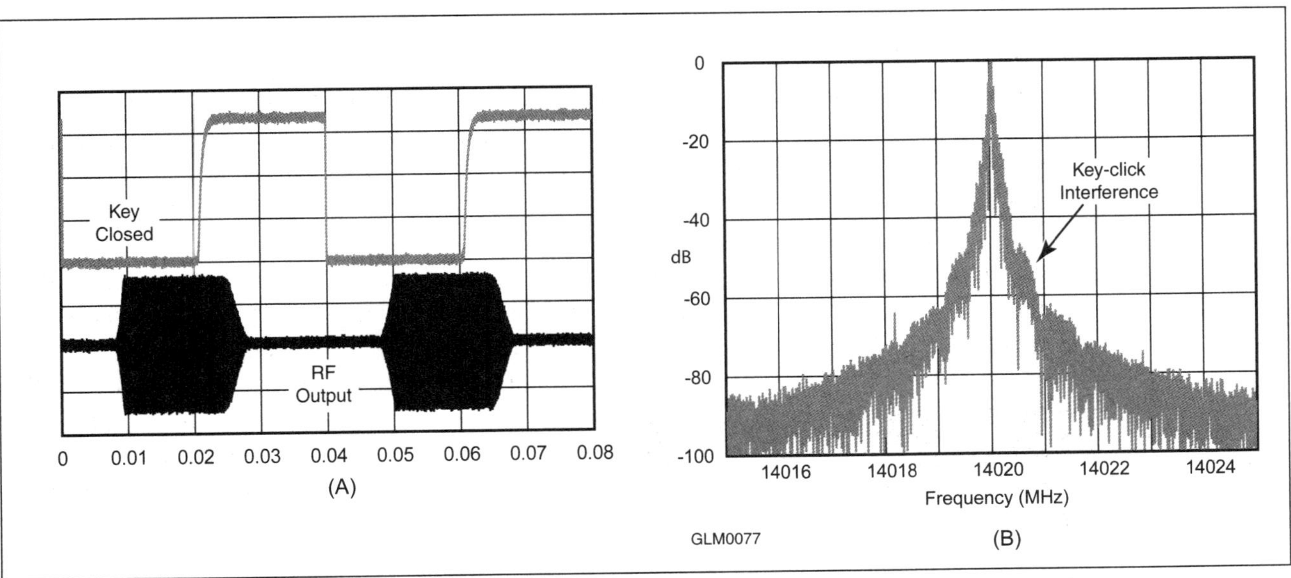

Figure 5.15 — CW waveforms can be inspected by using a monitoring oscilloscope. Key clicks that result from rising and falling edges that are too abrupt or not smooth cause interference on nearby frequencies.

tion is distortion of the received signal and interference to adjacent channels, just as it is for overmodulation of AM signals.

Most FM rigs have limiting circuits that prevent overdeviation caused by speaking too loudly. Your voice may be distorted, but it won't cause interference. Multimode rigs with adjustable microphone gain may allow overmodulation, however. Read your owner's manual to learn the proper operating procedure for your radio.

Key Clicks

Key clicks are sharp transient clicking sounds heard on adjacent frequencies as a transmitter turns on and off too rapidly during CW transmissions. Clicks can also be generated if the transmitter turns on and off erratically. These can be quite disruptive to nearby contacts. Key clicks can often be reduced by adjusting a transmitter configuration setting or by modifying the transmitter's keying control circuits. An oscilloscope can be used to monitor the CW waveform as shown in **Figure 5.15**. Rise and fall times of 4 ms or longer usually prevent clicks from being generated.

AMPLIFIERS

G4A04 — What is the effect on plate current of the correct setting of a vacuum-tube RF power amplifier's TUNE control?
A pronounced dip

G4A05 — Why is automatic level control (ALC) used with an RF power amplifier?
To prevent excessive drive

G4A08 — What is the correct adjustment for the LOAD or COUPLING control of a vacuum tube RF power amplifier?
Desired power output without exceeding maximum allowable plate current

G4A09 — What is the purpose of delaying RF output after activating a transmitter's keying line to an external amplifier?
To allow time for the amplifier to switch the antenna between the transceiver and the amplifier output

G7B01 — What is the purpose of neutralizing an amplifier?
To eliminate self-oscillations

G7B02 — Which of these classes of amplifiers has the highest efficiency?
Class C

G7B04 — In a Class A amplifier, what percentage of the time does the amplifying device conduct?
100%

G7B08 — How is the efficiency of an RF power amplifier determined?
Divide the RF output power by the DC input power

G7B11 — For which of the following modes is a Class C power stage appropriate for amplifying a modulated signal?
FM

Many HF operators use an amplifier (sometimes called a *linear*) so that they can make contacts when conditions are poor, over difficult propagation paths, or in situations when a strong signal is necessary, such as running a net. VHF and UHF amplifiers are most commonly available as solid-state "bricks" that require no tuning or adjustment — turn them on, hook up the rig and the antenna and go. On HF, high-power amplifiers often use vacuum tube circuits that require operator adjustment, although high power "no tune" solid-state amplifiers are rapidly gaining popularity.

An amplifier circuit or *stage* is designed to operate in one of several different *classes*. Each class is best suited for different radio uses and has different efficiency. The efficiency of an amplifier is defined as the RF output power divided by the dc input power. **[G7B08]** Hams use four common amplifier classes:

- *Class A* — The most linear (lowest signal distortion) of all classes and also the least efficient. Because Class A amplifiers pass the entire sinusoidal input cycle, they conduct 100% of the time. **[G7B04]**
- *Class B* — Also known as *push-pull* with a pair of amplifying devices each active during complementary halves of the signal's cycle.
- *Class AB* — Midway between Classes A and B, linearity is not as good as Class A, but efficiency is improved.
- *Class C* —This class of amplifier has the highest efficiency, but Class C amplifiers are only suitable for CW and FM because they have very poor linearity. **[G7B11, G7B02]**

Some linear amplifiers can be operated in either Class AB for SSB operation or in Class C for CW.

Along with the RF input from the transceiver, the transceiver should provide a *keying circuit* that tells the amplifier when to activate. When the keying circuit is inactive, signals from the antenna bypass the amplifier circuit through a transmit-receive *changeover relay* (TR relay) so they can be received. Transceivers often include a delay in the keying circuit timing so that the changeover relay is completely switched before the transceiver is allowed to supply any RF output. This prevents *hot-switching* in which the amplifier is already supplying RF at the time the changeover relay is switching. This can destroy the relay or other external devices. **[G4A09]**

Tuning and Driving a Vacuum-Tube Amplifier

Vacuum-tube amplifiers have three primary operator adjustments: BAND, TUNE and LOAD (or COUPLING). TUNE and LOAD controls adjust components in the output matching circuit, often a pi-network that was introduced in Chapter 4. (No-tune or auto-tune amplifiers do not require TUNE and LOAD adjustments because of their circuit design or because a microprocessor makes the adjustments automatically.) The BAND switch, found on both tube amplifiers and most solid-state amplifiers, configures the input and output impedance matching or filter circuits for the band on which signals will be applied to amplifier.

With the band switch set properly, a small amount of drive power is applied to the amplifier while watching the amplifier's plate current meter and adjusting the TUNE control for a minimum setting (or "dip"). This means the output matching circuit is resonant at the operating frequency. The LOAD control is adjusted to maximize (or "peak") output power and TUNE readjusted for the dip in plate current so that maximum output power is obtained without exceeding maximum plate current. Input power to the amplifier may also be adjusted during that process. **[G4A04, G4A08]**

Drive power is important, particularly for *grid-driven* amplifier circuits in which the input power is applied to the tube's control grid. It is easy to destroy an expensive tube by applying too much drive, observed as excessive grid current on the amplifier's metering circuits. Most modern amplifiers have protective circuits to prevent excessive grid drive. Excessive drive power or mistuning can also result in excessive plate current. This overheats the tube and can cause it to fail. Operate the amplifier according to the manufacturer's specifications and procedures to obtain the longest life from transmitting tubes. Similar cautions apply to solid-state amplifiers with power transistors that can be damaged or destroyed by excessive drive power.

Many amplifiers also generate an ALC signal that can be connected to your transmitter in order to limit excess drive that causes distorted output signals and splatter. You should read both the amplifier and transceiver manuals to be sure the signals are compatible and that you know how to use the ALC meter readings on your transceiver. **[G4A05]**

Neutralization

Self-oscillation because of positive feedback in an amplifier tube or circuit creates spurious output signals and can even damage the tube or amplifier components. The technique of preventing self-oscillation is called *neutralization*. **[G7B01]** Neutralization is performed by creating negative feedback. Negative feedback consists of connecting some of the output signal back to the input, but out-of-phase with the input signal to cancel the unwanted positive feedback. For an HF amplifier, this is done by connecting a small variable capacitor between the amplifier's output and input circuits. The amplifier's operating manual will show the appropriate procedure for making the adjustments. Once an amplifier is neutralized, no further adjustment is needed unless the amplifier tubes are replaced or some other circuit changes are made.

5.4 Receivers

G4A01 — What is the purpose of the notch filter found on many HF transceivers?
To reduce interference from carriers in the receiver passband

G4A02 — What is the benefit of using the opposite or "reverse" sideband when receiving CW?
It may be possible to reduce or eliminate interference from other signals

G4A03 — How does a noise blanker work?
By reducing receiver gain during a noise pulse

G4A07 — What happens as a receiver's noise reduction control level is increased?
Received signals may become distorted.

G4A13 — What is the purpose of using a receive attenuator?
To prevent receiver overload from strong incoming signals

G4D04 — What does an S-meter measure?
Received signal strength

G4D05 — How does a signal that reads 20 dB over S9 compare to one that reads S9 on a receiver, assuming a properly calibrated S meter?
It is 100 times more powerful

G4D06 — How much change in signal strength is typically represented by one S unit?
6 dB

G4D07 — How much must the power output of a transmitter be raised to change the S meter reading on a distant receiver from S8 to S9?
Approximately 4 times

G7C04 — How is a product detector used?
Used in a single sideband receiver to extract the modulated signal

G7C06 — Which of the following is an advantage of a digital signal processing (DSP) filter compared to an analog filter?
A wide range of filter bandwidths and shapes can be created

G7C08 — Which parameter affects receiver sensitivity?
Input amplifier gain; Demodulator stage bandwidth; Input amplifier noise figure

G8B01 — Which mixer input is varied or tuned to convert signals of different frequencies to an intermediate frequency (IF)?
Local oscillator

G8B02 — What is the term for interference from a signal at twice the IF frequency from the desired signal?
> Image response

G8B09 — Why is it good to match receiver bandwidth to the bandwidth of the operating mode?
> It results in the best signal-to-noise ratio

As the wise old radio saying goes, "You can't work 'em if you can't hear 'em!" That makes the receiver just about the most important part of the station. HF receivers also have more adjustments than HF transmitters by far — why? This section explains how receivers are constructed — tune in!

DSP and SDR techniques are rapidly replacing analog receiver electronic circuits. As a result, most receivers now combine analog RF circuitry with DSP techniques to take advantage of available technology at an affordable price. The functions described in this section can be performed by either analog circuits or mathematically in a digital microprocessor. In the coming years, most receivers will be all-digital.

BASIC SUPERHETERODYNE RECEIVERS

Most analog receivers in use by amateurs today are some type of *superheterodyne*, a design invented in the 1920s by Edwin Armstrong. As you learned earlier, the mixing together of signals to obtain sum and difference frequencies is called heterodyning. The "superhet" is built around that process.

Received signals are incredibly weak — on the order of nano or picowatts. Thus, a receiver must be quite sensitive to make it possible for an operator to hear such a signal. Simultaneously, a single signal must be picked out of a crowded spectrum where nearby signals might be billions of times stronger. So the receiver must be very selective, as well. Both of these requirements are satisfied by the basic superheterodyne receiver structure shown in **Figure 5.16**. Let's trace the signal through the receiver from antenna to speaker.

Received signals are first strengthened by the RF amplifier, and then applied to the RF input of a mixer. The local oscillator (LO) is adjusted so that the desired signal creates a mixing product at a fixed frequency, called the *intermediate frequency* (IF). **[G8B01]** An IF filter removes signals outside the receiver's passband and whatever signals remain are amplified by the IF amplifier. Most of the gain of a superhet is provided by the IF stages of the receiver. A detector or demodulator stage follows the IF to recover the modulating

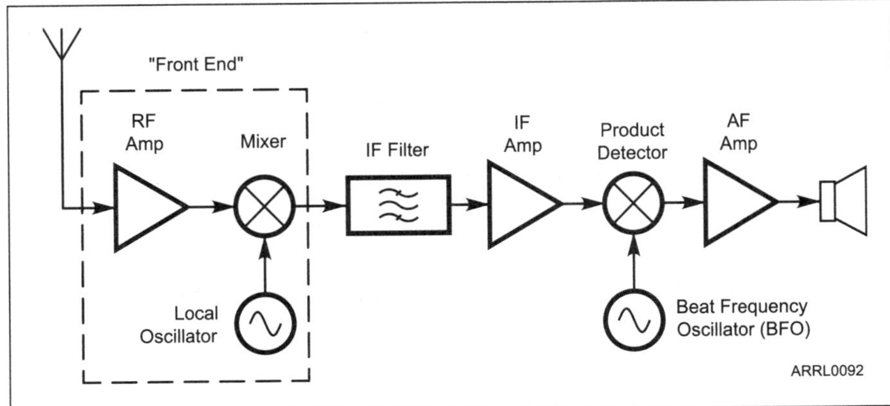

Figure 5.16 — A superheterodyne receiver converts signals to audio in two steps. The front end converts the frequency of a signal to the intermediate frequency (IF) where most of the gain of the receiver is provided. A second mixer — the product detector — converts the signal to audio frequencies.

information. The simplest possible superhet consists of a mixer connected to the antenna, an oscillator to act as the LO, and a detector that operates directly on the resulting IF signal. Each of these components — amplifier gain and noise figure as well as demodulator bandwidth — impact receiver sensitivity. [G7C08]

The single-frequency IF stages make it much easier to create high quality filters and high gain amplifiers without having to be tuned. Only the LO needs to be tuned in a superhet receiver. For example, to convert an RF signal on 14.250 MHz to an IF of 455 kHz, the LO must be tuned to either 14.250 − 455 kHz = 13.795 MHz or to 14.250 + 455 kHz = 14.705 MHz.

To cover the entire 20 meter band and assuming the difference mixing product is used, the LO would be tuned from 14.000 − 0.455 MHz = 13.545 MHz to 14.350 − 0.455 MHz = 13.895 MHz.

Once amplified to a more usable level, SSB and CW signals are demodulated by a *product detector*, a special type of mixer. [G7C04] If an AM signal is being received, either a product detector or an *envelope detector* is used to recover the modulating signal. The output of the product or envelope detector is an audio signal that is amplified by an audio frequency (AF) amplifier and applied to a speaker or headphones or sound card.

The RF amplifier and mixer comprise the receiver's "front end." This section of the receiver processes weak signals at their original frequencies, so it must work over a wide frequency range and for both strong and weak signals. A tunable filter or *preselector* is sometimes used between the antenna and RF amplifier to reject strong *out-of-band* signals, such as those from broadcasters or commercial stations. These out-of-band signals are not in the desired frequency band, but they could overload the circuitry. If additional sensitivity is needed, an additional stage of RF amplification called a *preamplifier* (or *preamp*) is used.

FM receivers are very similar to an AM/SSB/CW superhet, but they have key differences as shown in **Figure 5.17**. The only information that matters in an FM signal is the frequency, so a special, non-linear IF amplifier called a *limiter* replaces the linear IF amplifier in an AM receiver. A limiter amplifies the received signal until all of the amplitude modulated information, such as noise, is removed and only a square wave of varying frequency remains. The audio information is recovered by a *discriminator* or a *quadrature detector* that replaces the product detector. The audio is then amplified as before.

Like every design, the superheterodyne has some weaknesses. Because there are mixing products at both the sum and difference frequencies, undesired signals can also create their own mixing products at the IF. For example, if the IF is 455 kHz and the LO frequency is 13.800 MHz, signals at both 14.255 and 13.345 MHz will create a mixing product at 455 kHz. The first is 14.255 − 13.800 MHz = 455 kHz and the second is 13.800 − 13.345 MHz = 455 kHz. Assuming the receiver is supposed to receive the 14.255 MHz

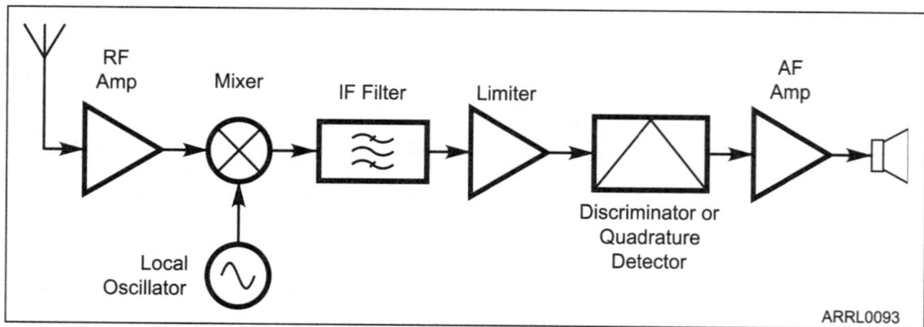

Figure 5.17 — Once the FM signal is converted to the IF, high-gain amplifiers called limiters change the signal to a square wave that only varies in frequency (not amplitude). A discriminator converts the frequency variations to audio.

signal, the undesired signal at 13.345 MHz is an *image response*. **[G8B02]** Filters in the receiver front end are required to remove signals that might produce images.

Another flaw is caused by the LO and other oscillator circuits inside the receiver. Leakage of these signals into the signal path can cause steady signals to appear. These signals are called *birdies*. Even if no signals are present at the receiver input, birdies will still be audible because they are caused by signals inside the receiver.

The receiver shown in Figures 5.16 and 5.17 is a *single-conversion* receiver, with only one mixer converting the signal from RF to IF. The IF stages provide most of the receiver's gain and almost all of its selectivity (the ability to reject unwanted signals). Depending on how many different frequency bands the receiver must cover and the demands for selectivity, superhet receivers may have one, two, or three IF stages, resulting in a single, double, or triple-conversion receiver. Filtering is applied at each IF, allowing the operator to select filter bandwidths appropriate for the desired signal. This gives the best received signal quality with the lowest unwanted noise and interference, maximizing the *signal-to-noise ratio* or (*SNR*). **[G8B09]**

DIGITAL SIGNAL PROCESSING (DSP)

The general term for converting signals from analog to digital form, operating on them with a microprocessor, and converting them back to analog is *digital signal processing* (*DSP*). **Figure 5.18** shows the basic structure of a digital signal processor in a communications receiver.

RF signals can be converted directly to digital data (*direct sampling*) or converted to a lower frequency with a mixer and converted at the receiver's IF. The conversion to digital form is performed by an *analog-to-digital converter* (ADC). A specialized microprocessor called a *digital signal processor* performs filtering and other receiving functions mathematically. The data is then converted back to analog form for the human operator by a *digital-to-analog converter* (DAC). If the receiver is intended to be used for digital modes, the data may be converted directly to characters instead of to analog form.

DSP technology has two major advantages over analog circuitry — performance and flexibility. Current DSP components can achieve performance as good as or better than the best analog filters. DSP receivers offer selectable preprogrammed filters and allow the operator to adjust the filter bandwidth and shape and even to define new filters. **[G7C06]** Functions that would be prohibitively expensive in analog circuitry can be implemented in DSP as a program without any additional hardware cost. DSP is limited only by processor speed and available memory as to how many options, functions, and adjustments can be created.

MANAGING RECEIVER GAIN

Receivers need to have a lot of gain to bring weak signals up to a level where their

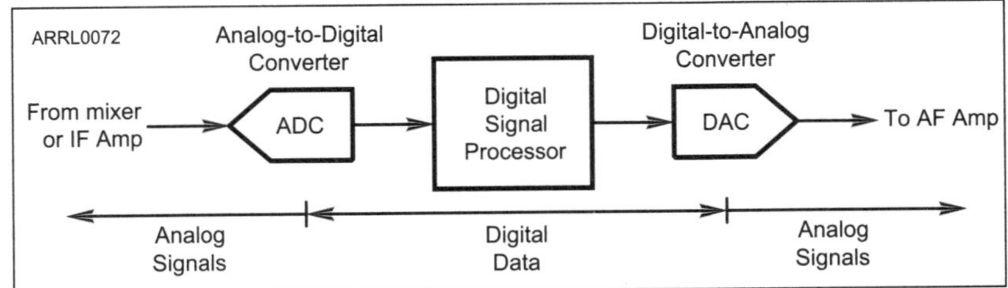

Figure 5.18 — DSP systems use an analog-to-digital converter (ADC) to change the signal to digital data. A special type of microprocessor then performs the mathematical operations on the data to accomplish filtering, noise reduction, or other functions. A digital-to-analog converter (DAC) changes the processed data back to analog form for output as audio.

information can be recovered by ear or by computer. Just as too little gain can cause weak signals to be missed, too much gain can cause its own set of problems. There are several controls and displays that the operator can use to get the gain setting "just right."

RF Gain and Automatic Gain Control

The amount of receiver gain is set by the RF gain control. If you are tuning your receiver and looking for weak signals, you will likely set the RF gain to maximum so that receiver sensitivity is highest. Once you've tuned in a signal, unless it's very weak, maximum gain isn't required and so RF gain can be adjusted for the most comfortable listening. Lower values of RF gain also reduce the volume of the background noise heard in the output audio.

The automatic gain control (AGC) circuits vary the gain of the RF and IF amplifiers so that the output volume of a signal stays relatively constant for both weak and strong signals. The AGC control of the receiver can be set so that the circuit responds quickly or slowly (or not at all) to volume changes, depending on the operator's preference. Fast AGC response is usually used for CW and data signals, while slow response works best for phone.

The AGC circuit adjusts receiver gain by changing a voltage that controls the IF amplifier gain. This voltage is also read by the *S-meter* of the receiver, which is used to measure received signal strength. ("S" stands for "signal.") **[G4D04]** The more the AGC circuit has to reduce gain to keep volume constant, the higher the reading on the S-meter, since stronger signals require less gain to produce the same output volume. You'll notice that turning down the RF gain also increases the S-meter reading because the RF gain control uses the same control voltage as the AGC circuit.

S-meters are calibrated in *S-units*, with a change of one S-unit usually equal to a 6 dB (fourfold) change in signal strength, although this may vary with manufacturer. **[G4D06, G4D07]** An AGC circuit may also respond differently at different signal strengths. Nevertheless, the S-meter is a useful indicator of signal strength, with a signal strength of S-9 being a strong signal. You'll notice that S-9 is at the midpoint of an S-meter display. To the right are additional markings of "20", "40" and "60." These correspond to "dB above S-9," so a reading of "S-9 + 20 dB" corresponds to a signal 20 dB (100 times) stronger than an S-9 signal. **[G4D05]**

Receiver Linearity

It is important that a receiver respond linearly to received signals, just as it is important for a transmitter to amplify linearly. If the received signal is overloaded, the input signals will be distorted, and new spurious signals will appear just as if the transmitting station were emitting them!

The most common form of receiver nonlinearity is *overload* or *gain compression*. (Overload is also called *front-end overload*.) This occurs when an input signal is simply too strong for the circuitry to handle and distortion results. The usual symptom is strong distortion of all signals when the overloading signal is present. The solution to overload is to either filter out the offending signal or reduce receiver gain using the *attenuator* circuit to reduce signal levels overall. Proper use of the attenuator and RF gain controls can dramatically reduce received noise and distortion caused by strong signals. **[G4A13]**

Accessory circuits in the receiver can also affect its linearity. Using a preamplifier makes it easier for strong signals to overload a receiver. Noise blankers that work by shutting off the receiver when a strong noise pulse is detected can confuse strong signals with the pulses, creating severe distortion as a result. Use these circuits only when necessary and to the minimum amount needed.

REJECTING INTERFERENCE AND NOISE

IF filters, whether analog or DSP, narrow the receiver's passband and remove unwanted signals. An assortment of filters is available to suit the common operating modes and styles. Once an interfering signal is in the receiver's passband, however, removing it can be difficult. You can apply several techniques to get rid of these signals.

• Notch filters remove signals in a very narrow band of frequencies, such as a single tone from an interfering carrier. **[G4A01]**

• Passband or IF shift adjusts the receiver's passband above or below the displayed carrier frequency to avoid interfering signals on adjacent frequencies. This results in a shift in tone of the received signal, but often improves intelligibility.

• Reverse sideband controls allow the operator to switch between receiving CW signals above the displayed carrier frequency (USB) and below it (LSB). This can help avoid nearby signals causing interference by placing them on the "other side" of the carrier frequency where filtering rejects them. **[G4A02]**

Most receivers also provide *noise blankers* and *noise reduction* features. Noise blankers operate by sensing short, sharp pulses in the IF signals and quickly reducing the gain of IF and audio amplifiers during the pulse. **[G4A03]** This is called "blanking." If the noise blanker is adjustable, it can be set to blank the receiver at different levels of noise. Noise blankers can confuse strong signals elsewhere on a band for a noise pulse, causing distortion of desired signals. This distortion can be minimized by using the minimum amount of blanking necessary or turning off the noise blanker entirely.

Noise reduction is performed on the receiver's output audio by DSP. This system attempts to remove hiss and noise from the audio that is not part of the desired speech, data, or CW. There may be more than one noise reduction setting optimized for different types of signals. Increasing the noise reduction level may cause some of the desired signal to be removed as well, causing distortion. **[G4A07]** Use the least noise reduction required to minimize distortion.

5.5 HF Station Installation

G4C01 — Which of the following might be useful in reducing RF interference to audio frequency circuits?

Bypass capacitor

G4C02 — Which of the following could be a cause of interference covering a wide range of frequencies?

Arcing at a poor electrical connection

G4C03 — What sound is heard from an audio device experiencing RF interference from a single sideband phone transmitter?

Distorted speech

G4C04 — What sound is heard from an audio device experiencing RF interference from a CW transmitter?

On-and-off humming or clicking

G4C05 — What is a possible cause of high voltages that produce RF burns?

The ground wire has high impedance on that frequency

G4C06 — What is a possible effect of a resonant ground connection?

High RF voltages on the enclosures of station equipment

G4C08 — Which of the following would reduce RF interference caused by common-mode current on an audio cable?

Place a ferrite choke on the cable

G4C09 — How can the effects of ground loops be minimized?
Bond equipment enclosures together

G4C10 — What could be a symptom caused by a ground loop in your station's audio connections?
You receive reports of "hum" on your station's transmitted signal

G4C11 — What technique helps to minimize RF "hot spots" in an amateur station?
Bonding all equipment enclosures together

G4C12 — Why must all metal enclosures of station equipment be grounded?
It ensures that hazardous voltages cannot appear on the chassis

G4E03 — Which of the following direct, fused power connections would be the best for a 100-watt HF mobile installation?
To the battery using heavy-gauge wire

G4E04 — Why should DC power for a 100-watt HF transceiver not be supplied by a vehicle's auxiliary power socket?
The socket's wiring may be inadequate for the current drawn by the transceiver

G4E05 — Which of the following most limits an HF mobile installation?
Efficiency of the electrically short antenna

G4E07 — Which of the following may cause receive interference to an HF transceiver installed in a vehicle?
The battery charging system; The fuel delivery system; The control computers

G6B10 — How does a ferrite bead or core reduce common-mode RF current on the shield of a coaxial cable?
By creating an impedance in the current's path

G8B05 — Which intermodulation products are closest to the original signal frequencies?
Odd-order

G8B12 — What process combines two signals in a non-linear circuit to produce unwanted spurious outputs?
Intermodulation

G8B13 — Which of the following is an odd-order intermodulation product of frequencies F1 and F2?
2F1-F2

Along with understanding the equipment itself, assembling it into a working station at home or in a vehicle creates another set of concerns. HF operating, with longer wavelengths and typically higher field strengths, makes grounding and interference control much more important. The General class exam focuses on three related areas: mobile installations, RF grounding and RF interference.

MOBILE INSTALLATIONS

To help you get rolling, review some of the mobile operating references on the *General Class License Manual* website (**arrl.org/general-class-license-manual**) before installing your mobile system. Don't hesitate to ask other mobile operators for advice — they're often glad to relate their own experiences and act as a mentor.

Power Connections

A mobile radio that can output 100 W requires a solid power connection capable of supplying 20 A or more with a minimum amount of voltage drop. Solid-state radios perform unpredictably when input voltage drops below the specified minimum power supply voltage.

Do not extend or replace the power cable provided by the manufacturer with smaller wire. The best power connection is direct to the battery using heavy gauge wire with a fuse in both the positive and negative leads. Do not use the auxiliary power socket, as that circuit is usually rated at only a few amperes which is insufficient to supply a 100 W HF radio. **[G4E03, G4E04]**

Do not assume that the vehicle's metal chassis is a suitable dc ground connection. Many vehicle bodies are constructed from independent sections, which leads to erratic ground connections over time. Some pieces may be made from plastic or other nonmetallic materials. Connect the radio power ground either directly to the battery or to the battery ground strap where it attaches to the engine block or vehicle chassis.

Antenna Connections

The most significant limitation of mobile operating is that electrically short (smaller in terms of a wavelength) antennas are less efficient than full-size antennas at a home station. This is particularly true on the lower frequency bands. **[G4E05]** When mobiling, the entire vehicle becomes part of the antenna system and attention to every detail can pay big benefits in signal strength. For example:
- Use the most efficient antenna you can.
- Make sure RF ground connections to the vehicle are solid.
- Mount the antenna where it is as clear as possible of metal surfaces.

Mobile Interference

When operating HF mobile, there are interference concerns quite different from those in the home station. Ignition noise caused by the spark plugs firing can be quite strong, although the noise blanker of modern radios can be quite effective at this reducing this type of noise. (Vehicles with diesel engines don't have this problem!) Another common problem is interfering signals generated by the vehicle's accessories and other systems. (See the sidebar, "Tame That High-Pitched Whine.") Common sources of interfering signals include the vehicle's onboard control computers, electric motor-driven devices such as fuel pumps and windows, and battery charging systems. **[G4E07]** Online mobile resources and manufacturer service bulletins can help you deal with mobile interference and noise problems.

GROUNDING AND BONDING

AC safety grounding is very important in the station. Make sure that all ac outlets are properly grounded to your ac service panel. Any equipment with an exposed metal enclosure must be grounded. This prevents hazardous voltages from appearing on the equipment chassis, creating a shock hazard. **[G4C12]**

To manage RF from your transmitted signal, bond equipment enclosures together as shown in **Figure 5.19**. Bonding means to connect two points together to minimize voltage

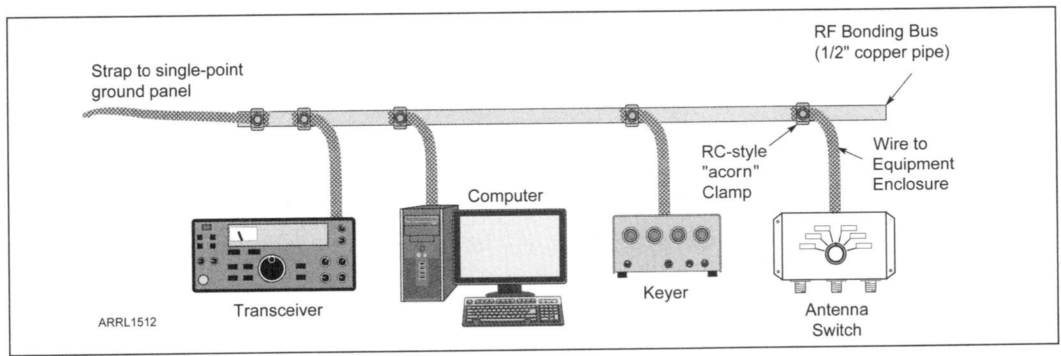

Figure 5.19 — This example of a typical RF bonding bus at the operating position helps keep all of the equipment at the same RF voltage.

differences between them. At RF, bonding keeps all equipment at as close to the same RF voltage as possible.

Keeping all of your equipment at the same RF voltage also minimizes "hot spots" where high RF voltage is present that can cause an "RF burn." It also reduces RF current flowing between pieces of equipment on power and signal cabling that can cause improper operation. For example, during digital operation, unwanted RF currents can cause audio distortion or erratic operation of computer interfaces, activate the transmitter improperly (such as when using VOX), and garble digital protocols which causes data or connections to be lost.

The basics for RF bonding in your station are:

• Connect all metal equipment enclosures directly together or to a common RF bonding bus. **[G4C11]**

• Keep all connections, straps and wires short.

• Use short, heavy conductors such as heavy wire (#12 or #14 AWG) or strap.

• Where strong RF signals are present, a piece of wide flashing or screen can be placed under the equipment and connected to the RF bonding bus.

If your station includes an external ground rod for lightning protection, make the connection as short as possible. If the ground connection approaches resonance at an odd number of 1/4 wavelengths at any frequency, it will present a high impedance, enabling RF voltages to exist on your equipment enclosures and connecting cables. **[G4C05, G4C06]** Avoiding a high impedance on the ground connection may be difficult, particularly for upper-floor or apartment stations. In such cases, keeping the equipment at the same RF voltage is the most effective strategy.

Ground loops are created by a continuous current path (the loop) around a series of equipment connections. This loop acts as a single-turn inductor that picks up voltages from magnetic fields generated by power transformers, ac wiring, and other low-frequency currents. The result is a "hum" in transmitted signals or that interferes with control or data signals. **[G4C10]** Ground loops can be avoided by connecting all ground conductors to the RF bonding bus. **[G4C09]** This minimizes the loop area and keeps voltage differences between equipment to a minimum.

The ARRL Technical Information Service's Safety web page (**arrl.org/safety**) provides an entire page of resources about grounding and RF management in your station with several *QST* magazine articles and web references. The ARRL book *Grounding and Bonding for the Radio Amateur* discusses ac safety, lightning protection, and RF management in the ham station. Each installation is a little different and you may have to experiment to get the results you expect.

RF INTERFERENCE (RFI)

Radiating a good signal means that you'll probably discover some unintentional listeners in nearby receivers and consumer electronics. A license study manual cannot provide a thorough discussion of the causes and effects of RF interference (RFI), but ARRL's Technical Information Service offers a lot of information. You can also learn more from *The ARRL Handbook*.

Here are some common causes and solutions of RF interference to consumer electronics and broadcast receivers:

• *Fundamental overload* — usually exhibited by radio or TV receivers unable to reject a strong signal that causes the internal circuits to act improperly, distorting or wiping out the intended signal. Prevent the offending signal from entering the equipment by using filters in the path of the signal.

• *Common-mode* — any type of electronic equipment with internal electronics, including telephones, computers, music players and so on, can be affected by strong local signals. The signal is picked up as common-mode current on the outside of cable shields or on all conductors of an unshielded connection. This can occur for power connections, speaker leads, telephone cable — any external wiring. The unwanted signal is then conducted into the equipment where it can cause erratic operation or audio noise.

- *Direct pickup* — occurs when the signal is received directly by the internal wiring of a device and can be very hard to eliminate without adding shielding to the device.
- *Harmonics* — spurious emissions from an amateur station may be received by radio or TV equipment. The solution is to use a low-pass filter to remove the spurious emissions at the amateur station. Remember to match the low-pass filter's impedance with the characteristic impedance of the feed line into which it is inserted. Harmonics are multiples of a fundamental frequency. So, if the fundamental frequency is 144 MHz, then the second harmonic is 288 MHz, the third is 432 MHz, etc. Note that there is no first harmonic. The first harmonic is the fundamental frequency.
- *Intermodulation* — Poor contacts between conductors picking up RF signals can create a nonlinear connection or circuit that acts as a mixer and mixing products from the signals. **[G8B12]** A diode or transistor exposed to the RF signals can behave similarly. If the mixing products are on the frequency that the receivers are tuned to, they will cause interference to the desired signal. The solution is to find and repair the poor contact or block RF signals from getting to the components. Odd-order harmonics are closest to the original frequencies. **[G8B05]**

Intermodulation products result whenever one or more signals are mixed together, and they follow a simple scheme of $mF_1 \pm nF_2$ where F is the frequency and m and n are any integer or zero. The second order intermodulation products are $2F_1$ and $2F_2$, while the third order IPs are $2F_1 \pm F_2$ and $2F_2 \pm F_1$. **[G8B13]**

- *Arcing* — Any spark or sustained arc creates radio noise over a wide range of frequencies and will interfere with both amateur and consumer reception. **[G4C02]** When created by the ac power lines, the result will be a crackling buzz. If the arc is from a motor or welding equipment, the buzz will come and go when the equipment is energized. In general, poor contact between any current-carrying conductors will cause interference. The solution for power line noise is to isolate it to a single installation and then request that the power company make the necessary repairs. Noise from specific equipment may require filtering of that equipment.

Common RFI Symptoms

RF interference is quite varied, but these symptoms of interference by a strong signal to audio equipment are probably some of the most common types of RFI:

- CW, FM or data — The interference will consist of on-and-off buzzes, humming, clicks or thumps when the interfering signal is transmitted. **[G4C04]**
- AM phone — Equipment experiencing overload or direct detection will often emit a replica of the speaker's voice.
- SSB voice — similar to AM phone, but the voice will be distorted or garbled. **[G4C03]**

Suppressing RFI

The best solution to many types of interference caused by proximity to an amateur station is to keep the RF signals from entering the equipment in the first place. If filters can be used, they are generally the most effective and least troublesome to install. The next approach is to block RF current flow by placing an impedance in its path. **[G6B10]** This is done by forming the conductor carrying the RF current into an RF choke by winding it around or through a ferrite core. **[G6B10]**

Ferrite beads and cores can also be placed on cables to prevent RF common-mode current from flowing on the outside of cable braids or shields ("common mode" interference). **[G4C08]** The same beads and cores can be used to prevent signals from computers and computer accessories from causing interference to amateur communications. Interference to audio equipment and appliance switch and sensor connections can sometimes be eliminated by placing a small (100 pF to 1 nF) *bypass capacitor* across balanced connections or from each connection to chassis ground. **[G4C01]** Do not place bypass capacitors across speaker or data connections. *The ARRL Handbook* provides detailed guidance on dealing with RFI along with ARRL's Technical Information Service web page mentioned previously.

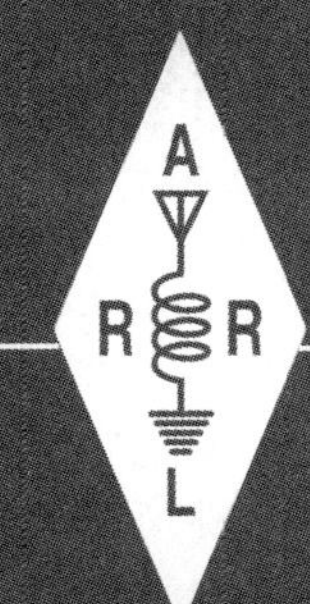

Chapter 6
Digital Modes

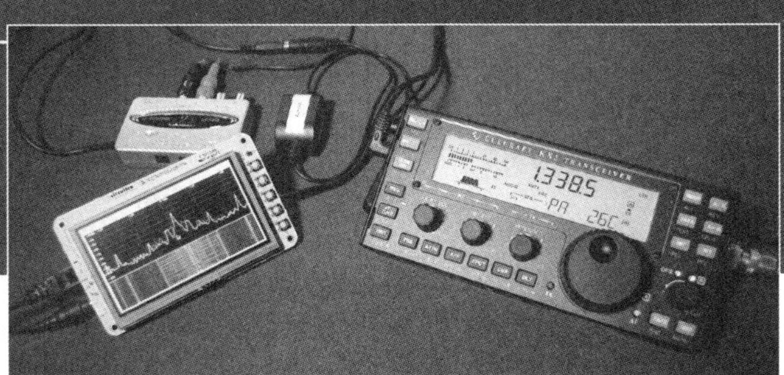

In this chapter, you'll learn about:
- **Digital data definitions**
- **Digital codes and protocols**
- **Rules for digital modes**
- **Digital operating procedures**
- **Receiving and transmitting digital signals**

Digital communications systems exchange digital data over the air between two computing systems. This includes email, data files, keyboard-to-keyboard typing, and control data, just to name a few examples. Amateur radio experimenters are developing new digital protocols and modes while more hams are using digital modes such as radioteletype, FT8, PSK31, and others every day. As a General class licensee you'll have access to all of amateur radio's digital technology, so it's important to learn about it as part of studying for your licensing exam.

6.1 Basics of Digital Modes

G2E08 — In what segment of the 20-meter band are most digital mode operations commonly found?
> Between 14.070 MHz and 14.100 MHz

G8A01 — How is direct binary FSK modulation generated?
> By changing an oscillator's frequency directly with a digital control signal

G8C11 — How are the two separate frequencies of a Frequency Shift Keyed (FSK) signal identified?
> Mark and space

G8C16 — Which of the following provide digital voice modes?
> DMR, D-STAR, and SystemFusion

Communications are considered to be digital modes if information is exchanged as individual characters encoded as digital bits. For example, the character "A" can be sent as "didah" in Morse code or the bit pattern 01000001 in the ASCII code. There are many digital modes used in amateur radio. Some are quite old, such as radioteletype which was invented in the 1930s. Others are adaptations of modes used commercially, and some, such as PSK31 and FT8, are purely amateur creations. New digital modes are being added regularly — an area in which amateur inventiveness shines brightly.

WHERE TO FIND DIGITAL ACTIVITY

Digital mode signals are restricted to the CW/data segments of each HF band. Most digital mode operation is found close to the top of the CW segment. Calling frequencies for the popular digital modes are incorporated into band plans and are usually the lowest frequency of operation with operators moving up in frequency as activity increases. For example, on 20 meters most PSK31 signals are found near 14.070 MHz. RTTY and other digital mode signals are found above that between 14.070 and 14.112 MHz. **[G2E08]** Segments of the HF bands where you'll find signals of the popular digital modes are listed in **Table 6.1**. When you are operating on 20 meters, be sure to keep your transmitted signal clear of 14.100 MHz, the frequency of the NCDXF system of international beacons.

To help you tell what mode you are hearing on the air, digital recordings of many modes are available for you to listen to at **sigidwiki.com/wiki/Category: Amateur_Radio**. To learn more about digital communications in amateur radio, check out the references at **arrl.org/general-class-license-manual**.

DEFINITIONS

Before diving into the details of the many amateur digital modes, it's helpful to define some useful terms.

• *Air link* — the part of the communication system that involves radio transmission and reception of signals.

• *Bit* — the fundamental unit of data; a 0 or 1 representing all or part of a binary number.

• *Bit rate* — the number of digital bits per second sent from one computing system to the other.

• *Baud or bauds* — the number of symbols per second that are sent from one computing system to the other, also known as *symbol rate*.

• *Duty cycle* — the ratio of time that the transmitter is on to the total of on time plus off time.

• *Protocol* — the rules that control the method used to exchange data between two systems.

Table 6.1

Digital Signal Band Plan

Where to Find Digital Signals on the HF Bands

Band (Meters)	Frequency Range (MHz)	Notes
160	1.800 – 1.810	FT8 is on 1.840 MHz
80	3.570 – 3.600	
60	5332, 5348, 5358.5, 5373 and 5405 kHz	Channel center frequencies.*
40	7.070 – 7.125	RTTY DX calling frequency 7.040 MHz
30	10.130 – 10.150	
20	14.070 – 14.0995 and 14.1005 – 14.112	PSK31 calling frequency 14.070 MHz
17	18.100 – 18.110	
15	21.070 – 21.110	
12	24.920 – 24.930	
10	28.070 – 28.189	

*On 60 meters, the FCC continues to require that all digital transmissions be centered on the channel-center frequencies, which the Report and Order defines as being 1.5 kHz above the suppressed carrier frequency of a transceiver operated in the Upper Sideband (USB) mode. This is typically the frequency shown on the frequency display. Automatic operation is not permitted.

• *Mode* — the combination of a protocol with a modulation method.

In some modes, such as RTTY or PSK31, bits are transmitted one at a time as audio tones over an air link. A *modem* (short for modulator-demodulator) translates the bits into tones (and back again). Typically, additional bits are added at lower levels of the system to help control the flow of data.

There is a lot of confusion about bit rate and baud. Is it 1200 bits per second or 1200 baud? *Bit rate* refers to the number of bits per second (bps) carried by the transmission. *Baud* (just "baud" or "bauds," not "baud rate") refers to the number of digital *symbols* sent each second. A symbol is defined as whatever combination of signal characteristics make up each distinct state of the transmitted signal. For example, a CW symbol is the ON or OFF state of the transmitted signal and in RTTY the symbols are represented by the mark and space tones.

In simple coding methods such as Baudot or ASCII, each symbol sent by the transmitter represents one bit. More sophisticated codes can encode more than one bit in every symbol. That is how modems exchange data at such high rates over a narrow voice channel — each symbol sent by the transmitter at 9600 baud represents 2 bits (19.2 kbps), 4 bits (38.4 kbps) or 6 bits (56.6 kbps) of data. If one bit is represented by each symbol, then bit rate and baud are the same. As more and more bits are encoded in each symbol, the bit rate will be higher than the symbol rate.

A digital mode combines a *protocol* and a method of modulation. A protocol is the set of rules that control the encoding, packaging, exchanging, and decoding of digital data. For example, packet radio uses the AX.25 protocol. The rules for that protocol specify how each frame is constructed and exchanged, what characters are allowed, and so forth. The protocol rules don't say what kind of transmitter to use or what the signal will sound like on the air. The method of modulation, such as SSB or FM for example, is determined by the equipment and frequencies available.

Modulation used for digital modes can be simple *on-off keying* (*OOK*) such as for CW or pulse-coded modulations. For the modes most hams think of as true digital modes, the data is transmitted as tones or as combinations of tones. The data may be represented by the tone frequency (*frequency shift keying* or *FSK*) or as phase differences (*phase shift keying* or *PSK*). Another popular method is to transmit two carriers with a 90° phase difference and vary their amplitude and/or phase relationship independently. This is called *I/Q modulation*. Each distinct combination of tones or amplitudes or phase shifts constitutes one symbol.

Maximum data rates and signal bandwidths are specified by the FCC rules in §97.307 to limit signal bandwidth on congested bands. FCC rules identify several types of digital codes (the method of encoding the characters for transmission) [§97.309]. If you intend to use a digital code other than those specified, you must first make sure that the protocol rules are public (amateurs are not allowed to use secret or private codes) and you must comply with bandwidth and symbol rate limitations.

FREQUENCY SHIFT KEYING (FSK)

Frequency shift keying is a method of digital communications in which the individual bits of data are encoded as tones. As the stream of bits is transmitted, different tone frequencies are used. If you listen to a slower modem or RTTY signal, you can hear the bits being exchanged as a rapidly changing pattern of two different tones shifting from one frequency to another. The frequencies in a two-tone FSK signal are called *mark* and *space*. [G8C11] Space represents 0 and mark represents 1.

In true or "direct" FSK, the frequency of the transmitter's VFO is controlled directly by a digital data signal from the computer representing the 1s and 0s of the code. [G8A01] *Audio frequency shift keying (AFSK)* is also used in which the audio tones modulate an SSB or FM transmitter through the microphone input. AFSK is a convenient method, but the operator must be careful to manage the audio level to avoid noise and distortion that could adversely affect signal quality or cause interference to nearby stations. Both FSK and AFSK sound the same on the air.

Whether FSK or AFSK is used, the rate at which symbols are sent affects the amount of frequency shift required. The faster the symbol rate (or keying rate), the greater the frequency shift required. This is because the closer the tones are in frequency, the longer it takes the receiving system to discriminate between them. Tones must be spaced far enough apart in frequency for the receiver to be able to determine which tone is being sent during the time interval in which the tone is present.

In *multiple frequency shift keying (MFSK)* more than two tones are used to create more codes. On the air, these modes often sound like a musical instrument playing random sequences of tones. By using more tones and controlling the sequences of tones that are allowed, MFSK modes can be made more error-resistant. A number in the mode's name, such as 8-MFSK, gives the number of tones used, eight tones in this example. Amateur modes include 8-MFSK, 16-MFSK, and 64-MFSK.

PHASE SHIFT KEYING (PSK)

The most common type of phase shift is to simply invert one of the tone waveforms, shifting its phase by 180°. The difference in phase can be measured with respect to the phase of the same signal at an earlier time or with respect to some other tone. The rapid changes in phase are heard by the human ear as a raspy noise or buzz — the signature of PSK signals on the air received by a CW or SSB receiver.

6.2 Character-Based Modes

G2E06 — What is the most common frequency shift for RTTY emissions in the amateur HF bands?
170 Hz

G8A06 — Which of the following is characteristic of QPSK31?
All these choices are correct

G8C04 — Which of the following describes Baudot code?
A 5-bit code with additional start and stop bits

G8C08 — Which of the following statements is true about PSK31?
Upper case letters use longer Varicode bit sequences and thus slow down transmission

G8C12 — Which type of code is used for sending characters in a PSK31 signal?
Varicode

The simplest use of digital communications is a mode in which individual characters are entered by an operator, then transmitted to another station where they are read by another operator. CW is an example of this type of communication. The speed of these modes is low but they are convenient to use and require little additional equipment beyond a sound card or a modem. This is often referred to as *keyboard-to-keyboard* or *chat* operation. Because these modes transmit a stream of characters without any additional data, they are often referred to as *unstructured* modes.

RADIOTELETYPE (RTTY)

RTTY is the oldest form of ham radio digital communication. Originally, bulky military and commercial surplus teleprinters and terminal units (modems) were used by hams to communicate using RTTY. Today a sound card and modem software does the conversion between audio tones and characters. RTTY is identified in the FCC rules as "narrowband, direct-printing telegraphy."

RTTY uses the Baudot code which represents (encodes) each text character as a sequence of 5 bits as shown in **Figure 6.1**. Baudot is the origin of the term baud. An initial bit (the *start bit*) and a pause between characters (the *stop bit*) are used to synchronize the transmitting and receiving stations. **[G8C04]** With only 5 bits for encoding data, there can be only 32 different characters, not enough for the entire English alphabet, numerals, and punctuation. Thus, two special codes, LTRS and FIGS, are used to switch between two sets of characters, increasing the number of available characters to 62 (not including the LTRS and FIGS codes).

The standard audio mark and space frequencies for encoding a RTTY signal are 2125 Hz (the mark tone) and 2295 Hz (the space tone). The difference between them is called the signal's *shift*. The rate of shifting between mark and space tones determines the character speed. On HF, the most common speed is 60 WPM (45 baud) with a 170 Hz shift. You should always answer a RTTY station at the same speed and shift it is using. **[G2E06]** Other tone pairs and shifts are used, but are not common.

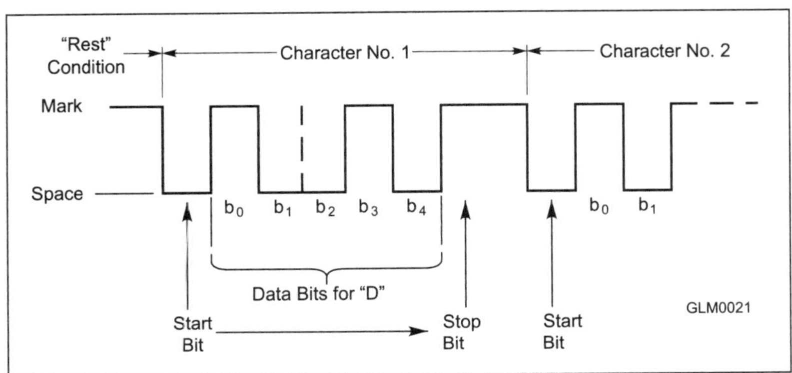

Figure 6.1 — The Baudot timing sequence for the bit pattern that encodes the letter "D." The start bit is sent first. Start and stop bits are required to allow the receiving and transmitting systems to synchronize. Mark and space are represented as audio tones in the transmitted signal.

PSK31

The most popular PSK mode is PSK31. The "31" stands for the symbol rate of the protocol, actually 31.25 baud. That may sound slow, but it is just right for keyboard-to-keyboard communication. PSK31 can support typing rates of up to 50 WPM under good conditions. A variation called QPSK31 (quadrature phase shift keying) sends two audio tones so that there are four possible phase shift combinations. That allows data to be encoded in a way that provides some error correction to improve performance in noisy conditions. Since there are two tones, you have to select the right sideband (USB or LSB) to decode the data, meaning the mode is *sideband sensitive*. QPSK31 and PSK31 have approximately the same bandwidth. **[G8A06]**

Instead of a fixed-length character code of 5, 7, or 8 bits, PSK uses a variable length code called *Varicode* (**en.wikipedia.org/wiki/Varicode**) that assigns shorter codes to common characters (such as "e") and longer codes for others, just like Morse code. **[G8C12]**

Note that in Varicode most capital letters and punctuation characters take more bits than lower case. That means it will take longer to send "MY NAME IS HIRAM" than "My name is Hiram." If you are used to RTTY operation which has no lower-case characters, be sure to turn off your CAPS LOCK key! **[G8C08]**

PSK31 sends a single tone, encoding each symbol as reversals of the tone's phase at regular intervals. Symbols are sent continually, with a reversal of phase from one interval to the next representing a "0" and no reversal a "1." (Two intervals of transmission are required to send one symbol.) If you listen to a PSK31 signal on the air, you'll hear a steady buzz with short variations as characters are transmitted. Zeroes are sent continuously when no other data is present so that the transmitter and receiver stay synchronized — you can hear the pauses as periods of consistent, unvarying buzz.

6.3 Packet-Based Modes and Systems

G2E02 — What is VARA?
> A digital protocol used with Winlink

G2E04 — Which of the following is good practice when choosing a transmitting frequency to answer a station calling CQ using FT8?
> Find a clear frequency during the alternate time slot to the calling station

G2E07 — Which of the following is required when using FT8?
> Computer time accurate to within approximately 1 second

G2E09 — How do you join a contact between two stations using the PACTOR protocol?
> Joining an existing contact is not possible, PACTOR connections are limited to two stations

G2E11 — What is the primary purpose of an Amateur Radio Emergency Data Network (AREDN) mesh network?
> To provide high-speed data services during an emergency or community event

G2E12 — Which of the following describes Winlink?
> All of the above

G2E13 — What is another name for a Winlink Remote Message Server?
> Gateway

G2E15 — Which of the following is a common location for FT8?
> Approximately 14.074 MHz to 14.077 MHz

G8A09 — What type of modulation is used by the FT8?
> 8-tone frequency shift keying

G8A12 — What is QPSK modulation?
> Modulation in which digital data is transmitted using 0-, 90-, 180- and 270-degrees phase shift to represent pairs of bits

G8C02 — Which digital mode is used as a low-power beacon for assessing HF propagation?
> WSPR

G8C03 — What part of a packet radio frame contains the routing and handling information?
> Header

G8C05 — In an ARQ mode, what is meant by a NAK response to a transmitted packet?
> Request retransmission of the packet

G8C07 — Which of the following narrow-band digital modes can receive signals with very low signal-to-noise ratios?

FT8

G8C09 — Which is true of mesh network microwave nodes?

If one node fails, a packet may still reach its target station via an alternate node

G8C10 — How does forward error correction (FEC) allow the receiver to correct data errors?

By transmitting redundant information with the data

G8C15 — What does an FT8 signal report of +3 mean?

The signal-to-noise ratio is equivalent to +3 dB in a 2.5 kHz bandwidth

Packet-based or *structured* modes are derived from early teletype-over-radio modes (TOR) and computer-to-computer network protocols. The networked protocols, developed in the early days of computing, are the basis of the modern protocols used for the internet and digital mobile telephones today. Hams adapted those protocols to be used over radio links, creating packet radio, PACTOR, and other communications systems.

As the modulation and coding techniques available to amateurs become more sophisticated, they also place more demands on the computer systems used to generate and receive them. One of the requirements is a minimum level of processing speed. More processing power enables the reception of weaker signals or more signals simultaneously. Modes such as JT65 and FT8 also require transmissions to occur in precisely defined periods so the receiving systems know when to begin decoding. Utility software is available to keep your computer precisely synchronized to within 1 second of standard time. **[G2E07]**

PACKET BASICS

Packet refers to the transmission of data in structured groups called *frames* as shown in **Figure 6.2**. While there are many different packet protocols, all of them use the same basic structure.

• *Header* — contains bit patterns that allow the receiver to synchronize with the packet's structure, control, and routing information, and for some protocols, error detection and correction information. **[G8C03]**

• *Data* — the data to be exchanged between computing systems, usually as ASCII characters. Data in packets is often compressed for efficiency.

• *Trailer* — additional control or status information and data used for error detection.

The process of packaging data within a packet structure is called *encapsulation*. Packets from one protocol can be treated as data by another protocol, so that entire protocols can be encapsulated. In fact, that is the basis for the popular TCP/IP protocol pair used on the internet. The Internet Protocol (IP) encapsulates packets from the Transport Control Protocol (TCP) and carries them to the destination.

By using error detection, it is possible for a protocol to provide *reliable transport* in which corrupted data is never accepted. The most common error detection mechanism is a *cyclic redundancy check* or *CRC*. A CRC is calculated from the contents of the packet and transmitted with the data. (A *checksum* is a weaker version of error detection than the CRC.) The receiving system performs the same calculation and if the results match, accepts

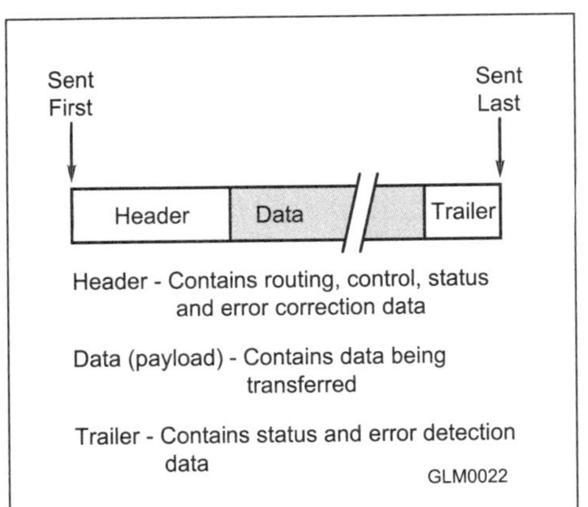

Figure 6.2 — Packet communication systems package data with control and routing information and add error detection information. Each package of header, data, and trailer is called a frame. Different packet protocols use different sets of information and methods of creating the frame.

the data as transmitted without error and responds with an ACK (acknowledged) message.

Forward error correction (FEC) goes beyond simply detecting errors. By including additional redundant encoded information with the data being transmitted, it is possible for the receiver to correct certain types of data errors. **[G8C10]**

If a mismatch is detected, the receiving system responds with a NAK (not acknowledged) message and the protocol requests that the packet be retransmitted. The transmitting system will continue to send a packet until it is received without errors or the limit for retransmission is exceeded. This type of protocol or mode is called *ARQ* for *Automatic Repeat reQuest*. Modes such as PACTORand packet radio use ARQ. **[G8C05]**

Because they were originally developed for connections over wired networks and not radio, ARQ protocols such as PACTOR are designed to transfer data between two stations: the transmitter and a single receiver. An ACK or NAK transmission can only be received from one receiving station during the connection. This means you can't "break in" to an ongoing contact between two stations using an ARQ mode. **[G2E09]**

So that a station can advertise its presence, ARQ protocols provide a "broadcast" mode to transmit without another station having established a connection. In addition, a monitoring or "MON" mode is provided so that other stations can listen to the conversation and even receive the data but without error correction. Using a monitoring mode allows you to determine if a frequency is occupied by two stations having an ARQ mode contact.

PACKET RADIO

Packet radio, used almost exclusively on VHF and UHF bands, is based on the computer network protocol X.25. Amateurs adapted it to radio transmission instead of transmission over wired networks and renamed the protocol AX.25. Packets are exchanged using VHF FM voice transceivers at 1,200 or 9,600 baud. Packet radio using AX.25 does not work well on HF because the data is easily disrupted by noise and fading, even at the slow maximum signaling rates of 300 baud permitted on HF.

PACTOR

The RTTY protocol is not designed to manage transmission errors. As a result, text is frequently garbled, particularly over noisy, fading HF signal paths. To improve communications reliability, *Teletype Over Radio (TOR)* systems were developed, such as AMTOR, G-TOR, and others. These systems send short bursts of characters with error detection and correction data. TOR modes are definitely more reliable, but the original versions were quite slow, particularly in the presence of interference or noise. PACTOR (Packet-based TOR) was developed to extend the capability of TOR modes.

PACTOR 1 uses FSK modulation while PACTOR 2, PACTOR 3, and PACTOR 4 use more advanced PSK modulation. While PSK shifts a single signal between two different phases, quadrature phase shift keying shifts two signals between four relative phases (0, 90, 180, and 270 degrees) to represent pairs of bits. **[G8A12]** FSK and PSK employ error detection methods and an ARQ protocol to insure the reliability of the transferred data. PACTOR is popular on HF radio today for exchanging large amounts of information. VARA is the preferred method of HF Data transmission for the popular Winlink amateur radio discussed in the next section.

THE WINLINK SYSTEM

Transferring email messages and digital files using digital modes on the HF bands has become a very common method of communication for personal and public service use. The Winlink system (**winlink.org**) has grown to a robust, worldwide system as a result. Winlink uses the internet to connect its system of email servers with gateway and mailbox stations around the world on HF, VHF, and UHF frequencies. **[G2E12, G2E13]**

Winklink stations do not connect an amateur directly with the internet but provide an effective means of email access for stations out of local internet connection range and for when the internet is not available due to disasters or local outages. Even without internet connectivity, Stations using *Winlink Express* can act as standalone *mailbox* stations or communicate directly with each other to transfer messages. A list of stations providing access to the Winlink system is published on the system's home page.

Winlink is not a mode — it is a communications system. Several modes are used to access the system. If you access a Winlink mailbox station on VHF you might use regular packet radio. On HF, the PACTOR and VARA modes are used. **[G2E02]**

Many amateurs upgrade to General class to take advantage of these and other messaging capabilities. If that sounds like something you'd like to try, remember that it is necessary to share the amateur bands with other users of the spectrum operating on different modes. All of us need to be good neighbors by following the time-honored practices of listening first, keeping our signals clean, and recognizing that no individual or system has exclusive rights to any frequency.

FT8 AND WSPR

FT8 and WSPR are modes supported by the *WSJT-X* software suite along with Q65, MSK144, and other digital modes. (*WSJT-X* software and extensive documentation are available from **wsjt.sourceforge.io/wsjtx.html**.) Both use precisely timed sequences of transmit and receive, 8-tone FSK modulation, and sophisticated error decoding and correction techniques to enable successful decoding at very low signal-to-noise ratios (SNR). **[G8A09, G8C07]** WSPR can decode signals at SNR levels approaching –30 dB — a signal 1,000 times weaker than the noise! FT8 is very popular because of its excellent performance with modest stations and high noise levels.

FT8 exchanges 75-bit messages (plus 12 bits for error detection codes) in a 50 Hz bandwidth. As FT8 is used today, there is a limited amount of information that can be exchanged, such as call signs, grid locators, and signal reports. Signal reports in FT8 are on the signal-to-noise ratio, so a report of +3 means the signal is 3 dB above the noise floor. **[G8C15]** Most frequently, you will find amateurs using FT8 between 14.074 and 14.077 MHz. **[G2E15]** Because *WSJT-X* is an open-source project, you should expect variations of FT8 to behave differently. Generally, when responding to a CQ on FT8, you should locate a clear frequency in the waterfall and select the time slot that doesn't interfere with the calling stations. **[G2E04]** Remember that time synchronization is important for FT4 and FT8.

WSPR ("whisper") is designed to experiment with and assess HF propagation paths at very low signal-to-noise ratios. WSPR does not support two-way QSOs and acts as a very narrow bandwidth beacon. Low-power WSPR transmitters generate coded packets and stations that receive and decode the packets report success on websites such as **wsprnet.org**. **[G8C02]**

AMATEUR WIRELESS NETWORKS

Table 6.2 lists wireless networking frequencies that overlap with amateur bands. Because wide bandwidth signals are allowed on these frequencies, amateurs are able to use them for many of the same purposes that unlicensed users are able to. For example, keyboard to keyboard texting, Voice Over IP phone conversations, video sharing, games, repeater linking, web servers, email messaging, and document editing and management are all possible. In fact, amateurs may use FCC Part 15 and commercial channels in these networks. However, the channels may be busy with wireless internet traffic. If you operate a wireless network on FCC Part 97 frequencies, you must comply with the prohibitions on encryption, which rules out accessing sites that employ HTTPS protocols (Secure HTTP), TLS (Transport Layer Security) and other security measures.

Table 6.2

Wireless Networking Frequencies

airMAX	Ubiquiti	ISM	Amateur
M900 900MHz	902 – 928	902 – 928	902 – 928
M2 2.4 GHz	2402 – 2462	2400 – 2500	2390 – 2459
M3 3 GHz1	3370 – 3730		3300 – 35003
M5 5GHz	5725 – 5850	5725 – 58752	5650 – 5925

[1]For export from USA
[2]U-NII: 5150 – 5350, 5470 – 5825 MHz
[3]ARRL Band Plan

There are two basic network topologies that hams utilize: mesh (also known as point-to-point or point-to-multipoint) and star configurations. The AREDN (Amateur Radio Emergency Data Network), discussed in the next section employs a mesh network, while HamWAN, HamNet, and Mi6WAN, employ the star configuration. An advantage of the mesh networking topology is that if one node fails, a packet may be able to find its destination by routing through another available node. [G8C09]

AREDN (AMATEUR RADIO EMERGENCY DATA NETWORK)

An AREDN network uses commercially available routers in the 900 MHz, 2.4, 3.4, and 5.8 GHz amateur bands. (See **arednmesh.org/content/supported-platform-matrix** for the current list of supported devices.) The stock firmware in the routers is replaced to become a fully functional node in a peer-to-peer network. The nodes are self-discovering, self-configuring, and self-advertising, which means it requires little networking knowledge to set up. Generally, AREDN networks are used during emergencies or to support community events like road races, parades, and other large gatherings. [G2E11]

A typical AREDN endpoint node consists of a wireless router to connect to the network and a wireless data access point, usually supporting both WiFi and Ethernet LAN connections (see **Figure 6.3**). The access point provides connectivity that is the same as in a typical home network and many AREDN nodes are part of a ham's home network. Relay nodes and backbone nodes consist of two or more wireless routers connected together with an Ethernet switch. No other equipment is required. Installed in advantageous loca-

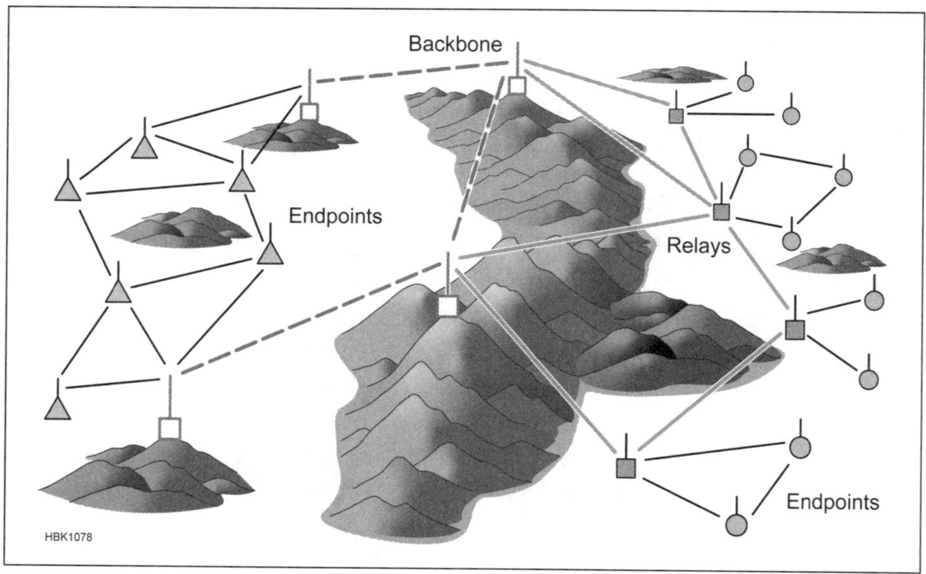

Figure 6.3 — The components of a typical AREDN network.

Figure 6.4 — The K6PVR backbone site in Southern California with user access points for 2 and 5 GHz. (Photo courtesy Orv Beach, W6BI)

tions, backbone nodes support long-distance links between relay nodes in different areas. **Figure 6.4** shows the K6PVR backbone site in the mountains of Southern California.

The current firmware also includes tunneling capability to allow RF "islands" to be connected through the internet. In this configuration, individual groups of nodes communicate with each and one or more has regular internet access. Tunneling protocols are then used to connect the groups of nodes together as if they were using a purely RF system of relays and backbone links.

6.4 Receiving and Transmitting Digital Modes

G2E01 — Which mode is normally used when sending RTTY signals via AFSK with an SSB transmitter?

LSB

G2E05 — What is the standard sideband for JT65, JT9, FT4, or FT8 digital signal when using AFSK?

USB

G2E14 — What could be wrong if you cannot decode an RTTY or other FSK signal even though it is apparently tuned in properly?

All of these choices are correct

G4A11 — Why should the ALC system be inactive when transmitting AFSK data signals?

The ALC action distorts the signal

G8B08 — Why is it important to know the duty cycle of the mode you are using when transmitting?

Some modes have high duty cycles that could exceed the transmitter's average power rating

G8B10 — What is the relationship between transmitted symbol rate and bandwidth?

Higher symbol rates require wider bandwidth

G8C13 — What is indicated on a waterfall display by one or more vertical lines on either side of a digital signal?

Overmodulation

Most digital modes on HF are transmitted as USB signals except for RTTY, which uses LSB. **[G2E01, G2E05]** Just as when trying to receive a USB voice signal on an LSB receiver, it is not possible to receive a digital signal on the wrong sideband because the relationship between the tones and the digital data will be inverted. Similarly, you'll need to have your receiving modem or software configured to the correct baud rate and the correct tone frequencies. Mistakes in any of these important settings will make it impossible to receive the data even if the signal is strong and seems to be tuned in correctly. **[G2E14]** Since PSK31 uses a single tone, either USB or LSB will work, although most amateurs use USB.

BANDWIDTH OF DIGITAL MODES

The FCC rules define the bandwidth of a digital mode signal in the same way as any other signal. [§97.3(a)(8)] However, the bandwidth of a signal changes with the symbol rate. As the symbol rate increases, so does the bandwidth needed for the signal needed to transmit them. **[G8B10] Table 6.3** shows the approximate bandwidths for several popular digital modes used on HF.

The most common method of generating and transmitting these modes is to connect the audio output from a computer sound card to the microphone input of an SSB transceiver. That means all of the modes must be capable of being transmitted within a standard SSB voice channel bandwidth, approximately 2.8 kHz. As SDR equipment becomes more common, wider bandwidth modes could be developed as long as they comply with the symbol rate limits in the FCC rules.

Table 6.3

Bandwidth Comparison of Digital Modes

Mode	Bandwidth (Hz)
PSK31	50
FT8	50
RTTY	200
MFSK16	300
JT65	350
DominoEX	524
Olivia	1,000
MT63	2,000
PACTOR-III	2,300
PACTOR-4	2,300

Bandwidths are approximate for the highest commonly used symbol rate and are not specifications

Staying in the Band

As discussed in the Radio Equipment and Signals chapter, be careful when you are operating near the edge of a data signal band segment! When using LSB for an FSK mode, the sidebands will be *below* the displayed carrier frequency on your radio. For example, if the carrier frequency displayed is 18103 kHz, when transmitting a RTTY signal's 2295 Hz tone, the RF signal's frequency will be 18103 − 2.295 = 18100.705 kHz. Similar calculations must be applied when using a digital mode on USB.

TRANSMITTER DUTY CYCLE

It is also important to know the typical duty cycle for a digital mode because most amateur transmitters are not designed to operate at full power output for an extended time. When you are operating CW, for example, the transmitter is turned on and off so it is only operating at full power about 40 to 50% of the time. When you are using SSB, the transmitter is producing full power only when your voice reaches maximum amplitude. For a typical SSB conversation, the transmitter is operating at full power only about 20 to 25% of the time.

Like FM, however, for some data modes your transmitter may be operating at full power the entire time you are transmitting. For Baudot radioteletype the transmitter is continually switching between the mark and space tones of the code, so the duty cycle is 100%. For PSK31 and similar modes, the transmitter is producing full power for virtually the entire transmit time, so the duty cycle is nearly 100%. Modes like JT65 and FT8 transmit for many seconds at full power, then stand by and listen for a response. ARQ modes like PACTOR have slightly reduced duty cycles because the transmitter sends some data and then waits to receive an acknowledgement.

Extended transmissions may be enough to exceed a transmitter's average power rating. [G8B08] If you aren't sure of a transceiver's rating for high-duty-cycle modes, it's good practice to reduce transmit power to prevent overheating. Reduce your transmitter power to about 50% of maximum output power for most digital modes.

DIGITAL MODE SIGNAL QUALITY

Digital mode operation involves the same concerns about signal quality as phone and CW. Digital signals are just as capable of generating interference to nearby channels, plus the audio signals between the computer and radio can also be a source of problems.

For digital modes that use an SSB transmitter to transmit AFSK, the most common problem is supplying too much or too little audio from the computer to the radio's microphone input. A microphone input is easy to overdrive, resulting in splatter and spurious outputs. Some radios have digital data inputs for connecting directly to a computer data interface. This eliminates the audio interface and level setting problems entirely.

If you are using a waterfall display (discussed later in this chapter), it will be quite obvious if a signal is distorted because there will be additional lines to each side of the main signal which may itself look broader than usual. Each of those vertical lines represents a spurious emission, usually caused by overmodulation of the transmitter from the audio level at the microphone input being too high. [G8C13] A distorted waveform is more difficult to decode and the spurious emissions occupy bandwidth that could be used by other stations. After adjusting transmit audio level yourself, have a friend check your signal to confirm that your audio level is set properly.

ALC AND DIGITAL MODES

Automatic level control (ALC) is used to prevent excessive drive to amplifier inputs. Inside a transceiver, ALC prevents overdrive of the output amplifier stage. The ALC signal from an external amplifier prevents a transceiver from putting out too much power for the amplifier's input. This sounds like a good thing but ALC and digital signals do not work well together.

ALC circuits reduce gain when power levels get too high so that higher amplitude input signals are amplified less than low ones. In effect, this compresses the signal similarly to how a speech processor works. For a voice signal, the resulting distortion is an acceptable trade for the higher average power because your ears can make up the difference. For a digital signal, however, the distortion caused by ALC makes the signal harder to decode and creates spurious emissions just like overmodulation does. [G4A11]

When using a digital mode, your ALC system should be either disabled or the microphone input level and gain turned down to the point where the ALC system does not activate. You can usually monitor ALC action on the same transceiver meter that monitors power output and SWR. Resist the temptation to turn up the gain because you will only be making your signal harder to understand and creating interference for others.

6.5 Digital Operating Procedures

G1E03 — What is required to conduct communications with a digital station operating under automatic control outside the automatic control band segments?

The station initiating the contact must be under local or remote control

G1E09 — Under what circumstances are messages that are sent via digital modes exempt from Part 97 third-party rules that apply to other modes of communication?

Under no circumstances

G1E11 — On what bands may automatically controlled stations transmitting RTTY or data emissions communicate with other automatically controlled digital stations?

Anywhere in the 6-meter or shorter wavelength bands, and in limited segments of some of the HF bands

G2E03 — What symptoms may result from other signals interfering with a PACTOR or VARA transmission?

All these choices are correct

G2E10 — Which of the following is a way to establish contact with a digital messaging system gateway station?

Transmit a connect message on the station's published frequency

G8C06 — What action results from a failure to exchange information due to excessive transmission attempts when using an ARQ mode?

The connection is dropped

G8C14 — Which of the following describes a waterfall display?

Frequency is horizontal, signal strength is intensity, time is vertical

INITIATING AND TERMINATING DIGITAL CONTACTS

Digital QSOs usually follow the general structure established by the long tradition of RTTY operating. A CQ on a keyboard-to-keyboard digital mode such as RTTY or PSK31 looks similar to the other modes:

CQ CQ CQ DE W1AW W1AW W1AW K

The usual method of responding looks like this:

W1AW W1AW W1AW DE WB8IMY WB8IMY WB8IMY K

As on CW, if signals are loud and clear, you may reduce the number of times you send the call signs.

Terminating an RTTY or PSK31 keyboard-to-keyboard connection is very much like ending a CW contact. Digital operators often use the same prosigns and abbreviations as for CW operation. For example, K is used at the end of a transmission to indicate the other station is to transmit as shown above. SK is used to indicate "signing off" or "end of contact."

If you are using a mode such as PACTOR or VARA, your software or modem will have a specific "disconnect" message or command such as BYE or D which initiates the contact termination sequence. If band conditions change and one station fades out, for example, after a preset number of unacknowledged message transmissions, the transmitting station will *timeout* and return to the disconnected state.

Connecting to Gateway and Mailbox Stations

Unmanned *gateway* and *mailbox* stations monitor a fixed frequency until another station attempts to connect to them. The exact method of establishing a connection will vary with the equipment and mode being used but beginning the contact starts with sending a CONNECT message to the station with which you want to connect. [G2E10] Because the listening station does not transmit until you do, you must be sure the transmit frequency is correct. Be sure your transceiver's frequency display is accurate and calibrated.

If your signal is received without errors, a connect message will be sent. Then a *training sequence* of packets may be exchanged to determine the type and version of protocol to use. If your signal is weak or experiencing interference, the connection may not be made or the available data rate may be too low for efficient use. Once the connection is established, a message can then be transferred.

Because these stations respond without a human control operator being present, the FCC classifies them as automatically-controlled digital stations and restricts them to certain segments of the amateur bands. Automatically controlled stations are permitted to contact other automatically controlled stations on the HF band segments in **Table 6.4** and anywhere RTTY and data are permitted on the 6-meter and shorter wavelength bands. [G1E11]

You may hear stations operating under automatic control outside the US amateur allocations. Stations in areas outside FCC administration may operate under automatic control on other amateur frequencies. A station operating under FCC rules must be operating under local or remote control (that is, with a control operator in charge of all transmissions) to contact these stations legally. [G1E03]

DURING THE CONTACT
Operating Displays

A waterfall display as seen in **Figure 6.5A** displays the presence of signals as a series of lines each representing a scan across the frequency range (the horizontal axis). The strength of the signals or noise present is represented as the brightness, intensity, or color of the line at each frequency. As new lines are captured and displayed, the older lines are moved down or to one side, giving the

Table 6.4

Automatic Control Band Segments for RTTY and Data

Band (Meters)	Frequency Range (MHz)
160	Not permitted
80	3.585 – 3.600
60	Not permitted
40	7.100 – 7.105
30	10.140 – 10.150
20	14.095 – 14.0995 and 14.1005 – 14.112
17	18.105 – 18.110
15	21.090 – 21.100
12	24.925 – 24.930
10	28.120 – 28.189
6	50.1 – 54.0
2	144.1 – 148

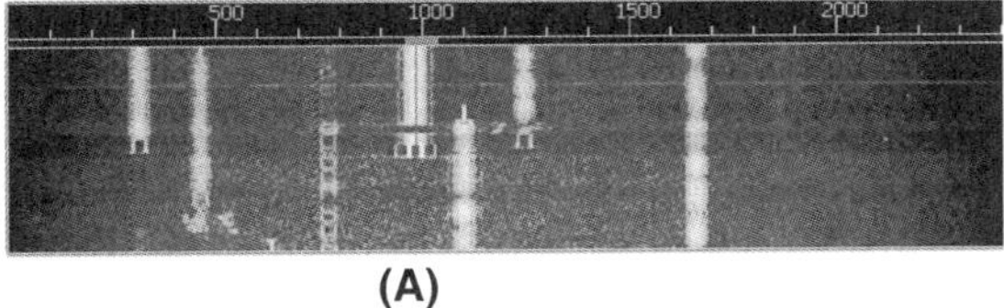

(A)

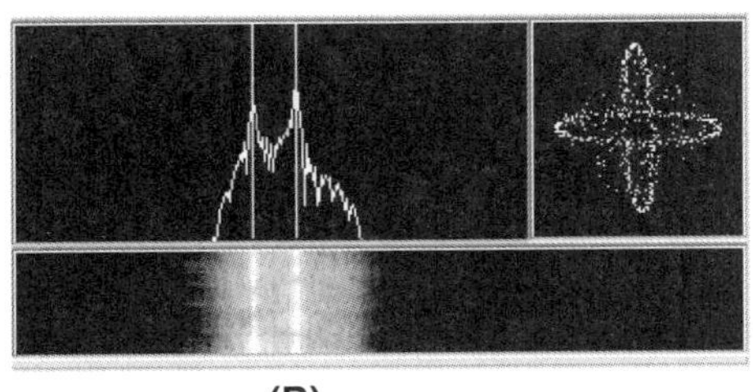

(B)

Figure 6.5 — At A, the waterfall display shows seven different digital signals being received in an audio frequency range of 0 to 2400 Hz. They appear as vertical traces. B shows an RTTY tuning display that includes a filter output window at the upper left (the signal is tuned properly when the tone peaks align with the vertical lines) and a crossed-ellipse display at the upper right for fine tuning. A waterfall display across the bottom is included as well.

impression of a "waterfall" as the information slows "flows" across the screen. **[G8C14]** Waterfall displays show the presence of any type of signal and a skilled operator can often tell what type of mode is in use from its appearance.

Figure 6.5B shows two common tuning aids for RTTY signals. On the left is a window showing the spectrum of the filtered received audio. Two vertical lines at the mark and space frequencies help tune in a signal so that the peaks are on the lines, indicating the right tone frequencies. At right is a crossed-ellipse display used for fine tuning. When the ellipses have approximately the same size and are at right angles, the signal is tuned in correctly.

Third-Party Traffic

Digital contacts are no different than voice or CW in the rules governing message content. All of the FCC rules about third-party messages apply to digital transmissions. **[G1E09]** This includes all information included in email, digital images, or web pages transmitted via amateur radio. This is why internet access through gateways and other services must be very limited. Commercial messages such as advertisements may not be transmitted via amateur radio and neither may information pertaining to your business or finances.

Interfering Signals

There are certain symptoms of interference you can recognize while using a digital mode. One of the most common is the "hidden transmitter" problem that occurs with all modes, not just digital. If you are located in a skip zone for one of the stations involved in an ongoing contact or that is trying to connect to the same digital station, you will not hear the hidden transmitter's signals but the receiving station might hear both of you. The resulting interference is completely unintentional but generally prevents both you and the hidden transmitter from completing a contact with the desired station.

Keyboard-to-keyboard modes, such as RTTY or PSK31, tolerate interference fairly well but it's your job to interpret any garbled information that appears in the decoded output. ARQ modes, such as PACTOR or VARA, do their best to automatically recover from reception difficulties but you should be aware of how they respond in the presence of interference. The result is generally one of these problems **[G2E03, G8C06]**:

• Failure to connect — the receiver won't be able to decode your connect request and your connect attempt will fail.

• Frequent retries or transmission delays — because of the interference, your transmissions will be received with errors and the data will be garbled so your station must retransmit the data multiple times, causing the data transfer progress to be slow or erratic.

• Timeouts or dropped connections — in cases of strong or persistent interference, the number of requested retransmissions may exceed a preset limit which causes the other station to drop the connection or disconnect from your station, ending the contact.

Those symptoms are a clue for you to listen to the channel or watch your operating displays to see if another signal is present. Remember, the interference may be accidental or the other station may not hear your signal at all! Use a different frequency or aim directional antennas in another direction.

Chapter 7

Antennas

In this chapter, you'll learn about:
- Antenna basics
- Dipoles and ground-planes
- Effects of antenna height and polarization
- How Yagis work
- Loop antennas
- Antennas with special characteristics
- Feed line basics
- SWR and impedance matching

Any conductor can act as an antenna, but selecting an efficient and useful antenna takes a little bit of know-how. It's not necessary for General class licensees to be antenna designers, but you should understand the basic principles of antennas. You're going to learn more detail about how simple antennas and feed lines work, then extend your understanding of common directional antennas. Building on what you already know from your Technician studies, the things you learn for your General exam will help you make better choices about what sort of antenna to use and what sort of performance to expect. Antenna basics are reviewed at the end of section 7.1 if you need a refresher.

7.1 Dipoles and Ground-planes

G4E01 — What is the purpose of a capacitance hat on a mobile antenna?
To electrically lengthen a physically short antenna

G4E02 — What is the purpose of a corona ball on an HF mobile antenna?
To reduce RF voltage discharge from the tip of the antenna while transmitting

G4E06 — What is one disadvantage of using a shortened mobile antenna as opposed to a full size antenna?
Operating bandwidth may be very limited

G9B02 — Which of the following is a common way to adjust the feed-point impedance of an elevated quarter-wave ground-plane vertical antenna to be approximately 50 ohms?
Slope the radials downward

G9B03 — Which of the following best describes the radiation pattern of a quarter-wave, ground-plane vertical antenna?
Omnidirectional in azimuth

G9B04 — What is the radiation pattern of a dipole antenna in free space in a plane containing the conductor?
It is a figure-eight at right angles to the antenna

G9B05 — How does antenna height affect the azimuthal radiation pattern of a horizontal dipole HF antenna at elevation angles higher than 46 degrees?

If the antenna is less than 1/2 wavelength high, the azimuthal pattern is almost omnidirectional

G9B06 — Where should the radial wires of a ground-mounted vertical antenna system be placed?

On the surface or buried a few inches below the ground

G9B07 — How does the feed point impedance of a horizontal 1/2 wave dipole antenna change as the antenna height is reduced to 1/10 wavelength above ground?

It steadily decreases

G9B08 — How does the feed point impedance of a ½ wave dipole change as the feed point is moved from the center toward the ends?

It steadily increases

G9B09 — Which of the following is an advantage of using a horizontally polarized as compared to a vertically polarized HF antenna?

Lower ground losses

G9B10 — What is the approximate length for a ½ wave dipole antenna cut for 14.250 MHz?

33 feet

G9B11 — What is the approximate length for a ½ wave dipole antenna cut for 3.550 MHz?

132 feet

G9B12 — What is the approximate length for a ¼ wave monopole antenna cut for 28.5 MHz?

8 feet

G9C04 — How does antenna gain in dBi compare to gain stated in dBd for the same antenna?

Gain in dBi is 2.15 dB higher

G9D01 — Which of the following antenna types will be most effective as a near vertical incidence skywave (NVIS) antenna for short-skip communications on 40 meters during the day?

A horizontal dipole placed between 1/10 and 1/4 wavelength above the ground

G9D02 — What is the feed-point impedance of an end-fed half-wave antenna?

Very high

G9D08 — How does a "screwdriver" mobile antenna adjust its feed-point impedance?

By varying the base loading inductance

G9D12 — What is the common name of a dipole with a single central support?

Inverted V

DIPOLES

The most fundamental antenna is a *dipole* (from "two electrical polarities") — a straight conductor that is ½ wavelength ($\lambda/2$) long with its feed point in the middle. (*Doublet* is another name for similar center-fed wire antennas that aren't generally a multiple of ½ wavelength long.) A dipole radiates strongest broadside to its axis in a plane containing the antenna's conductor. The weakest radiation is off the ends as shown in

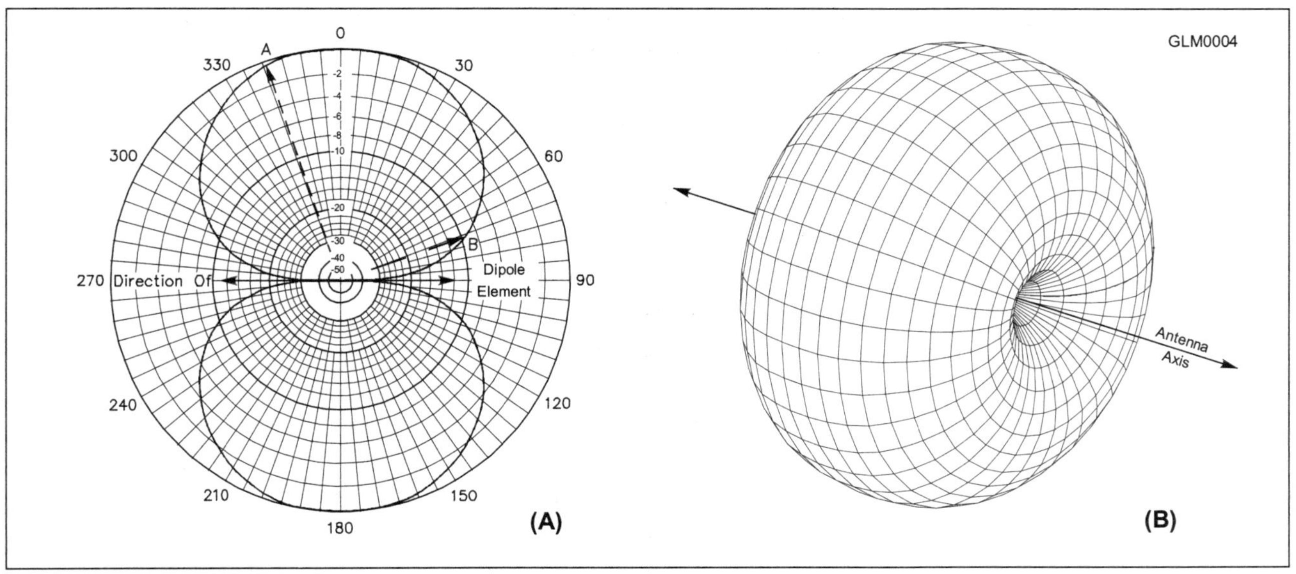

Figure 7.1 — Part A shows the radiation pattern in the plane of a dipole located in free space. The dipole element is located on the line from 270 to 90 degrees in this figure. Part B shows the three-dimensional radiation pattern in all directions around the dipole.

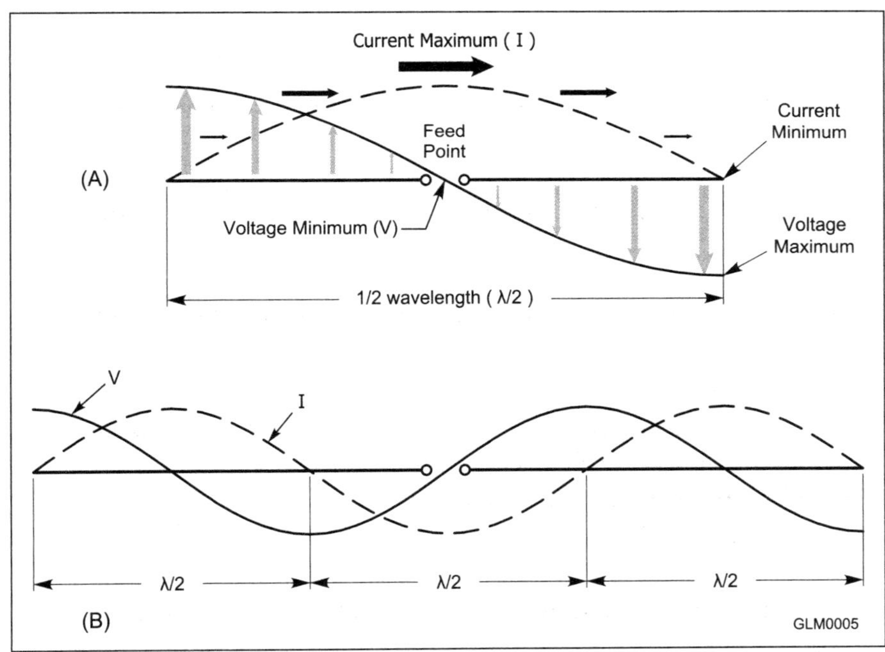

Figure 7.2 — The half-wave dipole at A has its maximum current in the middle and maximum voltage at each end. Feed point impedance is lowest in the middle. At odd harmonics of the fundamental frequency, the dipole's feed point impedance is low at the midpoint once again as shown at B.

Figure 7.1. This "figure-eight" is the shape of the azimuth pattern for a dipole in free space. **[G9B04]** When installed over actual ground, the resulting reflections will change both the azimuth and elevation radiation patterns as described later in this section.

Because a dipole has a well-defined radiation pattern and is so fundamental, it is often used as a reference antenna for gain measurements. Gain with respect to a dipole antenna's maximum radiation is given as dBd. If you use an isotropic antenna as the reference (a theoretical antenna that radiates equally in all directions), then gain is given in dBi. You can convert dBd to dBi by adding 2.15 dB and from dBi to dBd by subtracting 2.15 dB. **[G9C04]**

Current in a half-wave dipole is highest in the middle and zero at the ends. Voltage along the dipole is highest at the ends and lowest in the middle. (See **Figure 7.2**.) The feed point impedance (the ratio of RF voltage to current) at the center of a dipole in free space is approximately 72 Ω but it varies widely depending on its height above ground as we discuss later in this section. Impedance increases as the feed point is moved away from the center and is several thousand ohms at the ends. **[G9B08]** An example is the *end-fed* *half-wave (EFHW)* antenna that is popular for portable operating because it is lightweight and easy to install. **[G9D02]** The EFHW is just a half-wave dipole fed at one end.

In free space, ½ wavelength in feet equals 492 divided by frequency in MHz. If you cut a piece of wire that length, however, you'll generally find it somewhat too long to resonate at that frequency. At resonance, a ½-wave dipole made of ordinary wire will be shorter than the free-space ½ wavelength for several reasons. First, the physical thickness of the wire makes it look a bit longer electrically than it is physically. As the *length-to-diameter (l/d) ratio* of the wire gets smaller, meaning the wire gets thicker, the shorter it will be when it is resonant. Second, the dipole's height above ground also affects its resonant frequency. In addition, nearby conductors, insulation on the wire, the means by which the wire is secured to the insulators and to the feed line also affect the resonant length. For these reasons, a single universal formula for dipole length, such as the common 468/f, is not very useful. You should be start with a length near the free-space length and be prepared to trim the dipole to resonance using an SWR meter or antenna analyzer.

The exam only requires that you identify an approximate resonant length for a dipole. Use the free-space length, calculated as 492 / f (in MHz), and select the closest choice.

Example 1: What is the approximate length in feet of a 1/2-wave dipole resonant at 3.550 MHz? **[G9B11]**

$$\text{free-space length} = \frac{492}{3.55} = 139 \text{ ft}$$

The choices are 42, 84, 132, and 263 feet. The closest length and correct answer is 132 feet.

Example 2: What is the approximate length in feet of a ½-wave dipole for 14.250 MHz? **[G9B10]**

$$\text{free-space length} = \frac{492}{14.250} = 34.5 \text{ ft}$$

The choices are 8, 16, 24, and 33 feet. The closest length and correct answer is 33 feet.

Center-fed dipoles are easiest to use on the band for which they are resonant. The feed point impedance of such an antenna is a good match for the 50 or 75-Ω coaxial cable used by most hams. The feed point impedance of a half-wave dipole is also a good match for coax on odd multiples of the fundamental frequency. For example, a dipole for the 40-meter band (7 MHz) can also be used on 15 meters (21 MHz). On its third harmonic, the dipole acts like the three half-wave dipoles in Figure 7.2 connected end to end. On even-numbered harmonics and non-resonant bands, the feed point impedance of the dipole can be high, just as it is near the antenna's end.

A dipole needn't be straight to be effective. If you have a single antenna support, a dipole can be supported in the center where the feed line can be conveniently attached. This configuration is called an "inverted V." **[G9D12]** As long as the legs of the dipole form an angle of 90 degrees or more, the inverted V is nearly as effective as a horizontally installed dipole.

GROUND-PLANES (VERTICALS)

The ground-plane antenna is one-half of a dipole with the missing portion made up by an electrical mirror, called the *ground plane*. The ground plane can be made from sheet metal or a screen of *radial* wires. The basic ground-plane antenna is ¼-wavelength (λ/4) long with the feed point at the junction of the antenna and the ground plane. Currents in the ground plane create the effect of an electrical image of the physical portion of the antenna as shown in **Figure 7.3**. For HF ground-plane antennas mounted at ground level, the radial wires are laid on the surface of the ground or buried within a few inches of the surface. [**G9B06**]

Ground-planes are often called simply "verticals" because that is the usual way of constructing and installing them. Like a dipole, the ground-plane radiates best broadside to its axis. If installed vertically, this means the ground-plane antenna's pattern is omni-directional, uniform in all azimuth angles or directions. [**G9B03**] This is a very useful characteristic for VHF and UHF communications while mobile or portable and for an HF antenna where signals may come from any direction.

The feed point impedance at the base of the ideal ground-plane is 35 Ω, half of a complete dipole's impedance, because only half of the antenna is physically there and able to radiate energy. Sloping the radials of an elevated ground-plane antenna downward raises the feed point impedance. A droop angle between 30 and 45 degrees as shown in **Figure 7.4** results in the feed point impedance increasing to approximately 50 Ω, which matches coaxial cable. [**G9B02**]

If the droop angle continues to increase, the antenna functions more and more like a physical dipole and the feed point impedance eventually reaches the 72 Ω of the dipole. Also as with the dipole, moving the feed point away from the base — the midpoint of the combined physical antenna and its image — raises the impedance.

As with the dipole antenna, it is not useful to provide a one-size-fits-all formula for length of a ground-plane antenna. Since the ground-plane is one-half the size of a dipole, start with one-half the free-space length (246 / f in MHz) and be prepared to trim the antenna's length.

Example 3: What is the approximate length in feet of a ¼-wave monopole antenna cut for 28.5 MHz? [**G9B12**]

$$\text{free-space length} = \frac{246}{28.5} = 8.6 \text{ ft}$$

The choices on the exam question are 8, 11, 16 and 21 feet. The closest length and correct answer is 8 feet.

Mobile HF Antennas

Mobile HF antennas are often some form of ground-plane antenna. The most popular mobile antenna by far is the vertically-oriented *whip* — a thin steel rod mounted over the conducting surface of the vehicle, giving omnidirectional coverage. Whips are common on the VHF and UHF bands.

On HF, however, a full-sized λ/4 mobile whip is not feasible on bands below 28 and 24 MHz. To use practical whip antennas on the lower-frequency bands, *loading* tech-

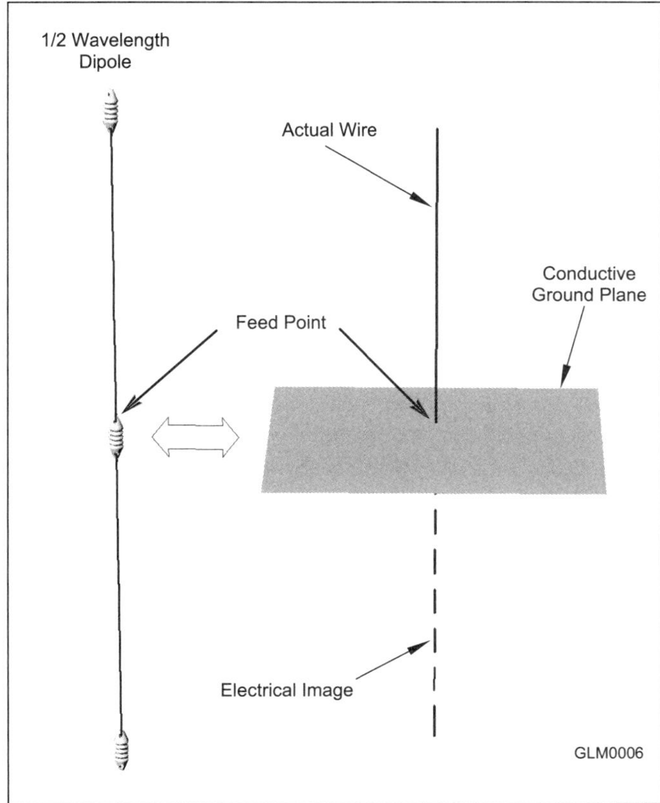

Figure 7.3 — The ground plane, whether made of solid metal or radial wires, creates an electrical mirror image of the ¼-wavelength antenna. This creates the electrical equivalent of a dipole antenna.

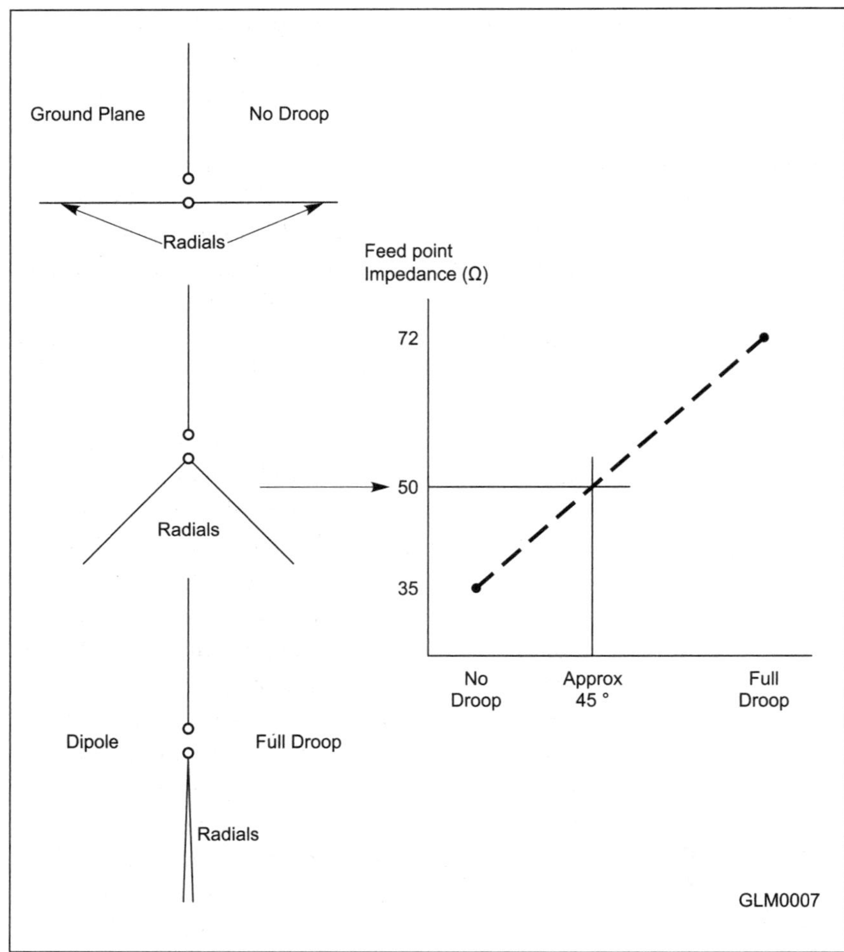

Figure 7.4 — The feed point impedance of a ground-plane antenna with radials perpendicular to the antenna is approximately 35 Ω, resulting in a 1.4:1 SWR with 50-Ω coaxial cable. Drooping or sloping the radials gradually raises the feed point impedance until, with the radials drooped so far as to become the other half of a dipole, feed point impedance becomes 72 Ω. A 50-Ω feed point is reached with radials drooping approximately 45 degrees.

niques are used to increase their electrical length. Some common loading techniques are:

• *Loading coils* — a coil is added at the base or somewhere along the length of the antenna.

• *Capacitance hats* — spokes or a wheel-shaped structure is added near the top of the antenna. **[G4E01]**

• *Linear loading* — part of the antenna is folded back on itself.

Another common feature on mobile whips is the corona ball at the tip of the antenna. While this does add a small amount of loading capacitance, its primary function is to eliminate any high-voltage discharges from the sharp tip of the antenna while transmitting. **[G4E02]**

While loading can cause an antenna to present reasonable feed point impedances, a loaded antenna is not as efficient as a full-sized straight whip and will have a small operating bandwidth without retuning. **[G4E06]** The "screwdriver" antenna design — a whip with an adjustable loading coil at the base, which varies its inductance — has gained popularity for HF mobile operation as a good compromise between performance and convenience. **[G9D08]**

EFFECTS OF GROUND

A dipole's feed point impedance and radiation pattern are both affected by its physical height above ground. The effects are caused by the presence of the electrical image of the antenna created in the electrically conducting ground below the antenna. The ground may not be a very good conductor, but the image is still present and affects antenna performance.

Feed point impedance is affected because the electrical image, like all mirror images, is electrically reversed from the actual dipole. As the image and antenna get closer together, the actual antenna begins to be "shorted out" by the image. Below ¼ wavelength in height, the dipole's feed point impedance steadily decreases until it is close to zero at ground level. **[G9B07]** Above ¼ wavelength, the impedance varies as suggested by **Figure 7.5**, eventually reaching a stable value at a height of several wavelengths.

Height above ground also affects radiation patterns because of reflection of the antenna's radiated energy by the ground. The actual radiation pattern is composed of energy received directly from the antenna and energy that has been reflected by the ground. The direct and reflected signals take different amounts of time to travel to the receiving antenna so they can add together, cancel each other, or any combination in between. This creates a new pattern of lobes and nulls not present for an antenna in free space.

Figure 7.6 shows what happens when a dipole is raised in steps from a very low height to more than one wavelength above ground. At heights below ½ wavelength, the dipole's pattern is almost omnidirectional and is maximum straight up. **[G9B05]** As a height of ½ wavelength is reached, the reflected and direct energy cancel in the vertical direction and add together at intermediate angles, creating a pattern of peaks and nulls in the radiation pattern for the antenna.

Selecting the proper antenna height is important to achieving the desired goals for the antenna! For example, many public service teams use HF to communicate regionally, using NVIS propagation. NVIS stands for *near-vertical incidence sky-wave*, a fancy way of saying, "Signals that go straight up!" Signals radiated at high vertical angles on low frequencies are usually reflected back to the ground over a wide area, ensuring good communication. Horizontal dipoles from ⅒ to ¼ wavelength high produce an omnidirectional, high-angle pattern ideal for NVIS use. **[G9D01]** Figure 7.6 shows the typical NVIS pattern of a dipole ⅛ wavelength above ground.

Polarization also affects the amount of signal that is lost from the resistance of the ground. Radio waves reflecting from the ground have lower losses when the polarization of the wave is parallel to the ground. That is, when the waves are horizontally polarized. Because the antenna's radiation pattern is made up of the reflected waves combining with the direct waves that are not reflected, lower reflection loss results in stronger maximum signal strength. **[G9B09]**

Ground-mounted vertical antennas, however, are able to generate stronger signals at low angles of radiation than horizontally polarized antennas at low heights. This means they are often preferred for DX contacts on the lower HF bands where it is impractical to raise horizontally polarized antennas to the height necessary for strong low-angle signals.

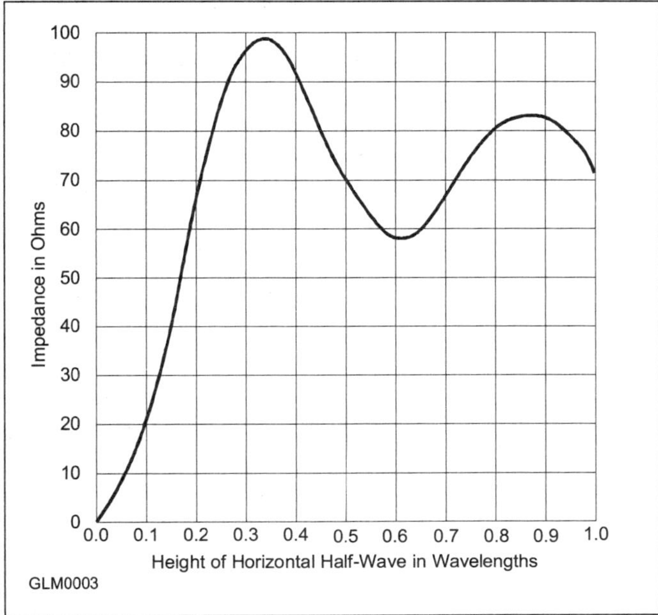

Figure 7.5 — The feed point impedance of a horizontal dipole over perfect ground varies dramatically with height. At ground level, the antenna is effectively "shorted out" by its electrical image. As the antenna is raised, the impedance gradually approaches the 72-Ω feed point impedance of a dipole in free space.

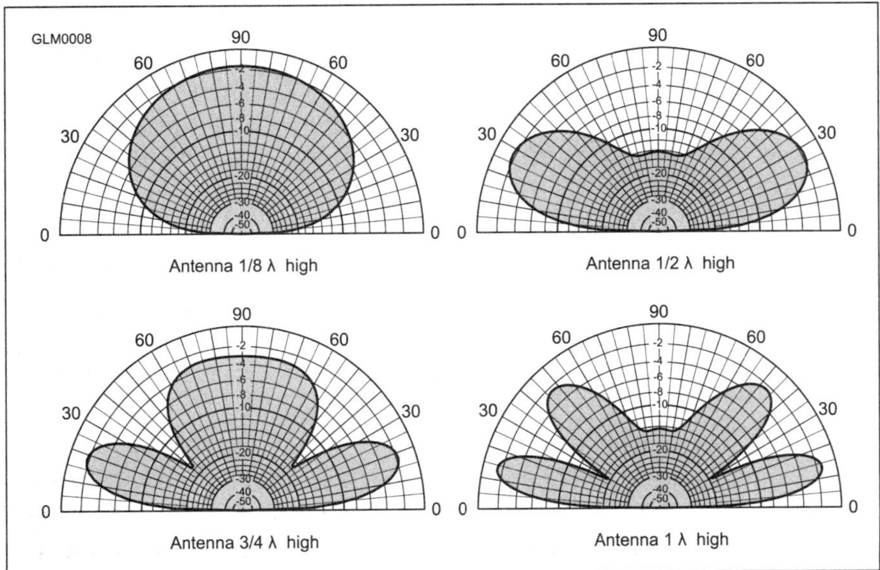

Figure 7.6 — As a low dipole starting at ⅛ wavelength above ground is raised, the effects of its electrical ground image cause the elevation pattern to flatten out. At multiples of ½ wavelength in height, the pattern has a null in the vertical direction because the direct and reflected signals cancel.

Elements are the conducting portions of an antenna that radiate or receive a signal. *Polarization* refers to the orientation of the electric field radiated by the antenna and is determined by the physical orientation of the elements with respect to the Earth's surface. If an element is horizontal, then the signal it radiates is horizontally polarized.

Feed point impedance is the ratio of RF voltage to current at an antenna's feed point. An antenna is *resonant* when its feed point impedance is completely resistive with no reactance.

An antenna's *radiation pattern* is a graph of signal strength in every direction or at every vertical angle. An *azimuthal* pattern shows signal strength in horizontal directions. An *elevation* pattern shows signal strength in vertical directions. An antenna transmits and receives with the same pattern. *Lobes* are regions in the radiation pattern where the antenna is radiating a signal. *Nulls* are the points at which radiation is at a minimum between lobes.

An *isotropic* antenna radiates equally in every possible direction, horizontal and vertical. Isotropic antennas do not exist in practice and are only used only as a reference. An *omnidirectional* antenna radiates a signal of equal strength in every horizontal direction. A *directional* antenna radiates preferentially in one or more directions.

Concentrating transmitted or received signals in a specific direction is called *gain*. Signal strength is increased in that direction for both receiving and transmitting. Antenna gain is specified in decibels (dB) with respect to an identified reference antenna.

The ratio of gain in the preferred or forward direction to the opposite direction is called *front-to-back ratio* (F/B). The ratio of gain in the preferred or forward direction to directions at right angles called the *front-to-side ratio* (F/S). All such ratios are measured in dB.

7.2 Yagi Antennas

G2D04 — Which of the following describes an azimuthal projection map?
A map that shows true bearings and distances from a specific location

G9C01 — Which of the following would increase the bandwidth of a Yagi antenna?
Larger-diameter elements

G9C02 — What is the approximate length of the driven element of a Yagi antenna?
1/2 wavelength

G9C03 — How do the lengths of a three-element Yagi reflector and director compare to that of the driven element?
The reflector is longer, and the director is shorter

G9C05 — What is the primary effect of increasing boom length and adding directors to a Yagi antenna?
Gain increases

G9C07 — What does "front-to-back ratio" mean in reference to a Yagi antenna?
The power radiated in the major lobe compared to that in the opposite direction

G9C08 — What is meant by the "main lobe" of a directive antenna?
The direction of maximum radiated field strength from the antenna

G9C10 — Which of the following can be adjusted to optimize forward gain, front-to-back ratio, or SWR bandwidth of a Yagi antenna?
All these choices are correct

G9C11 — What is a beta or hairpin match?

A shorted transmission line stub placed at the feed point of a Yagi antenna to provide impedance matching

G9C12 — Which of the following is a characteristic of using a gamma match with a Yagi antenna?

It does not require the driven element to be insulated from the boom

DIRECTIONAL ANTENNA BASICS

Directional antennas are used widely because they create gain as well as reject interference and noise from other than the desired direction. Being heard better by the station you're contacting means that you need to point your antenna's main lobe at the station. To point the antenna accurately if that station is beyond your line of sight, you'll need a special kind of map called an *azimuthal projection* map. This map shows the world in a circle centered on a particular location (such as your station) so that the paths to all other locations are shown as *great circle* paths, giving the true bearing and distance to any other point. By aiming your antenna in the direction shown on the azimuthal projection map, you will be beaming your signal directly at the other station. **[G2D04]**

The dipole, ground-plane, and random wire use a single radiating element. An *array* antenna uses two or more elements to create maximum field strength in a specific direction, called the *main lobe* or *major lobe* of the radiation pattern. **[G9C08]** There are two types of arrays: *driven* and *parasitic*. In a driven array, all of the antenna elements are connected to the transmitter and are called *driven elements*. In a parasitic array, one or more of the elements are not connected to the feed line but influence the antenna's pattern by interacting with the radiated energy from the driven element(s).

Whether an array is a driven or parasitic array, its radiation pattern is determined by *constructive* and *destructive interference*. When two waves interfere with each other, they can reinforce each other if they are in phase and cancel if they are out of phase. Partial cancellation occurs otherwise.

If two antenna elements are separated by more than a small fraction of a wavelength, the differences in travel time to a distant antenna from each are enough to result in cancellation that varies with the position of the distant antenna. **Figure 7.7** shows an example of

Aiming Antennas

There are two reasons you want to be able to aim an antenna: 1) to be heard better by a desired station, and 2) to hear a desired station better. The radiation pattern of a unidirectional antenna such as a Yagi usually has one main lobe and at least three nulls — two side nulls and one rear null. If you know where each of those nulls is pointing, it's a simple matter to use the pattern to accomplish your goals.

The device that does the actual mechanical moving is called a *rotator*. The rotator's control box in your shack has a meter or digital readout that you can calibrate to provide the compass heading of where the main lobe of the antenna is pointing — usually along the boom of the antenna. From that heading, you know that the side nulls will be at 90 degrees to either side where the ends of the elements face the signal. The rear null is usually aligned directly opposite to the direction of the main lobe. (The direction of the rear null may shift slightly from asymmetries in the antenna's installation or for signals arriving from different vertical angles.) To minimize noise or interference, try pointing one of these nulls at the source of the interference.

Once you have the antenna pointed in what you think is the right direction, don't hesitate to search or hunt for a slightly better signal somewhat off the direct path. It is not uncommon, particularly on HF, for the ionosphere to shift or *skew* the signal path by up to 15 degrees. To minimize noise or interference, you rarely know the exact location, so you'll have to find the best direction for a null by using your ears and your radio's S-meter.

cancellation for a pair of dipole antennas. The radiated fields from each antenna add and subtract at different angles around the antennas so that lobes and nulls are formed.

In a driven array, power is applied to all of the elements, such as in Figure 7.7. In a parasitic array, the antenna elements are so close together that energy from the driven element induces a current to flow in the parasitic element. That current radiates a field — called *re-radiation* — just as if it had been supplied by a feed line! By careful placement and tuning of the parasitic and driven elements, a directional antenna pattern can be created.

YAGI STRUCTURE

For the combination of economy, performance, and simplicity it's hard to beat the Yagi antenna. More accurately called the Yagi-Uda antenna, the design was first described in 1927. The Yagi remains the most popular of all directional antennas because of its simple

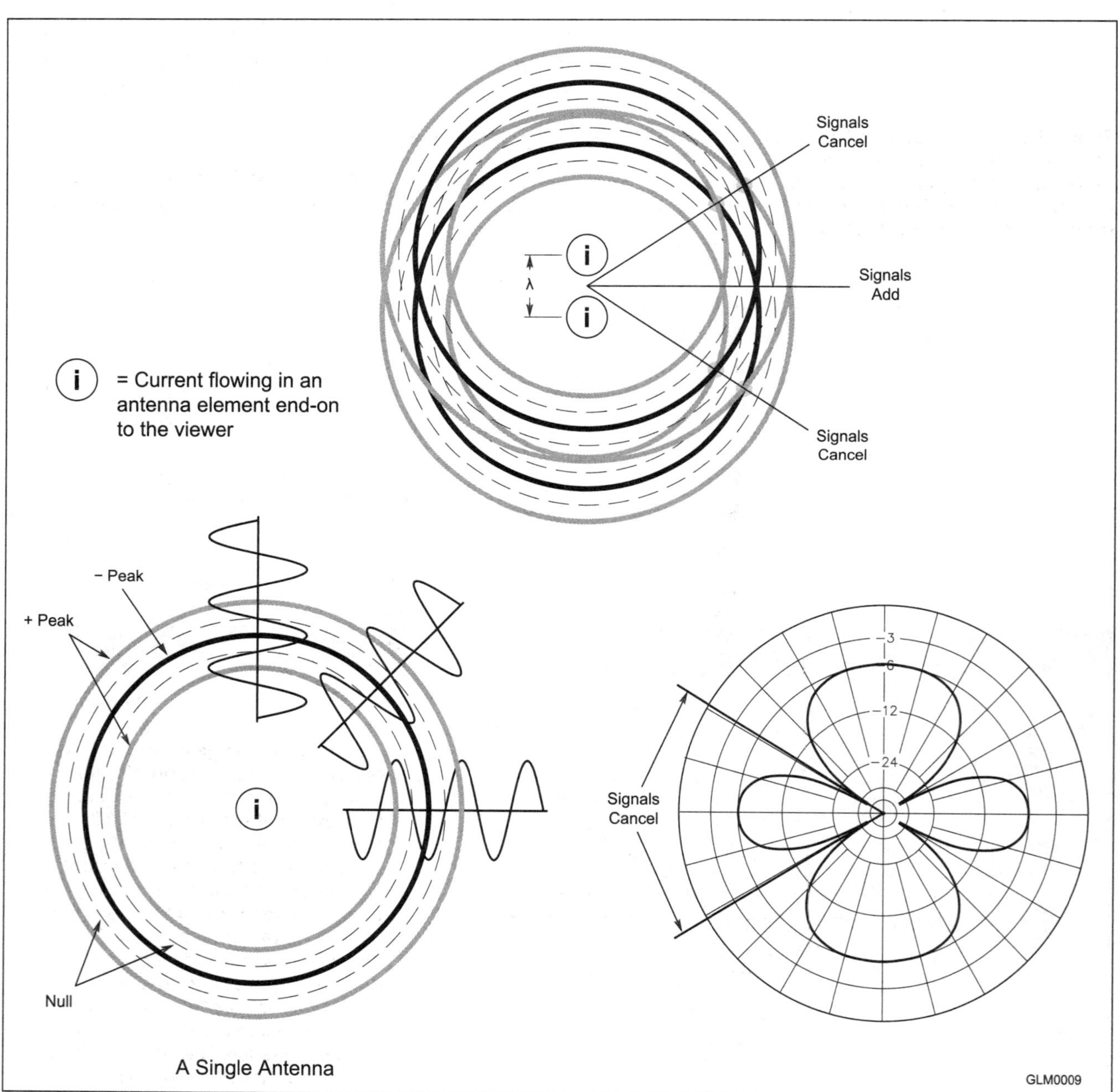

Figure 7.7 — For two antennas 1 wavelength apart (seen on-end) and fed identical, in-phase signals, the radiated signals add and cancel at different angles around the antennas. This creates the lobes and nulls of the radiation pattern seen at right.

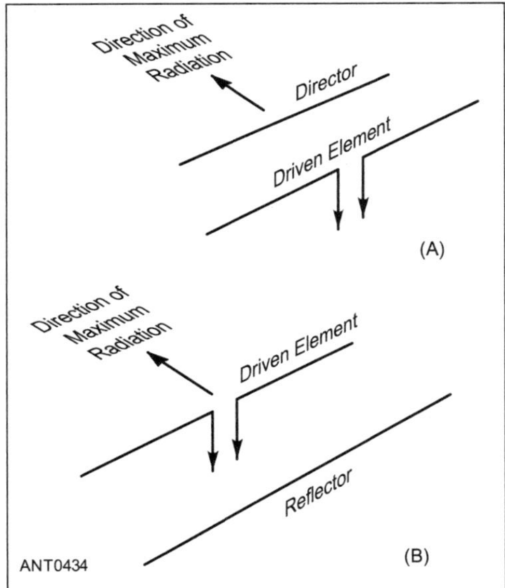

Figure 7.8 — Two-element Yagi antennas using a single parasitic element. At A the parasitic element acts as a director, and at B as a reflector. The arrows show the direction of maximum radiation.

construction and good performance. Even a simple Yagi can reduce interfering signals and noise from unwanted directions to the rear and sides of the antenna — an important feature on a crowded band such as 20 meters.

The Yagi is a parasitic array with a single driven element and at least one parasitic element as shown in **Figure 7.8**. The driven element (DE) is a resonant dipole, approximately ½ wavelength long. **[G9C02]** The elements are physically arranged to create gain in a single major or main lobe and cancel signals in the opposite direction. The parasitic elements placed in the direction of maximum gain are called *directors* and are slightly shorter than the driven element. **[G9C03]** Parasitic elements in the direction of minimum gain are called *reflectors* and are slightly longer than the driven element. For a Yagi antenna, the front-to-back ratio is the ratio of signal strength at the peak of the radiation pattern's major lobe to that in exactly the opposite direction. **[G9C07]**

DESIGN TRADEOFFS

Once the basic design principles are established, there are many ways to optimize a Yagi design to fit a specific need. Is it

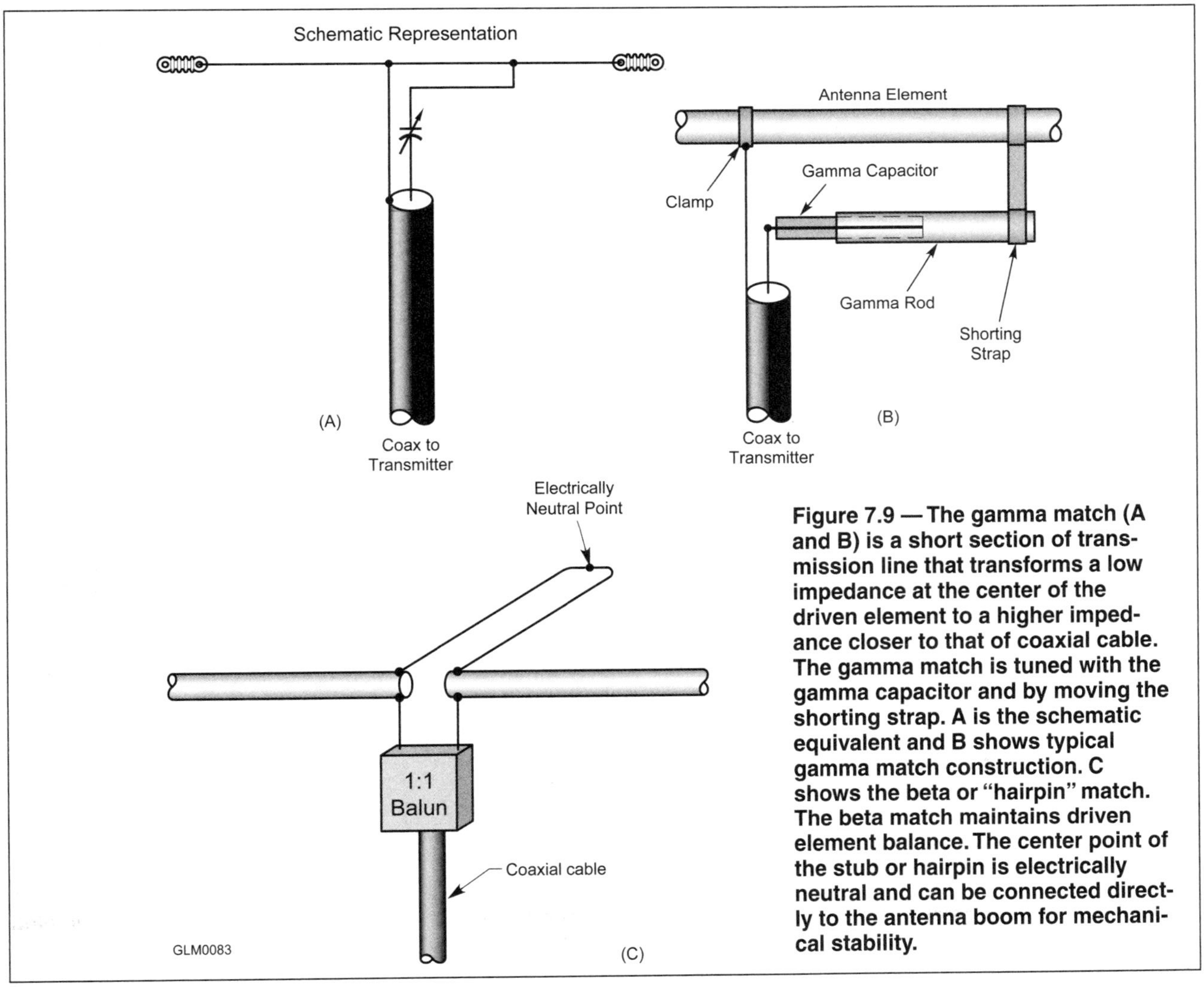

Figure 7.9 — The gamma match (A and B) is a short section of transmission line that transforms a low impedance at the center of the driven element to a higher impedance closer to that of coaxial cable. The gamma match is tuned with the gamma capacitor and by moving the shorting strap. A is the schematic equivalent and B shows typical gamma match construction. C shows the beta or "hairpin" match. The beta match maintains driven element balance. The center point of the stub or hairpin is electrically neutral and can be connected directly to the antenna boom for mechanical stability.

more important to have the maximum gain or the best front-to-back ratio? How much variation of SWR is allowed across the entire band? Making a "one size fits all" antenna is quite difficult!

The primary variables for Yagi antennas are the length and diameter of each element and their placement along the *boom* of the antenna (the central support). These affect gain, SWR, and front-to-back ratio in different ways:

• More directors increase gain.

• A longer boom with a fixed number of directors increases gain up to a maximum length beyond which gain is reduced. **[G9C05]**

• Larger diameter elements reduce SWR variation with frequency (increases SWR bandwidth). **[G9C01]**

• Placement and tuning of elements affects gain and feed point impedance (and SWR).

To be sure, there are other general rules of cause-and-effect, but these are typical of the decisions that antenna designers (and purchasers) should consider. **[G9C10]**

The process of modifying a design for a certain level of performance is called *optimizing*. Some antenna modeling programs can start with a basic design and then modify it so as to obtain the best gain, front-to-back ratio, feed point impedance and so on. For example, if you purchase a garden-variety commercial antenna, you could experiment with it to get more gain or better front-to-back ratio. Antenna design and modification is a very popular activity for hams.

IMPEDANCE MATCHING

Most Yagi designs that have desirable radiation patterns also have a feed point impedance somewhat below the 50 Ω of regular coaxial cable; typically the feed point impedance is 20 to 25 Ω. This results in an undesirable SWR of greater than 2:1. To change the feed point impedance back to 50 Ω, various impedance matching techniques are used.

The most common technique is the *gamma match* shown in **Figure 7.9A**. The gamma match is actually a short section of parallel-conductor transmission line that uses the driven element as one of its conductors. The transmission line transforms the low impedance of the feed point to a higher value. An adjustable capacitor — either an actual variable capacitor or a short piece of insulated wire inside a hollow gamma rod — is used to adjust the gamma match for an SWR of 1:1. A mechanical advantage of the gamma match over other techniques is that the driven element need not be insulated from the boom, simplifying construction. **[G9C12]**

There are other techniques of impedance matching Yagi antennas, such as *the beta match* (or "hairpin") shown in Figure 7.9C. The beta match is a short length or "stub" of parallel conductor transmission line connected directly across the driven element feed point. **[G9C11]** The stub acts as an inductive reactance that can compensate for any capacitive reactance at the feed point. The balun is used to maintain electrical balance between both halves of the driven element.

Other techniques, such as the omega match, impedance transformers, and transmission line stubs are described in references such as *The ARRL Antenna Book*. At VHF and UHF, it is also possible to use relatively large-diameter elements so that the feed point impedance is close to 50 Ω without any external matching devices.

For More Information
How Yagis Work

The following description of how a Yagi works is somewhat oversimplified but illustrates the general principles. The simplest two-element Yagi consists of a driven element (DE) and a reflector. The reflector is slightly longer than the DE by about 5% and placed about 0.15 to 0.2 wavelength behind the DE, opposite the direction of maximum signal.

The original signal from the DE travels to the reflector where it causes current to flow, re-radiating a signal. Re-radiated signals are 180 degrees out of phase with the original signal, so the re-radiated and DE signals cancel in the direction of the reflector (to the back of the antenna). To the front of the antenna, the extra travel time for the re-radiated signal from the reflector causes it to reinforce the DE signal.

Why is the reflector slightly longer than the DE? The physical separation and the 180 degrees of re-radiation phase shift don't quite add up to complete cancellation and reinforcement. Additional phase shift is needed and that comes from the reflector being slightly longer than ½ wavelength so that its impedance is inductive. The additional phase shift to the current in the reflector from the inductive reactance is just enough to cause the original and re-radiated signals to add and cancel in the desired directions.

A director element, placed in front of the DE by the same amount, increases forward gain. It works similarly but is somewhat shorter than the DE by about 5%. The resulting capacitive reactance subtracts a small amount of phase shift so that the DE and director signals add to the front of the antenna in the direction of the director.

Neglecting the effects of height above ground, a two-element Yagi with a driven element and a reflector has a gain of approximately 7 dBi (over an isotropic antenna) and about 5 dBd (over a dipole). The front-to-back ratio is 10 to 15 dB. By adding a single director, a three-element Yagi's forward gain improves to a theoretical maximum of 9.7 dBi and the front-to-back ratio to 30 to 35 dB. This is a very useful antenna!

Additional reflectors make little difference in either gain or front-to-back ratio. Therefore, most Yagi antennas have a single reflector. Adding more directors does not have a big effect on front-to-back ratio but does increase antenna gain, so it is not uncommon at HF to see Yagis with two to four directors. At VHF and UHF, there may be as many as a dozen or more directors, although each only adds a fraction of a dB in gain.

7.3 Loop Antennas

G9D03 — In which direction is the maximum radiation from a VHF/UHF "halo" antenna?

Omnidirectional in the plane of the halo

G9D10 — In which direction or directions does an electrically small loop (less than ¹⁄₁₀ wavelength in circumference) have nulls in its radiation pattern?

Broadside to the loop

Loop antennas completely enclose an area that can be circular, square, triangular or any simple open shape that is not too narrow. The feed line can be attached at a break in the loop or a smaller loop can be used to couple RF energy to the main loop.

LARGE LOOPS

A square loop with each leg ¼ wavelength (¼ λ) long is called a *quad loop*. Triangular or *delta loops* are usually symmetrical, with each leg ⅓ wavelength long. Some delta loops shorten one leg and lengthen the other two equally to remain symmetric.

A one-wavelength loop acts electrically like two dipoles connected end-to-end with the open ends brought together. The location at which a loop's feed line is attached becomes a high current point, just like at the middle of a dipole. No matter where the feed point is attached, a mirror image of the high current point then appears ½ wavelength from the feed point across the loop as shown in **Figure 7.10**.

The radiation pattern of the 1-wavelength loop in Figure 7.10 shows that the direction of maximum signal is broadside to the plane of the loop, whether round, quad or delta. If the loop is oriented horizontally, most of its signal will go straight up, making it a good antenna for local and regional contacts. Orienting the loop vertically aims the maximum

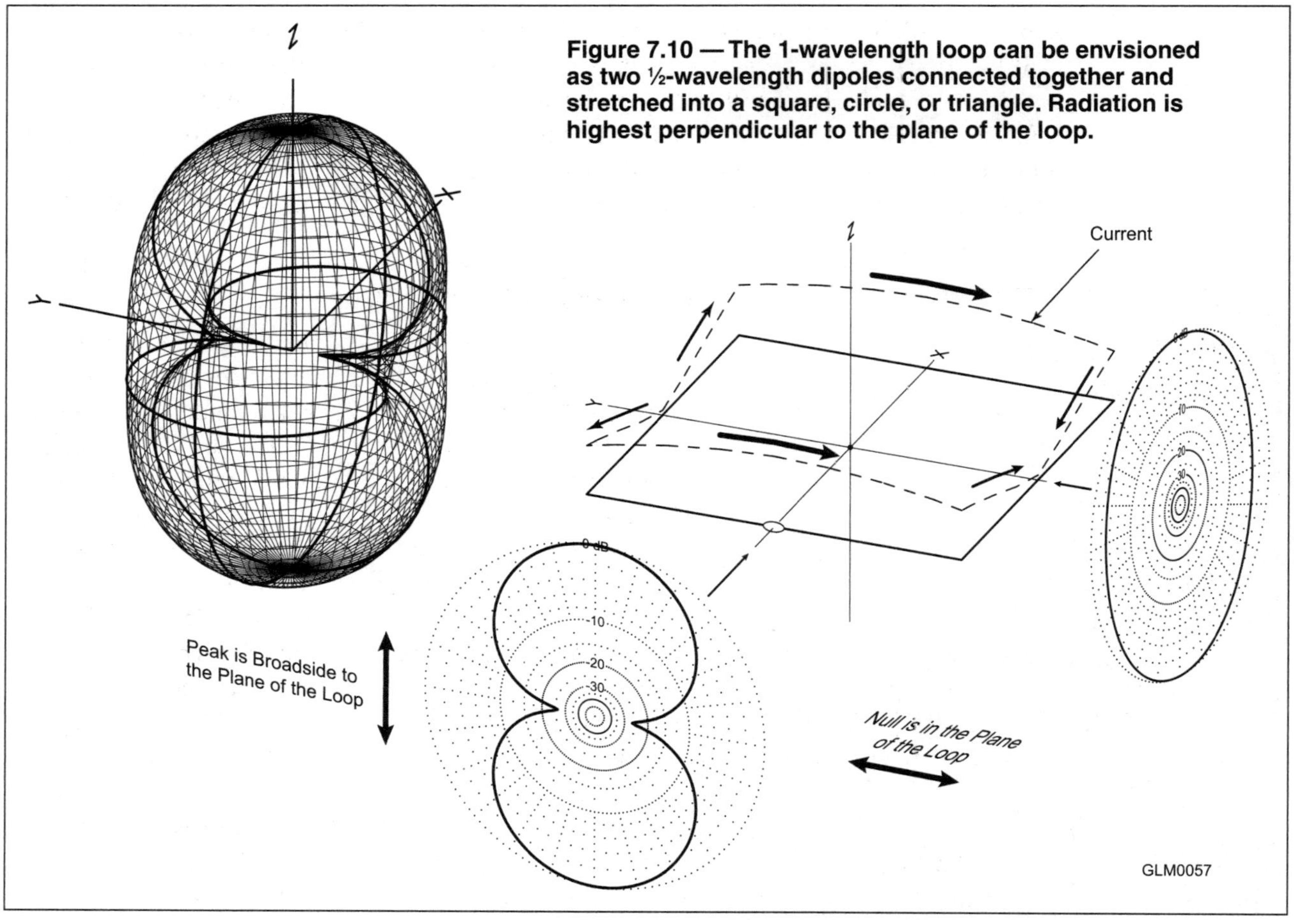

Figure 7.10 — The 1-wavelength loop can be envisioned as two ½-wavelength dipoles connected together and stretched into a square, circle, or triangle. Radiation is highest perpendicular to the plane of the loop.

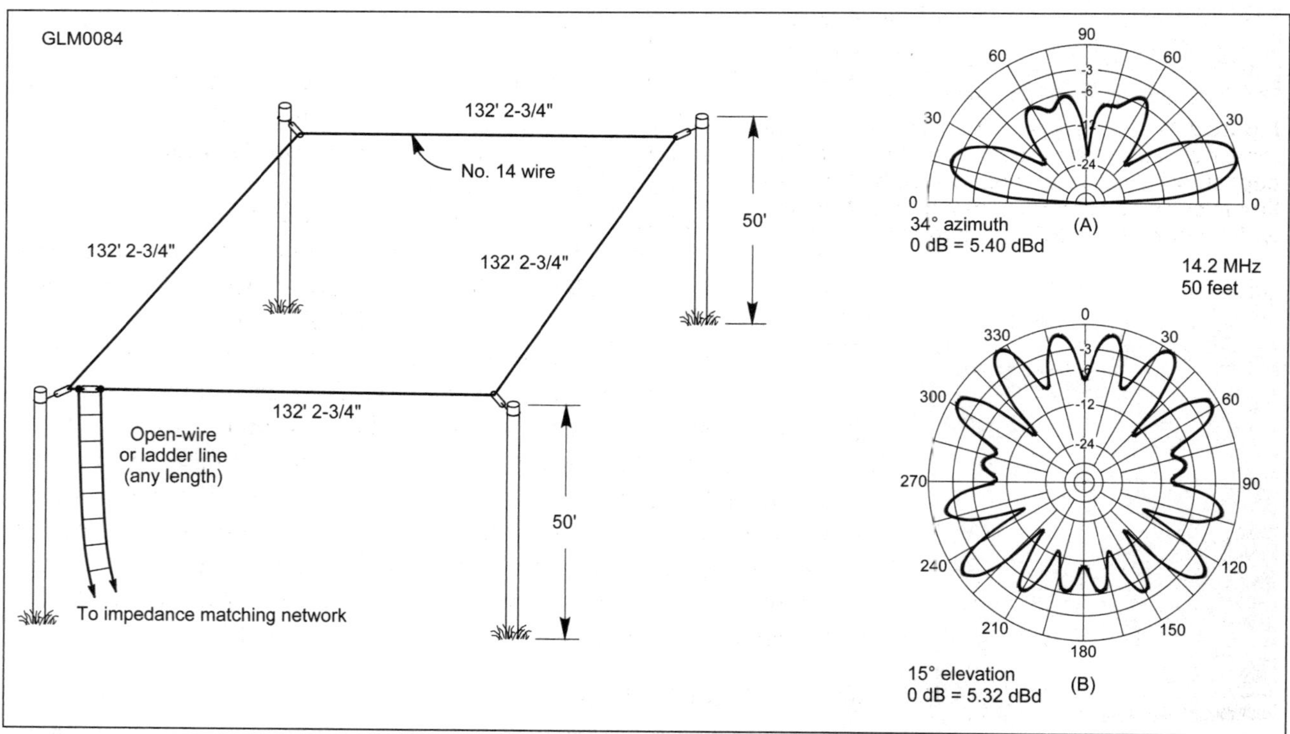

Figure 7.11 — A full-wave loop for 1.9 MHz. The loop is typically fed with open-wire or window line and an antenna tuner used in the station. At frequencies where the circumference is much greater than 1 wavelength, the radiation pattern becomes nearly omnidirectional at intermediate vertical angles as shown for 14.2 MHz at A and B.

signal toward the horizon, where it would be better for making DX contacts.

If the loop's circumference is much larger than 1 wavelength, the current patterns around the loop have more than two peaks and nulls. When the circumference reaches multiple wavelengths, there can be many current peaks and nulls. These create many lobes and nulls in the radiation pattern as shown in **Figure 7.11**. The result is an essentially omnidirectional pattern with the peak angle of radiation somewhat lower than a dipole at the same height.

Figure 7.12 — A typical small loop used for portable operation. The loop is tuned by a variable capacitor in the bottom enclosure and the feed line is connected to the small loop at the top which couples the RF signal to the main loop.

Figure 7.13 — A halo (shown here in the square "squalo" form) is a popular horizontally polarized antenna for VHF operation on 6 and 2 meters.

Quad and Delta Loop Beams

Loops can be used in arrays, just as dipoles can. In fact, a popular variation of the Yagi beam uses quad loops for elements. Not surprisingly, this beam antenna is called a *quad*. The quad has two or more full-sized loops mounted on a boom just like a Yagi's elements: reflector, driven element and director(s). The quad or delta loop beam driven elements are approximately 1 λ in circumference and operate on the same principles of re-radiation and phase shift as does the Yagi. The driven element of a quad is about ¼ wavelength per side and of a symmetrical delta loop about ⅓ wavelength per side. Quad and delta loop reflectors are about 5% longer in circumference than the driven element, and the directors about 5% shorter. A two-element quad or delta loop with a driven element and a reflector has approximately the same forward gain as a three-element Yagi. Front-to-back ratio is generally better for the Yagi. Quad and delta loop beams with the same number of elements have about the same gain.

SMALL LOOPS

When the circumference of the loop becomes less than ⅓ wavelength, the current in the loop becomes relatively uniform all the way around the loop. This causes the radiation pattern to develop sharp nulls broadside to the plane of the loop. **[G9D10]** Imagine the radiation pattern in Figure 7.10 but created by a small loop rotated 90 degrees from the loop in the figure. **Figure 7.12** shows a typical small loop being used for portable HF operation.

Small loops are in wide use as receiving antennas and portable or low-profile transmitting antennas. The sharp null broadside to the loop makes them effective for direction-finding by using the null to find the direction of minimum signal strength. Away from the null, small loops are nearly omnidirectional. For transmitting, small loops can be used for temporary or space-challenged setups and are usually oriented vertically as shown in the photo. Because of their size, small loops are not very efficient and much care must be taken to minimize losses in the antenna and feed line.

HALO ANTENNAS

The halo is not actually a continuous loop — it is a dipole bent into a circle or square (the "squalo") with the ends separated by a small gap. (See **Figure 7.13**.) Nevertheless, the halo is often viewed as a ½-wavelength loop. Like the continuous loops described above, the halo radiates most strongly in the plane of the antenna. Halos are usually mounted horizontally so they produce an omnidirectional pattern with the horizontal polarization preferred for VHF weak-signal operation. **[G9D03]** Halos for 6 and 2 meters can be mounted on a vehicle for mobile operation, as well.

7.4 Specialized Antennas

G9B01 — What is a characteristic of a random-wire HF antenna connected directly to the transmitter?
>Station equipment may carry significant RF current

G9C09 — In free space, how does the gain of two three-element, horizontally polarized Yagi antennas spaced vertically ½ wavelength apart typically compare to the gain of a single three-element Yagi?
>Approximately 3 dB higher

G9D04 — What is the primary function of antenna traps?
>To enable multiband operation

G9D05 — What is an advantage of vertically stacking horizontally polarized Yagi antennas?
>It narrows the main lobe in elevation

G9D06 — Which of the following is an advantage of a log-periodic antenna?
>Wide bandwidth

G9D07 — Which of the following describes a log-periodic antenna?
>Element length and spacing vary logarithmically along the boom

G9D09 — What is the primary use of a Beverage antenna?
>Directional receiving for MF and low HF bands

G9D11 — Which of the following is a disadvantage of multiband antennas?
>They have poor harmonic rejection

This section covers several interesting topics associated with specific types of antennas or special ways of using them. There are literally hundreds of different types of specialty antennas, but the following examples are common on the HF bands. You will also find that an ordinary antenna can be made to give unexpected results if constructed and installed in the just the right way!

RANDOM WIRES

It is not always practical to have a ½ or ¼-wavelength long resonant antenna. For portable operation and in other special circumstances, a *random wire* antenna can be used. The antenna is just what the name suggests, a random length of wire deployed however possible. The feed point impedance and radiation pattern of a random wire are unpredictable. The antenna's radiation pattern may have several lobes at different vertical and horizontal angles.

A true random wire is connected directly to the output of the transmitter (more commonly to the output of an antenna tuner) without a feed line. The station equipment and its ground connection are thus part of the antenna system as well. Using this type of an antenna may result in significant RF currents and voltages on the station equipment that could cause RF burns. **[G9B01]** Nevertheless, this simple antenna can give excellent results on any band for which the transmitter or tuner can accept the feed point impedance.

STACKED ANTENNAS

You may have seen an installation with a pair (or more!) of identical parallel Yagi antennas mounted one above the other or side-by-side. *Stacking* antennas in the manner of **Figure 7.14** results in more gain.

There is an additional benefit to stacking antennas. If you study the azimuthal radiation patterns of Yagis, you notice that as more and more directors are added, the *beamwidth* of the main lobe (the angle between the points on the main lobe at which gain is 3 dB less than maximum) narrows. If you look at the elevation pattern however, adding more directors doesn't have as great an effect. Vertically stacking antennas increases gain and narrows the elevation beamwidth. **[G9D05]**

Most *vertical stacks*, with the antennas directly above each other, space the antennas about λ/2 apart although spacings of up to more than 1 λ are sometimes used. Spaced λ/2 apart, the additional gain for a vertical stack of two horizontally-polarized beams is about 3 dB. **[G9C09]** Sometimes the antennas are aligned such that the elements are parallel but end-on to each other, in a *horizontal stack*. In this arrangement, the spacing is larger to keep the antennas from interacting too strongly.

LOG PERIODICS

If you don't look too closely at a TV antenna, you might think it is just another Yagi. Take a closer look and you'll be surprised — that's a *log periodic* antenna! Usually referred to as "logs," the log periodic antenna in **Figure 7.15** is designed to have a consistent radiation pattern and low SWR over a wide frequency bandwidth — as much as 10:1 — meaning the log periodic can be used over several bands. A log periodic will not have as much gain or front-to-back ratio as a Yagi antenna, however. **[G9D06]**

The "log" in log periodic refers to "logarithmic," and "periodic" means the spacing of the elements along the boom. The length and the spacing of the elements increases logarithmically from one end to the other. **[G9D07]** The result is that the part of the antenna doing the radiating and receiving shifts with frequency — the short elements are active at the high frequencies and the long elements at low frequencies. The elements are approximately the length of λ/2 dipoles at the frequency on which they are active. A log periodic antenna can be a good choice to cover several bands if only one rotatable antenna can be installed.

BEVERAGE ANTENNAS

Invented in 1922 by Harold Beverage, the Beverage is a receiving antenna designed not to have high gain, but to reject noise and interfering signals that are not from the desired direction. The result is lower

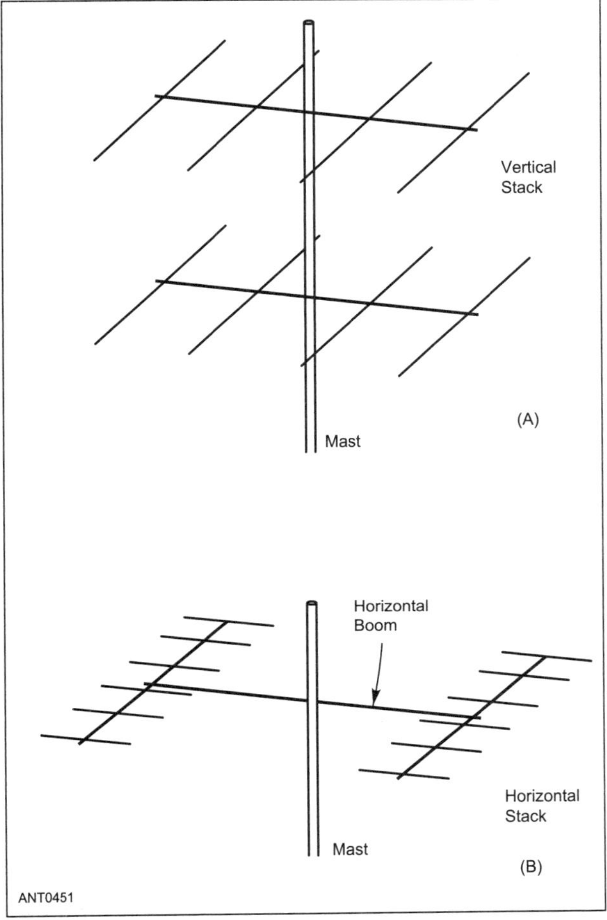

Figure 7.14 — Stacking antennas produces more gain in a main lobe that is carefully controlled. At A, two Yagis are stacked vertically on the same mast.

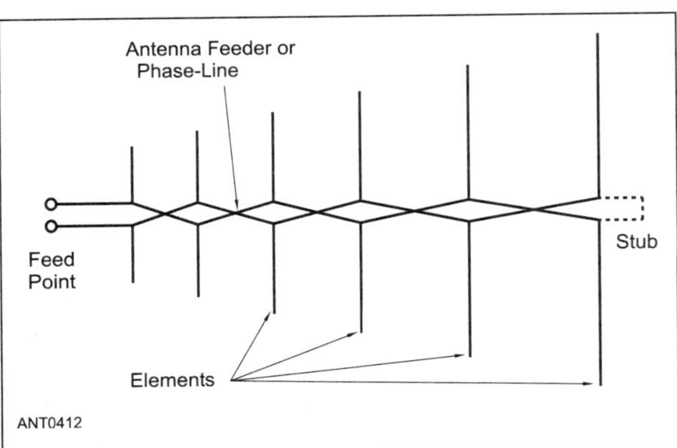

Figure 7.15 — The log periodic dipole array (LPDA) consists of dipoles fed by a common feed line that alternates polarity between elements. Traditional TV antennas sweep the elements slightly forward — there are many variations on the basic design.

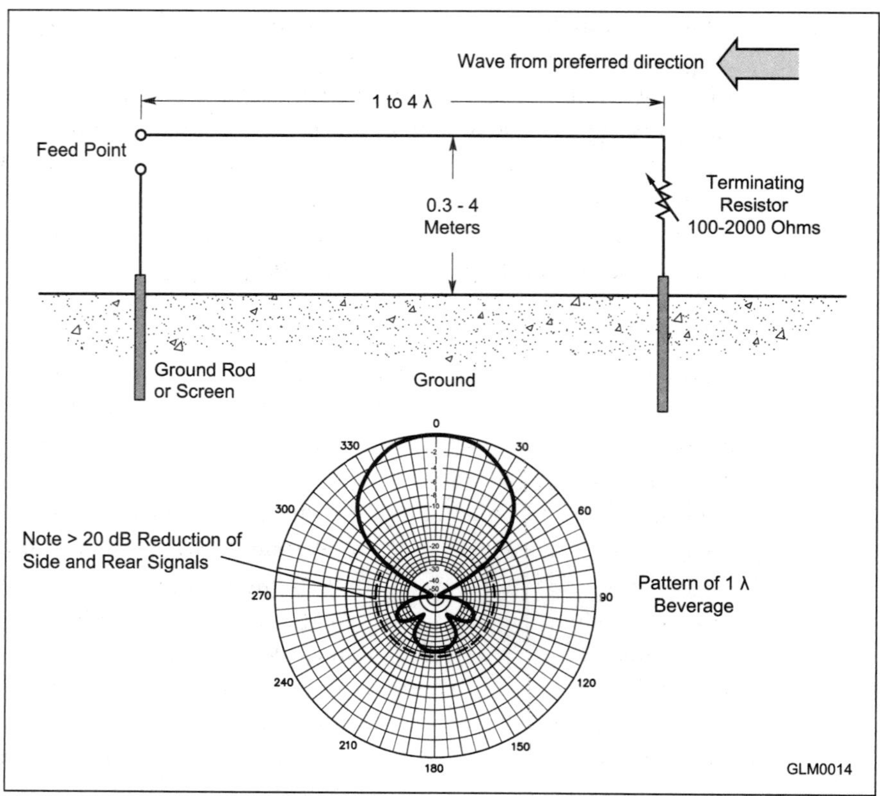

Figure 7.16 — In a Beverage antenna, signals arriving from the direction of the terminating resistor induce a traveling voltage wave along the wire transferred to the feed line at the feed point. Signals arriving from other directions are either absorbed by the terminating resistor or do not induce voltage waves in the antenna.

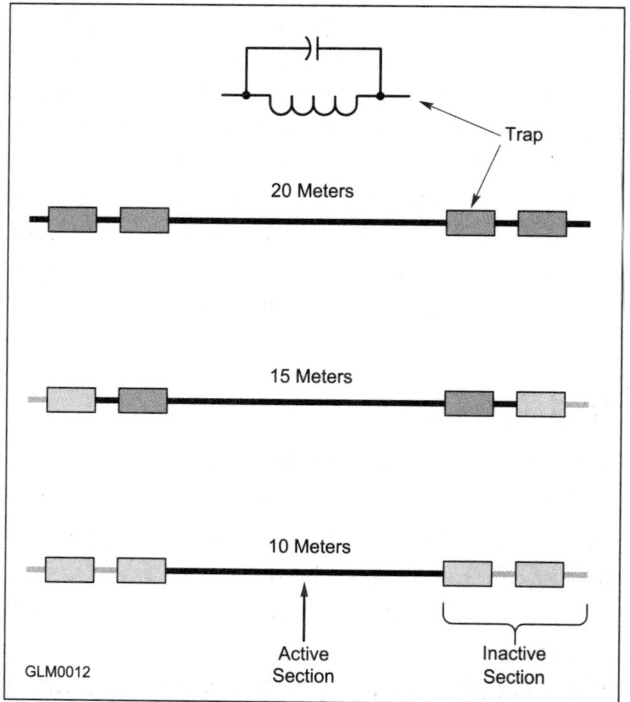

Figure 7.17 — Traps are parallel LC circuits. They may be made from discrete inductors and capacitors or may use coaxial cable or metal sleeves. The traps act like open circuits at their resonant frequency, causing different sections of the antenna to be active on different bands. This drawing shows a trap antenna that works on 10, 15, and 20 meters.

signal strength but a better signal-to-noise ratio. The Beverage of **Figure 7.16** is a *traveling wave antenna*. As the incoming wave moves along the antenna wire it builds up a voltage wave just as wind blowing across water builds up a water wave. When the wave reaches the end of the antenna, the energy is transferred to the feed line.

It consists of a long, low wire (usually less than 20 feet high) aligned with the preferred signal direction. Used exclusively for directional receiving on the lower HF bands (40 meters and longer wavelengths), the Beverage has high ground losses and is too inefficient for use as a transmitting antenna. **[G9D09]**

MULTIBAND ANTENNAS

So far, the discussion has been mainly about antennas that are designed for a single band. It is terrific to be able to put up a separate antenna for each band, but that's rarely practical. The solution is *multiband* antennas with good performance on more than one band, often several.

As discussed before, a half-wave dipole can be used on its odd harmonics without a tuner and gives good performance. A random wire or nonresonant antenna can also be used on multiple bands with a tuner. What hams generally mean by multiband antenna, however, is a design that reconfigures itself electrically for each band of operation.

The most basic multiband antenna, the *trap dipole*, is shown in **Figure 7.17**. Each trap is a parallel LC circuit. At resonance it acts like an open circuit, below resonance like an inductor, and above resonance like a capacitor. At their resonant frequencies, traps act like open electrical switches, effectively cutting off the rest of the antenna beyond their location. At lower frequencies, the traps add inductance to the antenna, making the antenna look electrically longer. At higher frequencies, the capacitance electrically shortens the antenna. **[G9D04]**

For the trap dipole in Figure 7.17, at the lowest frequency of operation the antenna acts like a regular dipole, shortened by the inductance of the trap. On the band where the trap is resonant, the outer segments of the antenna are electrically disconnected and only the inner segment is active. Some trap antenna designs are useful on higher frequencies as well. Yagis can also use traps to work on several bands. The three-element *tribander* Yagi with traps in the elements is a time-proven performer on 20, 15, and 10 meters.

There are a few drawbacks of using techniques such as traps to make antennas work on multiple bands. First, because the antenna does work on multiple bands, it will happily radiate harmonics and spurious signals just as if they were intentional. It is up to the transmitter operator to be sure those signals are not generated. **[G9D11]** Second, the traps have losses and do reduce the efficiency of the antenna to some degree. Third, because the antenna is shortened on the lowest or lower frequencies of operation, it will not radiate quite as well as a full-sized antenna. Nevertheless, using trap antennas is often an excellent compromise between performance and available space and budget for antennas.

7.5 Feed Lines

G4A06 — What is the purpose of an antenna tuner?
Increase power transfer from the transmitter to the feed line

G9A01 — Which of the following factors determine the characteristic impedance of a parallel conductor feed line?
The distance between the centers of the conductors and the radius of the conductors

G9A02 — What is the relationship between high standing wave ratio (SWR) and transmission line loss?
High SWR increases loss in a lossy transmission line

G9A03 — What is the nominal characteristic impedance of "window line" transmission line?
450 ohms

G9A04 — What causes reflected power at an antenna's feed point?
A difference between feed line impedance and antenna feed point impedance

G9A05 — How does the attenuation of coaxial cable change with increasing frequency?
Attenuation increases

G9A06 — In what units is RF feed line loss usually expressed?
Decibels per 100 feet

G9A07 — What must be done to prevent standing waves on a feed line connected to an antenna?
The antenna feed point impedance must be matched to the characteristic impedance of the feed line

G9A08 — If the SWR on an antenna feed line is 5:1, and a matching network at the transmitter end of the feed line is adjusted to present a 1:1 SWR to the transmitter, what is the resulting SWR on the feed line?
5:1

G9A09 — What standing wave ratio results from connecting a 50-ohm feed line to a 200-ohm resistive load?
4:1

G9A10 — What standing wave ratio results from connecting a 50-ohm feed line to a 10-ohm resistive load?
5:1

G9A11 — What is the effect of transmission line loss on SWR measured at the input to the line?
Higher loss reduces SWR measured at the input to the line

As a General class licensee, you'll be assembling more sophisticated collections of equipment, trying bigger and better antennas and using more and more feed lines — more accurately, transmission lines — to connect everything together. Getting the best performance out of your equipment requires a basic understanding of how feed lines work, the goal of this section. Let's start by reviewing what you learned for the Technician class exam.

CHARACTERISTIC IMPEDANCE

All feed lines have two conductors. Coaxial cable has an inner or center conductor and an outer shield or braid. The inner conductor is insulated from the outer conductor by air or by foamed or solid plastic. *Balanced* feed lines consist of two parallel conductors separated by insulating material in the form of strips or spacers. **Figure 7.18** shows some examples of common feed lines used by hams.

Just as pipes and tubes have different "acoustic impedances" to the flow of sound or air through them, feed lines have different *characteristic impedances* (Z_0) that characterize how electromagnetic energy is carried by the feed line. This is not the same as the resistance of the feed line's conductors.

The geometry of the feed line conductors determines the characteristic impedance. For parallel-conductor feed lines, the radius of the conductors and the distance between them determine Z_0. **[G9A01]** The most common type is *window line* that has solid plastic

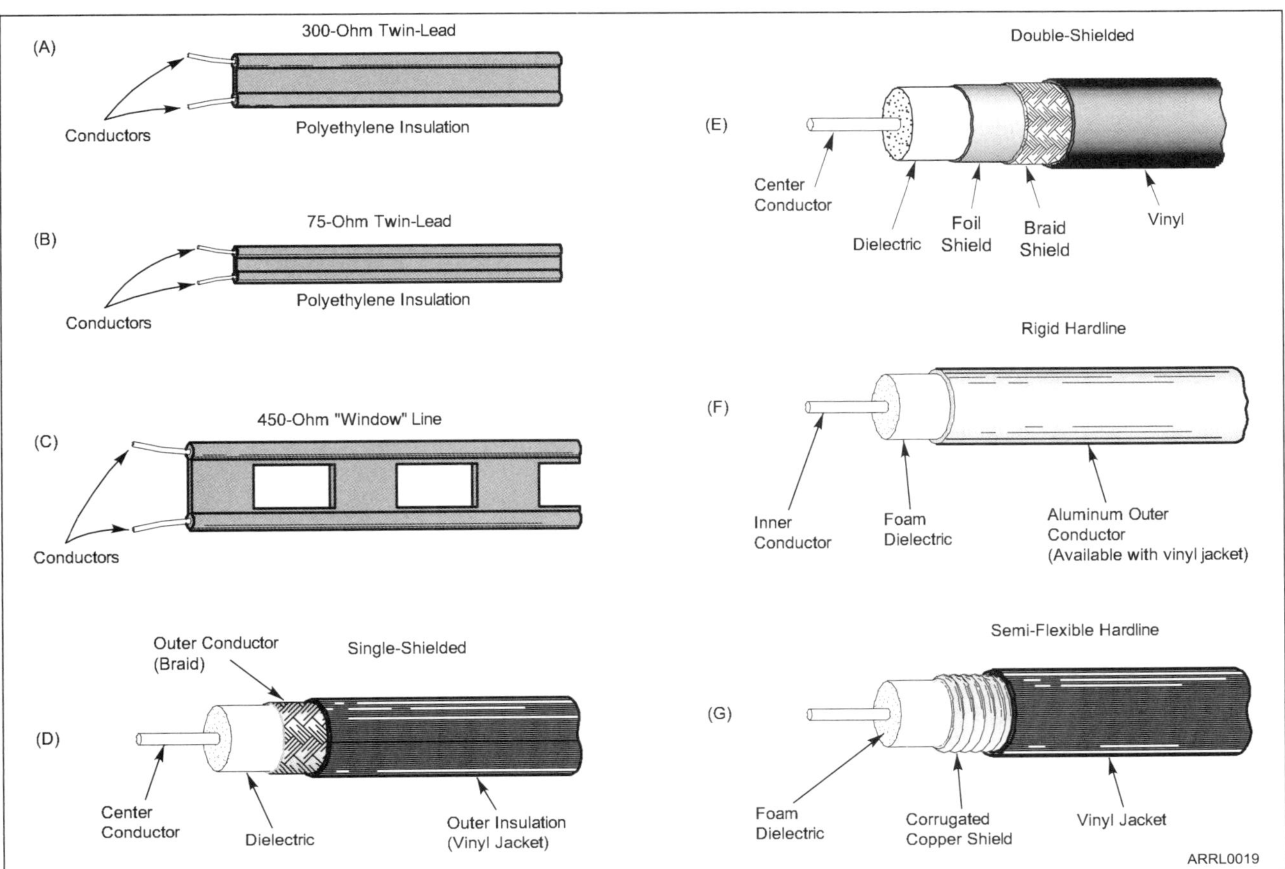

Figure 7.18 — Some common types of parallel conductor and coaxial cables used by amateurs. Parallel conductor line (A, B, C) has two parallel conductors separated by insulation (dielectric). Coaxial cable (D, E, F, G) or "coax" has a center conductor surrounded by insulation. The center conductor may be made from stranded or solid wire. The second conductor, called the shield, covers the insulation and is in turn covered by the plastic outer jacket. The shield may be made from braid, or from solid aluminum or copper.

insulation between the conductors with rectangular "windows" cut out of the insulation to reduce loss and weight. The typical impedance for window line is 450 Ω although there are several variations as low as 400 Ω. **[G9A03]**

In a coaxial feed line, Z_0 is determined by the diameters of the inner and outer conductors and the spacing between them. The characteristics of the insulating material has some effect on characteristic impedance, but has a larger effect on *feed line loss* and the *velocity of propagation*. The most common characteristic impedances for coaxial feed lines used by amateurs are 50 Ω and 75 Ω.

FORWARD AND REFLECTED POWER AND SWR

A feed line transfers all of its power to an antenna when the antenna and feed line impedances are *matched*. If the feed line and antenna impedances do not match, some of the power is *reflected* by the antenna. Power traveling toward the antenna is called *forward power*. Power reflected by the antenna is called *reflected power*. Power in a feed line is reflected at any point at which the impedance of the feed line changes. This can be at an antenna, at a connector, or from a different type of feed line. **[G9A04]**

The waves carrying forward power and reflected power form stationary interference patterns inside the feed line. These are *standing waves*. The ratio of the peak voltage in the standing wave to the minimum voltage is called the *standing wave ratio* (SWR) and is used to measure how well the antenna and feed line impedances are matched. SWR of 1:1, a "perfect match," indicates that none of the power is reflected, all of it transferred to the antenna. An SWR of infinity indicates that all of the power was reflected.

SWR is always greater than 1:1 (for example, 3:1 and not 1:3). SWR is equal to the ratio of the higher of antenna feed point impedance or feed line characteristic impedance to the lower. That means the ratio is always greater than or equal to 1:1.

Example 4: What is the SWR in a 50-Ω feed line connected to a 200-Ω load?

$$SWR = \frac{200}{50} = 4:1 \quad \textbf{[G9A09]}$$

Example 5: What is the SWR in a 50-Ω feed line connected to a 10-Ω load?

$$SWR = \frac{50}{10} = 5:1 \quad \textbf{[G9A10]}$$

Example 6: What standing wave ratio will result from the connection of a 50-Ω feed line to a non-reactive load having a 50-Ω impedance?

$$SWR = \frac{50}{50} = 1:1$$

Example 7: What would be the SWR if you feed a vertical antenna that has a 25-Ω feed point impedance with 50-Ω coaxial cable?

$$SWR = \frac{50}{25} = 2:1$$

Example 8: What would be the SWR if you feed an antenna that has a 300-Ω feed point impedance with 50-Ω coaxial cable?

$$SWR = \frac{300}{50} = 6:1$$

SWR can be measured anywhere along a feed line. It is most commonly measured at the transmitter where the feed line is connected. SWR meters (also called SWR bridges) are used to measure the SWR present in the feed line between the transmitter and the antenna.

Most amateur transmitting equipment is designed to work at full power with an SWR at the input to the feed line of 2:1 or lower. SWR greater than 2:1 may cause the transmitter to reduce power. The higher the SWR, the harder it is for a transmitter to transfer power to a feed line. High SWR may damage a transmitter. Antennas that are much too short or too long will not work well and will have extreme feed point impedances, causing high SWR. High SWR can be caused by a mismatch of the feed line and transmitter impedances, a mismatch of the antenna and feed line impedances, or by a faulty feed line.

IMPEDANCE MATCHING

Matching feed line and load (antenna) impedances eliminates standing waves from reflected power and maximizes power delivered to the load. **[G9A07]** This is not always practical however, so the impedance matching is more often done at the transmitter end of the feed line as shown in **Figure 7.19**.

The device used to reduce SWR at the transmitter connection to the feed line has many names: *impedance matcher, transmatch, antenna coupler,* and *antenna tuner.* Remember that an "antenna tuner" does not tune the antenna at all — it only changes the impedance of your antenna system at the end of the feed line to match that of your transmitter, or put another way, an antenna tuner increases the power transfer from the transmitter to the feed line. **[G4A06]**

Impedance matching devices are constructed from inductors and capacitors that are adjustable by the operator. The most common circuit configuration is the T network shown in Figure 7.19. This circuit can match a wide range of impedances at the feed line connection to 50 Ω that matches transmitter output impedance.

Regardless of what technique is used to transform impedances, it is important to remember that the SWR in the feed line between the impedance matching device and the antenna does not change! If the SWR in the feed line is 5:1 and an impedance matching device causes a 50-Ω load to be presented to the transmitter, the SWR is still 5:1 in the feed line. **[G9A08]**

Feed Line Loss

All feed lines dissipate a little of the energy they carry as heat — this is *attenuation* or *loss*. Loss occurs because of the resistance of the conductors and because the insulating material between the conductors absorbs some of the energy. Air-insulated cables such as parallel conductor feed lines and certain types of hardline have the lowest loss. Teflon insulation also has extremely low loss. Polyethylene, both solid and foamed, is used in most cables and has the highest loss, although it is still a very good insulating material.

Loss is measured in dB per unit of length, usually dB/100 feet of cable. **[G9A06]** Typical values for loss of different types of cable are given in **Table 7.1**. Loss increases with frequency for all types of feed lines. **[G9A05]** Small coaxial cables generally have higher loss at a given frequency than larger diameter cables.

As SWR increases, more power is reflected by the load. That reflected power must travel through the line and on each round trip, some of it is dissipated as heat due to feed line loss. Thus, increasing SWR in a feed line also increases the total loss in the line. **[G9A02]** Higher feed line loss also affects SWR measurement at the input to the line. The increased loss in the feed line means that less of reflected power returns to the input where it can be measured. This makes SWR look artificially low. The higher the feed line loss, the lower the measured SWR will be at the input to the line. **[G9A11]** In fact, a long length of lossy feed line can be used as a good dummy load!

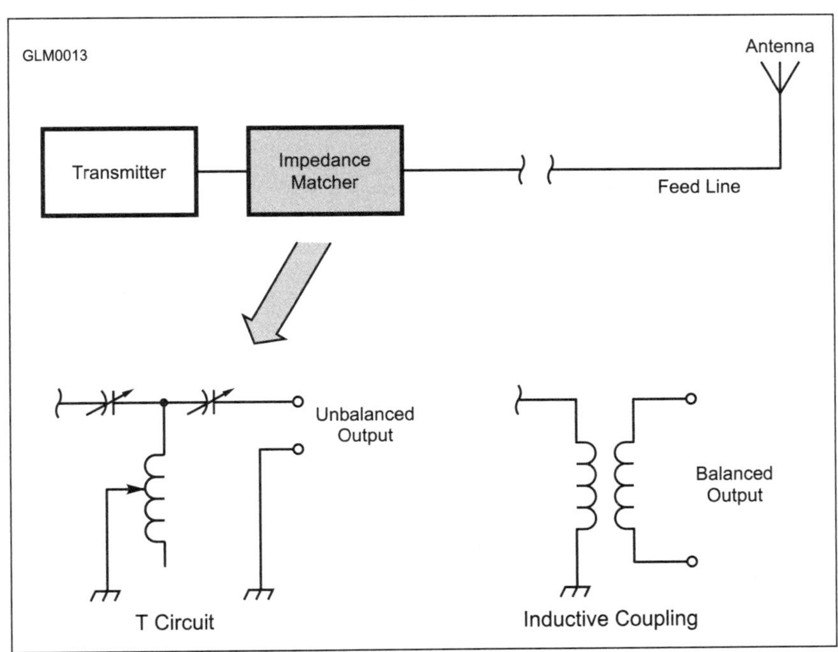

Figure 7.19 — The T network is a popular impedance matching circuit for HF antennas. Installed at the transmitter end of the feed line, a T network is designed to be used with unbalanced, coaxial feed lines. This circuit uses two variable capacitors and one variable inductor. To use balanced feed lines, such as window line, the output of a T network can be inductively coupled to the output so that neither of the feed line conductors is connected to ground.

Table 7.1
Feed Line Characteristics

Type	Impedance (Ω)	Loss per 100 ft (dB) at 28.4 MHz	Loss per 100 feet (dB) at 144 MHz
RG-174	50	4.4	10.2
RG-58	50	2.4	5.6
RG-8X	50	1.9	4.5
RG-213	50	1.2	2.8
9913	50	0.64	1.6
LMR-400	50	0.65	1.50
LMR-600	50	0.41	0.94
¾ inch CATV hardline	75	0.26	0.62

Chapter 8
Propagation

In this chapter, you'll learn about:
- **The structure of the ionosphere**
- **Reflection and absorption**
- **Sky-wave and ground-wave signals**
- **Sunspots and sunspot cycles**
- **How to assess propagation**
- **Solar phenomena**
- **Scatter propagation**

You've now studied electronics, signals, transmitters, receivers, and antennas. Only one thing is missing — how the waves get from point A to point B! That's propagation and it's the subject of this section. On the HF bands, propagation is strongly affected by what's happening on the sun so you'll need to learn a few things about solar phenomena. The effects of those events on the ionosphere are also important to HF operators. By learning some basic terms and relationships, HF propagation will be much easier to understand and use.

8.1 The Ionosphere

G2D06 — How is a directional antenna pointed when making a "long-path" contact with another station?

180 degrees from the station's short-path heading

G3B01 — What is a characteristic of skywave signals arriving at your location by both short-path and long-path propagation?

A slightly delayed echo might be heard

G3B09 — What is the approximate maximum distance along the Earth's surface normally covered in one hop using the F2 region?

2,500 miles

G3B10 — What is the approximate maximum distance along the Earth's surface normally covered in one hop using the E region?

1,200 miles

G3C01 — Which ionospheric region is closest to the surface of Earth?

The D region

G3C02 — What is meant by the term "critical frequency" at a given incidence angle?

The highest frequency which is refracted back to Earth

G3C03 — Why is skip propagation via the F2 region longer than that via the other ionospheric regions?

Because it is the highest

G3C04 —What does the term "critical angle" mean, as applied to radio wave propagation?

The highest takeoff angle that will return a radio wave to Earth under specific ionospheric conditions

G3C05 — Why is long-distance communication on the 40-, 60-, 80-, and 160-meter bands more difficult during the day?

The D region absorbs signals at these frequencies during daylight hours

G3C11 — Which ionospheric region is the most absorbent of signals below 10 MHz during daylight hours?

The D region

The upper reaches of the Earth's atmosphere get thinner and thinner with distance above the Earth. Beginning at about 30 miles in height, the remaining gas is thin enough that solar ultraviolet (UV) radiation can break the molecules of gas into individual atoms and then knock electrons away from them. The loss of an electron causes the neutral atom to become a positively charged *ion* and the electron becomes a *free electron*. This process is called *ionization*. These ions and the electrons can respond to voltages just as electrons do in a conductor. This region of the atmosphere becomes a very weak conductor called the *ionosphere*, extending up to 300 miles above the Earth.

Because of various physical processes, the ionosphere organizes itself naturally into several regions in which the density of the free electrons is higher than at adjacent altitudes. The main regions of the ionosphere are the D, E, and F layers as shown in **Figure 8.1**. (The words *region* and *layer* mean the same thing.)

• The *D layer* (30 to 60 miles in altitude) is only present when illuminated by the sun. It disappears at night because the ions and free electrons are close enough together to recombine quickly when no UV is present, returning to a neutral condition. **[G3C01]**

• The *E layer* (60 to 70 miles in altitude) acts similarly to the D region. Because it is higher and less dense than the D region, it lasts longer after sunset but still disappears at night, returning to its neutral state.

• The *F layer* (100 to 300 miles in altitude) is the least dense of the three and can remain partially ionized at night. During the day, the F region splits into the F1 and F2 layers, which combine back into the single F layer at night. The height of the F region and the F1 and F2 layers varies quite a bit with local time, season, latitude, and solar activity. At any particular location, the stronger the illumination from the sun, the higher the F2 layer will be, so its maximum height is reached at noon when the sun is overhead.

REFLECTION

The ionosphere is a weak conductor, so if affects radio waves passing through it. **Figure 8.2** illustrates how it bends or *refracts* radio waves. The ability of the ionosphere to bend radio waves depends on how strongly the region's gases are ionized and the frequency of the wave. The greater the region's ionization, the more the wave will be bent. The higher the frequency of the wave, the less it is bent. In fact, at VHF and UHF, the waves are hardly bent at all and are usually lost to space. (Scatter propagation, discussed later, is an exception.)

At HF, the waves can often be bent enough to return to Earth as if they were reflected from a mirror high in the ionosphere. Figure 8.2 illustrates how the height of this "mirror" is determined, called the region's *virtual height*. Remember that radio waves are actually refracted by the ionosphere, however.

Each reflection from the ionosphere is called a *hop* and allows radio waves to be received hundreds or thousands of miles away. Signals received in this way are called *sky-wave* and propagation via the ionosphere is called *skip*.

The higher the region from which the reflection takes place, the longer the hop. Waves

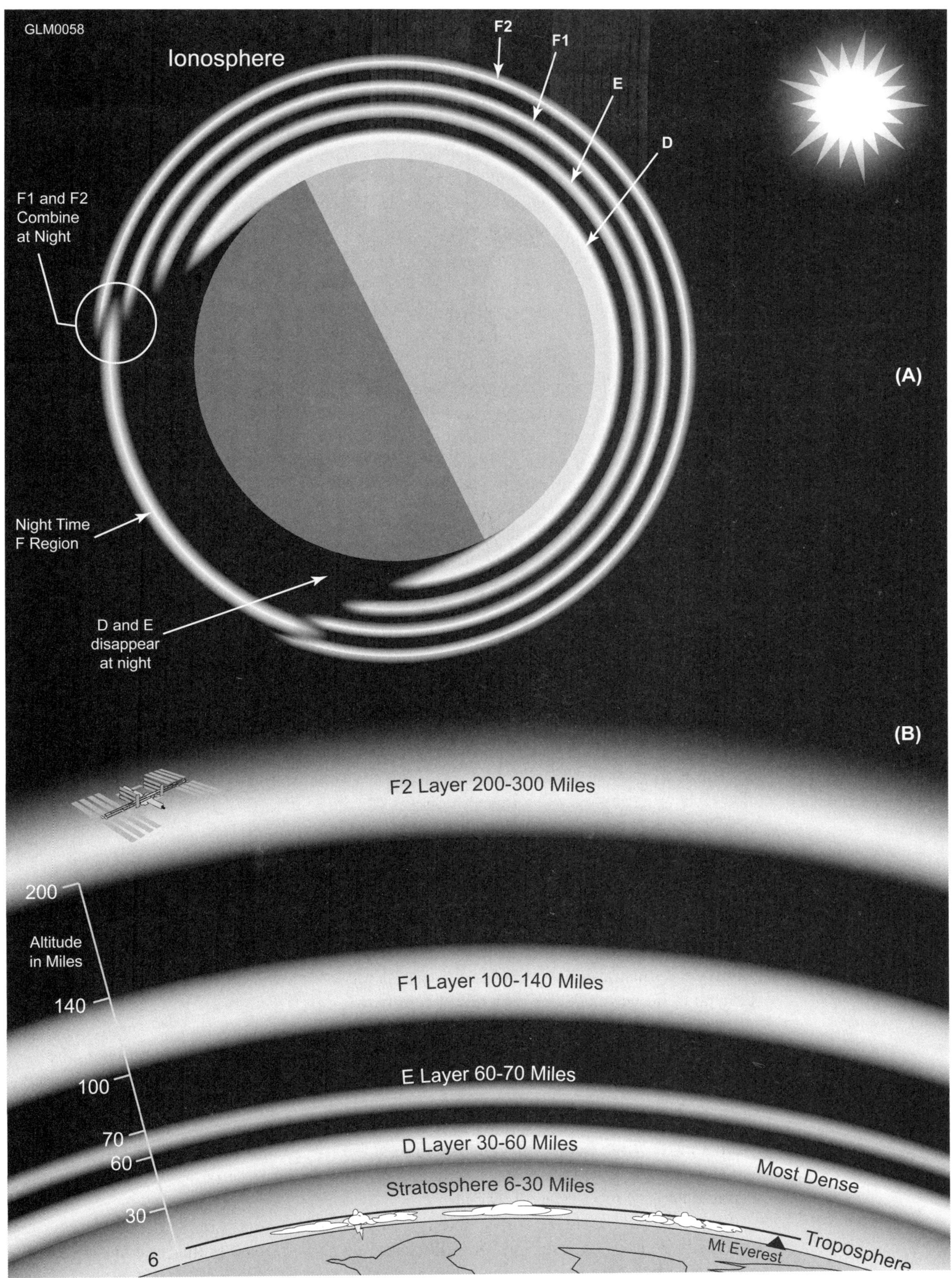

Figure 8.1 — The ionosphere consists of several regions of ionized particles at different heights above the Earth. At night, the D and E regions disappear and the F1 and F2 regions combine to form a single F region.

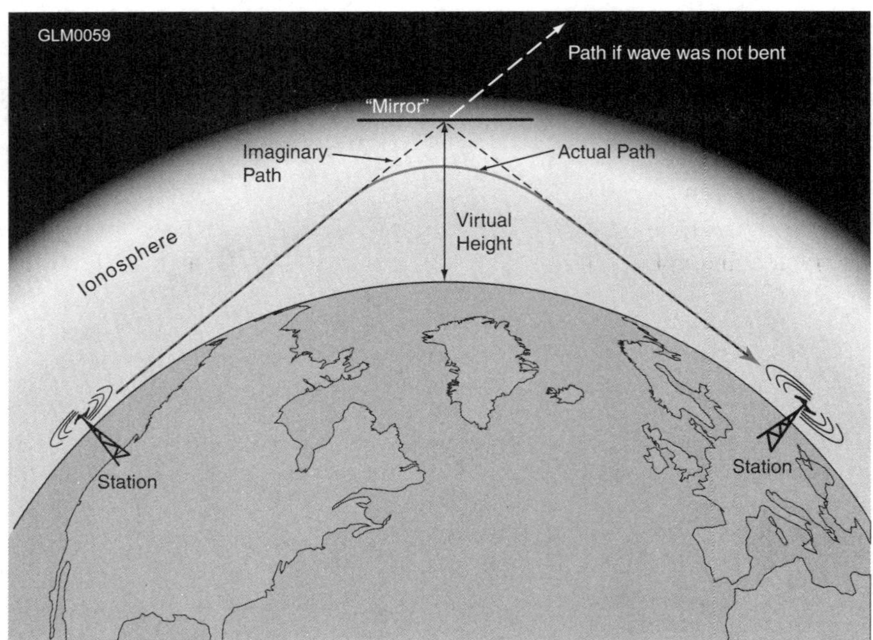

Figure 8.2 — Radio waves are refracted (bent) in the ionosphere, so they return to Earth far from the transmitting station. Without refraction in the ionosphere, radio waves would pass into space. (Not to scale)

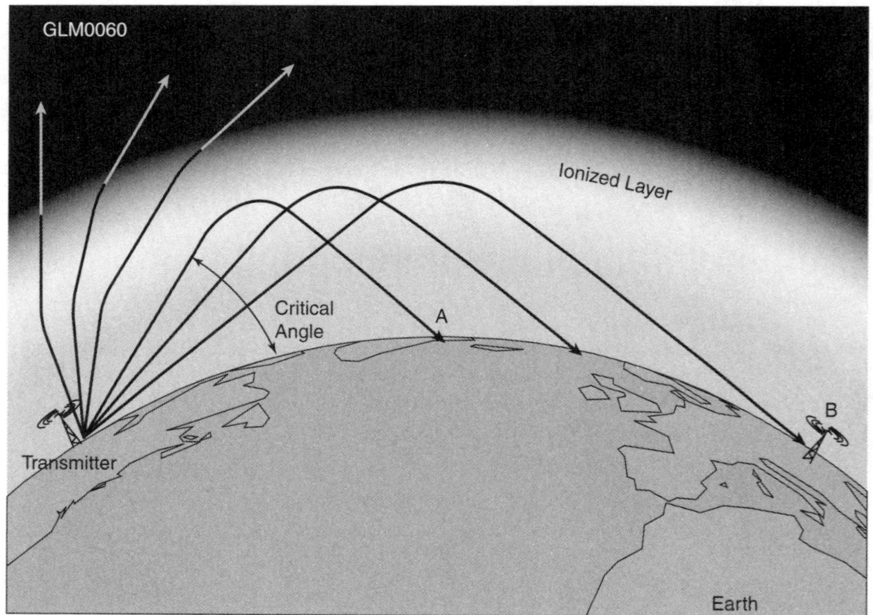

Figure 8.3 — Waves that leave the transmitting antenna above the critical angle are refracted in the ionosphere, but not enough to return to Earth. Waves at and below the critical angle will return to Earth. The lowest angle waves return to Earth at the greatest distance, which is why low angles of radiation are often best for contacting DX stations. (Not to scale)

reflected from the uppermost F2 layer normally travel up to 2,500 miles before returning to the ground. Hops that use the E layer are shorter, up to 1,200 miles, because of the lower reflecting height. **[G3B09, G3B10, G3C03]**

Some combinations of frequency and ionization level result in weak bending. In these cases, the wave must leave the Earth's surface at a low enough angle for the bending of the wave to send it back. The highest takeoff angle at which a wave can be returned to Earth is the *critical angle*. If the wave enters the ionosphere at a steeper angle, it might be diffracted, but not to return it to Earth, and it is lost to space, as shown in **Figure 8.3**. The critical angle depends on ionospheric conditions and frequency. **[G3C04]**

The companion to critical angle is *critical frequency*, the highest frequency on which a wave transmitted straight up will be returned to Earth. **[G3C02]** Measuring the critical frequency with ionosonde equipment gives the height of all the ionosphere's regions and helps provide a day-to-day picture of the ionosphere's status and activity. (An ionosonde is a special type of radar instrument for measuring ionospheric parameters.)

ABSORPTION AND NOISE

The enemy of propagation is *absorption*. In the D and E regions, waves passing through the denser gas are partially absorbed, even as they are refracted. In fact, the D region is not very good at refraction. In the HF bands below 10 MHz, the AM broadcast bands, and at lower frequencies, the D region completely absorbs radio waves during the day, preventing those waves from returning to Earth until after dark. **[G3C05, G3C11]** In general, absorption increases in the daytime and when solar UV is more intense.

Noise is another enemy of propagation, covering up weak signals. It is much stronger at frequencies below VHF. This is due to storms and other processes in the atmosphere. The lower you go in frequency, the stronger the noise or "static" becomes. Atmospheric noise also varies with the seasons. This is most noticeable on the lower frequency HF bands in the summer when atmospheric noise is strongest.

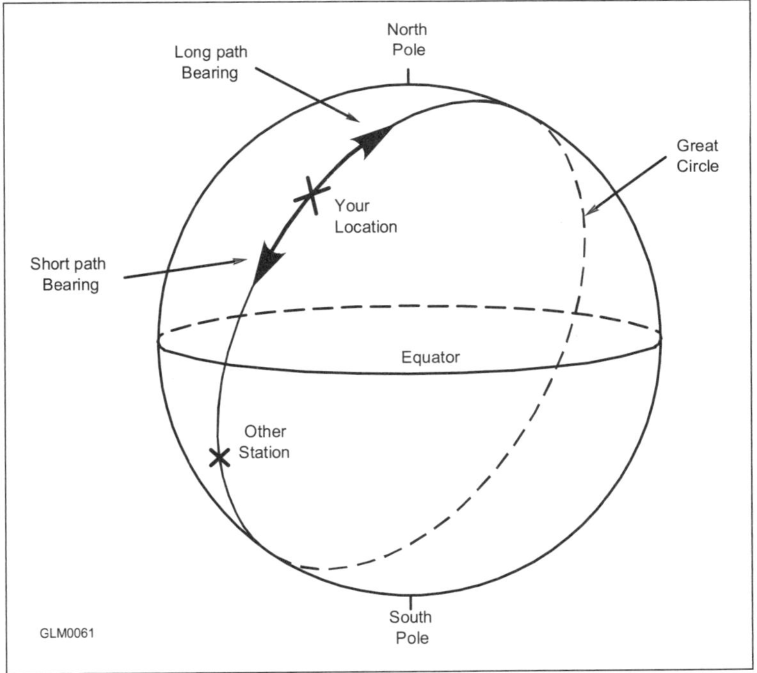

Figure 8.4 — This sketch of the Earth shows both great circle paths drawn between two stations. The bearings for the short path and the long path are shown from the Northern Hemisphere station.

LONG PATH AND SHORT PATH

As you become more skilled in observing and understanding propagation, you'll begin to take advantage of unusual and short-term propagation effects. One of the most exciting is *long path* in which stations are contacted over a path that takes "the long way 'round." Most contacts are made via the *short path*, which is the shorter of the two great circle paths between stations. When the ionosphere along the short path does not support propagation, sometimes the long path will. The bearing of the long path is 180 degrees away from the short path bearing as illustrated by **Figure 8.4**. **[G2D06]**

Occasionally, propagation over both the long and short paths will be supported. Unless the long and short paths are almost equal (such as between stations located at each other's *antipode*) there will be an echo as the more delayed signal arrives a fraction of a second later. **[G3B01]** Occasionally, *round-the-world* propagation is supported and you can hear your own signal coming all the way around to your location about 1/7 of a second later!

For More Information

Sky-wave propagation can consist of multiple hops because the Earth's surface also reflects radio waves. The ocean's highly conductive saltwater is a particularly good reflector of radio waves. Propagation between Europe and the United States, for example, requires up to seven hops depending on location and time of day!

Hops can also be considerably shorter than those maximum figures if the ionosphere is sufficiently ionized so that the critical angle is high. Signals received via sky-wave at much shorter than maximum hop distances are called *short skip*. Short skip is also a good indicator that there is sufficient ionization to support longer skip distances on higher frequency bands. For example, short skip on the 10-meter band is a good indication that sky-wave propagation may be available on the 6-meter band at low takeoff angles.

Sky-wave signals also have a characteristic sound caused by the variations in density and height they encounter in the ionosphere. The ionosphere is not a smooth, stable medium through which the waves travel. The ionosphere is in motion itself and there are large variations in density and ionization at different heights and locations. This allows a sky-wave signal to take multiple paths before returning to Earth. Receiving several of these *multipath* signals at once gives the signal a characteristic echo or flutter as the quality of reflection changes or as signals combine from different paths.

Ground-wave signals travel along the surface of the Earth between stations. Rock and soil and concrete are not very good conductors and so a ground-wave signal loses strength much more rapidly than signals traveling through air. The higher the frequency of the wave, the greater the loss as it travels. Ground-wave propagation on 40 meters, for example, may be up to 100 miles, but on 10 meters, only a few miles at best.

Depending on the critical angle for a particular frequency, a ring-shaped region around the transmitting station can occur between the ranges of maximum ground-wave and minimum sky-wave. This region is called the *skip zone*, and stations located in the skip zone are hard to contact on that particular frequency. (See the section on Scatter Modes later in this chapter.)

8.2 The Sun

G3A01 — How does a higher sunspot number affect HF propagation?
Higher sunspot numbers generally indicate a greater probability of good propagation at higher frequencies

G3A04 — Which of the following are the least reliable bands for long-distance communications during periods of low solar activity?
15 meters, 12 meters, and 10 meters

G3A05 — What is the solar flux index?
A measure of solar radiation with a wavelength of 10.7 centimeters

G3A07 — At what point in the solar cycle does the 20-meter band usually support worldwide propagation during daylight hours?
At any point

G3A10 — What causes HF propagation conditions to vary periodically in a 26- to 28-day cycle?
Rotation of the Sun's surface layers around its axis

G3A12 — What does the K-index measure?
The short-term stability of Earth's geomagnetic field

G3A13 — What does the A-index measure?
The long-term stability of Earth's geomagnetic field

G3B12 — Which of the following is typical of the lower HF frequencies during the summer?
High levels of atmospheric noise or static

SUNSPOTS AND CYCLES

In the previous discussion, you learned that the ionosphere is dependent on solar UV to separate the electrons from their host atoms. The sun is always generating UV radiation (even at night!) but there is a considerable amount of variation over time. A lot of this variation has been shown to be caused by sunspots, the slightly cooler (and comparatively darker) regions of the sun's surface.

The number of sunspots and sunspot groups present on the solar disk at a particular time is the *sunspot number*. Sunspot number is used as an important parameter in assessing overall solar activity. Solar activity rises and falls along with the presence of sunspots in an approximately 11-year cycle. In mid 2023, when this book is being published, Cycle 25 is heating up and propagation on 10 meters and other bands is increasing. The chart in **Figure 8.5** shows how the sunspot number has varied during the past several cycles.

When more sunspots are observed on the face of the sun, more UV is being generated, creating more intense ionization in the ionosphere and improving propagation on the higher frequency bands above 10 MHz and

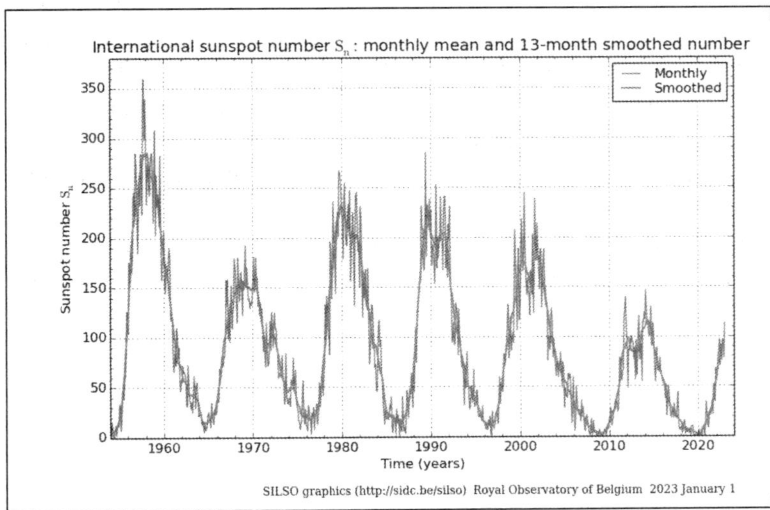

Figure 8.5 — One complete sunspot cycle lasts about 11 years, ramping up and down gradually. This graph shows the monthly mean sunspot numbers for several past cycles through December 2022. Courtesy of the Royal Observatory of Belgium.)

Table 8.1

Daytime/Nighttime HF Propagation

HF Band (meters)	Daytime	Nighttime
160, 80, 60	Local and regional to 100 – 200 miles	Local to long distance with DX best near sunset or sunrise at one or both ends of the contact
40, 30	Local and regional to 300 – 400 miles	Short-range (20 or 30 miles) and medium distances (150 miles) to worldwide
20, 17	Regional to long distance, opening at or near sunrise and closing at night	20 meters is often open to the west at night and may be open 24 hours a day
15, 12, 10	Primarily long distance (1,000 miles and more), opening to the east after sunrise and to the west in the afternoon	10 meters is often used for local communications 24 hours a day

even into the lower VHF range. **[G3A01]** At the peak of the sunspot cycle, there may be sufficient solar UV to cause higher frequency bands such as 10 meters to stay open for long-distance contacts at night. The high ionization takes a toll on the low frequency bands such as 80 and 160 meters because it increases absorption. Conversely, at the bottom of the sunspot cycle when solar activity is low, the lower HF bands have good propagation and the higher HF bands above 20 MHz (15 meters and up) are often closed. **[G3A04]** One band that seems to do well at all times in the sunspot cycle is 20 meters (14 MHz), supporting daytime communications worldwide nearly every day! **[G3A07]**

Sunspots also seem to move across the sun's surface because the sun rotates once every 28 days. That is why propagation conditions (good and bad) on the HF bands often repeat themselves in 28-day cycles as sunspots rotate back into view from Earth. **[G3A10]**

There are strong daily and seasonal variations in HF propagation at any point in the sunspot cycle. **Table 8.1** shows the typical variations in propagation on a daily basis across the HF bands for average solar activity. The seasons also affect propagation as the hemispheres receive more or less solar illumination. In summer, the higher illumination and absorption make daytime HF propagation more difficult, driving up atmospheric noise and static, shifting activity toward the evenings. **[G3B12]** The opposite happens in the winter. Propagation around the equinoxes in March and September can be very interesting at any time of the sunspot cycle.

MEASURING SOLAR ACTIVITY

Solar activity is so important to propagation and communications that it is monitored around the clock by solar observatories all over the world. The results are available from websites, email distribution and radio broadcast announcements. By using this information, along with their experience and software tools to

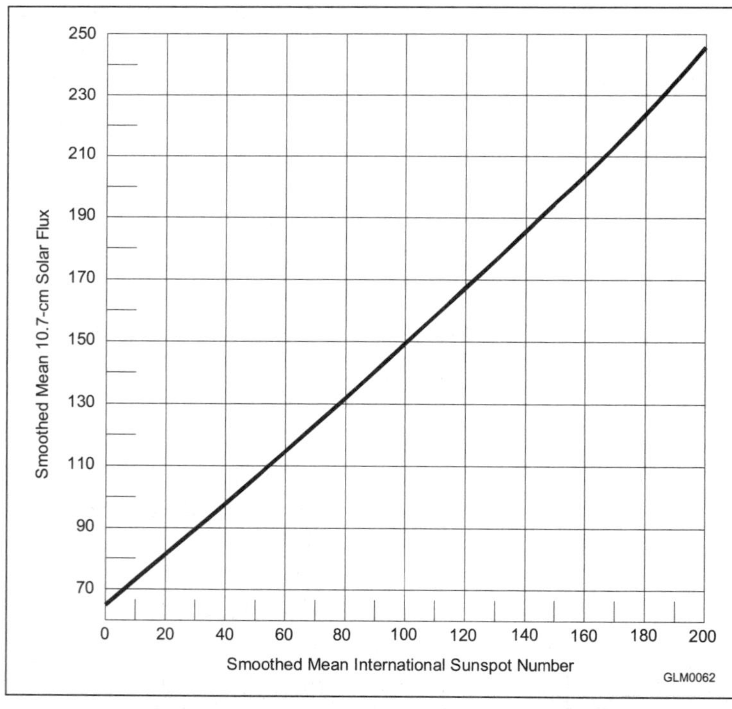

Figure 8.6 — This graph shows the approximate correlation between solar flux and sunspot number. Note that the minimum solar flux is 65, corresponding to a sunspot number of 0.

predict propagation, amateurs can confidently plan their on-the-air activity and be alerted of sudden changes in conditions.

Along with the sunspot number, there are three primary indices that are used to measure solar activity:

- *Solar-Flux Index (SFI)* — describes the amount of 2800 MHz (10.7 cm wavelength) radio energy coming from the sun. This index corresponds well to the amount of solar UV that is hard to measure at ground level. SFI starts at a minimum of 65 and has no maximum value. Higher levels indicate higher solar activity and generally better HF propagation above 10 MHz. **Figure 8.6** shows the correlation between SFI and sunspot number. **[G3A05]**

- *K index* — K values from 0 to 9 represent the short-term stability of the Earth's *magnetic* or *geomagnetic field*, updated every three hours at the National Institute of Standards and Technology (NIST) in Boulder, Colorado. Steady values indicate a stable geomagnetic field. Higher values indicate that the geomagnetic field is disturbed, which disrupts HF communications. **[G3A12]**

- *A index* — based on the previous eight K index values from around the world, the A index gives a good picture of long-term geomagnetic field stability. A index values range from 0 (stable) to 400 (greatly disturbed). **[G3A13]**

All three indices and other solar data is available from the NASA website **spaceweather.com** and the NOAA Space Weather Prediction Center (**swpc.noaa.gov/communities/radio-communications**).

ASSESSING PROPAGATION

G3A02 — What effect does a sudden ionospheric disturbance have on the daytime ionospheric propagation?
> It disrupts signals on lower frequencies more than those on higher frequencies

G3A03 — Approximately how long does it take the increased ultraviolet and X-ray radiation from a solar flare to affect radio propagation on Earth?
> 8 minutes

G3A06 — What is a geomagnetic storm?
> A temporary disturbance in Earth's geomagnetic field

G3A08 — How can a geomagnetic storm affect HF propagation?
> Degrade high-latitude HF propagation

G3A09 — How can high geomagnetic activity benefit radio communications?
> Creates auroras that can reflect VHF signals

G3A11 — How long does it take a coronal mass ejection to affect radio propagation on Earth?
> 15 hours to several days

G3A14 — How is long distance radio communication usually affected by the charged particles that reach Earth from solar coronal holes?
> HF communication is disturbed

G3B02 — What factors affect the MUF?
> All these choices are correct

G3B03 — Which frequency will have the least attenuation for long-distance skip propagation?
> Just below the MUF

G3B04 — Which of the following is a way to determine current propagation on a desired band from your station?
> Use a network of automated receiving stations on the internet to see where your transmissions are being received

G3B05 — How does the ionosphere affect radio waves with frequencies below the

MUF and above the LUF?

They are refracted back to Earth

G3B06 — What usually happens to radio waves with frequencies below the LUF?

They are attenuated before reaching the destination

G3B07 — What does LUF stand for?

The Lowest Usable Frequency for communications between two specific points

G3B08 — What does MUF stand for?

The Maximum Usable Frequency for communications between two points

G3B11 — What happens to HF propagation when the LUF exceeds the MUF?

Propagation via ordinary skywave communications is not possible over that path

Given the solar activity indices and a reasonably good model of the Earth's geomagnetic field, scientists and communications engineers have developed fairly effective software tools for predicting propagation. Amateurs make extensive use of these programs and as a General class ham operating on HF, you'll want to give them a try.

Two key terms used by prediction programs are of particular importance to hams: *maximum usable frequency (MUF) and lowest usable frequency (LUF)*. **[G3B07, G3B08]** Both the MUF and LUF depend on the specific path between two points — their location and distance apart. MUF and LUF also vary with time of day, season, the amount of solar radiation and ionospheric stability. **[G3B02]**

The MUF represents the highest frequency at which propagation exists between two points. Waves at or below the MUF will be refracted back toward the Earth. Note that MUF accounts for propagation at all points along the path between the two stations. The MUF will be different for every path from your station. It must account for variations in the ionosphere at every likely reflection as the wave hops its way from place to place. Waves above the MUF will at some point in the journey penetrate the ionosphere and be lost to space. MUF must also take into account the likely takeoff angles from your antenna system, since this affects the ability of the ionosphere to reflect your signal.

The LUF specifies the lowest frequency for which propagation exists between two points. Waves below the LUF will be completely absorbed by the ionosphere. **[G3B06]** To make contact with a distant station, you will have to use a frequency between the LUF and the MUF so the wave is bent back to Earth but isn't absorbed. **[G3B05]** If the MUF drops below the LUF, then no propagation exists between those two points via ordinary skywave. **[G3B11]**

Operating near the MUF often gives excellent results because absorption is lowest just below the MUF. **[G3B03]** Low takeoff angles also raise the MUF because the waves need less bending to complete a hop.

One way to check the actual band conditions between two points is to listen for propagation beacons. There is an international network of beacon stations maintained by the Northern California DX Foundation (**ncdxf.org**) that transmit continuously. In addition, sites like **PSKReporter. info/pskmap.html** and **WSPRNet.org** provide real time propagation information. **[G3B04]**

SOLAR DISTURBANCES

It would be wonderful if the sun just beamed steadily, pumping up the ionosphere and never causing any trouble up there. That's not the case, unfortunately. The sun is very

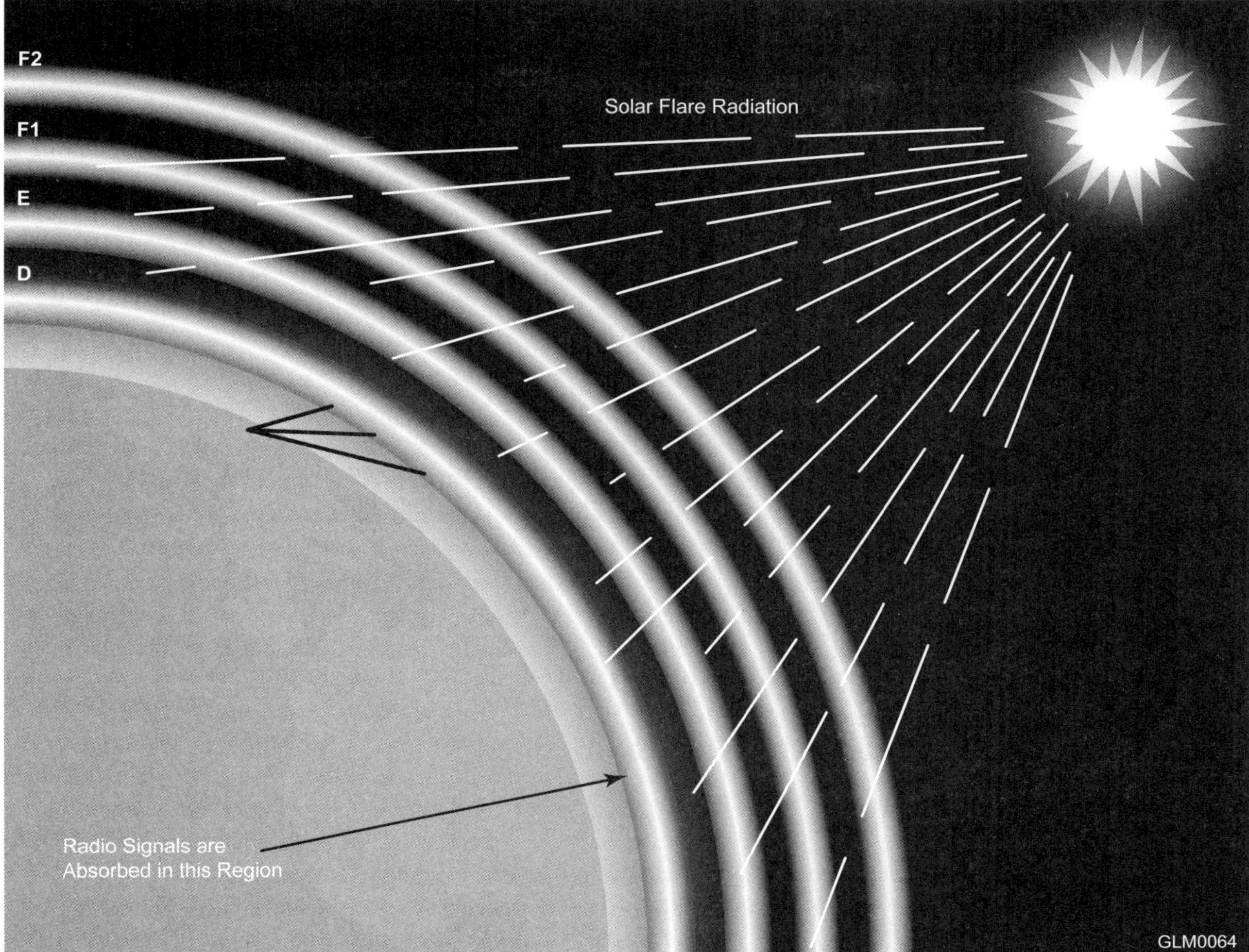

Figure 8.7 — Approximately eight minutes after a solar flare occurs on the sun, the ultraviolet and X-ray radiation released by the flare reaches the Earth. This radiation causes increased ionization and radio wave absorption in the D region.

dynamic, particularly during the years of peak activity during the sunspot cycle. There are several common events on the sun that disrupt HF propagation. Their characteristics are measured by solar observatories and included in regular bulletins and broadcasts to alert users of the HF spectrum.

- *Solar flare* — a large eruption of energy and solar material when magnetic field disruptions occur on the surface of the sun.
- *Coronal hole* — a weak area in the sun's corona (the outer layer) through which plasma (ionized gas and charged particles) escapes the sun's magnetic field and streams away into space at high velocities.
- *Coronal mass ejection (CME)* — an ejection of large amounts of material from the corona. A CME may direct the material in a relatively narrow stream or in a wide spray.

Sudden Ionospheric Disturbances

UV and X-ray radiation from a solar flare travels at the speed of light to impact the ionosphere about 8 minutes later. **[G3A03]** When the radiation hits the ionosphere, the level of ionization increases rapidly, particularly in the D region (see **Figure 8.7**). This increases absorption dramatically, causing a *sudden ionospheric disturbance* (SID) also known as a *radio blackout*. After a large flare, the HF bands can be completely devoid of sky-wave signals for a period of many seconds to hours, returning gradually to normal. The lower bands are more strongly affected so communication may still be possible on a higher band. **[G3A02]** SIDs affect only the sunlit side of the Earth, so dark-side communications may be relatively unaffected.

Geomagnetic Disturbances

The sun continually gives off a stream of charged particles called the *solar wind*. The interaction between the solar wind and the Earth's geomagnetic field creates a region of space called the *magnetosphere*. Charged particles and other material from coronal holes and coronal mass ejections travel considerably slower and take longer to reach Earth, up to 15 to 40 hours. **[G3A11]** When the charged particles arrive they can be trapped in and disturb the Earth's magnetosphere near the north and south magnetic poles. By depositing their energy into the Earth's geomagnetic field they increase ionization in the E region of the ionosphere, causing auroral displays and creating a *geomagnetic storm*. **[G3A06]**

The sudden change in the geomagnetic field disrupts the upper layers of the ionosphere, causing propagation on the higher HF bands to be affected first. Long-distance paths that traverse high latitudes, particularly those that pass near the magnetic poles, may be completely wiped out for a period of hours to days. **[G3A08, G3A14]**

Auroras are actually the glow of gases ionized by the incoming charged particles as they flow vertically down into the atmosphere, guided by the magnetic field. The resulting conductive sheets that light up the night sky also reflect radio waves above 20 MHz. In particular, auroral propagation is strongest on 6 and 2 meters, modulating the signals with a characteristic hiss or buzz. **[G3A09]**

8.3 Scatter Modes

G3C06 — What is a characteristic of HF scatter?
Signals have a fluttering sound

G3C07 — What makes HF scatter signals often sound distorted?
Energy is scattered into the skip zone through several different paths

G3C08 — Why are HF scatter signals in the skip zone usually weak?
Only a small part of the signal energy is scattered into the skip zone

G3C09 — What type of propagation allows signals to be heard in the transmitting station's skip zone?
Scatter

G3C10 — What is near vertical incidence skywave (NVIS) propagation?
Short distance MF or HF propagation at high elevation angles

As you may have experienced on VHF, radio waves often propagate by reflections from terrestrial objects and disturbances in the atmosphere. The same is true for HF radio waves on a larger scale. In particular, the ionosphere is not nearly so neatly organized into horizontal layers or regions as we imagine. There are regions that are tilted at significant angles and that reflect waves somewhat horizontally. Other regions may have significant variations in density that support localized reflections, such as the sporadic E (E-skip) propagation common on 6 meters. These are scatter modes of propagation and can be quite useful when regular sky-wave is unavailable.

SCATTER CHARACTERISTICS

If a signal's frequency is very close to the MUF, reflections from features on the Earth's surface such as the ocean or a mountain range may return some of the wave back toward the transmitting station. This is called *backscatter* and is illustrated in **Figure 8.8**. Waves can also be scattered from within the ionosphere, allowing signals to be heard from sta-

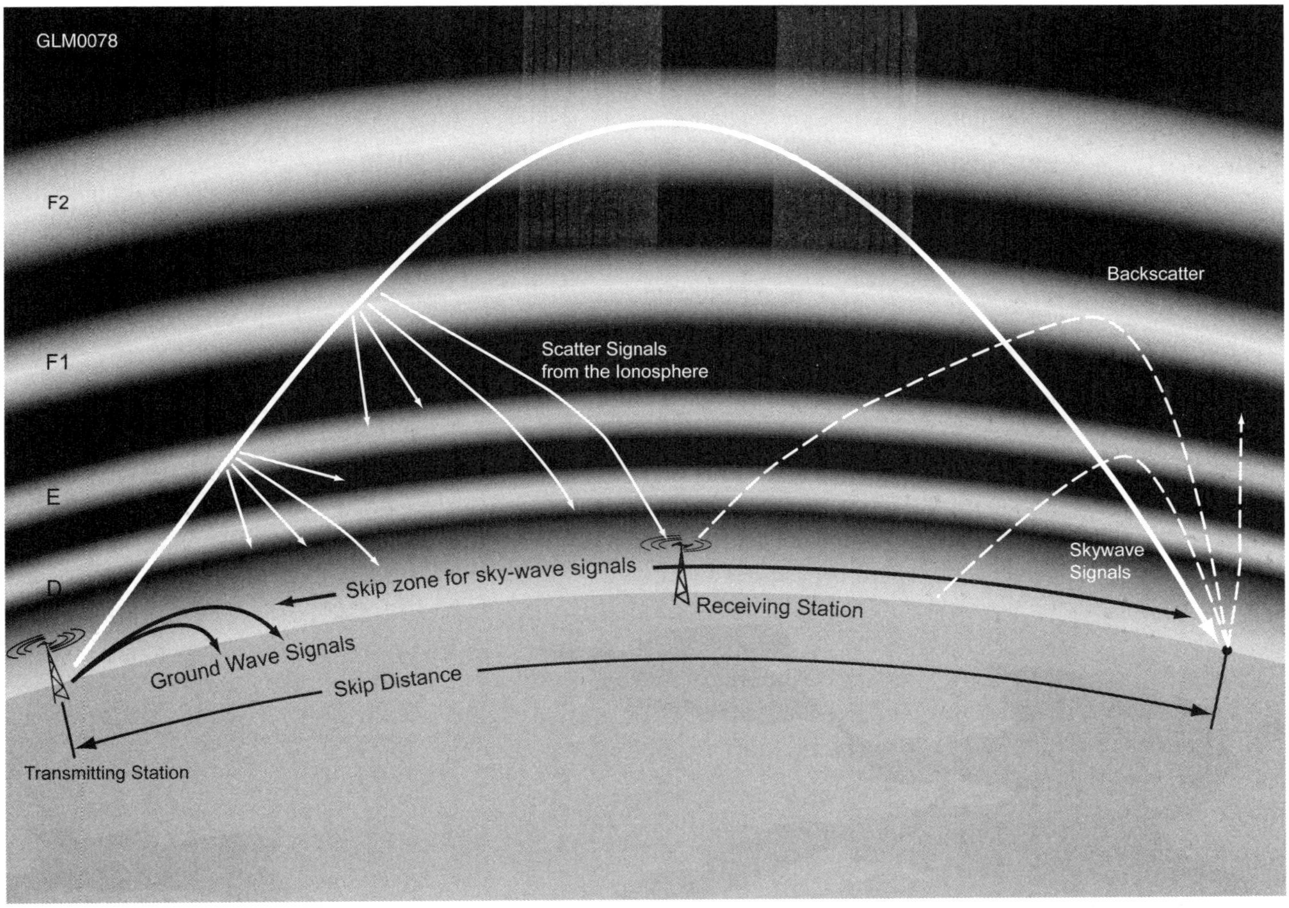

Figure 8.8 — On striking the ground after ionospheric reflection, radio waves may be reflected back toward the transmitting station. Backscatter consists of signals reflected by the ground back into the skip zone. Backscatter supports communication between stations that would otherwise be in each other's skip zone.

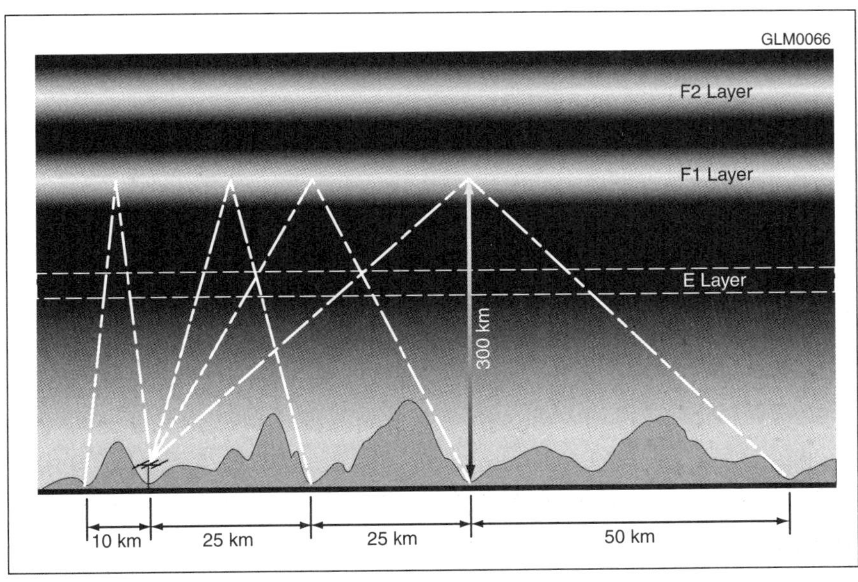

Figure 8.9 — Near vertical incidence sky-wave (NVIS) communications relies on signals below the critical frequency transmitted at high vertical angles. The signals are reflected by the ionosphere back to Earth in the region around the transmitter.

tions too distant to be heard by ground wave and on frequencies too high for short hop sky-wave propagation. Scatter and backscatter help fill in the skip zone where signals would otherwise not be heard. **[G3C09]**

Signals received via HF scatter are usually weaker than those received by normal sky-wave propagation because the reflection is not very efficient and tends to spread out the signal, delivering only a small fraction of the signal to the receiving station. Scatter signals into the skip zone often sound distorted because the reflected waves may arrive at the receiver by many different paths, resulting in multipath interference, just as on VHF and UHF. The usual effect is a fluttering or wavering characteristic. **[G3C06, G3C07, G3C08]**

NVIS

You will recall that for waves below the critical frequency, the ionosphere reflects waves arriving at any angle — even vertical. At most locations, the critical frequency is always above 5 MHz and frequently rises above the 40-meter band. Higher frequencies can be used during the day as the critical frequency rises due to solar illumination.

For a signal below the critical frequency, when it is radiated vertically the reflection scatters the signal back to Earth throughout a region of up to 200 to 300 miles centered on the transmitter. Communication using this special scatter mode is called *near vertical incidence sky-wave* (*NVIS*). **[G3C10]** To make use of NVIS as shown in **Figure 8.9**, horizontally polarized dipoles are placed low to the ground so that their radiation pattern is almost omnidirectional and concentrated at high elevation angles. (See the **Antennas and Feed Lines** chapter for more information on this subject.)

Chapter 9

Electrical and RF Safety

Radio is basically quite safe, but no activity is completely without risk. As a General class licensee, you'll be using more different types of equipment, working with larger antennas and towers, and building more complex stations. With this broader set of privileges comes an increased responsibility to be aware of potential hazards. This will help you to take the necessary steps to protect yourself and others.

9.1 Electrical Safety

With the exception of mobile and portable operating, radio equipment gets its power from the ac power grid. Since that ac line voltage from the wall doesn't care whether a powerful radio or a tiny indicator light is connected, the same safety practices apply for both low-power and high-power stations.

PREVENTING ELECTRICAL SHOCK

It's important to have a master OFF/ON switch for your station and workbench, just as in a shop full of power tools and machinery. If you are shocked, your rescuers should have been trained to remove power first so they are not also exposed to shock. The switch should be clearly labeled and somewhat away from the equipment. Don't place the OFF/ON switch in an obscure, hard-to-find or reach location. Show your family how to turn off power at the master switch and at your home's circuit-breaker box.

Don't put yourself in a position to be shocked or hard to rescue. Don't work on "live" equipment unless absolutely necessary. Avoid working alone on energized equipment. Never assume equipment is off or de-energized — check with a meter or tester first. If you are working on feed lines or antennas, be sure that a transmitter or amplifier can't be activated while you're working. Keep one hand in your pocket while probing or testing energized equipment, wear shoes with an insulated sole and remove unnecessary jewelry.

When working inside equipment, remove, insulate, or otherwise secure loose wires and cables. Remember that the residual charge on a capacitor can present hazardous voltages for a long time and use bleeder resistors to drain it off. A *grounding stick* (shown in **Figure 9.1**) should be used to positively remove charge from capacitors and be sure that all exposed conductors are at ground potential.

Shocks result from current flow through the body, and shocks that result from ac current are the most dangerous. Remember that it is not voltage that causes the shock, but current flow. **Table 9.1** (from OSHA Publication 3075, "Controlling Electrical Hazards" — **osha.gov/Publications/3075.html**) shows that even shocks from small currents can be painful. Electrical current of more than a few milliamperes can cause involuntary muscle spasms that in turn cause falls and sudden large movements. Burns can be caused by large ac or dc currents through the body or along the skin.

The most dangerous currents are those that travel through the heart, such as arm-to-arm or arm-to-foot. The current flow disrupts the heart's normal beating rhythm. Low-frequency ac current, such as 50 or 60 Hz household power, is the most dangerous because it penetrates the body easily and is of a frequency that can disrupt the heart.

After a shock, the heart may resynchronize to its usual rhythm, enter an uncoordinated state called *fibrillation*, or stop beating altogether. Depending on the body's resistance, voltages as low as 30 V can cause enough current flow to be dangerous.

Both fibrillation and lack of beating cause immediate unconsciousness from which you'll need assistance to recover. It is a good idea for you and every other adult to get CPR training from your local fire or police department or from the American Red Cross (**redcross.org**). It could come in handy not just for you, but as a lifesaver to anyone in need. A comprehensive discussion of electrical injury is available on the website **medlineplus.gov/ency/article/000053.htm**.

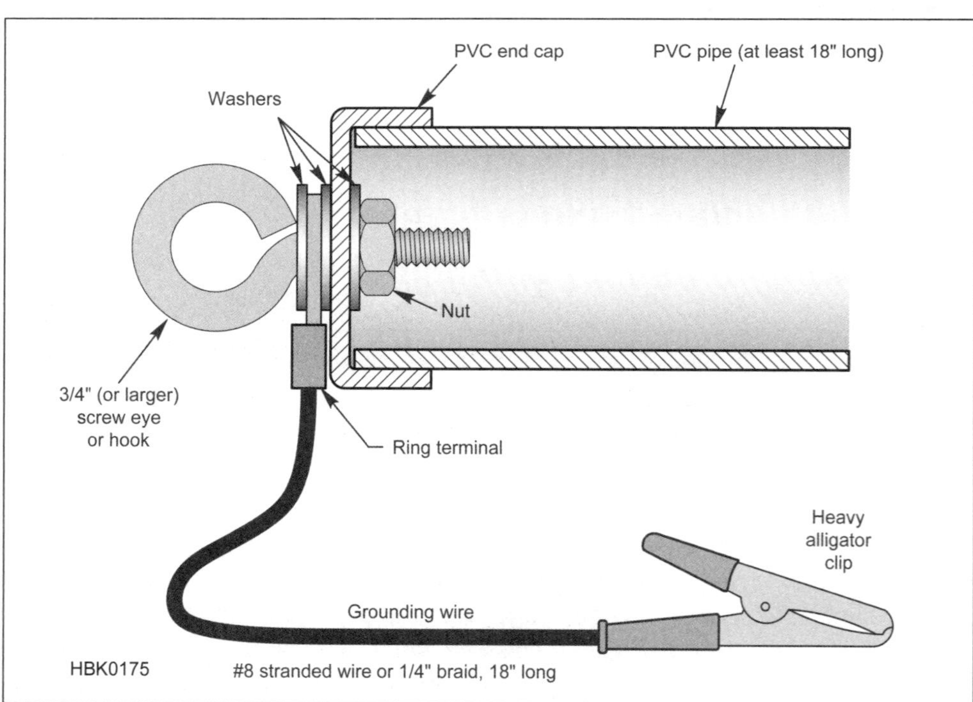

Figure 9.1 — A grounding stick is touched to all circuitry inside an enclosure to insure that no high voltage is present. The alligator clip is attached to an electrical ground and the eyebolt is put in contact with the circuitry.

Table 9.1

Effects of Electric Current Through the Body of an Average Person

Current	Effect (1 sec contact)
Below 1 mA	Generally not perceptible.
1 mA	Faint tingle
5 mA	Slight shock felt; not painful but disturbing. Average individual can let go. Strong involuntary reactions can lead to other injuries.
6 – 25 milliamperes (women)	Painful shock, loss of muscular control*
9 – 30 milliamperes (men)	The freezing current or "let-go" range.* Individual cannot let go, but can be thrown away from the circuit if the extensor muscles are stimulated.
50 – 150 milliamperes	Extreme pain, respiratory arrest, severe muscular contractions. Death is possible.
1,000 – 4,300 milliamperes	Rhythmic pumping action of the heart ceases. Muscular contraction and nerve damage occur; death likely.
10,000 milliamperes	Cardiac arrest, severe burns; death probable

*If the extensor muscles are excited by the shock, the person may be thrown away from the power source.

Source: W.B. Kouwenhoven, "Human Safety and Electric Shock," Electrical Safety Practices, Monograph, 112, Instrument Society of America, p. 93. November 1968.

SOLDERING SAFETY

G0B10 — Which of the following is a danger from lead-tin solder?

Lead can contaminate food if hands are not washed carefully after handling the solder

Soldering is part of the electronic experience and has been for more than 100 years. Solder is primarily lead-based, with tin added to lower the melting point. Lead is a known toxin and so it is prudent to avoid unnecessary exposure. Solder in a well-ventilated area to avoid breathing the small amounts of lead vapor that result from melting the solder. The rosin flux smoke is also likely not good for you in high doses. After you are finished soldering, wash your hands to remove any solder or flux residue. **[G0B10]**

Soldering and Lead

In 2006, a new set of environmental regulations called "Reduction of Hazardous Substances" or RoHS went into effect. The goal of those regulations is to reduce the amount of toxic materials used in electronics manufacturing, reducing them when the equipment is discarded or recycled, as well. Part of the regulations require that solder become lead-free.

Most amateurs will never be exposed by soldering to enough lead to pose a health hazard, but as industry changes, so will amateur practices. Lead-based solder will continue to be available for some time, but newer equipment will likely contain the new solders. Consult the owner's manual or manufacturer of your equipment to find out what type of solder was used. Mixing types of solder may lead to unreliable solder joints and erratic operation.

WIRING PRACTICES

G0B01 — Which wire or wires in a four-conductor 240 VAC circuit should be attached to fuses or circuit breakers?
Only the hot wires

G0B02 — According to the National Electrical Code, what is the minimum wire size that may be used for wiring with a 20-ampere circuit breaker?
AWG number 12

G0B03 — Which size of fuse or circuit breaker would be appropriate to use with a circuit that uses AWG number 14 wiring?
15 amperes

G0B05 — Which of the following conditions will cause a ground fault circuit interrupter (GFCI) to disconnect AC power?
Current flowing from one or more of the hot wires directly to ground

G0B06 — Which of the following is covered by the National Electrical Code?
Electrical safety of the station

G0B12 — What is the purpose of a power supply interlock?
To ensure that dangerous voltages are removed if the cabinet is opened

When you are performing electrical maintenance in your home or in the station, how can you tell what practices are safe? The *National Electrical Code Handbook* contains detailed descriptions of how to handle ac wiring in your home and station in a safe manner. [G0B06] (You may be able to get a copy at the library.)

Local building codes should also be followed so that your home is properly wired to meet any special local conditions. This may be important for insurance purposes, as well. If you are in doubt about your ability to do the work properly, hire a licensed professional electrician!

When wiring or repairing an ac power cord plug, be sure to follow the standard wire color conventions as shown in **Figure 9.2** and **Figure 9.3**:

• Hot (the wire or wires carrying voltage) is black or red insulation, connect to the brass terminal or screw

• Neutral is white insulation, connect to the silver terminal or screw

• Ground is green insulation or bare wire, connect to the green or bare copper terminal or screw

Whether you are installing a new power circuit in your home or selecting a power cord, use cable and wire sufficiently rated for the expected current load as shown in

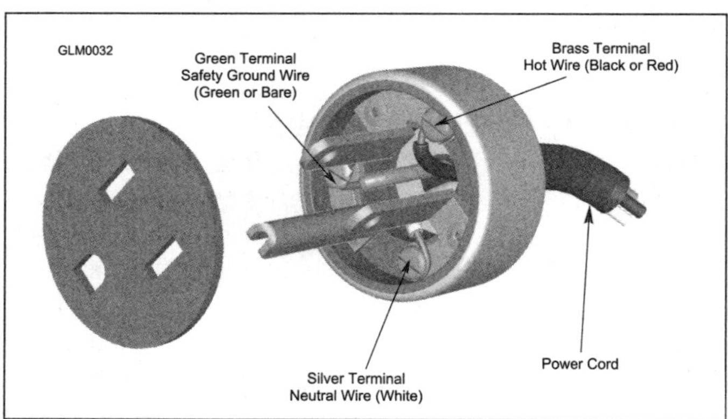

Figure 9.2 — The correct wiring of a 120-V ac line cord to a new plug: Connect the black or red wire (hot) to the brass terminal, the white wire (neutral) to the silver terminal, and the green or bare wire (ground) to the green terminal.

Figure 9.3 — Standard wiring conventions for 120-V and 240-V ac plugs and receptacles. It is critically important to follow the correct wiring techniques for ac power wiring. The white wire is neutral, the green wire is ground, and the black or red wire is the hot lead. Note that 240 V circuits have two hot wires and a ground.

Table 9.2. The rating of wire to carry current is called its *ampacity*. For house ac wiring, the two most common sizes are #12 AWG for 20 A circuits and #14 AWG for 15 A circuits. **[G0B02, G0B03]** When you are finished with the wiring job, verify that you have the connections correct by using an ac circuit tester.

Be sure there is a fuse or circuit breaker in the hot conductor for 120 V circuits or both

Protective Components

Protective components are used to prevent equipment damage or safety hazards such as fire or electrical shock caused by equipment malfunction. Those that are aimed at preventing shock hazards act when they detect current or voltage where it shouldn't be or indications that current is going where it's not supposed to go. Power control devices such as fuses and circuit breakers prevent equipment damage and fire by interrupting potentially large currents and disconnecting substantial voltages.

Fuses and Circuit Breakers

Fuses interrupt excessive current flow by melting a short length of metal. When the metal melts or "blows," the current path is broken. The rating of a fuse is the maximum current it can carry without blowing. Fuses also have a voltage rating showing how much voltage they will withstand. Do not substitute a fuse rated at 12 V for one with a 120/240 V rating or the result may be that the fuse arcs over instead of removing voltage from the circuit. "Slow-blow" fuses can withstand temporary overloads, but will blow if the overload is sustained.

Circuit breakers act like fuses and "trip" when current overloads occur, opening the circuit and interrupting current flow. Unlike fuses, circuit breakers can be reset once the current overload is removed. If a circuit breaker repeatedly trips, it is an indication that too much power is being drawn on that circuit. Either move some of the loads to a different circuit or increase the circuit's current capacity by increasing the wire size and circuit breaker rating.

Use properly sized fuses and circuit breakers. Equipment manufacturers will specify the required fuse rating. Along with minimum wire size, building codes specify the size of the circuit breakers required at the power distribution panel. Never replace a fuse or circuit breaker with one of a larger current rating — fix the problem!

When installing fuses or circuit breakers in an ac power wiring circuit, be sure to place them only in the correct lines. Power is generally delivered to your home as a two-wire, 240 V circuit as shown in **Figure 9.4**. There is 120 V between each of the hot wires and the neutral wire. Most of your household circuits are connected between one of the hot wires and the neutral wire. Large household appliances and amplifiers should be connected between the two hot wires supplying 240 V because the higher voltage reduces the required amount of current for the same power consumption. 240-V household appliances may use two hot wires and a ground (three wire) or a separate neutral and ground (four-wire).

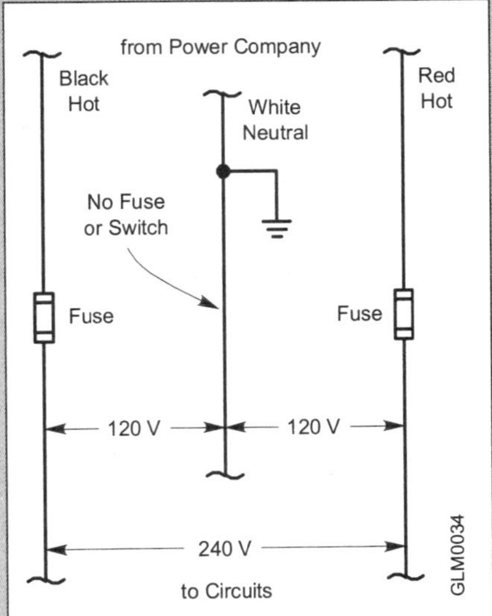

Figure 9.4 — Fuses and circuit breakers should be placed in the hot wire or wires of ac power wiring. Never install a fuse or circuit breaker in the neutral or ground wire of ac wiring. If a neutral or ground wire is disconnected, ac voltage is not removed from the equipment and may still present a shock or fire hazard.

Table 9.2

Current Carrying Capacity of Some Common Wire Sizes

Copper Wire Size (AWG)	Allowable Ampacity (A)	Max Fuse or Circuit Breaker (A)
6	55	50
8	40	40
10	30	30
12	25 (20)*	20
14	20 (15)*	15

*The National Electrical Code limits the fuse or circuit breaker size (and as such, the maximum allowable circuit load) to 15 A for AWG #14 copper wire and to 20 A for AWG #12 copper wire conductors.

Figure 9.5 — Ground fault circuit interrupter (GFCI) circuit breakers are used in ac power circuits to prevent shock hazards. They are usually found in bathrooms, kitchens and other areas of the home with running water.

hot conductors of a 240 V circuit using three or four wires. **[G0B01]** Never install a fuse or circuit breaker in the neutral or ground circuit. Opening the neutral or ground does not remove voltage from the equipment and an electrical hazard may still be present.

Ground fault circuit interrupter (GFCI) circuit breakers (**Figure 9.5**) are used in ac power circuits to prevent shock hazards. A GFCI circuit breaker will trip if an imbalance is sensed in the currents carried by the hot and neutral conductors. Current imbalances indicate the presence of an electrical shock hazard because the unbalanced current must be flowing through an unintended path, such as through a person from the hot wire to ground! GFCI breakers can be sensitive to just a few milliamperes (mA) of imbalance between hot and neutral, well below the threshold for electrical injury. **[G0B05]**

A *safety interlock* is a switch that prevents dangerous voltages or intense RF from being present when a cabinet or enclosure is opened. **[G0B12]** One type of interlock physically disconnects high voltage (HV) or RF when activated. A second type shorts or grounds a HV circuit when activated, possibly blowing a circuit breaker or fuse in a power supply. Never bypass an interlock during testing unless specifically instructed to do so and then only in the way directed by the instructions. Be sure to enable the interlock before returning the equipment to service.

Don't run antenna feed lines over power lines or service drops from a transformer to the house. Even though they are "just" 240 V ac lines, they pack plenty of punch! If you are shooting lines through or over trees to support a wire antenna, be sure the projected flight path is completely safe and clear of people and power lines. Power lines can be hidden in or just beyond trees.

GENERATOR SAFETY

G0B09 — Which of the following is true of an emergency generator installation?

The generator should be operated in a well-ventilated area

Emergency and portable operation often makes use of an electrical generator driven by a gasoline, diesel, or propane engine. With generators easier and more convenient to use than ever, it's easy to overlook basic safety procedures.

Fueling and ventilation problems cause more injuries associated with generators than from any other cause. A generator should never be operated in an enclosed space or basement, or even a garage, where people are present or nearby. Install it outdoors, away from living areas, as shown in **Figure 9.6**. Carbon monoxide (CO) in the exhaust can quickly

Figure 9.6 — Install your generator in a well ventilated area, away from living areas.

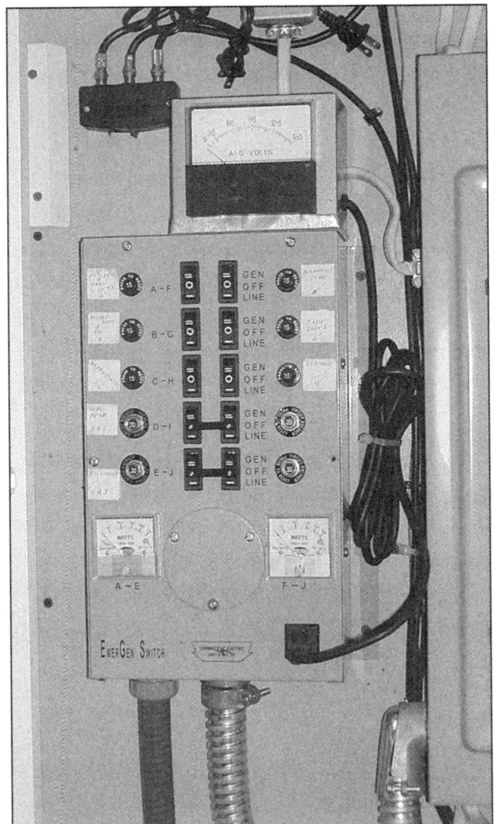

Figure 9.7 — A transfer switch connects your household circuits to the ac line or to a generator and isolates the generator from the line. This device eliminates the dangerous practice of "back-feeding" generator power into the ac line or the possibility of damaging the generator if ac power is restored.

build up to toxic levels. (For more information about CO safety, visit **epa.gov/indoor-air-quality-iaq/ carbon-monoxides-impact-indoor- air-quality**.) Even outside, exhaust fumes can be drawn into air intakes or windows or build up in poorly ventilated areas. If you plan on using a generator regularly, install CO detector alarms in living and working areas. **[G0B09]**

Flammable liquid fuels pose their own hazards. Generators should always be shut off when refueling to avoid igniting fumes or splashed liquid from the spark plug. Even if the generator engine is shut off, the engine block or exhaust may remain hot enough to pose an ignition hazard. Refueling should be done by a team of two, with one person equipped with a fire extinguisher. Store fuel well away from the generator, particularly from its hot exhaust, in approved containers. A fire extinguisher should be kept near the generator and separated from the fuel.

The metal frames of the generator housing and the engine act as an electrical ground, but they are not physically connected to the Earth. The best way to provide a generator safety ground is to use a ground rod near the generator and connected to the frame with heavy gauge wire. Most generators provide a special ground terminal just for this purpose.

If the generator is to be used at your home, connecting it to your household circuits requires special precautions. If you intend to connect the generator output directly to your home's wiring system, you must have the ability to disconnect your power service from the utility lines. This is usually accomplished by a pair of large circuit breakers labeled "Main." Opening these breakers completely disconnects your power distribution panel from the external electrical service. With these breakers open, you can then safely use a generator to power your home.

By not opening the main breakers, power supplied to your home's system is also connected back to the utility grid. The power system transformer that normally supplies your home works just as well in reverse — the voltage from your generator will be stepped up to lethal levels and placed on the utility lines. Known as *back-feeding*, this poses a serious hazard to electrical workers working on the system and to neighbors whose homes are likely still connected to the power system. If your generator is connected and running when power is restored, the resulting conflict between the utility and generator power is likely to cause damage to your generator.

The best way to connect a generator to your home is by using a *transfer switch* that transfers the power source for your distribution panel from the utility lines to a special connector for your generator. Once the transfer switch is thrown, the power from your generator is connected only to your home's wiring and nothing else. The type of transfer switch in **Figure 9.7** switches selected household circuits between the ac line and the generator. A transfer switch should be installed by a licensed professional electrician.

LIGHTNING

G4C07 — Why should soldered joints not be used in lightning protection ground connections?

A soldered joint will likely be destroyed by the heat of a lightning strike

G0B04 — Where should the station's lightning protection ground system be located?

Outside the building

G0B11 — Which of the following is required for lightning protection ground rods?

They must be bonded together with all other grounds

G0B13 — Where should lightning arrestors be located?

Where the feed lines enter the building

The goal of lightning protection is to provide fire prevention for your home and to reduce or prevent electrical damage to your equipment. When installing your station, a metal entry panel where signal and control cables enter the house is a good place to provide a lightning ground (see **Figure 9.8**). The panel should be grounded to a nearby ground rod with a heavy, short metal strap. **[G0B04]** Lightning arrestors should be installed at the entry panel. **[G0B13]** The ground rod must then be bonded to the ac service entry ground rod outside the building with a heavy conductor. Towers should be grounded with separate 8-foot ground rods for each tower leg, with the ground rods bonded to the tower and each other.

Grounding wires and straps should be as short and direct as possible. All towers, masts and antenna mounts should be grounded. Lightning grounds should be bonded to other safety grounds. **[G0B11]** Do not use solder to make the connections since solder joints would likely melt and be destroyed if hit with a lightning-sized current. Use mechanical clamps, brazing, or welding to be sure the ground connection is heavy enough. **[G4C07]**

Finally, you should also determine whether your renter's or homeowner's insurance covers lightning damage. Be sure to check for coverage of "external structures" and other types of property improvements that may be recognized by the insurance underwriters.

Figure 9.8 — A metal entrance panel serves as a common grounding point for all cables and feed lines entering your home. The ground rod to which the panel is attached must also be connected to the ac service entry ground rod with a heavy bonding wire. This helps to prevent damage from lightning.

9.2 RF Exposure

G0A01 — What is one way that RF energy can affect human body tissue?

It heats body tissue

G0A02 — Which of the following is used to determine RF exposure from a transmitted signal?

All these choices are correct

G0A03 — How can you determine that your station complies with FCC RF exposure regulations?

All these choices are correct

G0A04 — What does "time averaging" mean when evaluating RF radiation exposure?

The total RF exposure averaged over a certain period

G0A05 — What must you do if an evaluation of your station shows that the RF energy radiated by your station exceeds permissible limits for possible human absorption?

Take action to prevent human exposure to the excessive RF fields

G0A06 — What must you do if your station fails to meet the FCC RF exposure exemption criteria?

Perform an RF Exposure Evaluation in accordance with FCC OET Bulletin 65

G0A07 — What is the effect of modulation duty cycle on RF exposure?

A lower duty cycle permits greater power levels to be transmitted

G0A08 — Which of the following steps must an amateur operator take to ensure compliance with RF safety regulations?

Perform a routine RF exposure evaluation and prevent access to any identified high exposure areas

G0A09 — What type of instrument can be used to accurately measure an RF field strength?

A calibrated field strength meter with a calibrated antenna

G0A10 — What is one thing that can be done if evaluation shows that a neighbor might receive more than the allowable limit of RF exposure from the main lobe of a directional antenna?

Take precautions to ensure that the antenna cannot be pointed in their direction when they are present

G0A11 — What precaution should be taken if you install an indoor transmitting antenna?

Make sure that MPE limits are not exceeded in occupied areas

G0A12 — What stations are subject to the FCC rules on RF exposure?

All stations with a time-averaged transmission of more than one milliwatt

Exposure to RF at low levels is not hazardous. At high power levels, for some frequencies, the amount of energy that the body absorbs can be a problem. The *maximum permissible exposure (MPE)* is the maximum intensity of RF radiation to which a human being may be exposed. There are a number of factors to consider when estimating human exposure: minimum distance of humans to any part of the antenna, transmitted power, feed line loss, antenna gain, frequency, exposure time, and duty cycle. **[G0A02]** The two primary factors that determine how much RF energy the body will absorb are power density and frequency. This section discusses how to take into account the various factors and arrive at a reasonable estimate of what RF exposure results from your transmissions and whether any safety precautions are required. All stations with a time-averaged transmission of more than one milliwatt are subject to the FCC's RF exposure rules. **[G0A12]** If you find that your station exceeds the exemption criteria listed below, you will need to evaluate it according to the FCC OET Bulletin 65. **[G0A06]**

POWER DENSITY

Heating from exposure to RF signals is caused when tissue absorbs RF energy. **[G0A01]** The intensity of the RF energy is called *power density* and it is measured in mW/cm^2 (milliwatts per square centimeter), which is power per unit of area. RF field strength is also measured in V/m and A/m, and at frequencies below 30 MHz all of these should be determined.

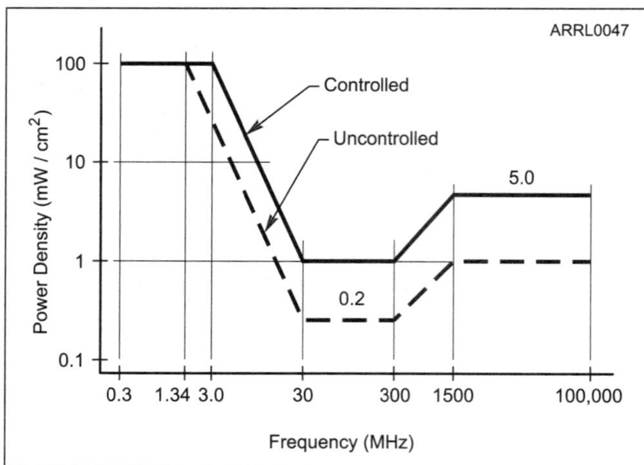

Figure 9.9 — Maximum Permissible Exposure (MPE) limits vary with frequency because the body responds differently to energy at different frequencies. The occupational (controlled) and general public (uncontrolled) limits refer to the characteristics of the people being exposed to the RF energy. The controlled limits apply to trained occupational exposure and amateurs. The uncontrolled limits apply to the general public.

Power density is highest near antennas and in the directions in which antennas have the most gain. Increasing transmitter power increases power density around the antenna. Increasing distance from an antenna generally lowers power density.

ABSORPTION AND LIMITS

The rate at which energy is absorbed from the field to which the body is exposed is called the *specific absorption rate* (SAR). SAR is the best indicator of RF exposure but is unfortunately very difficult to determine. The SAR varies with frequency, power density, and the duty cycle of transmission. Injury can be caused when the combination of frequency and power result in excessive SAR that can lead to unacceptable tissue temperature rise.

SAR depends on the frequency and the size of the body or body part affected and is highest when the body and body parts are resonant. The limbs (arms and legs) and torso experience the highest

Table 9.3A

(From §1.1310) Limits for Maximum Permissible Exposure (MPE)
Limits for Occupational/Controlled Exposure

Frequency Range (MHz)	Electric Field Strength (V/m)	Magnetic Field Strength (A/m)	Power Density (mW/cm2)	Averaging Time (minutes)
0.3-3.0	614	1.63	(100)*	6
3.0-30	1842/f	4.89/f	(900/f2)*	6
30-300	61.4	0.163	1.0	6
300-1500	—	—	f/300	6
1500-100,000	—	—	5	6

f = frequency in MHz
* = Plane-wave equivalent power density (see Notes 1 and 2 in Table 9.3B).

Table 9.3B

Limits for General Population/Uncontrolled Exposure

Frequency Range (MHz)	Electric Field Strength (V/m)	Magnetic Field Strength (A/m)	Power Density (mW/cm²)	Averaging Time (minutes)
0.3-1.34	614	1.63	(100)*	30
1.34-30	824/f	2.19/f	(180/f2)*	30
30-300	27.5	0.073	0.2	30
300-1500	—	—	f/1500	30
1500-100,000	—	—	1.0	30

f = frequency in MHz
* = Plane-wave equivalent power density (see Notes 1 and 2).

Note 1: This means the equivalent far-field strength that would have the E or H-field component calculated or measured. It does not apply well in the near field of an antenna. The equivalent far-field power density can be found in the near or far field regions from the relationships:

$P_d = |E_{total}|^2 / 3770$ mW/cm² or from $P_d = |H_{total}|^2 \times 37.7$ mW/cm².
Note 2: $|E_{total}|^2 = |E_x|^2 + |E_y|^2 + |E_z|^2$, and $|H_{total}|^2 = |H_x|^2 + |H_y|^2 + |H_z|^2$

SAR for RF fields in the VHF spectrum from 30 to 300 MHz. The head is more absorptive at UHF frequencies from 300 MHz to 3 GHz. The frequencies with highest whole-body SAR are between 30 and 1500 MHz. At frequencies above and below the ranges of highest absorption, the body as a whole responds less and less to the RF energy, just like an antenna responds poorly to signals away from its resonant frequency.

Safe exposure levels based on demonstrated hazards have been adopted by the FCC in the form of maximum permissible exposure (MPE) values (that may be used instead of whole-body SAR limits) that vary with frequency as shown in **Figure 9.9** and **Tables 9.3A** and **9.3B**. These are much easier to measure or calculate and they take into account the variations in the body's absorption of RF energy at different frequencies.

AVERAGING AND DUTY CYCLE

Exposure to RF energy is averaged over fixed time intervals. Time-averaging evaluates the total RF exposure over a fixed time interval. **[G0A04]**

Exposure Population

The MPE levels specified by the FCC varies according to the characteristics of the exposed populations. The two populations are called "occupational" and "general population."

The occupational group consists of people who are aware of their exposure and have the appropriate training to control it. For this population, a less stringent MPE applies. Licensed radio amateurs and the members of their households are considered by the FCC to be part of the occupational group. For this population, a less stringent MPE applies. Amateurs receive their training by preparing for their license exams. They are responsible for training the members of their households about RF exposure. The averaging time for the occupational population is 6 minutes.

The general public consists of everyone else. They are assumed to have no awareness of their exposure and no training on controlling their exposure. The MPEs for this group are more restrictive and amateurs are expected to make allowances for anyone who wanders by their stations or lives nearby. The averaging period for the general public is 30 minutes.

Duty Cycle

Duty cycle is the ratio of the time the transmitter is on to the total time during the exposure. Duty cycle has a maximum of 100%. (*Duty factor* is the same as duty cycle expressed as a fraction, instead of percent, such as 0.25 instead of 25%.) The less time the transmitter is on), the lower the average exposure, permitting greater short-term exposure levels for a given average exposure. **[G0A07]** This is the *operational duty cycle*. For most amateur operating, listening and transmitting time are about the same, so operational duty cycle is rarely higher than 50%.

Along with operational duty cycle, the different modes themselves have different *emission duty cycles* as shown in **Table 9.4**. For example, a normal SSB signal without

---

Table 9.4

Emission Duty Cycle of Modes Commonly Used by Amateurs

Mode	Duty Cycle	Notes
Conversational SSB	20%	1
Conversational SSB	40%	2
SSB AFSK data	100%	
SSB SSTV	100%	
Voice AM, 50% modulation	50%	3
Voice AM, 100% modulation	25%	
Voice AM, no modulation	100%	
Voice FM	100%	
Digital FM	100%	
ATV, video portion, image	60%	
ATV, video portion, black screen	80%	
Conversational CW	40%	
Carrier	100%	4

Notes
1) Includes voice characteristics and syllabic duty cycle. No speech processing.
2) Includes voice characteristics and syllabic duty cycle. Heavy speech processing.
3) Full-carrier, double-sideband modulation, referenced to PEP. Typical for voice speech. Can range from 25% to 100% depending on modulation.
4) A full carrier is commonly used for tune-up purposes.

	Frequency (MHz)	Maximum ERP (Watts)
VLF	0.3 – 1.34	$1920 \times R^2$
HF	1.34 – 30	$3450 \times R^2 / f^2$
VHF	30 – 300	$3.83 \times R^2$
UHF	300 – 1500	$0.0128 \times R^2 \times f$
MW	1500 – 100,000	$19.2 \times R^2$

Note: R is distance in meters and f is frequency in MHz.
Example Calculations:

On 14.1 MHz at 10 meters from the antenna, the maximum exempt ERP is $3450 \times 10^2 / 14.1^2 = 1735$ W.

On 22.2 MHz at 10 meters from the antenna, the maximum exempt ERP is $3450 \times 10^2 / 22.2^2 = 433$ W.

On 50.1 MHz at 5 meters from the antenna, the maximum exempt ERP is $3.83 \times 5^2 = 96$ W.

On 146 MHz at 0.5 meters from the antenna, the maximum exempt ERP is $3.83 \times 0.5^2 = 0.96$ W.

Table 9.5B
Minimum Exemption Distances ($\lambda/2\pi$)

Band (MHz)	Distance	Band (MHz)	Distance
1.8	87.0 ft	24.9	6.3 ft
3.6	43.5 ft	28.2	5.6 ft
3.9	40.2 ft	50.1	3.1 ft
7.1	22.1 ft	146	1.1 ft
10.1	15.5 ft	223	8.4 in
14.1	11.1 ft	440	4.3 in
18.1	8.7 ft	902	2.1 in
21.2	7.4 ft	1296	1.5 in

speech processing to raise average power is considered to have an emission duty cycle of 20%. In contrast, FM is a constant-power mode so its emission duty cycle is 100%. Transmitted power multiplied by the emission duty cycle multiplied by the operating duty cycle gives the average power output.

Example 1: A station is using SSB without speech processing, transmitting and listening for equal amounts of time and with transmitted power of 150 W. The average power output = $150 \times 20\% \times 50\% = 15$ W.

Example 2: A station is sending a series of messages using SSB AFSK to transmit a digital signal at 100 W transmitted power, listening only ¼ of the time. The average power output = $100 \times 75\% \times 100\% = 75$ W.

Antenna System

You must also take into account the of gain provided by your antenna and any significant loss from the feed line. High gain antennas increase a signal's radiated power density considerably in the direction that gain is focused. For example, let's modify the two examples above by using an antenna with 3.8 dBd of gain. In Example 1, the effective radiated power (ERP) is increased to 600 W by the antenna, increasing average power to 60 W ERP. In Example 2, the same antenna would increase the average ERP to 300 W, larger than the transmitter's average power output.

ESTIMATING EXPOSURE AND STATION EVALUATION

All fixed amateur stations must evaluate their capability to cause RF exposure, no matter whether they use high or low power. **[G0A08] Table 9.5A** lists effective radiated power (ERP — relative to a half-wave dipole) threshold formulas based on frequency and the separation distance between any person and any part of the antenna. If your station doesn't exceed the ERP threshold, then it qualifies for an evaluation exemption.

If you need to evaluate your station, you can perform the evaluation by actually measuring the RF field strength with calibrated field strength meters and calibrated antennas.

Multitransmitter Environments

In a multitransmitter environment, such as at a commercial repeater site, each transmitter operator may be jointly responsible (with all other site operators) for ensuring that the total RF exposure from the site does not exceed the MPE limits. Any transmitter (including the antenna) that produces more than 5% of the total permissible exposure limit for transmissions at that frequency must be included in the site evaluation. (This is 5% of the permitted power density or 5% of the square of the E or H-field MPE limit. It is *not* 5% of the total exposure, which sometimes can be unknown.) The situation described by this question is common for amateur repeater installations, which often share a transmitting site.

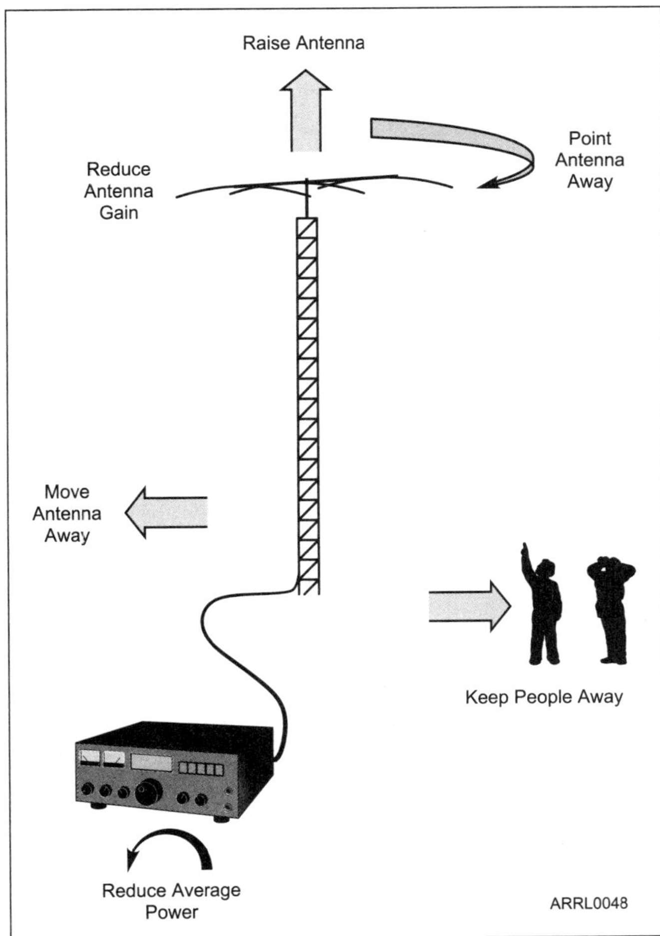

Figure 9.10 — There are many ways to reduce RF exposure to nearby people. Whatever lowers the power density in areas where people are present will work. Raising the antenna will even benefit your signal strength to other stations as it lowers power density on the ground!

[G0A09] You can also use computer modeling or calculations based on FCC OET Bulletin 65 to determine the exposure levels. However, it's easiest for most hams to use ARRL's online calculator, at **arrl.org/rf-exposure-calculator**. **[G0A03]** The calculator cannot be used for devices operated within 20 cm of anyone. SAR limits would then apply.

If you choose to use the ARRL calculators, you will need to know:

• Power at the antenna, including adjustments for duty cycle and feed line loss

• Antenna type (or gain) and height above ground

• Operating frequency in MHz and mode

The current FCC rules allow for "exemptions" from performing more detailed exposure evaluations. However, there is no exemption from complying with the FCC exposure regulations! **Table 9.5B** gives the minimum distances from the antenna for which the FCC exemptions can be used for most amateur bands. To determine if you are exempt from further, more detailed, evaluation, you can use the expressions in Table 9.5A for your frequency range of interest to calculate the threshold ERP that will ensure compliance with the exposure rules. The calculation result tells you the maximum power that can be emitted from the antenna (ERP) in order to maintain the exemption.

If you make changes to your station, such as changing to a higher power transmitter, increasing antenna gain or changing antenna height, or you find that people are able to be closer to your antenna than you originally thought, you must re-evaluate the RF exposure from your station. If you reduce output power without making any other changes to a station already in compliance, you need not re-evaluate RF exposure.

EXPOSURE SAFETY MEASURES

The measures you can take if your evaluation results exceed MPE limits are summarized in **Figure 9.10**. These are all "good practice" suggestions and can save time and expense if they are followed before doing your evaluation. All of them might satisfy the basic requirement to prevent human exposure to the excessive RF field, depending on your particular station setup. **[G0A05]**

• Locate or move antennas away from where people can be exposed to excessive RF fields. Raise the antenna or place it away from where people will be. Keep the ends (high voltage) and center (high current) of antennas away from where people could come in contact with them. Locate the antenna away from property lines and place a fence around the base of ground-mounted vertical antennas or any location that you determine to have exposure levels that exceed the MPE limits regardless of the antenna type.

• Don't point directive antennas where people are likely to be. Use gain antennas to direct the RF energy away from people. **[G0A10]** Remember that high-gain antennas

If there is a word guaranteed to cause apprehension, it is "radiation." Amateur radio uses the word in a much broader sense — radiation pattern, feed line radiation, antennas radiate — and that can be confusing to the layman. It is true that radio frequency energy is a form of radiation, but it is far different from the radiation used for cancer treatment or emitted by radioactive materials.

Radiation from antennas is not the same as ionizing radiation from radioactivity. Radio frequencies are far too low for a photon of radio energy to cause an electron to leave the atom (ionize) as was discussed in the earlier section on ionospheric propagation. That is the difference between *ionizing* and *non-ionizing radiation* of which radio waves are the latter type.

Before radio waves can be considered ionizing, their frequency would have to be increased far beyond microwaves, through visible light and on to the upper reaches of the ultraviolet and X-ray spectrum. The radiation from radioactivity is atomic particles such as the nucleus of a helium atom (alpha radiation), an electron (beta radiation), neutrons, or gamma-ray photons with frequencies even higher than X-rays. These are billions of times more energetic than the radio waves used by amateurs.

Biologic (athermal) effects such as genetic damage have never been observed at amateur frequencies and power levels. That requires the energy of ionizing radiation. The only demonstrated hazard from exposure to RF energy is heating (thermal effects) and that occurs only in very strong fields. RF "burns" are caused by touching conducting surfaces that have a high RF voltage present and are a very localized instance of heating that carries no more risk than thermal burns from hot objects.

have a narrower beam, but exposure in the beam will be more intense. Take special care with high-gain VHF/UHF/microwave antennas (such as long Yagis and dish antennas) and transmitters — don't transmit when you or other people are close to the antenna.

• If you have to use stealth or attic or other indoor antennas, make sure MPE limits are not exceeded in your home's living quarters. **[G0A11]**

• On VHF and UHF, place mobile antennas on the roof or trunk of the car to maximize shielding of the passengers.

• If using an HF mobile antenna that might be bumper mounted, be observant that individuals are not close to the antenna when operating from a fixed location such as at a park.

• From the transmitter's perspective, use a dummy load or dummy antenna when testing a transmitter. You can also reduce the power and duty cycle of your transmissions. This is often quite effective and has a minimal effect on your signal.

9.3 Outdoor Safety

G0B07 — Which of these choices should be observed when climbing a tower using a safety harness?

Confirm that the harness is rated for the weight of the climber and that it is within its allowable service life

G0B08 — What should be done before climbing a tower that supports electrically powered devices?

Make sure all circuits that supply power to the tower are locked out and tagged

Focusing on electrical safety associated with wiring and equipment is certainly justified, but there are many components of an amateur radio station outside the station, as well. Outdoor safety involves mostly mechanical concerns that can be just as important as electrical safety indoors. A complete treatment of antenna and antenna support safety is available in *The ARRL Antenna Book*.

INSTALLING ANTENNAS

The most important rule for installing antennas is violated every year, usually with tragic results: *Place all antennas and feed lines well clear of power lines!* Poles and transmission lines like those in **Figure 9.11** are a common sight and must be given wide clearance. Safety rules dictate that no part of your antenna system should be closer than 10 feet from power lines and a good rule of thumb is to separate all parts of the antenna and support from the power lines by at least 150% of total height of tower or mast plus antenna. For example, if the combination of antenna and support mast is 40 feet tall, they should be 60 feet from the power lines. This effectively prevents an antenna from toppling over or blowing into power lines. Similarly, should a power line come down, it will be less likely to contact your antenna.

GOOD MAINTENANCE PRACTICES

Whether you're working in a tree or on your roof or a tower, following basic safety rules will help get the job done properly without risking life and limb. Ignore that little voice saying, "Oh, I can just run up there in five minutes and do the job — why go to all the bother?"

First, both the climbers and any helpers should wear appropriate protective gear at all times. The climber must have a proper safety harness such as the one shown in **Figure 9.12**. Other needed gear includes a hard hat, gloves, sun block, and even goggles. Wear boots or work shoes to protect your feet and prevent sore arches from standing on tower rungs for extended periods. Plan for extra time on the job to handle the unexpected

Figure 9.12 — A harness specifically designed for tower climbing makes working on the tower more comfortable as well as providing essential safety features.

Figure 9.11 — Utility poles and power lines must be given wide clearance from your antenna system.

Figure 9.13 — Before working on a tower or antenna, disconnect and if possible lock out the ac power circuits for your radio equipment.

chores.

Before climbing or starting work, run through a safety checklist every time:

- Inspect all tower guying and support hardware.
- Crank-up towers must be fully nested and blocked.
- Double-check all belts and lanyards.
- Inspect all ropes and load-bearing hardware such as pulleys.
- Turn off and unplug all ac equipment, locking the circuits out and tagging them if possible (**Figure 9.13**). [G0B08]
- Transmitters should be off and disconnected from the feed line to avoid shock or excessive RF exposure.
- Check the weather report and don't be caught on the tower in a storm!

As you are climbing up or down, remember to take your time — it's not a race! Be sure your climbing gear is fully secure:

- Belts and harnesses must be within their service life and adequately rated for weight **[G0B07]**
- Carabiners should close completely and securely
- Always use a safety lanyard or redundant lanyards

And remember that often forgotten rule to follow the manufacturer's directions!

For More Information

Building permits are generally required for lattice, crank-up and tilt-over towers. When erecting a tower near an airport, be sure to comply with FCC and FAA rules about maximum structure height near an airport. Make sure you follow grounding rules for external metal structures. Check with your local building codes.

If the mast or tower requires guying, keep all lines and guys above head height wherever possible. If the guy anchor is low to the ground, flag or fence guy lines where they are lower than head height.

If you are working with or are part of the ground crew, that is an important part of the team. Round up enough crew to do the job safely. If you don't have enough people, postpone the work. With everybody present and paying attention, review the job in detail and agree on who gives instructions. Make sure you can communicate clearly. Handheld unlicensed FRS radios or ham radios are a lot easier to use than yelling and pointing. If you're going to use hand signals, make sure everybody understands them and uses the same ones!

Perhaps the most ignored safety advice is to follow the manufacturer's directions! Read the directions thoroughly before starting the job. The manufacturer wants you to have good results from their product and for you to be able to install it safely. Make sure you understand every step and that every part is on hand. When the mast is halfway up or the antenna is pulled up to the top of the tower is no time to discover that you didn't really understand the instructions or that a crucial part is missing!

Once the antenna is up, people should not be able to come in contact with it. Place a fence around a ground-mounted antenna if there is a chance that people could come in contact with the antenna while you are transmitting. This also helps reduce RF exposure and reduces the chance of your antenna being knocked over.

General Class (Element 3) Syllabus
Effective July 1, 2023 to June 30, 2027

SUBELEMENT G1 — COMMISSION'S RULES
[5 Exam Questions — 5 Groups] 57 Questions

G1A – General class control operator frequency privileges; primary and secondary allocations

G1B – Antenna structure limitations; good engineering and good amateur practice; beacon operation; prohibited transmissions; retransmitting radio signals

G1C – Transmitter power regulations; data emission standards; 60-meter operation requirements

G1D – Volunteer Examiners and Volunteer Examiner Coordinators; temporary identification; element credit; remote operation

G1E – Control categories; repeater regulations; third-party rules; ITU regions; automatically controlled digital station

SUBELEMENT G2 — OPERATING PROCEDURES
[5 Exam Questions — 5 Groups] 60 Questions

G2A – Phone operating procedures: USB/LSB conventions, breaking into a contact, transmitter setup for voice operation; answering DX stations

G2B – Operating effectively; band plans; drills and emergencies; RACES operation

G2C – CW operating procedures and procedural signals; Q signals; full break-in

G2D – Volunteer Monitor Program; HF operations

G2E – Digital mode operating procedures

SUBELEMENT G3 — RADIO WAVE PROPAGATION
[3 Exam Questions — 3 Groups] 37 Questions

G3A – Sunspots and solar radiation; geomagnetic field and stability indices

G3B – Maximum Usable Frequency; Lowest Usable Frequency; short path and long path propagation; determining propagation conditions; ionospheric refraction

G3C – Ionospheric regions; critical angle and frequency; HF scatter; near vertical incidence skywave (NVIS)

SUBELEMENT G4 — AMATEUR RADIO PRACTICES
[5 Exam Questions — 5 groups] 60 Questions

G4A – Station configuration and operation

G4B –Tests and test equipment

G4C – Interference to consumer electronics; grounding and bonding

G4D – Speech processors; S meters; sideband operation near band edges

G4E – Mobile and portable HF stations; alternative energy source operation

SUBELEMENT G5 — ELECTRICAL PRINCIPLES
[3 Exam Questions — 3 Groups] 40 Questions

G5A – Reactance; inductance; capacitance; impedance; impedance transformation; resonance

G5B – The decibel; current and voltage dividers; electrical power calculations; sine wave root-mean-square (RMS) values; PEP calculations

G5C – Resistors, capacitors, and inductors in series and parallel; transformers

SUBELEMENT G6 — CIRCUIT COMPONENTS
[2 Exam Questions — 2 Groups] 24 Questions

G6A – Resistors; capacitors; inductors; rectifiers; solid-state diodes and transistors; vacuum tubes; batteries

G6B – Analog and digital integrated circuits (ICs); microwave ICs (MMICs); display devices; RF connectors; ferrite cores

SUBELEMENT G7 — PRACTICAL CIRCUITS
[3 Exam Questions — 3 Groups] 38 Questions

G7A – Power supplies; schematic symbols

G7B – Digital circuits; amplifiers and oscillators

G7C – Transceiver design; filters; oscillators; digital signal processing (DSP)

SUBELEMENT G8 — SIGNALS AND EMISSIONS
[3 Exam Questions — 3 Groups] 43 Questions

G8A – Carriers and modulation: AM, FM, and single sideband; modulation envelope; digital modulation; overmodulation; link budgets and link margins

G8B – Frequency changing; bandwidths of various modes; deviation; intermodulation

G8C – Digital emission modes

SUBELEMENT G9 — ANTENNAS AND FEED LINES
[4 Exam Questions — 4 Groups] 46 Questions

G9A – Feed lines: characteristic impedance and attenuation; standing wave ratio (SWR) calculation, measurement, and effects; antenna feed point matching

G9B – Basic dipole and monopole antennas

G9C – Directional antennas

G9D – Specialized antenna types and applications

SUBELEMENT G0 — ELECTRICAL AND RF SAFETY
[2 Exam Questions — 2 Groups] 25 Questions

G0A – RF safety principles, rules, and guidelines; routine station evaluation

G0B – Station safety: electrical shock, grounding, fusing, interlocks, and wiring; antenna and tower safety

General Class (Element 3) Question Pool

Effective for VEC examinations on July 1, 2023 through June 30, 2027

SUBELEMENT G1 — COMMISSION'S RULES
[5 Exam Questions — 5 Groups]
G1A — General class control operator frequency privileges; primary and secondary allocations

G1A01 [97.301(d)]
On which HF and/or MF amateur bands are there portions where General class licensees cannot transmit?
A. 60 meters, 30 meters, 17 meters, and 12 meters
B. 160 meters, 60 meters, 15 meters, and 12 meters
C. 80 meters, 40 meters, 20 meters, and 15 meters
D. 80 meters, 20 meters, 15 meters, and 10 meters

G1A02 [97.305]
On which of the following bands is phone operation prohibited?
A. 160 meters
B. 30 meters
C. 17 meters
D. 12 meters

G1A03 [97.305]
On which of the following bands is image transmission prohibited?
A. 160 meters
B. 30 meters
C. 20 meters
D. 12 meters

G1A04 [97.303(h)]
Which of the following amateur bands is restricted to communication only on specific channels, rather than frequency ranges?
A. 11 meters
B. 12 meters
C. 30 meters
D. 60 meters

G1A05 [97.301(d)]
On which of the following frequencies are General class licensees prohibited from operating as control operator?
A. 7.125 MHz to 7.175 MHz
B. 28.000 MHz to 28.025 MHz
C. 21.275 MHz to 21.300 MHz
D. All of the above

G1A01
(C)
Page 3-7

G1A02
(B)
Page 3-7

G1A03
(B)
Page 3-7

G1A04
(D)
Page 3-7

G1A05
(A)
Page 3-7

G1A06
(C)
Page 3-7

G1A06 [97.303]
Which of the following applies when the FCC rules designate the amateur service as a secondary user on a band?
A. Amateur stations must record the call sign of the primary service station before operating on a frequency assigned to that station
B. Amateur stations may use the band only during emergencies
C. Amateur stations must not cause harmful interference to primary users and must accept interference from primary users
D. Amateur stations may only operate during specific hours of the day, while primary users are permitted 24-hour use of the band

G1A07
(D)
Page 3-7

G1A07 [97.305(a)]
On which amateur frequencies in the 10-meter band may stations with a General class control operator transmit CW emissions?
A. 28.000 MHz to 28.025 MHz only
B. 28.000 MHz to 28.300 MHz only
C. 28.025 MHz to 28.300 MHz only
D. The entire band

G1A08
(B)
Page 3-8

G1A08 [97.301(b)]
Which HF bands have segments exclusively allocated to Amateur Extra licensees?
A. All HF bands
B. 80 meters, 40 meters, 20 meters, and 15 meters
C. All HF bands except 160 meters and 10 meters
D. 60 meters, 30 meters, 17 meters, and 12 meters

G1A09
(C)
Page 3-8

G1A09 [97.301(d)]
Which of the following frequencies is within the General class portion of the 15-meter band?
A. 14250 kHz
B. 18155 kHz
C. 21300 kHz
D. 24900 kHz

G1A10
(D)
Page 3-8

G1A10 [97.205(b)]
What portion of the 10-meter band is available for repeater use?
A. The entire band
B. The portion between 28.1 MHz and 28.2 MHz
C. The portion between 28.3 MHz and 28.5 MHz
D. The portion above 29.5 MHz

G1A11
(B)
Page 3-8

G1A11 [97.301]
When General class licensees are not permitted to use the entire voice portion of a band, which portion of the voice segment is available to them?
A. The lower frequency portion
B. The upper frequency portion
C. The lower frequency portion on frequencies below 7.3 MHz, and the upper portion on frequencies above 14.150 MHz
D. The upper frequency portion on frequencies below 7.3 MHz, and the lower portion on frequencies above 14.150 MHz

G1B01 [97.15(a)]
What is the maximum height above ground for an antenna structure not near a public use airport without requiring notification to the FAA and registration with the FCC?
A. 50 feet
B. 100 feet
C. 200 feet
D. 250 feet

G1B01
(C)
Page 3-1

G1B02 [97.203(b)]
With which of the following conditions must beacon stations comply?
A. No more than one beacon station may transmit in the same band from the same station location
B. The frequency must be coordinated with the National Beacon Organization
C. The frequency must be posted on the internet or published in a national periodical
D. All these choices are correct

G1B02
(A)
Page 3-8

G1B03 [97.3(a)(9)]
Which of the following is a purpose of a beacon station as identified in the FCC rules?
A. Observation of propagation and reception
B. Automatic identification of repeaters
C. Transmission of bulletins of general interest to amateur radio licensees
D. All these choices are correct

G1B03
(A)
Page 3-8

G1B04 [97.113(c)]
Which of the following transmissions is permitted for all amateur stations?
A. Unidentified transmissions of less than 10 seconds duration for test purposes only
B. Automatic retransmission of other amateur signals by any amateur station
C. Occasional retransmission of weather and propagation forecast information from US government stations
D. Encrypted messages, if not intended to facilitate a criminal act

G1B04
(C)
Page 3-14

G1B05 [97.111(5)(b)]
Which of the following one-way transmissions are permitted?
A. Unidentified test transmissions of less than 10 seconds in duration
B. Transmissions to assist with learning the International Morse code
C. Regular transmissions offering equipment for sale, if intended for amateur radio use
D. All these choices are correct

G1B05
(B)
Page 3-14

G1B06 [97.15(b), PRB-1, 101 FCC 2d 952 (1985)]
Under what conditions are state and local governments permitted to regulate amateur radio antenna structures?
A. Under no circumstances, FCC rules take priority
B. At any time and to any extent necessary to accomplish a legitimate purpose of the state or local entity, provided that proper filings are made with the FCC
C. Only when such structures exceed 50 feet in height and are clearly visible 1,000 feet from the structure
D. Amateur Service communications must be reasonably accommodated, and regulations must constitute the minimum practical to accommodate a legitimate purpose of the state or local entity

G1B06
(D)
Page 3-1

G1B07
(B)
Page 3-14

G1B07 [97.113(a)(4)]
What are the restrictions on the use of abbreviations or procedural signals in the amateur service?
A. Only "Q" signals are permitted
B. They may be used if they do not obscure the meaning of a message
C. They are not permitted
D. They are limited to those expressly listed in Part 97 of the FCC rules

G1B08
(B)
Page 3-14

G1B08 [97.111(a)(1)]
When is it permissible to communicate with amateur stations in countries outside the areas administered by the Federal Communications Commission?
A. Only when the foreign country has a formal third-party agreement filed with the FCC
B. When the contact is with amateurs in any country except those whose administrations have notified the ITU that they object to such communications
C. Only when the contact is with amateurs licensed by a country which is a member of the United Nations, or by a territory possessed by such a country
D. Only when the contact is with amateurs licensed by a country which is a member of the International Amateur Radio Union, or by a territory possessed by such a country

G1B09
(D)
Page 3-8

G1B09 [97.203(d)]
On what HF frequencies are automatically controlled beacons permitted?
A. On any frequency if power is less than 1 watt
B. On any frequency if transmissions are in Morse code
C. 21.08 MHz to 21.09 MHz
D. 28.20 MHz to 28.30 MHz

G1B10
(C)
Page 3-8

G1B10 [97.203(c)]
What is the power limit for beacon stations?
A. 10 watts PEP output
B. 20 watts PEP output
C. 100 watts PEP output
D. 200 watts PEP output

G1B11
(A)
Page 3-15

G1B11 [97.101(a)]
Who or what determines "good engineering and good amateur practice," as applied to the operation of an amateur station in all respects not covered by the Part 97 rules?
A. The FCC
B. The control operator
C. The IEEE
D. The ITU

G1C — Transmitter power regulations; data emission standards; 60-meter operation requirements

G1C01
(A)
Page 3-15

G1C01 [97.313(c)(1)]
What is the maximum transmitter power an amateur station may use on 10.140 MHz?
A. 200 watts PEP output
B. 1000 watts PEP output
C. 1500 watts PEP output
D. 2000 watts PEP output

G1C02
(C)
Page 3-15

G1C02 [97.313]
What is the maximum transmitter power an amateur station may use on the 12-meter band?
A. 50 watts PEP output
B. 200 watts PEP output
C. 1500 watts PEP output
D. An effective radiated power equivalent to 100 watts from a half-wave dipole

G1C03 [97.303(h)(1)]
What is the maximum bandwidth permitted by FCC rules for amateur radio stations transmitting on USB frequencies in the 60-meter band?
A. 2.8 kHz
B. 5.6 kHz
C. 1.8 kHz
D. 3 kHz

G1C04 [97.303(i)]
Which of the following is required by the FCC rules when operating in the 60-meter band?
A. If you are using an antenna other than a dipole, you must keep a record of the gain of your antenna
B. You must keep a record of the date, time, frequency, power level, and stations worked
C. You must keep a record of all third-party traffic
D. You must keep a record of the manufacturer of your equipment and the antenna used

G1C05 [97.313]
What is the limit for transmitter power on the 28 MHz band for a General Class control operator?
A. 100 watts PEP output
B. 1000 watts PEP output
C. 1500 watts PEP output
D. 2000 watts PEP output

G1C06 [97.313]
What is the limit for transmitter power on the 1.8 MHz band?
A. 200 watts PEP output
B. 1000 watts PEP output
C. 1200 watts PEP output
D. 1500 watts PEP output

G1C07 [97.309(a)(4)]
What must be done before using a new digital protocol on the air?
A. Type-certify equipment to FCC standards
B. Obtain an experimental license from the FCC
C. Publicly document the technical characteristics of the protocol
D. Submit a rule-making proposal to the FCC describing the codes and methods of the technique

G1C08 [97.307(f)(3)]
What is the maximum symbol rate permitted for RTTY or data emission transmitted at frequencies below 28 MHz?
A. 56 kilobaud
B. 19.6 kilobaud
C. 1200 baud
D. 300 baud

G1C09 [97.313(i)]
What is the maximum power limit on the 60-meter band?
A. 1500 watts PEP
B. 10 watts RMS
C. ERP of 100 watts PEP with respect to a dipole
D. ERP of 100 watts PEP with respect to an isotropic antenna

G1C03
(A)
Page 3-15

G1C04
(A)
Page 2-5

G1C05
(C)
Page 3-15

G1C06
(D)
Page 3-15

G1C07
(C)
Page 3-17

G1C08
(D)
Page 3-17

G1C09
(C)
Page 3-15

G1C10
(C)
Page 3-17

G1C10 [97.305(c) and 97.307(f)(4)]
What is the maximum symbol rate permitted for RTTY or data emission transmissions on the 10-meter band?
A. 56 kilobaud
B. 19.6 kilobaud
C. 1200 baud
D. 300 baud

G1C11
(D)
Page 3-15

G1C11 [97.313]
What measurement is specified by FCC rules that regulate maximum power?
A. RMS output from the transmitter
B. RMS input to the antenna
C. PEP input to the antenna
D. PEP output from the transmitter

G1D — Volunteer Examiners and Volunteer Examiner Coordinators; temporary identification; element credit; remote operation

G1D01
(A)
Page 3-3

G1D01 [97.501, 97.505(a)]
Who may receive partial credit for the elements represented by an expired amateur radio license?
A. Any person who can demonstrate that they once held an FCC-issued General, Advanced, or Amateur Extra class license that was not revoked by the FCC
B. Anyone who held an FCC-issued amateur radio license that expired not less than 5 and not more than 15 years ago
C. Any person who previously held an amateur license issued by another country, but only if that country has a current reciprocal licensing agreement with the FCC
D. Only persons who once held an FCC issued Novice, Technician, or Technician Plus license

G1D02
(C)
Page 3-3

G1D02 [97.509(b)(3)(i)]
What license examinations may you administer as an accredited Volunteer Examiner holding a General class operator license?
A. General and Technician
B. None, only Amateur Extra class licensees may be accredited
C. Technician only
D. Amateur Extra, General, and Technician

G1D03
(C)
Page 3-4

G1D03 [97.9(b)]
On which of the following band segments may you operate if you are a Technician class operator and have an unexpired Certificate of Successful Completion of Examination (CSCE) for General class privileges?
A. Only the Technician band segments until your upgrade is posted in the FCC database
B. Only on the Technician band segments until you have a receipt for the FCC application fee payment
C. On any General or Technician class band segment
D. On any General or Technician class band segment except 30 meters and 60 meters

G1D04
(A)
Page 3-4

G1D04 [97.509(3)(i)(c)]
Who must observe the administration of a Technician class license examination?
A. At least three Volunteer Examiners of General class or higher
B. At least two Volunteer Examiners of General class or higher
C. At least two Volunteer Examiners of Technician class or higher
D. At least three Volunteer Examiners of Technician class

G1D05 [97.7]
When operating a US station by remote control from outside the country, what license is required of the control operator?
A. A US operator/primary station license
B. Only an appropriate US operator/primary license and a special remote station permit from the FCC
C. Only a license from the foreign country, as long as the call sign includes identification of portable operation in the US
D. A license from the foreign country and a special remote station permit from the FCC

G1D06 [97.119(f)(2)]
Until an upgrade to General class is shown in the FCC database, when must a Technician licensee identify with "AG" after their call sign?
A. Whenever they operate using General class frequency privileges
B. Whenever they operate on any amateur frequency
C. Whenever they operate using Technician frequency privileges
D. A special identifier is not required if their General class license application has been filed with the FCC

G1D07 [97.509(b)(1)]
Volunteer Examiners are accredited by what organization?
A. The Federal Communications Commission
B. The Universal Licensing System
C. A Volunteer Examiner Coordinator
D. The Wireless Telecommunications Bureau

G1D08 [97.509(b)(3)]
Which of the following criteria must be met for a non-US citizen to be an accredited Volunteer Examiner?
A. The person must be a resident of the US for a minimum of 5 years
B. The person must hold an FCC granted amateur radio license of General class or above
C. The person's home citizenship must be in ITU region 2
D. None of these choices is correct; a non-US citizen cannot be a Volunteer Examiner

G1D09 [97.9(b)]
How long is a Certificate of Successful Completion of Examination (CSCE) valid for exam element credit?
A. 30 days
B. 180 days
C. 365 days
D. For as long as your current license is valid

G1D10 [97.509(b)(2)]
What is the minimum age that one must be to qualify as an accredited Volunteer Examiner?
A. 16 years
B. 18 years
C. 21 years
D. There is no age limit

G1D05	(A) Page 3-1
G1D06	(A) Page 3-4
G1D07	(C) Page 3-4
G1D08	(B) Page 3-4
G1D09	(C) Page 3-4
G1D10	(B) Page 3-4

G1D11 [97.505]
What action is required to obtain a new General class license after a previously held license has expired and the two-year grace period has passed?
A. They must have a letter from the FCC showing they once held an amateur or commercial license
B. There are no requirements other than being able to show a copy of the expired license
C. Contact the FCC to have the license reinstated
D. The applicant must show proof of the appropriate expired license grant and pass the current Element 2 exam

G1D12 [97.507]
When operating a station in South America by remote control over the internet from the US, what regulations apply?
A. Those of both the remote station's country and the FCC
B. Those of the remote station's country and the FCC's third-party regulations
C. Only those of the remote station's country
D. Only those of the FCC

G1E — Control categories; repeater regulations; third-party rules; ITU regions; automatically controlled digital station

G1E01 [97.115(b)(2)]
Which of the following would disqualify a third party from participating in sending a message via an amateur station?
A. The third party's amateur license has been revoked and not reinstated
B. The third party is not a US citizen
C. The third party is speaking in a language other than English
D. All these choices are correct

G1E02 [97.205(b)]
When may a 10-meter repeater retransmit the 2-meter signal from a station that has a Technician class control operator?
A. Under no circumstances
B. Only if the station on 10-meters is operating under a Special Temporary Authorization allowing such retransmission
C. Only during an FCC-declared general state of communications emergency
D. Only if the 10-meter repeater control operator holds at least a General class license

G1E03 [97.221]
What is required to conduct communications with a digital station operating under automatic control outside the automatic control band segments?
A. The station initiating the contact must be under local or remote control
B. The interrogating transmission must be made by another automatically controlled station
C. No third-party traffic may be transmitted
D. The control operator of the interrogating station must hold an Amateur Extra class license

G1E04 [97.13(b), 97.303, 97.311(b)]
Which of the following conditions require a licensed amateur radio operator to take specific steps to avoid harmful interference to other users or facilities?
A. When operating within one mile of an FCC Monitoring Station
B. When using a band where the Amateur Service is secondary
C. When a station is transmitting spread spectrum emissions
D. All these choices are correct

G1E05 [97.115(a)(2), 97.117]
What are the restrictions on messages sent to a third party in a country with which there is a Third-Party Agreement?
A. They must relate to emergencies or disaster relief
B. They must be for other licensed amateurs
C. They must relate to amateur radio, or remarks of a personal character, or messages relating to emergencies or disaster relief
D. The message must be limited to no longer than 1 minute in duration and the name of the third party must be recorded in the station log

G1E06 [97.301, ITU Radio Regulations]
The frequency allocations of which ITU region apply to radio amateurs operating in North and South America?
A. Region 4
B. Region 3
C. Region 2
D. Region 1

G1E07 [97.111]
In what part of the 2.4 GHz band may an amateur station communicate with non-licensed Wi-Fi stations?
A. Anywhere in the band
B. Channels 1 through 4
C. Channels 42 through 45
D. No part

G1E08 [97.313(j)]
What is the maximum PEP output allowed for spread spectrum transmissions?
A. 100 milliwatts
B. 10 watts
C. 100 watts
D. 1500 watts

G1E09 [97.115]
Under what circumstances are messages that are sent via digital modes exempt from Part 97 third-party rules that apply to other modes of communication?
A. Under no circumstances
B. When messages are encrypted
C. When messages are not encrypted
D. When under automatic control

G1E10 [97.101]
Why should an amateur operator normally avoid transmitting on 14.100, 18.110, 21.150, 24. 930 and 28.200 MHz?
A. A system of propagation beacon stations operates on those frequencies
B. A system of automatic digital stations operates on those frequencies
C. These frequencies are set aside for emergency operations
D. These frequencies are set aside for bulletins from the FCC

G1E05
(C)
Page 3-13

G1E06
(C)
Page 3-1

G1E07
(D)
Page 3-8

G1E08
(B)
Page 3-15

G1E09
(A)
Page 6-14

G1E10
(A)
Page 3-8

G1E11
(D)
Page 6-14

G1E11 [97.221, 97.305]
On what bands may automatically controlled stations transmitting RTTY or data emissions communicate with other automatically controlled digital stations?
A. On any band segment where digital operation is permitted
B. Anywhere in the non-phone segments of the 10-meter or shorter wavelength bands
C. Only in the non-phone Extra Class segments of the bands
D. Anywhere in the 6-meter or shorter wavelength bands, and in limited segments of some of the HF bands

G1E12
(A)
Page 3-13

G1E12 [97.115]
When may third-party messages be transmitted via remote control?
A. Under any circumstances in which third party messages are permitted by FCC rules
B. Under no circumstances except for emergencies
C. Only when the message is intended for licensed radio amateurs
D. Only when the message is intended for third parties in areas where licensing is controlled by the FCC

SUBELEMENT G2 — OPERATING PROCEDURES
[5 Exam Questions — 5 Groups]

G2A — Phone operating procedures: USB/LSB conventions, breaking into a contact, transmitter setup for voice operation; answering DX stations

G2A01
(A)
Page 2-9

G2A01
Which mode is most commonly used for voice communications on frequencies of 14 MHz or higher?
A. Upper sideband
B. Lower sideband
C. Suppressed sideband
D. Double sideband

G2A02
(B)
Page 2-9

G2A02
Which mode is most commonly used for voice communications on the 160-, 75-, and 40-meter bands?
A. Upper sideband
B. Lower sideband
C. Suppressed sideband
D. Double sideband

G2A03
(A)
Page 2-9

G2A03
Which mode is most commonly used for SSB voice communications in the VHF and UHF bands?
A. Upper sideband
B. Lower sideband
C. Suppressed sideband
D. Double sideband

G2A04
(A)
Page 2-9

G2A04
Which mode is most commonly used for voice communications on the 17- and 12-meter bands?
A. Upper sideband
B. Lower sideband
C. Suppressed sideband
D. Double sideband

G2A05
Which mode of voice communication is most commonly used on the HF amateur bands?
A. Frequency modulation
B. Double sideband
C. Single sideband
D. Single phase modulation

G2A06
Which of the following is an advantage of using single sideband, as compared to other analog voice modes on the HF amateur bands?
A. Very high-fidelity voice modulation
B. Less subject to interference from atmospheric static crashes
C. Ease of tuning on receive and immunity to impulse noise
D. Less bandwidth used and greater power efficiency

G2A07
Which of the following statements is true of single sideband (SSB)?
A. Only one sideband and the carrier are transmitted; the other sideband is suppressed
B. Only one sideband is transmitted; the other sideband and carrier are suppressed
C. SSB is the only voice mode authorized on the 20-, 15-, and 10-meter amateur bands
D. SSB is the only voice mode authorized on the 160-, 75-, and 40-meter amateur bands

G2A08
What is the recommended way to break into a phone contact?
A. Say "QRZ" several times, followed by your call sign
B. Say your call sign once
C. Say "Breaker Breaker"
D. Say "CQ" followed by the call sign of either station

G2A09
Why do most amateur stations use lower sideband on the 160-, 75-, and 40-meter bands?
A. Lower sideband is more efficient than upper sideband at these frequencies
B. Lower sideband is the only sideband legal on these frequency bands
C. Because it is fully compatible with an AM detector
D. It is commonly accepted amateur practice

G2A10
Which of the following statements is true of VOX operation versus PTT operation?
A. The received signal is more natural sounding
B. It allows "hands free" operation
C. It occupies less bandwidth
D. It provides more power output

G2A11
Generally, who should respond to a station in the contiguous 48 states calling "CQ DX"?
A. Any caller is welcome to respond
B. Only stations in Germany
C. Any stations outside the lower 48 states
D. Only contest stations

G2A12
What control is typically adjusted for proper ALC setting on a single sideband transceiver?
A. RF clipping level
B. Transmit audio or microphone gain
C. Antenna inductance or capacitance
D. Attenuator level

<table>
<tr><td>G2A05
(C)
Page 2-9</td></tr>
<tr><td>G2A06
(D)
Page 2-9</td></tr>
<tr><td>G2A07
(B)
Page 2-9</td></tr>
<tr><td>G2A08
(B)
Page 2-5</td></tr>
<tr><td>G2A09
(D)
Page 2-9</td></tr>
<tr><td>G2A10
(B)
Page 2-13</td></tr>
<tr><td>G2A11
(C)
Page 2-5</td></tr>
<tr><td>G2A12
(B)
Page 5-8</td></tr>
</table>

G2B01
(C)
Page 2-1

G2B01 [97.101(b), (c)]
Which of the following is true concerning access to frequencies?
A. Nets have priority
B. QSOs in progress have priority
C. Except during emergencies, no amateur station has priority access to any frequency
D. Contest operations should yield to non-contest use of frequencies

G2B02
(B)
Page 2-16

G2B02
What is the first thing you should do if you are communicating with another amateur station and hear a station in distress break in?
A. Inform your local emergency coordinator
B. Acknowledge the station in distress and determine what assistance may be needed
C. Immediately decrease power to avoid interfering with the station in distress
D. Immediately cease all transmissions

G2B03
(C)
Page 2-1

G2B03
What is good amateur practice if propagation changes during a contact creating interference from other stations using the frequency?
A. Advise the interfering stations that you are on the frequency and that you have priority
B. Decrease power and continue to transmit
C. Attempt to resolve the interference problem with the other stations in a mutually acceptable manner
D. Switch to the opposite sideband

G2B04
(B)
Page 2-1

G2B04
When selecting a CW transmitting frequency, what minimum separation from other stations should be used to minimize interference to stations on adjacent frequencies?
A. 5 Hz to 50 Hz
B. 150 Hz to 500 Hz
C. 1 kHz to 3 kHz
D. 3 kHz to 6 kHz

G2B05
(C)
Page 2-1

G2B05
When selecting an SSB transmitting frequency, what minimum separation should be used to minimize interference to stations on adjacent frequencies?
A. 5 Hz to 50 Hz
B. 150 Hz to 500 Hz
C. 2 kHz to 3 kHz
D. Approximately 6 kHz

G2B06
(A)
Page 2-1

G2B06
How can you avoid harmful interference on an apparently clear frequency before calling CQ on CW or phone?
A. Send "QRL?" on CW, followed by your call sign; or, if using phone, ask if the frequency is in use, followed by your call sign
B. Listen for 2 minutes before calling CQ
C. Send the letter "V" in Morse code several times and listen for a response, or say "test" several times and listen for a response
D. Send "QSY" on CW or if using phone, announce "the frequency is in use," then give your call sign and listen for a response

G2B07
Which of the following complies with commonly accepted amateur practice when choosing a frequency on which to initiate a call?
A. Listen on the frequency for at least two minutes to be sure it is clear
B. Identify your station by transmitting your call sign at least 3 times
C. Follow the voluntary band plan
D. All these choices are correct

G2B08
What is the voluntary band plan restriction for US stations transmitting within the 48 contiguous states in the 50.1 MHz to 50.125 MHz band segment?
A. Only contacts with stations not within the 48 contiguous states
B. Only contacts with other stations within the 48 contiguous states
C. Only digital contacts
D. Only SSTV contacts

G2B09 [97.407(a)]
Who may be the control operator of an amateur station transmitting in RACES to assist relief operations during a disaster?
A. Only a person holding an FCC-issued amateur operator license
B. Only a RACES net control operator
C. A person holding an FCC-issued amateur operator license or an appropriate government official
D. Any control operator when normal communication systems are operational

G2B10
Which of the following is good amateur practice for net management?
A. Always use multiple sets of phonetics during check-in
B. Have a backup frequency in case of interference or poor conditions
C. Transmit the full net roster at the beginning of every session
D. All these choices are correct

G2B11 [97.407(d)(4)]
How often may RACES training drills and tests be routinely conducted without special authorization?
A. No more than 1 hour per month
B. No more than 2 hours per month
C. No more than 1 hour per week
D. No more than 2 hours per week

G2C — CW operating procedures and procedural signals; Q signals; full break-in

G2C01
Which of the following describes full break-in CW operation (QSK)?
A. Breaking stations send the Morse code prosign "BK"
B. Automatic keyers, instead of hand keys, are used to send Morse code
C. An operator must activate a manual send/receive switch before and after every transmission
D. Transmitting stations can receive between code characters and elements

G2C02
What should you do if a CW station sends "QRS?"
A. Send slower
B. Change frequency
C. Increase your power
D. Repeat everything twice

G2B07
(C)
Page 2-2

G2B08
(A)
Page 2-5

G2B09
(A)
Page 2-16

G2B10
(B)
Page 2-5

G2B11
(C)
Page 2-13

G2C01
(D)
Page 2-13

G2C02
(A)
Page 2-13

G2C03
(C)
Page 2-13

G2C03
What does it mean when a CW operator sends "KN" at the end of a transmission?
A. No US stations should call
B. Operating full break-in
C. Listening only for a specific station or stations
D. Closing station now

G2C04
(D)
Page 2-2

G2C04
What does the Q signal "QRL?" mean?
A. "Will you keep the frequency clear?"
B. "Are you operating full break-in?" or "Can you operate full break-in?"
C. "Are you listening only for a specific station?"
D. "Are you busy?" or "Is this frequency in use?"

G2C05
(B)
Page 2-13

G2C05
What is the best speed to use when answering a CQ in Morse code?
A. The fastest speed at which you are comfortable copying, but no slower than the CQ
B. The fastest speed at which you are comfortable copying, but no faster than the CQ
C. At the standard calling speed of 10 wpm
D. At the standard calling speed of 5 wpm

G2C06
(D)
Page 2-13

G2C06
What does the term "zero beat" mean in CW operation?
A. Matching the speed of the transmitting station
B. Operating split to avoid interference on frequency
C. Sending without error
D. Matching the transmit frequency to the frequency of a received signal

G2C07
(A)
Page 2-11

G2C07
When sending CW, what does a "C" mean when added to the RST report?
A. Chirpy or unstable signal
B. Report was read from an S meter rather than estimated
C. 100 percent copy
D. Key clicks

G2C08
(C)
Page 2-13

G2C08
What prosign is sent to indicate the end of a formal message when using CW?
A. SK
B. BK
C. AR
D. KN

G2C09
(C)
Page 2-13

G2C09
What does the Q signal "QSL" mean?
A. Send slower
B. We have already confirmed the contact
C. I have received and understood
D. We have worked before

G2C10
(D)
Page 2-11

G2C10
What does the Q signal "QRN" mean?
A. Send more slowly
B. Stop sending
C. Zero beat my signal
D. I am troubled by static

G2C11
What does the Q signal "QRV" mean?
A. You are sending too fast
B. There is interference on the frequency
C. I am quitting for the day
D. I am ready to receive

G2D — Volunteer Monitor Program; HF operations

G2D01
What is the Volunteer Monitor Program?
A. Amateur volunteers who are formally enlisted to monitor the airwaves for rules violations
B. Amateur volunteers who conduct amateur licensing examinations
C. Amateur volunteers who conduct frequency coordination for amateur VHF repeaters
D. Amateur volunteers who use their station equipment to help civil defense organizations in times of emergency

G2D02
Which of the following are objectives of the Volunteer Monitor Program?
A. To conduct efficient and orderly amateur licensing examinations
B. To provide emergency and public safety communications
C. To coordinate repeaters for efficient and orderly spectrum usage
D. To encourage amateur radio operators to self-regulate and comply with the rules

G2D03
What procedure may be used by Volunteer Monitors to localize a station whose continuous carrier is holding a repeater on in their area?
A. Compare vertical and horizontal signal strengths on the input frequency
B. Compare beam headings on the repeater input from their home locations with that of other Volunteer Monitors
C. Compare signal strengths between the input and output of the repeater
D. All these choices are correct

G2D04
Which of the following describes an azimuthal projection map?
A. A map that shows accurate land masses
B. A map that shows true bearings and distances from a specific location
C. A map that shows the angle at which an amateur satellite crosses the equator
D. A map that shows the number of degrees longitude that an amateur satellite appears to move westward at the equator with each orbit

G2D05
Which of the following indicates that you are looking for an HF contact with any station?
A. Sign your call sign once, followed by the words "listening for a call" -- if no answer, change frequency and repeat
B. Say "QTC" followed by "this is" and your call sign -- if no answer, change frequency and repeat
C. Repeat "CQ" a few times, followed by "this is," then your call sign a few times, then pause to listen, repeat as necessary
D. Transmit an unmodulated carried for approximately 10 seconds, followed by "this is" and your call sign, and pause to listen -- repeat as necessary

G2C11
(D)
Page 2-13

G2D01
(A)
Page 3-2

G2D02
(D)
Page 3-2

G2D03
(B)
Page 3-2

G2D04
(B)
Page 7-8

G2D05
(C)
Page 2-5

G2D06
(C)
Page 8-1

G2D06
How is a directional antenna pointed when making a "long-path" contact with another station?
A. Toward the rising sun
B. Along the gray line
C. 180 degrees from the station's short-path heading
D. Toward the north

G2D07
(D)
Page 2-2

G2D07
Which of the following are examples of the NATO Phonetic Alphabet?
A. Able, Baker, Charlie, Dog
B. Adam, Boy, Charles, David
C. America, Boston, Canada, Denmark
D. Alpha, Bravo, Charlie, Delta

G2D08
(D)
Page 2-5

G2D08
Why do many amateurs keep a station log?
A. The FCC requires a log of all international contacts
B. The FCC requires a log of all international third-party traffic
C. The log provides evidence of operation needed to renew a license without retest
D. To help with a reply if the FCC requests information about your station

G2D09
(C)
Page 2-5

G2D09
Which of the following is required when participating in a contest on HF frequencies?
A. Submit a log to the contest sponsor
B. Send a QSL card to the stations worked, or QSL via Logbook of The World
C. Identify your station according to normal FCC regulations
D. All these choices are correct

G2D10
(B)
Page 3-15

G2D10
What is QRP operation?
A. Remote piloted model control
B. Low-power transmit operation
C. Transmission using Quick Response Protocol
D. Traffic relay procedure net operation

G2D11
(A)
Page 2-11

G2D11
Why are signal reports typically exchanged at the beginning of an HF contact?
A. To allow each station to operate according to conditions
B. To be sure the contact will count for award programs
C. To follow standard radiogram structure
D. To allow each station to calibrate their frequency display

G2E — Digital mode operating procedures

G2E01
(D)
Page 6-11

G2E01
Which mode is normally used when sending RTTY signals via AFSK with an SSB transmitter?
A. USB
B. DSB
C. CW
D. LSB

G2E02
What is VARA?
A. A low signal-to-noise digital mode used for EME (moonbounce)
B. A digital protocol used with Winlink
C. A radio direction finding system used on VHF and UHF
D.A DX spotting system using a network of software defined radios

G2E03
What symptoms may result from other signals interfering with a PACTOR or VARA transmission?
A. Frequent retries or timeouts
B. Long pauses in message transmission
C. Failure to establish a connection between stations
D. All these choices are correct

G2E04
Which of the following is good practice when choosing a transmitting frequency to answer a station calling CQ using FT8?
A. Always call on the station's frequency
B. Call on any frequency in the waterfall except the station's frequency
C. Find a clear frequency during the same time slot as the calling station
D. Find a clear frequency during the alternate time slot to the calling station

G2E05
What is the standard sideband for JT65, JT9, FT4, or FT8 digital signal when using AFSK?
A. LSB
B. USB
C. DSB
D. SSB

G2E06
What is the most common frequency shift for RTTY emissions in the amateur HF bands?
A. 85 Hz
B. 170 Hz
C. 425 Hz
D. 850 Hz

G2E07
Which of the following is required when using FT8?
A. A special hardware modem
B. Computer time accurate to within approximately 1 second
C. Receiver attenuator set to -12 dB
D. A vertically polarized antenna

G2E08
In what segment of the 20-meter band are most digital mode operations commonly found?
A. At the bottom of the slow-scan TV segment, near 14.230 MHz
B. At the top of the SSB phone segment, near 14.325 MHz
C. In the middle of the CW segment, near 14.100 MHz
D. Between 14.070 MHz and 14.100 MHz

G2E09
How do you join a contact between two stations using the PACTOR protocol?
A. Send broadcast packets containing your call sign while in MONITOR mode
B. Transmit a steady carrier until the PACTOR protocol times out and disconnects
C. Joining an existing contact is not possible, PACTOR connections are limited to two stations
D. Send a NAK code

G2E10
(D)
Page 6-14

G2E10
Which of the following is a way to establish contact with a digital messaging system gateway station?
A. Send an email to the system control operator
B. Send QRL in Morse code
C. Respond when the station broadcasts its SSID
D. Transmit a connect message on the station's published frequency

G2E11
(C)
Page 6-6

G2E11
What is the primary purpose of an Amateur Radio Emergency Data Network (AREDN) mesh network?
A. To provide FM repeater coverage in remote areas
B. To provide real time propagation data by monitoring amateur radio transmissions worldwide
C. To provide high-speed data services during an emergency or community event
D. To provide DX spotting reports to aid contesters and DXers

G2E12
(D)
Page 6-6

G2E12
Which of the following describes Winlink?
A. An amateur radio wireless network to send and receive email on the internet
B. A form of Packet Radio
C. A wireless network capable of both VHF and HF band operation
D. All of the above

G2E13
(B)
Page 6-6

G2E13
What is another name for a Winlink Remote Message Server?
A. Terminal Node Controller
B. Gateway
C. RJ-45
D. Printer/Server

G2E14
(D)
Page 6-11

G2E14
What could be wrong if you cannot decode an RTTY or other FSK signal even though it is apparently tuned in properly?
A. The mark and space frequencies may be reversed
B. You may have selected the wrong baud rate
C. You may be listening on the wrong sideband
D. All these choices are correct

G2E15
(C)
Page 6-6

G2E15
Which of the following is a common location for FT8?
A. Anywhere in the voice portion of the band
B. Anywhere in the CW portion of the band
C. Approximately 14.074 MHz to 14.077 MHz
D. Approximately 14.110 MHz to 14.113 MHz

SUBELEMENT G3 — RADIO WAVE PROPAGATION
[3 Exam Questions — 3 Groups]

G3A — Sunspots and solar radiation; geomagnetic field and stability indices

G3A01
How does a higher sunspot number affect HF propagation?
A. Higher sunspot numbers generally indicate a greater probability of good propagation at higher frequencies
B. Lower sunspot numbers generally indicate greater probability of sporadic E propagation
C. A zero sunspot number indicates that radio propagation is not possible on any band
D. A zero sunspot number indicates undisturbed conditions

G3A02
What effect does a sudden ionospheric disturbance have on the daytime ionospheric propagation?
A. It enhances propagation on all HF frequencies
B. It disrupts signals on lower frequencies more than those on higher frequencies
C. It disrupts communications via satellite more than direct communications
D. None, because only areas on the night side of the Earth are affected

G3A03
Approximately how long does it take the increased ultraviolet and X-ray radiation from a solar flare to affect radio propagation on Earth?
A. 28 days
B. 1 to 2 hours
C. 8 minutes
D. 20 to 40 hours

G3A04
Which of the following are the least reliable bands for long-distance communications during periods of low solar activity?
A. 80 meters and 160 meters
B. 60 meters and 40 meters
C. 30 meters and 20 meters
D. 15 meters, 12 meters, and 10 meters

G3A05
What is the solar flux index?
A. A measure of the highest frequency that is useful for ionospheric propagation between two points on Earth
B. A count of sunspots that is adjusted for solar emissions
C. Another name for the American sunspot number
D. A measure of solar radiation with a wavelength of 10.7 centimeters

G3A06
What is a geomagnetic storm?
A. A sudden drop in the solar flux index
B. A thunderstorm that affects radio propagation
C. Ripples in the geomagnetic force
D. A temporary disturbance in Earth's geomagnetic field

G3A07
(D)
Page 8-7

G3A07
At what point in the solar cycle does the 20-meter band usually support worldwide propagation during daylight hours?
A. At the summer solstice
B. Only at the maximum point
C. Only at the minimum point
D. At any point

G3A08
(D)
Page 8-9

G3A08
How can a geomagnetic storm affect HF propagation?
A. Improve high-latitude HF propagation
B. Degrade ground wave propagation
C. Improve ground wave propagation
D. Degrade high-latitude HF propagation

G3A09
(A)
Page 8-9

G3A09
How can high geomagnetic activity benefit radio communications?
A. Creates auroras that can reflect VHF signals
B. Increases signal strength for HF signals passing through the polar regions
C. Improve HF long path propagation
D. Reduce long delayed echoes

G3A10
(C)
Page 8-7

G3A10
What causes HF propagation conditions to vary periodically in a 26- to 28-day cycle?
A. Long term oscillations in the upper atmosphere
B. Cyclic variation in Earth's radiation belts
C. Rotation of the Sun's surface layers around its axis
D. The position of the Moon in its orbit

G3A11
(D)
Page 8-9

G3A11
How long does it take a coronal mass ejection to affect radio propagation on Earth?
A. 28 days
B. 14 days
C. 4 to 8 minutes
D. 15 hours to several days

G3A12
(B)
Page 8-7

G3A12
What does the K-index measure?
A. The relative position of sunspots on the surface of the Sun
B. The short-term stability of Earth's geomagnetic field
C. The short-term stability of the Sun's magnetic field
D. The solar radio flux at Boulder, Colorado

G3A13
(C)
Page 8-7

G3A13
What does the A-index measure?
A. The relative position of sunspots on the surface of the Sun
B. The amount of polarization of the Sun's electric field
C. The long-term stability of Earth's geomagnetic field
D. The solar radio flux at Boulder, Colorado

G3A14
How is long distance radio communication usually affected by the charged particles that reach Earth from solar coronal holes?
A. HF communication is improved
B. HF communication is disturbed
C. VHF/UHF ducting is improved
D. VHF/UHF ducting is disturbed

G3B — Maximum Usable Frequency; Lowest Usable Frequency; short path and long path propagation; determining propagation conditions; ionospheric refraction

G3B01
What is a characteristic of skywave signals arriving at your location by both short-path and long-path propagation?
A. Periodic fading approximately every 10 seconds
B. Signal strength increased by 3 dB
C. The signal might be cancelled causing severe attenuation
D. A slightly delayed echo might be heard

G3B02
What factors affect the MUF?
A. Path distance and location
B. Time of day and season
C. Solar radiation and ionospheric disturbances
D. All these choices are correct

G3B03
Which frequency will have the least attenuation for long-distance skip propagation?
A. Just below the MUF
B. Just above the LUF
C. Just below the critical frequency
D. Just above the critical frequency

G3B04
Which of the following is a way to determine current propagation on a desired band from your station?
A. Use a network of automated receiving stations on the internet to see where your transmissions are being received
B. Check the A-index
C. Send a series of dots and listen for echoes
D. All these choices are correct

G3B05
How does the ionosphere affect radio waves with frequencies below the MUF and above the LUF?
A. They are refracted back to Earth
B. They pass through the ionosphere
C. They are amplified by interaction with the ionosphere
D. They are refracted and trapped in the ionosphere to circle Earth

G3B06
What usually happens to radio waves with frequencies below the LUF?
A. They are refracted back to Earth
B. They pass through the ionosphere
C. They are attenuated before reaching the destination
D. They are refracted and trapped in the ionosphere to circle Earth

G3A14
(B)
Page 8-9

G3B01
(D)
Page 8-1

G3B02
(D)
Page 8-9

G3B03
(A)
Page 8-9

G3B04
(A)
Page 8-9

G3B05
(A)
Page 8-10

G3B06
(C)
Page 8-10

G3B07
(A)
Page 8-10

G3B07
What does LUF stand for?
A. The Lowest Usable Frequency for communications between two specific points
B. Lowest Usable Frequency for communications to any point outside a 100-mile radius
C. The Lowest Usable Frequency during a 24-hour period
D. Lowest Usable Frequency during the past 60 minutes

G3B08
(B)
Page 8-10

G3B08
What does MUF stand for?
A. The Minimum Usable Frequency for communications between two points
B. The Maximum Usable Frequency for communications between two points
C. The Minimum Usable Frequency during a 24-hour period
D. The Maximum Usable Frequency during a 24-hour period

G3B09
(C)
Page 8-1

G3B09
What is the approximate maximum distance along the Earth's surface normally covered in one hop using the F2 region?
A. 180 miles
B. 1,200 miles
C. 2,500 miles
D. 12,000 miles

G3B10
(B)
Page 8-10

G3B10
What is the approximate maximum distance along the Earth's surface normally covered in one hop using the E region?
A. 180 miles
B. 1,200 miles
C. 2,500 miles
D. 12,000 miles

G3B11
(A)
Page 8-10

G3B11
What happens to HF propagation when the LUF exceeds the MUF?
A. Propagation via ordinary skywave communications is not possible over that path
B. HF communications over the path are enhanced
C. Double-hop propagation along the path is more common
D. Propagation over the path on all HF frequencies is enhanced

G3B12
(D)
Page 8-7

G3B12
Which of the following is typical of the lower HF frequencies during the summer?
A. Poor propagation at any time of day
B. World-wide propagation during daylight hours
C. Heavy distortion on signals due to photon absorption
D. High levels of atmospheric noise or static

G3C — Ionospheric regions; critical angle and frequency; HF scatter; near vertical incidence skywave (NVIS)

G3C01
(A)
Page 8-1

G3C01
Which ionospheric region is closest to the surface of Earth?
A. The D region
B. The E region
C. The F1 region
D. The F2 region

G3C02
What is meant by the term "critical frequency" at a given incidence angle?
A. The highest frequency which is refracted back to Earth
B. The lowest frequency which is refracted back to Earth
C. The frequency at which the signal-to-noise ratio approaches unity
D. The frequency at which the signal-to-noise ratio is 6 dB

G3C03
Why is skip propagation via the F2 region longer than that via the other ionospheric regions?
A. Because it is the densest
B. Because of the Doppler effect
C. Because it is the highest
D. Because of temperature inversions

G3C04
What does the term "critical angle" mean, as applied to radio wave propagation?
A. The long path azimuth of a distant station
B. The short path azimuth of a distant station
C. The lowest takeoff angle that will return a radio wave to Earth under specific ionospheric
   conditions
D. The highest takeoff angle that will return a radio wave to Earth under specific ionospheric
   conditions

G3C05
Why is long-distance communication on the 40-, 60-, 80-, and 160-meter bands more difficult during
the day?
A. The F region absorbs signals at these frequencies during daylight hours
B. The F region is unstable during daylight hours
C. The D region absorbs signals at these frequencies during daylight hours
D. The E region is unstable during daylight hours

G3C06
What is a characteristic of HF scatter?
A. Phone signals have high intelligibility
B. Signals have a fluttering sound
C. There are very large, sudden swings in signal strength
D. Scatter propagation occurs only at night

G3C07
What makes HF scatter signals often sound distorted?
A. The ionospheric region involved is unstable
B. Ground waves are absorbing much of the signal
C. The E region is not present
D. Energy is scattered into the skip zone through several different paths

G3C08
Why are HF scatter signals in the skip zone usually weak?
A. Only a small part of the signal energy is scattered into the skip zone
B. Signals are scattered from the magnetosphere, which is not a good reflector
C. Propagation is via ground waves, which absorb most of the signal energy
D. Propagation is via ducts in the F region, which absorb most of the energy

G3C02
(A)
Page 8-1

G3C03
(C)
Page 8-1

G3C04
(D)
Page 8-2

G3C05
(C)
Page 8-2

G3C06
(B)
Page 8-12

G3C07
(D)
Page 8-12

G3C08
(A)
Page 8-12

G3C09
What type of propagation allows signals to be heard in the transmitting station's skip zone?
A. Faraday rotation
B. Scatter
C. Chordal hop
D. Short-path

G3C10
What is near vertical incidence skywave (NVIS) propagation?
A. Propagation near the MUF
B. Short distance MF or HF propagation at high elevation angles
C. Long path HF propagation at sunrise and sunset
D. Double hop propagation near the LUF

G3C11
Which ionospheric region is the most absorbent of signals below 10 MHz during daylight hours?
A. The F2 region
B. The F1 region
C. The E region
D. The D region

SUBELEMENT G4 — AMATEUR RADIO PRACTICES
[5 Exam Questions — 5 groups]
G4A — Station configuration and operation

G4A01
What is the purpose of the notch filter found on many HF transceivers?
A. To restrict the transmitter voice bandwidth
B. To reduce interference from carriers in the receiver passband
C. To eliminate receiver interference from impulse noise sources
D. To remove interfering splatter generated by signals on adjacent frequencies

G4A02
What is the benefit of using the opposite or "reverse" sideband when receiving CW?
A. Interference from impulse noise will be eliminated
B. More stations can be accommodated within a given signal passband
C. It may be possible to reduce or eliminate interference from other signals
D. Accidental out-of-band operation can be prevented

G4A03
How does a noise blanker work?
A. By temporarily increasing received bandwidth
B. By redirecting noise pulses into a filter capacitor
C. By reducing receiver gain during a noise pulse
D. By clipping noise peaks

G4A04
What is the effect on plate current of the correct setting of a vacuum-tube RF power amplifier's TUNE control?
A. A pronounced peak
B. A pronounced dip
C. No change will be observed
D. A slow, rhythmic oscillation

G4A05
Why is automatic level control (ALC) used with an RF power amplifier?
A. To balance the transmitter audio frequency response
B. To reduce harmonic radiation
C. To prevent excessive drive
D. To increase overall efficiency

G4A06
What is the purpose of an antenna tuner?
A. Reduce the SWR in the feed line to the antenna
B. Reduce the power dissipation in the feedline to the antenna
C. Increase power transfer from the transmitter to the feed line
D. All these choices are correct

G4A07
What happens as a receiver's noise reduction control level is increased?
A. Received signals may become distorted
B. Received frequency may become unstable
C. CW signals may become severely attenuated
D. Received frequency may shift several kHz

G4A08
What is the correct adjustment for the LOAD or COUPLING control of a vacuum tube RF power amplifier?
A. Minimum SWR on the antenna
B. Minimum plate current without exceeding maximum allowable grid current
C. Highest plate voltage while minimizing grid current
D. Desired power output without exceeding maximum allowable plate current

G4A09
What is the purpose of delaying RF output after activating a transmitter's keying line to an external amplifier?
A. To prevent key clicks on CW
B. To prevent transient overmodulation
C. To allow time for the amplifier to switch the antenna between the transceiver and the amplifier output
D. To allow time for the amplifier power supply to reach operating level

G4A10
What is the function of an electronic keyer?
A. Automatic transmit/receive switching
B. Automatic generation of dots and dashes for CW operation
C. To allow time for switching the antenna from the receiver to the transmitter
D. Computer interface for PSK and RTTY operation

G4A11
Why should the ALC system be inactive when transmitting AFSK data signals?
A. ALC will invert the modulation of the AFSK mode
B. The ALC action distorts the signal
C. When using digital modes, too much ALC activity can cause the transmitter to overheat
D. All these choices are correct

G4A05
(C)
Page 5-14

G4A06
(C)
Page 7-19

G4A07
(A)
Page 5-16

G4A08
(D)
Page 5-14

G4A09
(C)
Page 5-14

G4A10
(B)
Page 2-13

G4A11
(B)
Page 6-11

G4A12
(C)
Page 2-2

G4A12
Which of the following is a common use of the dual-VFO feature on a transceiver?
A. To allow transmitting on two frequencies at once
B. To permit full duplex operation -- that is, transmitting and receiving at the same time
C. To transmit on one frequency and listen on another
D. To improve frequency accuracy by allowing variable frequency output (VFO) operation

G4A13
(A)
Page 5-16

G4A13
What is the purpose of using a receive attenuator?
A. To prevent receiver overload from strong incoming signals
B. To reduce the transmitter power when driving a linear amplifier
C. To reduce power consumption when operating from batteries
D. To reduce excessive audio level on strong signals

G4B — Tests and test equipment

G4B01
(D)
Page 4-42

G4B01
What item of test equipment contains horizontal and vertical channel amplifiers?
A. An ohmmeter
B. A signal generator
C. An ammeter
D. An oscilloscope

G4B02
(D)
Page 4-42

G4B02
Which of the following is an advantage of an oscilloscope versus a digital voltmeter?
A. An oscilloscope uses less power
B. Complex impedances can be easily measured
C. Greater precision
D. Complex waveforms can be measured

G4B03
(A)
Page 4-42

G4B03
Which of the following is the best instrument to use for checking the keying waveform of a CW transmitter?
A. An oscilloscope
B. A field strength meter
C. A sidetone monitor
D. A wavemeter

G4B04
(D)
Page 4-43

G4B04
What signal source is connected to the vertical input of an oscilloscope when checking the RF envelope pattern of a transmitted signal?
A. The local oscillator of the transmitter
B. An external RF oscillator
C. The transmitter balanced mixer output
D. The attenuated RF output of the transmitter

G4B05
(D)
Page 4-43

G4B05
Why do voltmeters have high input impedance?
A. It improves the frequency response
B. It allows for higher voltages to be safely measured
C. It improves the resolution of the readings
D. It decreases the loading on circuits being measured

G4B06
What is an advantage of a digital multimeter as compared to an analog multimeter?
A. Better for measuring computer circuits
B. Less prone to overload
C. Higher precision
D. Faster response

G4B07
What signals are used to conduct a two-tone test?
A. Two audio signals of the same frequency shifted 90 degrees
B. Two non-harmonically related audio signals
C. Two swept frequency tones
D. Two audio frequency range square wave signals of equal amplitude

G4B08
What transmitter performance parameter does a two-tone test analyze?
A. Linearity
B. Percentage of suppression of the carrier and undesired sideband for SSB
C. Percentage of frequency modulation
D. Percentage of carrier phase shift

G4B09
When is an analog multimeter preferred to a digital multimeter?
A. When testing logic circuits
B. When high precision is desired
C. When measuring the frequency of an oscillator
D. When adjusting circuits for maximum or minimum values

G4B10
Which of the following can be determined with a directional wattmeter?
A. Standing wave ratio
B. Antenna front-to-back ratio
C. RF interference
D. Radio wave propagation

G4B11
Which of the following must be connected to an antenna analyzer when it is being used for SWR measurements?
A. Receiver
B. Transmitter
C. Antenna and feed line
D. All these choices are correct

G4B12
What effect can strong signals from nearby transmitters have on an antenna analyzer?
A. Desensitization which can cause intermodulation products which interfere with impedance readings
B. Received power that interferes with SWR readings
C. Generation of harmonics which interfere with frequency readings
D. All these choices are correct

<table>
<tr><td>G4B06</td></tr>
<tr><td>(C)</td></tr>
<tr><td>Page 4-43</td></tr>
<tr><td>G4B07</td></tr>
<tr><td>(B)</td></tr>
<tr><td>Page 5-8</td></tr>
<tr><td>G4B08</td></tr>
<tr><td>(A)</td></tr>
<tr><td>Page 5-8</td></tr>
<tr><td>G4B09</td></tr>
<tr><td>(D)</td></tr>
<tr><td>Page 4-43</td></tr>
<tr><td>G4B10</td></tr>
<tr><td>(A)</td></tr>
<tr><td>Page 4-43</td></tr>
<tr><td>G4B11</td></tr>
<tr><td>(C)</td></tr>
<tr><td>Page 4-43</td></tr>
<tr><td>G4B12</td></tr>
<tr><td>(B)</td></tr>
<tr><td>Page 4-43</td></tr>
</table>

G4B13
Which of the following can be measured with an antenna analyzer?
A. Front-to-back ratio of an antenna
B. Power output from a transmitter
C. Impedance of coaxial cable
D. Gain of a directional antenna

G4C — Interference to consumer electronics; grounding and bonding

G4C01
Which of the following might be useful in reducing RF interference to audio frequency circuits?
A. Bypass inductor
B. Bypass capacitor
C. Forward-biased diode
D. Reverse-biased diode

G4C02
Which of the following could be a cause of interference covering a wide range of frequencies?
A. Not using a balun or line isolator to feed balanced antennas
B. Lack of rectification of the transmitter's signal in power conductors
C. Arcing at a poor electrical connection
D. Using a balun to feed an unbalanced antenna

G4C03
What sound is heard from an audio device experiencing RF interference from a single sideband phone transmitter?
A. A steady hum whenever the transmitter is on the air
B. On-and-off humming or clicking
C. Distorted speech
D. Clearly audible speech

G4C04
What sound is heard from an audio device experiencing RF interference from a CW transmitter?
A. On-and-off humming or clicking
B. A CW signal at a nearly pure audio frequency
C. A chirpy CW signal
D. Severely distorted audio

G4C05
What is a possible cause of high voltages that produce RF burns?
A. Flat braid rather than round wire has been used for the ground wire
B. Insulated wire has been used for the ground wire
C. The ground rod is resonant
D. The ground wire has high impedance on that frequency

G4C06
What is a possible effect of a resonant ground connection?
A. Overheating of ground straps
B. Corrosion of the ground rod
C. High RF voltages on the enclosures of station equipment
D. A ground loop

G4C07
Why should soldered joints not be used in lightning protection ground connections?
A. A soldered joint will likely be destroyed by the heat of a lightning strike
B. Solder flux will prevent a low conductivity connection
C. Solder has too high a dielectric constant to provide adequate lightning protection
D. All these choices are correct

G4C08
Which of the following would reduce RF interference caused by common-mode current on an audio cable?
A. Place a ferrite choke on the cable
B. Connect the center conductor to the shield of all cables to short circuit the RFI signal
C. Ground the center conductor of the audio cable causing the interference
D. Add an additional insulating jacket to the cable

G4C09
How can the effects of ground loops be minimized?
A. Connect all ground conductors in series
B. Connect the AC neutral conductor to the ground wire
C. Avoid using lock washers and star washers when making ground connections
D. Bond equipment enclosures together

G4C10
What could be a symptom caused by a ground loop in your station's audio connections?
A. You receive reports of "hum" on your station's transmitted signal
B. The SWR reading for one or more antennas is suddenly very high
C. An item of station equipment starts to draw excessive amounts of current
D. You receive reports of harmonic interference from your station

G4C11
What technique helps to minimize RF "hot spots" in an amateur station?
A. Building all equipment in a metal enclosure
B. Using surge suppressor power outlets
C. Bonding all equipment enclosures together
D. Placing low-pass filters on all feed lines

G4C12
Why must all metal enclosures of station equipment be grounded?
A. It prevents a blown fuse in the event of an internal short circuit
B. It prevents signal overload
C. It ensures that the neutral wire is grounded
D. It ensures that hazardous voltages cannot appear on the chassis

G4D — Speech processors; S meters; sideband operation near band edges

G4D01
What is the purpose of a speech processor in a transceiver?
A. Increase the apparent loudness of transmitted voice signals
B. Increase transmitter bass response for more natural-sounding SSB signals
C. Prevent distortion of voice signals
D. Decrease high-frequency voice output to prevent out-of-band operation

G4C07
(A)
Page 9-8

G4C08
(A)
Page 5-21

G4C09
(D)
Page 5-22

G4C10
(A)
Page 5-22

G4C11
(C)
Page 5-22

G4C12
(D)
Page 5-22

G4D01
(A)
Page 5-8

G4D02
(B)
Page 5-8

G4D02
How does a speech processor affect a single sideband phone signal?
A. It increases peak power
B. It increases average power
C. It reduces harmonic distortion
D. It reduces intermodulation distortion

G4D03
(D)
Page 5-8

G4D03
What is the effect of an incorrectly adjusted speech processor?
A. Distorted speech
B. Excess intermodulation products
C. Excessive background noise
D. All these choices are correct

G4D04
(C)
Page 5-16

G4D04
What does an S meter measure?
A. Carrier suppression
B. Impedance
C. Received signal strength
D. Transmitter power output

G4D05
(D)
Page 5-16

G4D05
How does a signal that reads 20 dB over S9 compare to one that reads S9 on a receiver, assuming a properly calibrated S meter?
A. It is 10 times less powerful
B. It is 20 times less powerful
C. It is 20 times more powerful
D. It is 100 times more powerful

G4D06
(A)
Page 5-16

G4D06
How much change in signal strength is typically represented by one S unit?
A. 6 dB
B. 12 dB
C. 15 dB
D. 18 dB

G4D07
(C)
Page 5-16

G4D07
How much must the power output of a transmitter be raised to change the S meter reading on a distant receiver from S8 to S9?
A. Approximately 1.5 times
B. Approximately 2 times
C. Approximately 4 times
D. Approximately 8 times

G4D08
(C)
Page 5-8

G4D08
What frequency range is occupied by a 3 kHz LSB signal when the displayed carrier frequency is set to 7.178 MHz?
A. 7.178 MHz to 7.181 MHz
B. 7.178 MHz to 7.184 MHz
C. 7.175 MHz to 7.178 MHz
D. 7.1765 MHz to 7.1795 MHz

G4D09
What frequency range is occupied by a 3 kHz USB signal with the displayed carrier frequency set to 14.347 MHz?
A. 14.347 MHz to 14.647 MHz
B. 14.347 MHz to 14.350 MHz
C. 14.344 MHz to 14.347 MHz
D. 14.3455 MHz to 14.3485 MHz

G4D10
How close to the lower edge of a band's phone segment should your displayed carrier frequency be when using 3 kHz wide LSB?
A. At least 3 kHz above the edge of the segment
B. At least 3 kHz below the edge of the segment
C. At least 1 kHz below the edge of the segment
D. At least 1 kHz above the edge of the segment

G4D11
How close to the upper edge of a band's phone segment should your displayed carrier frequency be when using 3 kHz wide USB?
A. At least 3 kHz above the edge of the band
B. At least 3 kHz below the edge of the band
C. At least 1 kHz above the edge of the segment
D. At least 1 kHz below the edge of the segment

G4E — Mobile and portable HF stations; alternative energy source operation

G4E01
What is the purpose of a capacitance hat on a mobile antenna?
A. To increase the power handling capacity of a whip antenna
B. To reduce radiation resistance
C. To electrically lengthen a physically short antenna
D. To lower the radiation angle

G4E02
What is the purpose of a corona ball on an HF mobile antenna?
A. To narrow the operating bandwidth of the antenna
B. To increase the "Q" of the antenna
C. To reduce the chance of damage if the antenna should strike an object
D. To reduce RF voltage discharge from the tip of the antenna while transmitting

G4E03
Which of the following direct, fused power connections would be the best for a 100-watt HF mobile installation?
A. To the battery using heavy-gauge wire
B. To the alternator or generator using heavy-gauge wire
C. To the battery using insulated heavy duty balanced transmission line
D. To the alternator or generator using insulated heavy duty balanced transmission line

G4E04
Why should DC power for a 100-watt HF transceiver not be supplied by a vehicle's auxiliary power socket?
A. The socket is not wired with an RF-shielded power cable
B. The socket's wiring may be inadequate for the current drawn by the transceiver
C. The DC polarity of the socket is reversed from the polarity of modern HF transceivers
D. Drawing more than 50 watts from this socket could cause the engine to overheat

G4D09
(B)
Page 5-8

G4D10
(A)
Page 5-8

G4D11
(B)
Page 5-8

G4E01
(C)
Page 7-1

G4E02
(D)
Page 7-1

G4E03
(A)
Page 5-22

G4E04
(B)
Page 5-22

G4E05
(C)
Page 5-22

G4E05
Which of the following most limits an HF mobile installation?
A. "Picket fencing"
B. The wire gauge of the DC power line to the transceiver
C. Efficiency of the electrically short antenna
D. FCC rules limiting mobile output power on the 75-meter band

G4E06
(C)
Page 7-1

G4E06
What is one disadvantage of using a shortened mobile antenna as opposed to a full-size antenna?
A. Short antennas are more likely to cause distortion of transmitted signals
B. Q of the antenna will be very low
C. Operating bandwidth may be very limited
D. Harmonic radiation may increase

G4E07
(D)
Page 5-22

G4E07
Which of the following may cause receive interference to an HF transceiver installed in a vehicle?
A. The battery charging system
B. The fuel delivery system
C. The control computers
D. All these choices are correct

G4E08
(A)
Page 4-37

G4E08
In what configuration are the individual cells in a solar panel connected together?
A. Series-parallel
B. Shunt
C. Bypass
D. Full-wave bridge

G4E09
(B)
Page 4-37

G4E09
What is the approximate open-circuit voltage from a fully illuminated silicon photovoltaic cell?
A. 0.02 VDC
B. 0.5 VDC
C. 0.2 VDC
D. 1.38 VDC

G4E10
(B)
Page 4-37

G4E10
Why should a series diode be connected between a solar panel and a storage battery that is being charged by the panel?
A. To prevent overload by regulating the charging voltage
B. To prevent discharge of the battery through the panel during times of low or no illumination
C. To limit the current flowing from the panel to a safe value
D. To prevent damage to the battery due to excessive voltage at high illumination levels

G4E11
(D)
Page 4-38

G4E11
What precaution should be taken when connecting a solar panel to a lithium iron phosphate battery?
A. Ground the solar panel outer metal framework
B. Ensure the battery is placed terminals-up
C. A series resistor must be in place
D. The solar panel must have a charge controller

SUBELEMENT G5 — ELECTRICAL PRINCIPLES
[3 Exam Questions — 3 Groups]

G5A — Reactance; inductance; capacitance; impedance; impedance transformation; resonance

G5A01
What happens when inductive and capacitive reactance are equal in a series LC circuit?
A. Resonance causes impedance to be very high
B. Impedance is equal to the geometric mean of the inductance and capacitance
C. Resonance causes impedance to be very low
D. Impedance is equal to the arithmetic mean of the inductance and capacitance

G5A02
What is reactance?
A. Opposition to the flow of direct current caused by resistance
B. Opposition to the flow of alternating current caused by capacitance or inductance
C. Reinforcement of the flow of direct current caused by resistance
D. Reinforcement of the flow of alternating current caused by capacitance or inductance

G5A03
Which of the following is opposition to the flow of alternating current in an inductor?
A. Conductance
B. Reluctance
C. Admittance
D. Reactance

G5A04
Which of the following is opposition to the flow of alternating current in a capacitor?
A. Conductance
B. Reluctance
C. Reactance
D. Admittance

G5A05
How does an inductor react to AC?
A. As the frequency of the applied AC increases, the reactance decreases
B. As the amplitude of the applied AC increases, the reactance increases
C. As the amplitude of the applied AC increases, the reactance decreases
D. As the frequency of the applied AC increases, the reactance increases

G5A06
How does a capacitor react to AC?
A. As the frequency of the applied AC increases, the reactance decreases
B. As the frequency of the applied AC increases, the reactance increases
C. As the amplitude of the applied AC increases, the reactance increases
D. As the amplitude of the applied AC increases, the reactance decreases

G5A07
What is the term for the inverse of impedance?
A. Conductance
B. Susceptance
C. Reluctance
D. Admittance

G5A01
(C)
Page 4-23

G5A02
(B)
Page 4-20

G5A03
(D)
Page 4-20

G5A04
(C)
Page 4-20

G5A05
(D)
Page 4-20

G5A06
(A)
Page 4-20

G5A07
(D)
Page 4-23

G5A08
(C)
Page 4-23

G5A08
What is impedance?
A. The ratio of current to voltage
B. The product of current and voltage
C. The ratio of voltage to current
D. The product of current and reactance

G5A09
(B)
Page 4-20

G5A09
What unit is used to measure reactance?
A. Farad
B. Ohm
C. Ampere
D. Siemens

G5A10
(D)
Page 4-23

G5A10
Which of the following devices can be used for impedance matching at radio frequencies?
A. A transformer
B. A Pi-network
C. A length of transmission line
D. All these choices are correct

G5A11
(B)
Page 4-23

G5A11
What letter is used to represent reactance?
A. Z
B. X
C. B
D. Y

G5A12
(D)
Page 4-23

G5A12
What occurs in an LC circuit at resonance?
A. Current and voltage are equal
B. Resistance is cancelled
C. The circuit radiates all its energy in the form of radio waves
D. Inductive reactance and capacitive reactance cancel

G5B — The decibel; current and voltage dividers; electrical power calculations; sine wave root-mean-square (RMS) values; PEP calculations

G5B01
(B)
Page 4-1

G5B01
What dB change represents a factor of two increase or decrease in power?
A. Approximately 2 dB
B. Approximately 3 dB
C. Approximately 6 dB
D. Approximately 9 dB

G5B02
(C)
Page 4-15

G5B02
How does the total current relate to the individual currents in a circuit of parallel resistors?
A. It equals the average of the branch currents
B. It decreases as more parallel branches are added to the circuit
C. It equals the sum of the currents through each branch
D. It is the sum of the reciprocal of each individual voltage drop

G5B03
How many watts of electrical power are consumed if 400 VDC is supplied to an 800-ohm load?
A. 0.5 watts
B. 200 watts
C. 400 watts
D. 3200 watts

G5B04
How many watts of electrical power are consumed by a 12 VDC light bulb that draws 0.2 amperes?
A. 2.4 watts
B. 24 watts
C. 6 watts
D. 60 watts

G5B05
How many watts are consumed when a current of 7.0 milliamperes flows through a 1,250-ohm resistance?
A. Approximately 61 milliwatts
B. Approximately 61 watts
C. Approximately 11 milliwatts
D. Approximately 11 watts

G5B06
What is the PEP produced by 200 volts peak-to-peak across a 50-ohm dummy load?
A. 1.4 watts
B. 100 watts
C. 353.5 watts
D. 400 watts

G5B07
What value of an AC signal produces the same power dissipation in a resistor as a DC voltage of the same value?
A. The peak-to-peak value
B. The peak value
C. The RMS value
D. The reciprocal of the RMS value

G5B08
What is the peak-to-peak voltage of a sine wave with an RMS voltage of 120 volts?
A. 84.8 volts
B. 169.7 volts
C. 240.0 volts
D. 339.4 volts

G5B09
What is the RMS voltage of a sine wave with a value of 17 volts peak?
A. 8.5 volts
B. 12 volts
C. 24 volts
D. 34 volts

G5B03
(B)
Page 4-1

G5B04
(A)
Page 4-1

G5B05
(A)
Page 4-1

G5B06
(B)
Page 4-5

G5B07
(C)
Page 4-5

G5B08
(D)
Page 4-5

G5B09
(B)
Page 4-5

G5B10
(C)
Page 4-1

G5B10
What percentage of power loss is equivalent to a loss of 1 dB?
A. 10.9 percent
B. 12.2 percent
C. 20.6 percent
D. 25.9 percent

G5B11
(B)
Page 4-5

G5B11
What is the ratio of PEP to average power for an unmodulated carrier?
A. 0.707
B. 1.00
C. 1.414
D. 2.00

G5B12
(B)
Page 4-5

G5B12
What is the RMS voltage across a 50-ohm dummy load dissipating 1200 watts?
A. 173 volts
B. 245 volts
C. 346 volts
D. 692 volts

G5B13
(B)
Page 4-6

G5B13
What is the output PEP of an unmodulated carrier if the average power is 1060 watts?
A. 530 watts
B. 1060 watts
C. 1500 watts
D. 2120 watts

G5B14
(B)
Page 4-6

G5B14
What is the output PEP of 500 volts peak-to-peak across a 50-ohm load?
A. 8.75 watts
B. 625 watts
C. 2500 watts
D. 5000 watts

G5C — Resistors, capacitors, and inductors in series and parallel; transformers

G5C01
(C)
Page 4-14

G5C01
What causes a voltage to appear across the secondary winding of a transformer when an AC voltage source is connected across its primary winding?
A. Capacitive coupling
B. Displacement current coupling
C. Mutual inductance
D. Mutual capacitance

G5C02
(A)
Page 4-14

G5C02
What is the output voltage if an input signal is applied to the secondary winding of a 4:1 voltage step-down transformer instead of the primary winding?
A. The input voltage is multiplied by 4
B. The input voltage is divided by 4
C. Additional resistance must be added in series with the primary to prevent overload
D. Additional resistance must be added in parallel with the secondary to prevent overload

G5C03
What is the total resistance of a 10-, a 20-, and a 50-ohm resistor connected in parallel?
A. 5.9 ohms
B. 0.17 ohms
C. 17 ohms
D. 80 ohms

G5C04
What is the approximate total resistance of a 100- and a 200-ohm resistor in parallel?
A. 300 ohms
B. 150 ohms
C. 75 ohms
D. 67 ohms

G5C05
Why is the primary winding wire of a voltage step-up transformer usually a larger size than that of
the secondary winding?
A. To improve the coupling between the primary and secondary
B. To accommodate the higher current of the primary
C. To prevent parasitic oscillations due to resistive losses in the primary
D. To ensure that the volume of the primary winding is equal to the volume of the secondary
    winding

G5C06
What is the voltage output of a transformer with a 500-turn primary and a 1500-turn secondary when
120 VAC is applied to the primary?
A. 360 volts
B. 120 volts
C. 40 volts
D. 25.5 volts

G5C07
What transformer turns ratio matches an antenna's 600-ohm feed point impedance to a 50-ohm
coaxial cable?
A. 3.5 to 1
B. 12 to 1
C. 24 to 1
D. 144 to 1

G5C08
What is the equivalent capacitance of two 5.0-nanofarad capacitors and one 750-picofarad capacitor
connected in parallel?
A. 576.9 nanofarads
B. 1,733 picofarads
C. 3,583 picofarads
D. 10.750 nanofarads

G5C09
What is the capacitance of three 100-microfarad capacitors connected in series?
A. 0.33 microfarads
B. 3.0 microfarads
C. 33.3 microfarads
D. 300 microfarads

G5C03
(A)
Page 4-15

G5C04
(D)
Page 4-16

G5C05
(B)
Page 4-14

G5C06
(A)
Page 4-14

G5C07
(A)
Page 4-23

G5C08
(D)
Page 4-16

G5C09
(C)
Page 4-16

G5C10
(C)
Page 4-16

G5C10
What is the inductance of three 10-millihenry inductors connected in parallel?
A. 0.30 henries
B. 3.3 henries
C. 3.3 millihenries
D. 30 millihenries

G5C11
(C)
Page 4-16

G5C11
What is the inductance of a circuit with a 20-millihenry inductor connected in series with a 50-millihenry inductor?
A. 7 millihenries
B. 14.3 millihenries
C. 70 millihenries
D. 1,000 millihenries

G5C12
(B)
Page 4-16

G5C12
What is the capacitance of a 20-microfarad capacitor connected in series with a 50-microfarad capacitor?
A. 0.07 microfarads
B. 14.3 microfarads
C. 70 microfarads
D. 1,000 microfarads

G5C13
(C)
Page 4-16

G5C13
Which of the following components should be added to a capacitor to increase the capacitance?
A. An inductor in series
B. An inductor in parallel
C. A capacitor in parallel
D. A capacitor in series

G5C14
(D)
Page 4-16

G5C14
Which of the following components should be added to an inductor to increase the inductance?
A. A capacitor in series
B. A capacitor in parallel
C. An inductor in parallel
D. An inductor in series

SUBELEMENT G6 — CIRCUIT COMPONENTS
[2 Exam Questions — 2 Groups]

G6A — Resistors; capacitors; inductors; rectifiers; solid-state diodes and transistors; vacuum tubes; batteries

G6A01
(C)
Page 4-38

G6A01
What is the minimum allowable discharge voltage for maximum life of a standard 12-volt lead-acid battery?
A. 6 volts
B. 8.5 volts
C. 10.5 volts
D. 12 volts

G6A02
(B)
Page 4-38

G6A02
What is an advantage of batteries with low internal resistance?
A. Long life
B. High discharge current
C. High voltage
D. Rapid recharge

G6A03
What is the approximate forward threshold voltage of a germanium diode?
A. 0.1 volt
B. 0.3 volts
C. 0.7 volts
D. 1.0 volts

G6A04
Which of the following is characteristic of an electrolytic capacitor?
A. Tight tolerance
B. Much less leakage than any other type
C. High capacitance for a given volume
D. Inexpensive RF capacitor

G6A05
What is the approximate forward threshold voltage of a silicon junction diode?
A. 0.1 volt
B. 0.3 volts
C. 0.7 volts
D. 1.0 volts

G6A06
Why should wire-wound resistors not be used in RF circuits?
A. The resistor's tolerance value would not be adequate
B. The resistor's inductance could make circuit performance unpredictable
C. The resistor could overheat
D. The resistor's internal capacitance would detune the circuit

G6A07
What are the operating points for a bipolar transistor used as a switch?
A. Saturation and cutoff
B. The active region (between cutoff and saturation)
C. Peak and valley current points
D. Enhancement and depletion modes

G6A08
Which of the following is characteristic of low voltage ceramic capacitors?
A. Tight tolerance
B. High stability
C. High capacitance for given volume
D. Comparatively low cost

G6A09
Which of the following describes MOSFET construction?
A. The gate is formed by a back-biased junction
B. The gate is separated from the channel by a thin insulating layer
C. The source is separated from the drain by a thin insulating layer
D. The source is formed by depositing metal on silicon

G6A10
Which element of a vacuum tube regulates the flow of electrons between cathode and plate?
A. Control grid
B. Suppressor grid
C. Screen grid
D. Trigger electrode

| G6A03
| (B)
| Page 4-25

| G6A04
| (C)
| Page 4-13

| G6A05
| (C)
| Page 4-25

| G6A06
| (B)
| Page 4-20

| G6A07
| (A)
| Page 4-25

| G6A08
| (D)
| Page 4-13

| G6A09
| (B)
| Page 4-25

| G6A10
| (A)
| Page 4-27

G6A11
(C)
Page 4-23

G6A11
What happens when an inductor is operated above its self-resonant frequency?
A. Its reactance increases
B. Harmonics are generated
C. It becomes capacitive
D. Catastrophic failure is likely

G6A12
(A)
Page 4-27

G6A12
What is the primary purpose of a screen grid in a vacuum tube?
A. To reduce grid-to-plate capacitance
B. To increase efficiency
C. To increase the control grid resistance
D. To decrease plate resistance

G6B — Analog and digital integrated circuits (ICs); microwave ICs (MMICs); display devices; RF connectors; ferrite cores

G6B01
(C)
Page 4-11

G6B01
What determines the performance of a ferrite core at different frequencies?
A. Its conductivity
B. Its thickness
C. The composition, or "mix," of materials used
D. The ratio of outer diameter to inner diameter

G6B02
(B)
Page 4-29

G6B02
What is meant by the term MMIC?
A. Multi-Mode Integrated Circuit
B. Monolithic Microwave Integrated Circuit
C. Metal Monolayer Integrated Circuit
D. Mode Modulated Integrated Circuit

G6B03
(A)
Page 4-29

G6B03
Which of the following is an advantage of CMOS integrated circuits compared to TTL integrated circuits?
A. Low power consumption
B. High power handling capability
C. Better suited for RF amplification
D. Better suited for power supply regulation

G6B04
(C)
Page 4-39

G6B04
What is a typical upper frequency limit for low SWR operation of 50-ohm BNC connectors?
A. 50 MHz
B. 500 MHz
C. 4 GHz
D. 40 GHz

G6B05
(D)
Page 4-11

G6B05
What is an advantage of using a ferrite core toroidal inductor?
A. Large values of inductance may be obtained
B. The magnetic properties of the core may be optimized for a specific range of frequencies
C. Most of the magnetic field is contained in the core
D. All these choices are correct

G6B06
What kind of device is an integrated circuit operational amplifier?
A. Digital
B. MMIC
C. Programmable Logic
D. Analog

G6B07
Which of the following describes a type N connector?
A. A moisture-resistant RF connector useful to 10 GHz
B. A small bayonet connector used for data circuits
C. A low noise figure VHF connector
D. A nickel plated version of the PL-259

G6B08
How is an LED biased when emitting light?
A. In the tunnel-effect region
B. At the Zener voltage
C. Reverse biased
D. Forward biased

G6B09
How does a liquid crystal display compare to an LED display?
A. Higher contrast in high ambient lighting
B. Wider dynamic range
C. Higher power consumption
D. Shorter lifetime

G6B10
How does a ferrite bead or core reduce common-mode RF current on the shield of a coaxial cable?
A. By creating an impedance in the current's path
B. It converts common-mode current to differential mode current
C. By creating an out-of-phase current to cancel the common-mode current
D. Ferrites expel magnetic fields

G6B11
What is an SMA connector?
A. A type-S to type-M adaptor
B. A small threaded connector suitable for signals up to several GHz
C. A connector designed for serial multiple access signals
D. A type of push-on connector intended for high-voltage applications

G6B12
Which of these connector types is commonly used for low frequency or dc signal connections to a
transceiver?
A. PL-259
B. BNC
C. RCA Phono
D. Type N

G6B06
(D)
Page 4-29

G6B07
(A)
Page 4-39

G6B08
(D)
Page 4-32

G6B09
(A)
Page 4-32

G6B10
(A)
Page 5-22

G6B11
(B)
Page 4-39

G6B12
(C)
Page 4-39

SUBELEMENT G7 — PRACTICAL CIRCUITS
[3 Exam Questions — 3 Groups]

G7A — Power supplies; schematic symbols

G7A01
What is the function of a power supply bleeder resistor?
A. It acts as a fuse for excess voltage
B. It discharges the filter capacitors when power is removed
C. It removes shock hazards from the induction coils
D. It eliminates ground loop current

G7A02
Which of the following components are used in a power supply filter network?
A. Diodes
B. Transformers and transducers
C. Capacitors and inductors
D. All these choices are correct

G7A03
Which type of rectifier circuit uses two diodes and a center-tapped transformer?
A. Full-wave
B. Full-wave bridge
C. Half-wave
D. Synchronous

G7A04
What is characteristic of a half-wave rectifier in a power supply?
A. Only one diode is required
B. The ripple frequency is twice that of a full-wave rectifier
C. More current can be drawn from the half-wave rectifier
D. The output voltage is two times the peak input voltage

G7A05
What portion of the AC cycle is converted to DC by a half-wave rectifier?
A. 90 degrees
B. 180 degrees
C. 270 degrees
D. 360 degrees

G7A06
What portion of the AC cycle is converted to DC by a full-wave rectifier?
A. 90 degrees
B. 180 degrees
C. 270 degrees
D. 360 degrees

G7A07
What is the output waveform of an unfiltered full-wave rectifier connected to a resistive load?
A. A series of DC pulses at twice the frequency of the AC input
B. A series of DC pulses at the same frequency as the AC input
C. A sine wave at half the frequency of the AC input
D. A steady DC voltage

G7A01
(B)
Page 4-33

G7A02
(C)
Page 4-33

G7A03
(A)
Page 4-33

G7A04
(A)
Page 4-33

G7A05
(B)
Page 4-33

G7A06
(D)
Page 4-33

G7A07
(A)
Page 4-33

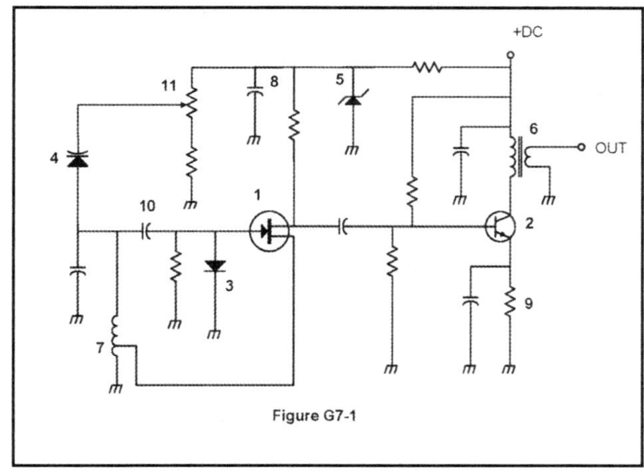

Figure G7-1

G7A08
Which of the following is characteristic of a switchmode power supply as compared to a linear power supply?
A. Faster switching time makes higher output voltage possible
B. Fewer circuit components are required
C. High-frequency operation allows the use of smaller components
D. Inherently more stable

G7A09
Which symbol in figure G7-1 represents a field effect transistor?
A. Symbol 2
B. Symbol 5
C. Symbol 1
D. Symbol 4

G7A10
Which symbol in figure G7-1 represents a Zener diode?
A. Symbol 4
B. Symbol 1
C. Symbol 11
D. Symbol 5

G7A11
Which symbol in figure G7-1 represents an NPN junction transistor?
A. Symbol 1
B. Symbol 2
C. Symbol 7
D. Symbol 11

G7A12
Which symbol in Figure G7-1 represents a solid core transformer?
A. Symbol 4
B. Symbol 7
C. Symbol 6
D. Symbol 1

G7A13
Which symbol in Figure G7-1 represents a tapped inductor?
A. Symbol 7
B. Symbol 11
C. Symbol 6
D. Symbol 1

G7A08
(C)
Page 4-33

G7A09
(C)
Page 4-8

G7A10
(D)
Page 4-8

G7A11
(B)
Page 4-8

G7A12
(C)
Page 4-8

G7A13
(A)
Page 4-8

G7B01
(B)
Page 5-14

G7B01
What is the purpose of neutralizing an amplifier?
A. To limit the modulation index
B. To eliminate self-oscillations
C. To cut off the final amplifier during standby periods
D. To keep the carrier on frequency

G7B02
(D)
Page 5-14

G7B02
Which of these classes of amplifiers has the highest efficiency?
A. Class A
B. Class B
C. Class AB
D. Class C

G7B03
(B)
Page 4-29

G7B03
Which of the following describes the function of a two-input AND gate?
A. Output is high when either or both inputs are low
B. Output is high only when both inputs are high
C. Output is low when either or both inputs are high
D. Output is low only when both inputs are high

G7B04
(A)
Page 5-14

G7B04
In a Class A amplifier, what percentage of the time does the amplifying device conduct?
A. 100%
B. More than 50% but less than 100%
C. 50%
D. Less than 50%

G7B05
(C)
Page 4-29

G7B05
How many states does a 3-bit binary counter have?
A. 3
B. 6
C. 8
D. 16

G7B06
(A)
Page 4-29

G7B06
What is a shift register?
A. A clocked array of circuits that passes data in steps along the array
B. An array of operational amplifiers used for tri-state arithmetic operations
C. A digital mixer
D. An analog mixer

G7B07
(D)
Page 5-3

G7B07
Which of the following are basic components of a sine wave oscillator?
A. An amplifier and a divider
B. A frequency multiplier and a mixer
C. A circulator and a filter operating in a feed-forward loop
D. A filter and an amplifier operating in a feedback loop

G7B08
(B)
Page 5-14

G7B08
How is the efficiency of an RF power amplifier determined?
A. Divide the DC input power by the DC output power
B. Divide the RF output power by the DC input power
C. Multiply the RF input power by the reciprocal of the RF output power
D. Add the RF input power to the DC output power

G7B09
What determines the frequency of an LC oscillator?
A. The number of stages in the counter
B. The number of stages in the divider
C. The inductance and capacitance in the tank circuit
D. The time delay of the lag circuit

G7B10
Which of the following describes a linear amplifier?
A. Any RF power amplifier used in conjunction with an amateur transceiver
B. An amplifier in which the output preserves the input waveform
C. A Class C high efficiency amplifier
D. An amplifier used as a frequency multiplier

G7B11
For which of the following modes is a Class C power stage appropriate for amplifying a modulated signal?
A. SSB
B. FM
C. AM
D. All these choices are correct

G7C — Transceiver design; filters; oscillators; digital signal processing (DSP)

G7C01
What circuit is used to select one of the sidebands from a balanced modulator?
A. Carrier oscillator
B. Filter
C. IF amplifier
D. RF amplifier

G7C02
What output is produced by a balanced modulator?
A. Frequency modulated RF
B. Audio with equalized frequency response
C. Audio extracted from the modulation signal
D. Double-sideband modulated RF

G7C03
What is one reason to use an impedance matching transformer at a transmitter output?
A. To minimize transmitter power output
B. To present the desired impedance to the transmitter and feed line
C. To reduce power supply ripple
D. To minimize radiation resistance

G7C04
How is a product detector used?
A. Used in test gear to detect spurious mixing products
B. Used in a transmitter to perform frequency multiplication
C. Used in an FM receiver to filter out unwanted sidebands
D. Used in a single sideband receiver to extract the modulated signal

G7B09
(C)
Page 5-3

G7B10
(B)
Page 5-8

G7B11
(B)
Page 5-14

G7C01
(B)
Page 5-8

G7C02
(D)
Page 5-8

G7C03
(B)
Page 4-23

G7C04
(D)
Page 5-16

G7C05
(D)
Page 5-3

G7C05
Which of the following is characteristic of a direct digital synthesizer (DDS)?
A. Extremely narrow tuning range
B. Relatively high-power output
C. Pure sine wave output
D. Variable output frequency with the stability of a crystal oscillator

G7C06
(A)
Page 5-16

G7C06
Which of the following is an advantage of a digital signal processing (DSP) filter compared to an analog filter?
A. A wide range of filter bandwidths and shapes can be created
B. Fewer digital components are required
C. Mixing products are greatly reduced
D. The DSP filter is much more effective at VHF frequencies

G7C07
(A)
Page 5-3

G7C07
What term specifies a filter's attenuation inside its passband?
A. Insertion loss
B. Return loss
C. Q
D. Ultimate rejection

G7C08
(D)
Page 5-16

G7C08
Which parameter affects receiver sensitivity?
A. Input amplifier gain
B. Demodulator stage bandwidth
C. Input amplifier noise figure
D. All these choices are correct

G7C09
(B)
Page 5-3

G7C09
What is the phase difference between the I and Q RF signals that software-defined radio (SDR) equipment uses for modulation and demodulation?
A. Zero
B. 90 degrees
C. 180 degrees
D. 45 degrees

G7C10
(B)
Page 5-3

G7C10
What is an advantage of using I-Q modulation with software-defined radios (SDRs)?
A. The need for high resolution analog-to-digital converters is eliminated
B. All types of modulation can be created with appropriate processing
C. Minimum detectible signal level is reduced
D. Automatic conversion of the signal from digital to analog

G7C11
(D)
Page 5-3

G7C11
Which of these functions is performed by software in a software-defined radio (SDR)?
A. Filtering
B. Detection
C. Modulation
D. All these choices are correct

G7C12
(C)
Page 5-3

G7C12
What is the frequency above which a low-pass filter's output power is less than half the input power?
A. Notch frequency
B. Neper frequency
C. Cutoff frequency
D. Rolloff frequency

G7C13
What term specifies a filter's maximum ability to reject signals outside its passband?
A. Notch depth
B. Rolloff
C. Insertion loss
D. Ultimate rejection

G7C14
The bandwidth of a band-pass filter is measured between what two frequencies?
A. Upper and lower half-power
B. Cutoff and rolloff
C. Pole and zero
D. Image and harmonic

SUBELEMENT G8 — SIGNALS AND EMISSIONS
[3 Exam Questions — 3 Groups]

G8A — Carriers and modulation: AM, FM, and single sideband; modulation envelope; digital modulation; overmodulation; link budgets and link margins

G8A01
How is direct binary FSK modulation generated?
A. By keying an FM transmitter with a sub-audible tone
B. By changing an oscillator's frequency directly with a digital control signal
C. By using a transceiver's computer data interface protocol to change frequencies
D. By reconfiguring the CW keying input to act as a tone generator

G8A02
What is the name of the process that changes the phase angle of an RF signal to convey information?
A. Phase convolution
B. Phase modulation
C. Phase transformation
D. Phase inversion

G8A03
What is the name of the process that changes the instantaneous frequency of an RF wave to convey information?
A. Frequency convolution
B. Frequency transformation
C. Frequency conversion
D. Frequency modulation

G8A04
What emission is produced by a reactance modulator connected to a transmitter RF amplifier stage?
A. Multiplex modulation
B. Phase modulation
C. Amplitude modulation
D. Pulse modulation

G8A05
What type of modulation varies the instantaneous power level of the RF signal?
A. Power modulation
B. Phase modulation
C. Frequency modulation
D. Amplitude modulation

G7C13
(D)
Page 5-4

G7C14
(A)
Page 5-4

G8A01
(B)
Page 6-1

G8A02
(B)
Page 5-1

G8A03
(D)
Page 5-1

G8A04
(B)
Page 5-4

G8A05
(D)
Page 5-1

G8A06
(D)
Page 6-4

G8A06
Which of the following is characteristic of QPSK31?
A. It is sideband sensitive
B. Its encoding provides error correction
C. Its bandwidth is approximately the same as BPSK31
D. All these choices are correct

G8A07
(A)
Page 5-1

G8A07
Which of the following phone emissions uses the narrowest bandwidth?
A. Single sideband
B. Vestigial sideband
C. Phase modulation
D. Frequency modulation

G8A08
(D)
Page 5-8

G8A08
Which of the following is an effect of overmodulation?
A. Insufficient audio
B. Insufficient bandwidth
C. Frequency drift
D. Excessive bandwidth

G8A09
(A)
Page 6-6

G8A09
What type of modulation is used by FT8?
A. 8-tone frequency shift keying
B. Vestigial sideband
C. Amplitude compressed AM
D. 8-bit direct sequence spread spectrum

G8A10
(C)
Page 5-8

G8A10
What is meant by the term "flat-topping," when referring to an amplitude-modulated phone signal?
A. Signal distortion caused by insufficient collector current
B. The transmitter's automatic level control (ALC) is properly adjusted
C. Signal distortion caused by excessive drive or speech levels
D. The transmitter's carrier is properly suppressed

G8A11
(A)
Page 5-8

G8A11
What is the modulation envelope of an AM signal?
A. The waveform created by connecting the peak values of the modulated signal
B. The carrier frequency that contains the signal
C. Spurious signals that envelop nearby frequencies
D. The bandwidth of the modulated signal

G8A12
(D)
Page 6-6

G8A12
What is QPSK modulation?
A. Modulation using quasi-parallel to serial conversion to reduce bandwidth
B. Modulation using quadra-pole sideband keying to generate spread spectrum signals
C. Modulation using Fast Fourier Transforms to generate frequencies at the first, second, third, and
   fourth harmonics of the carrier frequency to improve noise immunity
D. Modulation in which digital data is transmitted using 0-, 90-, 180- and 270-degrees phase shift
   to represent pairs of bits

G8A13
(C)
Page 5-1

G8A13
What is a link budget?
A. The financial costs associated with operating a radio link
B. The sum of antenna gains minus system losses
C. The sum of transmit power and antenna gains minus system losses as seen at the receiver
D. The difference between transmit power and receiver sensitivity

G8A14
What is link margin?
A. The opposite of fade margin
B. The difference between received power level and minimum required signal level at the input to
   the receiver
C. Transmit power minus receiver sensitivity
D. Receiver sensitivity plus 3 dB

G8B — Frequency changing; bandwidths of various modes; deviation; intermodulation

G8B01
Which mixer input is varied or tuned to convert signals of different frequencies to an intermediate
frequency (IF)?
A. Image frequency
B. Local oscillator
C. RF input
D. Beat frequency oscillator

G8B02
What is the term for interference from a signal at twice the IF frequency from the desired signal?
A. Quadrature response
B. Image response
C. Mixer interference
D. Intermediate interference

G8B03
What is another term for the mixing of two RF signals?
A. Heterodyning
B. Synthesizing
C. Frequency inversion
D. Phase inversion

G8B04
What is the stage in a VHF FM transmitter that generates a harmonic of a lower frequency signal to
reach the desired operating frequency?
A. Mixer
B. Reactance modulator
C. Balanced converter
D. Multiplier

G8B05
Which intermodulation products are closest to the original signal frequencies?
A. Second harmonics
B. Even-order
C. Odd-order
D. Intercept point

G8B06
What is the total bandwidth of an FM phone transmission having 5 kHz deviation and 3 kHz
modulating frequency?
A. 3 kHz
B. 5 kHz
C. 8 kHz
D. 16 kHz

G8A14
(B)
Page 5-1

G8B01
(B)
Page 5-16

G8B02
(B)
Page 5-17

G8B03
(A)
Page 5-4

G8B04
(D)
Page 5-4

G8B05
(C)
Page 5-22

G8B06
(D)
Page 5-8

G8B07
(B)
Page 5-8

G8B07
What is the frequency deviation for a 12.21 MHz reactance modulated oscillator in a 5 kHz deviation, 146.52 MHz FM phone transmitter?
A. 101.75 Hz
B. 416.7 Hz
C. 5 kHz
D. 60 kHz

G8B08
(B)
Page 6-12

G8B08
Why is it important to know the duty cycle of the mode you are using when transmitting?
A. To aid in tuning your transmitter
B. Some modes have high duty cycles that could exceed the transmitter's average power rating
C. To allow time for the other station to break in during a transmission
D. To prevent overmodulation

G8B09
(D)
Page 5-17

G8B09
Why is it good to match receiver bandwidth to the bandwidth of the operating mode?
A. It is required by FCC rules
B. It minimizes power consumption in the receiver
C. It improves impedance matching of the antenna
D. It results in the best signal-to-noise ratio

G8B10
(B)
Page 6-12

G8B10
What is the relationship between transmitted symbol rate and bandwidth?
A. Symbol rate and bandwidth are not related
B. Higher symbol rates require wider bandwidth
C. Lower symbol rates require wider bandwidth
D. Bandwidth is half the symbol rate

G8B11
(C)
Page 5-4

G8B11
What combination of a mixer's Local Oscillator (LO) and RF input frequencies is found in the output?
A. The ratio
B. The average
C. The sum and difference
D. The arithmetic product

G8B12
(A)
Page 5-22

G8B12
What process combines two signals in a non-linear circuit to produce unwanted spurious outputs?
A. Intermodulation
B. Heterodyning
C. Detection
D. Rolloff

G8B13
(C)
Page 5-22

G8B13
Which of the following is an odd-order intermodulation product of frequencies F1 and F2?
A. 5F1-3F2
B. 3F1-F2
C. 2F1-F2
D. All these choices are correct

G8C — Digital emission modes

G8C01
(C)
Page 3-8

G8C01
On what band do amateurs share channels with the unlicensed Wi-Fi service?
A. 432 MHz
B. 902 MHz
C. 2.4 GHz
D. 10.7 GHz

G8C02
Which digital mode is used as a low-power beacon for assessing HF propagation?
A. WSPR
B. MFSK16
C. PSK31
D. SSB-SC

G8C03
What part of a packet radio frame contains the routing and handling information?
A. Directory
B. Preamble
C. Header
D. Trailer

G8C04
Which of the following describes Baudot code?
A. A 7-bit code with start, stop, and parity bits
B. A code using error detection and correction
C. A 5-bit code with additional start and stop bits
D. A code using SELCAL and LISTEN

G8C05
In an ARQ mode, what is meant by a NAK response to a transmitted packet?
A. Request retransmission of the packet
B. Packet was received without error
C. Receiving station connected and ready for transmissions
D. Entire file received correctly

G8C06
What action results from a failure to exchange information due to excessive transmission attempts when using an ARQ mode?
A. The checksum overflows
B. The connection is dropped
C. Packets will be routed incorrectly
D. Encoding reverts to the default character set

G8C07
Which of the following narrow-band digital modes can receive signals with very low signal-to-noise ratios?
A. MSK144
B. FT8
C. AMTOR
D. MFSK32

G8C08
Which of the following statements is true about PSK31?
A. Upper case letters are sent with more power
B. Upper case letters use longer Varicode bit sequences and thus slow down transmission
C. Error correction is used to ensure accurate message reception
D. Higher power is needed as compared to RTTY for similar error rates

G8C02
(A)
Page 6-6

G8C03
(C)
Page 6-6

G8C04
(C)
Page 6-4

G8C05
(A)
Page 6-6

G8C06
(B)
Page 6-14

G8C07
(B)
Page 6-7

G8C08
(B)
Page 6-4

G8C09
(B)
Page 6-7

G8C09
Which is true of mesh network microwave nodes?
A. Having more nodes increases signal strengths
B. If one node fails, a packet may still reach its target station via an alternate node
C. Links between two nodes in a network may have different frequencies and bandwidths
D. More nodes reduce overall microwave out of band interference

G8C10
(C)
Page 6-7

G8C10
How does forward error correction (FEC) allow the receiver to correct data errors?
A. By controlling transmitter output power for optimum signal strength
B. By using the Varicode character set
C. By transmitting redundant information with the data
D. By using a parity bit with each character

G8C11
(D)
Page 6-1

G8C11
How are the two separate frequencies of a Frequency Shift Keyed (FSK) signal identified?
A. Dot and dash
B. On and off
C. High and low
D. Mark and space

G8C12
(A)
Page 6-4

G8C12
Which type of code is used for sending characters in a PSK31 signal?
A. Varicode
B. Viterbi
C. Volumetric
D. Binary

G8C13
(D)
Page 6-12

G8C13
What is indicated on a waterfall display by one or more vertical lines on either side of a data mode
or RTTY signal?
A. Long path propagation
B. Backscatter propagation
C. Insufficient modulation
D. Overmodulation

G8C14
(C)
Page 6-14

G8C14
Which of the following describes a waterfall display?
A. Frequency is horizontal, signal strength is vertical, time is intensity
B. Frequency is vertical, signal strength is intensity, time is horizontal
C. Frequency is horizontal, signal strength is intensity, time is vertical
D. Frequency is vertical, signal strength is horizontal, time is intensity

G8C15
(C)
Page 6-7

G8C15
What does an FT8 signal report of +3 mean?
A. The signal is 3 times the noise level of an equivalent SSB signal
B. The signal is S3 (weak signals)
C. The signal-to-noise ratio is equivalent to +3dB in a 2.5 kHz bandwidth
D. The signal is 3 dB over S9

G8C16
(D)
Page 6-1

G8C16
Which of the following provide digital voice modes?
A. WSPR, MFSK16, and EasyPAL
B. FT8, FT4, and FST4
C. Winlink, PACTOR II, and PACTOR III
D. DMR, D-STAR, and SystemFusion

SUBELEMENT G9 — ANTENNAS AND FEED LINES
[4 Exam Questions — 4 Groups]

G9A — Feed lines: characteristic impedance and attenuation; standing wave ratio (SWR) calculation, measurement, and effects; antenna feed point matching

G9A01
Which of the following factors determine the characteristic impedance of a parallel conductor feed line?
A. The distance between the centers of the conductors and the radius of the conductors
B. The distance between the centers of the conductors and the length of the line
C. The radius of the conductors and the frequency of the signal
D. The frequency of the signal and the length of the line

G9A02
What is the relationship between high standing wave ratio (SWR) and transmission line loss?
A. There is no relationship between transmission line loss and SWR
B. High SWR increases loss in a lossy transmission line
C. High SWR makes it difficult to measure transmission line loss
D. High SWR reduces the relative effect of transmission line loss

G9A03
What is the nominal characteristic impedance of "window line" transmission line?
A. 50 ohms
B. 75 ohms
C. 100 ohms
D. 450 ohms

G9A04
What causes reflected power at an antenna's feed point?
A. Operating an antenna at its resonant frequency
B. Using more transmitter power than the antenna can handle
C. A difference between feed line impedance and antenna feed point impedance
D. Feeding the antenna with unbalanced feed line

G9A05
How does the attenuation of coaxial cable change with increasing frequency?
A. Attenuation is independent of frequency
B. Attenuation increases
C. Attenuation decreases
D. Attenuation follows Marconi's Law of Attenuation

G9A06
In what units is RF feed line loss usually expressed?
A. Ohms per 1,000 feet
B. Decibels per 1,000 feet
C. Ohms per 100 feet
D. Decibels per 100 feet

G9A07
What must be done to prevent standing waves on a feed line connected to an antenna?
A. The antenna feed point must be at DC ground potential
B. The feed line must be an odd number of electrical quarter wavelengths long
C. The feed line must be an even number of physical half wavelengths long
D. The antenna feed point impedance must be matched to the characteristic impedance of the feed line

G9A01
(A)
Page 7-19

G9A02
(B)
Page 7-19

G9A03
(D)
Page 7-20

G9A04
(C)
Page 7-20

G9A05
(B)
Page 7-20

G9A06
(D)
Page 7-20

G9A07
(D)
Page 7-20

G9A08
(B)
Page 7-20

G9A08
If the SWR on an antenna feed line is 5:1, and a matching network at the transmitter end of the feed line is adjusted to present a 1:1 SWR to the transmitter, what is the resulting SWR on the feed line?
A. 1:1
B. 5:1
C. Between 1:1 and 5:1 depending on the characteristic impedance of the line
D. Between 1:1 and 5:1 depending on the reflected power at the transmitter

G9A09
(A)
Page 7-20

G9A09
What standing wave ratio results from connecting a 50-ohm feed line to a 200-ohm resistive load?
A. 4:1
B. 1:4
C. 2:1
D. 1:2

G9A10
(D)
Page 7-20

G9A10
What standing wave ratio results from connecting a 50-ohm feed line to a 10-ohm resistive load?
A. 2:1
B. 1:2
C. 1:5
D. 5:1

G9A11
(A)
Page 7-20

G9A11
What is the effect of transmission line loss on SWR measured at the input to the line?
A. Higher loss reduces SWR measured at the input to the line
B. Higher loss increases SWR measured at the input to the line
C. Higher loss increases the accuracy of SWR measured at the input to the line
D. Transmission line loss does not affect the SWR measurement

G9B — Basic dipole and monopole antennas

G9B01
(B)
Page 7-16

G9B01
What is a characteristic of a random-wire HF antenna connected directly to the transmitter?
A. It must be longer than 1 wavelength
B. Station equipment may carry significant RF current
C. It produces only vertically polarized radiation
D. It is more effective on the lower HF bands than on the higher bands

G9B02
(B)
Page 7-1

G9B02
Which of the following is a common way to adjust the feed point impedance of an elevated quarter-wave ground-plane vertical antenna to be approximately 50 ohms?
A. Slope the radials upward
B. Slope the radials downward
C. Lengthen the radials beyond one wavelength
D. Coil the radials

G9B03
(D)
Page 7-1

G9B03
Which of the following best describes the radiation pattern of a quarter-wave ground-plane vertical antenna?
A. Bi-directional in azimuth
B. Isotropic
C. Hemispherical
D. Omnidirectional in azimuth

G9B04
What is the radiation pattern of a dipole antenna in free space in a plane containing the conductor?
A. It is a figure-eight at right angles to the antenna
B. It is a figure-eight off both ends of the antenna
C. It is a circle (equal radiation in all directions)
D. It has a pair of lobes on one side of the antenna and a single lobe on the other side

G9B05
How does antenna height affect the azimuthal radiation pattern of a horizontal dipole HF antenna at elevation angles higher than about 45 degrees?
A. If the antenna is too high, the pattern becomes unpredictable
B. Antenna height has no effect on the pattern
C. If the antenna is less than 1/2 wavelength high, the azimuthal pattern is almost omnidirectional
D. If the antenna is less than 1/2 wavelength high, radiation off the ends of the wire is eliminated

G9B06
Where should the radial wires of a ground-mounted vertical antenna system be placed?
A. As high as possible above the ground
B. Parallel to the antenna element
C. On the surface or buried a few inches below the ground
D. At the center of the antenna

G9B07
How does the feed point impedance of a horizontal 1/2 wave dipole antenna change as the antenna height is reduced to 1/10 wavelength above ground?
A. It steadily increases
B. It steadily decreases
C. It peaks at about 1/8 wavelength above ground
D. It is unaffected by the height above ground

G9B08
How does the feed point impedance of a 1/2 wave dipole change as the feed point is moved from the center toward the ends?
A. It steadily increases
B. It steadily decreases
C. It peaks at about 1/8 wavelength from the end
D. It is unaffected by the location of the feed point

G9B09
Which of the following is an advantage of using a horizontally polarized as compared to a vertically polarized HF antenna?
A. Lower ground losses
B. Lower feed point impedance
C. Shorter radials
D. Lower radiation resistance

G9B10
What is the approximate length for a 1/2 wave dipole antenna cut for 14.250 MHz?
A. 8 feet
B. 16 feet
C. 24 feet
D. 33 feet

G9B04
(A)
Page 7-1

G9B05
(C)
Page 7-2

G9B06
(C)
Page 7-2

G9B07
(B)
Page 7-2

G9B08
(A)
Page 7-2

G9B09
(A)
Page 7-2

G9B10
(D)
Page 7-2

G9B11
What is the approximate length for a 1/2 wave dipole antenna cut for 3.550 MHz?
A. 42 feet
B. 84 feet
C. 132 feet
D. 263 feet

G9B12
What is the approximate length for a 1/4 wave monopole antenna cut for 28.5 MHz?
A. 8 feet
B. 11 feet
C. 16 feet
D. 21 feet

G9C — Directional antennas

G9C01
Which of the following would increase the bandwidth of a Yagi antenna?
A. Larger-diameter elements
B. Closer element spacing
C. Loading coils in series with the element
D. Tapered-diameter elements

G9C02
What is the approximate length of the driven element of a Yagi antenna?
A. 1/4 wavelength
B. 1/2 wavelength
C. 3/4 wavelength
D. 1 wavelength

G9C03
How do the lengths of a three-element Yagi reflector and director compare to that of the driven element?
A. The reflector is longer, and the director is shorter
B. The reflector is shorter, and the director is longer
C. They are all the same length
D. Relative length depends on the frequency of operation

G9C04
How does antenna gain in dBi compare to gain stated in dBd for the same antenna?
A. Gain in dBi is 2.15 dB lower
B. Gain in dBi is 2.15 dB higher
C. Gain in dBd is 1.25 dBd lower
D. Gain in dBd is 1.25 dBd higher

G9C05
What is the primary effect of increasing boom length and adding directors to a Yagi antenna?
A. Gain increases
B. Beamwidth increases
C. Front-to-back ratio decreases
D. Resonant frequency is lower

G9C06 [Deleted]

G9C07
What does "front-to-back ratio" mean in reference to a Yagi antenna?
A. The number of directors versus the number of reflectors
B. The relative position of the driven element with respect to the reflectors and directors
C. The power radiated in the major lobe compared to that in the opposite direction
D. The ratio of forward gain to dipole gain

G9C08
What is meant by the "main lobe" of a directive antenna?
A. The magnitude of the maximum vertical angle of radiation
B. The point of maximum current in a radiating antenna element
C. The maximum voltage standing wave point on a radiating element
D. The direction of maximum radiated field strength from the antenna

G9C09
In free space, how does the gain of two three-element, horizontally polarized Yagi antennas spaced vertically ½ wavelength apart typically compare to the gain of a single three-element Yagi?
A. Approximately 1.5 dB higher
B. Approximately 3 dB higher
C. Approximately 6 dB higher
D. Approximately 9 dB higher

G9C10
Which of the following can be adjusted to optimize forward gain, front-to-back ratio, or SWR bandwidth of a Yagi antenna?
A. The physical length of the boom
B. The number of elements on the boom
C. The spacing of each element along the boom
D. All these choices are correct

G9C11
What is a beta or hairpin match?
A. A shorted transmission line stub placed at the feed point of a Yagi antenna to provide impedance matching
B. A 1/4 wavelength section of 75-ohm coax in series with the feed point of a Yagi to provide impedance matching
C. A series capacitor selected to cancel the inductive reactance of a folded dipole antenna
D. A section of 300-ohm twin-lead transmission line used to match a folded dipole antenna

G9C12
Which of the following is a characteristic of using a gamma match with a Yagi antenna?
A. It does not require the driven element to be insulated from the boom
B. It does not require any inductors or capacitors
C. It is useful for matching multiband antennas
D. All these choices are correct

G9D — Specialized antenna types and applications

G9D01
Which of the following antenna types will be most effective as a near vertical incidence skywave (NVIS) antenna for short-skip communications on 40 meters during the day?
A. A horizontal dipole placed between 1/10 and 1/4 wavelength above the ground
B. A vertical antenna placed between 1/4 and 1/2 wavelength above the ground
C. horizontal dipole placed at approximately 1/2 wavelength above the ground
D. A vertical dipole placed at approximately 1/2 wavelength above the ground

G9C07
(C)
Page 7-8

G9C08
(D)
Page 7-8

G9C09
(B)
Page 7-16

G9C10
(D)
Page 7-8

G9C11
(A)
Page 7-9

G9C12
(A)
Page 7-9

G9D01
(A)
Page 7-2

G9D02
(D)
Page 7-2

G9D02
What is the feed point impedance of an end-fed half-wave antenna?
A. Very low
B. Approximately 50 ohms
C. Approximately 300 ohms
D. Very high

G9D03
(C)
Page 7-13

G9D03
In which direction is the maximum radiation from a VHF/UHF "halo" antenna?
A. Broadside to the plane of the halo
B. Opposite the feed point
C. Omnidirectional in the plane of the halo
D. On the same side as the feed point

G9D04
(A)
Page 7-16

G9D04
What is the primary function of antenna traps?
A. To enable multiband operation
B. To notch spurious frequencies
C. To provide balanced feed point impedance
D. To prevent out-of-band operation

G9D05
(D)
Page 7-16

G9D05
What is an advantage of vertically stacking horizontally polarized Yagi antennas?
A. It allows quick selection of vertical or horizontal polarization
B. It allows simultaneous vertical and horizontal polarization
C. It narrows the main lobe in azimuth
D. It narrows the main lobe in elevation

G9D06
(A)
Page 7-16

G9D06
Which of the following is an advantage of a log-periodic antenna?
A. Wide bandwidth
B. Higher gain per element than a Yagi antenna
C. Harmonic suppression
D. Polarization diversity

G9D07
(A)
Page 7-16

G9D07
Which of the following describes a log-periodic antenna?
A. Element length and spacing vary logarithmically along the boom
B. Impedance varies periodically as a function of frequency
C. Gain varies logarithmically as a function of frequency
D. SWR varies periodically as a function of boom length

G9D08
(B)
Page 7-2

G9D08
How does a "screwdriver" mobile antenna adjust its feed point impedance?
A. By varying its body capacitance
B. By varying the base loading inductance
C. By extending and retracting the whip
D. By deploying a capacitance hat

G9D09
(A)
Page 7-16

G9D09
What is the primary use of a Beverage antenna?
A. Directional receiving for MF and low HF bands
B. Directional transmitting for low HF bands
C. Portable direction finding at higher HF frequencies
D. Portable direction finding at lower HF frequencies

G9D10
In which direction or directions does an electrically small loop (less than $\frac{1}{10}$ wavelength in circumference) have nulls in its radiation pattern?
A. In the plane of the loop
B. Broadside to the loop
C. Broadside and in the plane of the loop
D. Electrically small loops are omnidirectional

G9D11
Which of the following is a disadvantage of multiband antennas?
A. They present low impedance on all design frequencies
B. They must be used with an antenna tuner
C. They must be fed with open wire line
D. They have poor harmonic rejection

G9D12
What is the common name of a dipole with a single central support?
A. Inverted V
B. Inverted L
C. Sloper
D. Lazy H

G9D13 [Deleted]

SUBELEMENT G0 — ELECTRICAL AND RF SAFETY
[2 Exam Questions — 2 Groups]

G0A — RF safety principles, rules, and guidelines; routine station evaluation

G0A01
What is one way that RF energy can affect human body tissue?
A. It heats body tissue
B. It causes radiation poisoning
C. It causes the blood count to reach a dangerously low level
D. It cools body tissue

G0A02
Which of the following is used to determine RF exposure from a transmitted signal?
A. Its duty cycle
B. Its frequency
C. Its power density
D. All these choices are correct

G0A03 [97.13(c)(1)]
How can you determine that your station complies with FCC RF exposure regulations?
A. By calculation based on FCC OET Bulletin 65
B. By calculation based on computer modeling
C. By measurement of field strength using calibrated equipment
D. All these choices are correct

G0A04
What does "time averaging" mean when evaluating RF radiation exposure?
A. The average amount of power developed by the transmitter over a specific 24-hour period
B. The average time it takes RF radiation to have any long-term effect on the body
C. The total time of the exposure
D. The total RF exposure averaged over a certain period

G9D10	(B) Page 7-13
G9D11	(D) Page 7-16
G9D12	(A) Page 7-2
G0A01	(A) Page 9-8
G0A02	(D) Page 9-8
G0A03	(D) Page 9-8
G0A04	(D) Page 9-9

G0A05
(A)
Page 9-9

G0A05 [97.13(c)(2), 1.1307(b)]
What must you do if an evaluation of your station shows that the RF energy radiated by your station exceeds permissible limits for possible human absorption?
A. Take action to prevent human exposure to the excessive RF fields
B. File an Environmental Impact Statement (EIS-97) with the FCC
C. Secure written permission from your neighbors to operate above the controlled MPE limits
D. All these choices are correct

G0A06
(A)
Page 9-9

G0A06 [97.13(c)(2), 1.1307(1)(b)(3)(i)]
What must you do if your station fails to meet the FCC RF exposure exemption criteria?
A. Perform an RF Exposure Evaluation in accordance with FCC OET Bulletin 65
B. Contact the FCC for permission to transmit
C. Perform an RF exposure evaluation in accordance with World Meteorological Organization guidelines
D. Use an FCC-approved band-pass filter

G0A07
(A)
Page 9-9

G0A07
What is the effect of modulation duty cycle on RF exposure?
A. A lower duty cycle permits greater power levels to be transmitted
B. A higher duty cycle permits greater power levels to be transmitted
C. Low duty cycle transmitters are exempt from RF exposure evaluation requirements
D. High duty cycle transmitters are exempt from RF exposure requirements

G0A08
(C)
Page 9-9

G0A08 [97.13(c)(2)]
Which of the following steps must an amateur operator take to ensure compliance with RF safety regulations?
A. Post a copy of FCC Part 97.13 in the station
B. Notify neighbors within a 100-foot radius of the antenna of the existence of the station and power levels
C. Perform a routine RF exposure evaluation and prevent access to any identified high exposure areas
D. All these choices are correct

G0A09
(B)
Page 9-9

G0A09
What type of instrument can be used to accurately measure an RF field strength?
A. A receiver with digital signal processing (DSP) noise reduction
B. A calibrated field strength meter with a calibrated antenna
C. An SWR meter with a peak-reading function
D. An oscilloscope with a high-stability crystal marker generator

G0A10
(C)
Page 9-9

G0A10
What should be done if evaluation shows that a neighbor might experience more than the allowable limit of RF exposure from the main lobe of a directional antenna?
A. Change to a non-polarized antenna with higher gain
B. Use an antenna with a higher front-to-back ratio
C. Take precautions to ensure that the antenna cannot be pointed in their direction when they are present
D. All these choices are correct

G0A11
(C)
Page 9-9

G0A11
What precaution should be taken if you install an indoor transmitting antenna?
A. Locate the antenna close to your operating position to minimize feed-line radiation
B. Position the antenna along the edge of a wall to reduce parasitic radiation
C. Make sure that MPE limits are not exceeded in occupied areas
D. Make sure the antenna is properly shielded

G0A12 [1.1307(1)(b)(3)(i)(A)]
What stations are subject to the FCC rules on RF exposure?
A. All commercial stations; amateur radio stations are exempt
B. Only stations with antennas lower than one wavelength above the ground
C. Only stations transmitting more than 500 watts PEP
D. All stations with a time-averaged transmission of more than one milliwatt

G0B — Station safety: electrical shock, grounding, fusing, interlocks, and wiring; antenna and tower safety

G0B01
Which wire or wires in a four-conductor 240 VAC circuit should be attached to fuses or circuit breakers?
A. Only the hot wires
B. Only the neutral wire
C. Only the ground wire
D. All wires

G0B02
According to the National Electrical Code, what is the minimum wire size that may be used safely for wiring with a 20-ampere circuit breaker?
A. AWG number 20
B. AWG number 16
C. AWG number 12
D. AWG number 8

G0B03
Which size of fuse or circuit breaker would be appropriate to use with a circuit that uses AWG number 14 wiring?
A. 30 amperes
B. 25 amperes
C. 20 amperes
D. 15 amperes

G0B04
Where should the station's lightning protection ground system be located?
A. As close to the station equipment as possible
B. Outside the building
C. Next to the closest power pole
D. Parallel to the water supply line

G0B05
Which of the following conditions will cause a ground fault circuit interrupter (GFCI) to disconnect AC power?
A. Current flowing from one or more of the hot wires to the neutral wire
B. Current flowing from one or more of the hot wires directly to ground
C. Overvoltage on the hot wires
D. All these choices are correct

G0B06
Which of the following is covered by the National Electrical Code?
A. Acceptable bandwidth limits
B. Acceptable modulation limits
C. Electrical safety of the station
D. RF exposure limits of the human body

G0B07
(B)
Page 9-14

G0B07
Which of these choices should be observed when climbing a tower using a safety harness?
A. Always hold on to the tower with one hand
B. Confirm that the harness is rated for the weight of the climber and that it is within its
   allowable service life
C. Ensure that all heavy tools are securely fastened to the harness
D. All these choices are correct

G0B08
(B)
Page 9-14

G0B08
What should be done before climbing a tower that supports electrically powered devices?
A. Notify the electric company that a person will be working on the tower
B. Make sure all circuits that supply power to the tower are locked out and tagged
C. Unground the base of the tower
D. All these choices are correct

G0B09
(A)
Page 9-6

G0B09
Which of the following is true of an emergency generator installation?
A. The generator should be operated in a well-ventilated area
B. The generator must be insulated from ground
C. Fuel should be stored near the generator for rapid refueling in case of an emergency
D. All these choices are correct

G0B10
(A)
Page 9-3

G0B10
Which of the following is a danger from lead-tin solder?
A. Lead can contaminate food if hands are not washed carefully after handling the solder
B. High voltages can cause lead-tin solder to disintegrate suddenly
C. Tin in the solder can "cold flow," causing shorts in the circuit
D. RF energy can convert the lead into a poisonous gas

G0B11
(D)
Page 9-8

G0B11
Which of the following is required for lightning protection ground rods?
A. They must be bonded to all buried water and gas lines
B. Bends in ground wires must be made as close as possible to a right angle
C. Lightning grounds must be connected to all ungrounded wiring
D. They must be bonded together with all other grounds

G0B12
(C)
Page 9-4

G0B12
What is the purpose of a power supply interlock?
A. To prevent unauthorized changes to the circuit that would void the manufacturer's warranty
B. To shut down the unit if it becomes too hot
C. To ensure that dangerous voltages are removed if the cabinet is opened
D. To shut off the power supply if too much voltage is produced

G0B13
(A)
Page 9-8

G0B13
Where should lightning arrestors be located?
A. Where the feed lines enter the building
B. On the antenna, opposite the feed point
C. In series with each ground lead
D. At the closest power pole ground electrode

PreppComm
Amateur Radio
www.preppcomm.com
Real preppers use PreppComm™
Morse Code Multi-Band Transceiver
MORSE CODE RADIO TEXTING SYSTEM
Emergency Comm That Works™

MOSLEY ANTENNAS
Mosley
AIRCRAFT GRADE ALUMINUM ELEMENTS & BOOMS and STAINLESS STEEL HARDWARE
STRONG!
Snow, ice or rain are no match for Mosley Quality!
...built to last!
..."a better Antenna!"
Call 800-325-4016
REQUEST A CATALOG
www.mosley-electronics.com
or
www.mosleyelectronics.com

Air Boss Antenna Launcher
$99.99
See Video
www.olahtechnologies.com
When you want your antenna on top
Free shipping to lower 48
Every AirBoss Earns It's Sticker
My Grandfather (KR4LO) instilled in me that you have an obligation to every customer to provide a good quality working product to every buyer. You can buy with confidence knowing that every AirBoss undergoes quality control prior to leaving my shop. All AirBosses are pressure tested and sinker tested prior to receiving its sticker and being packaged.
olahtechnologies@gmail.com

Upgrade to Amateur Extra with
The ARRL Extra Class License Manual
EXTRA CLASS LICENSE MANUAL
www.arrl.org/shop

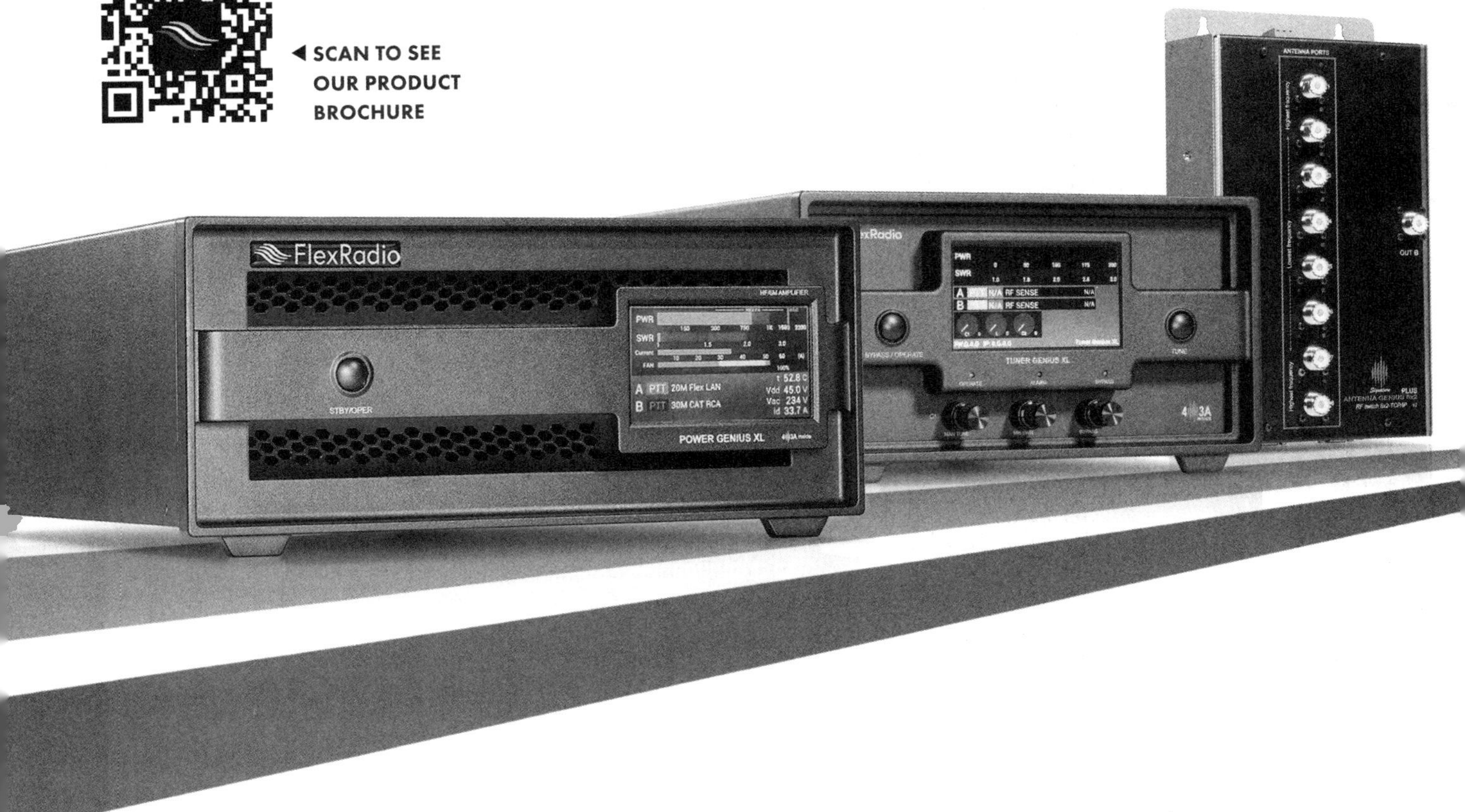

HAM RADIO OUTLET®

WWW.HAMRADIO.COM

*Free Shipping and Fast Delivery!

IC-9700 | *All Mode Tri-Band Transceiver*

• VHF/UHF/1.2GHz • Direct Sampling Now Enters the VHF/UHF Arena • 4.3" Touch Screen Color TFT LCD • Real-Time, High-Speed Spectrum Scope & Waterfall Display • Smooth Satellite Operation

IC-7851 | *HF/50MHz Transceiver*

• 1.2kHz "Optimum" roofing filter • New local oscillator design • Improved phase noise • Improved spectrum scope • Dual scope function • Enhanced mouse operation for spectrum scope

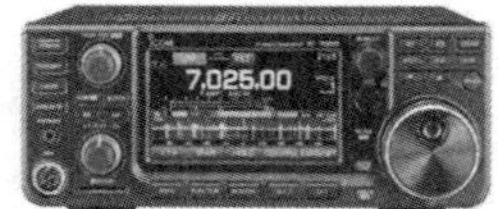

IC-7300 | *HF/50MHz Transceiver*

• RF Direct Sampling System • New "IP+" Function • Class Leading RMDR and Phase Noise Characteristics • 15 Discrete Band-Pass Filters • Built-In Automatic Antenna Tuner

IC-7610 | *HF/50 MHz All Mode Transceiver*

• Large 7-inch color display with high resolution real-time spectrum scope and waterfall • Independent direct sampling receivers capable of receiving two bands/two modes simultaneously

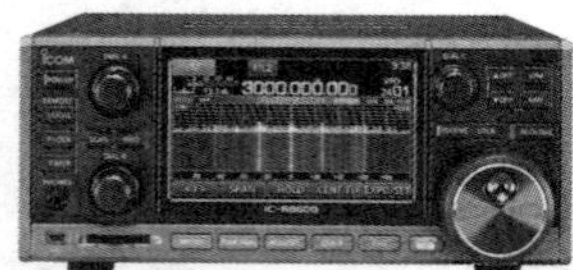

IC-R8600 | *Wideband SDR Receiver*

10 kHz to 3 GHz Super Wideband Coverage • Real-time Spectrum Scope w/Waterfall Function • Remote Control Function through IP Network or USB Cable • Decodes Digital Incl P25, NXDN™, D-STAR • SD Card Slot for Receiver Recorder

IC-718 | *HF Transceiver*

• 160-10M** • 100W • 12V operation • Simple to use • CW Keyer Built-in • One touch band switching • Direct frequency input • VOX Built-in • Band stacking register • IF shift • 101 memories

IC-705 | *HF/50/144/430 MHz All Mode Transceiver*

• RF Direct Sampling • Real-Time Spectrum Scope and Waterfall Display • Large Color Touch Screen • Supports QRP/QRPp • Bluetooth® and Wireless LAN Built-in

IC-7100 | *All Mode Transceiver*

• HF/50/144/430/440 MHz Multi-band, Multi-mode, IF DSP • D-STAR DV Mode (Digital Voice + Data) • Intuitive Touch Screen Interface • Built-in RTTY Functions

IC-2730A | *VHF/UHF Dual Band Transceiver*

• VHF/VHF, UHF/UHF simultaneous receive • 50 watts of output on VHF and UHF • Optional VS-3 Bluetooth® headset • Easy-to-See large white backlight LCD • Controller attachment to the main Unit

ID-5100A Deluxe
VHF/UHF Dual Band Digital Transceiver

• Analog FM/D-Star DV Mode • SD Card Slot for Voice & Data Storage • 50W Output on VHF/UHF Bands • Integrated GPS Receiver • AM Airband Dualwatch

IC-V3500 | *144MHz FM Mobile*

• 65W of Power for Long Range Communications • 4.5 Watts Loud & Clear Audio • Modern White Display & Simple Operation • Weather Channel Receive & Alert Function

IC-2300H | *VHF FM Transceiver*

• 65W RF Output Power • 4.5W Audio Output • MIL-STD 810 G Specifications • 207 alphanumeric Memory Channels • Built-in CTCSS/DTCS Encode/Decode • DMS

IC-V86 | *VHF 7W HT*

• 7W OutputPower Plus New Antenna Provides 1.5 Times More Coverage • More Audio, 1500 mW Audio Output • IP54 & MIL-STD 810G–Rugged Design Against Dust & Water • 19 Hours of Long Lasting Battery Life • 200 Memory Channels, 1 Call Channel & 6 Scan Edges

IC-T10 | *Rugged 144/430 MHz Dual Band*

• Disaster Ready - Excellent Fit for Your Emergency Bag • Loud Audio - New Speaker Design • Long Bettery Life - Up to 11 Hours • FM Broadcast & Weather Channels

ID-52A | *VHF/UHF D-STAR Portable*

• Bluetooth® Communication • Simultaneous Reception in V/V, U/U, V/U and DV/DV • Enriched D-STAR® Features Including the Terminal Mode/Access Point Mode • UHF (225~374.995MHz) Air Band Reception

5 Ways to Shop!

• RETAIL LOCATIONS – Store hours 10:00AM - 5:30PM - Closed Sunday
• PHONE – Toll-free phone hours 9:30AM - 5:30PM
• ONLINE – WWW.HAMRADIO.COM
• FAX – All store locations
• MAIL – All store locations

ICOM

FOLLOW HRO ON SOCIAL MEDIA

twitter.com/HamRadioOutlet
facebook.com/HROHamRadioOutlet
instagram.com/HamRadioOutlet
youtube.com/HamRadioOutlet

HAM RADIO OUTLET

WWW.HAMRADIO.COM

Family owned and operated since 1971

FTDX101MP | *200W HF/50MHz Transceiver*

• Hybrid SDR Configuration • Unparalleled 70 dB Max. Attenuation VC-Tune • New Generation Scope Display 3DSS • ABI (Active Band Indicator) & MPVD (Multi-Purpose VFO Outer Dial) • PC Remote Control Software to Expand the Operating Range • Includes External Power With Matching Front Speaker

FTDX10 | *HF/50MHz 100 W SDR Transceiver*

• Narrow Band and Direct Sampling SDR • Down Conversion, 9MHz IF Roofing Filters Produce Excellent Shape Factor • 5" Full-Color Touch Panel w/3D Spectrum Stream • High Speed Auto Antenna Tuner • Microphone Amplifier w/3-Stage Parametric Equalizer • Remote Operation w/optional LAN Unit (SCU-LAN10)

FT-991A | *HF/VHF/UHF All ModeTransceiver*

Real-time Spectrum Scope with Automatic Scope Control • Multi-color waterfall display • State of the art 32-bit Digital Signal Processing System • 3kHz Roofing Filter for enhanced performance • 3.5 Inch Full Color TFT USB Capable • Internal Automatic Antenna Tuner • High Accuracy TCXO

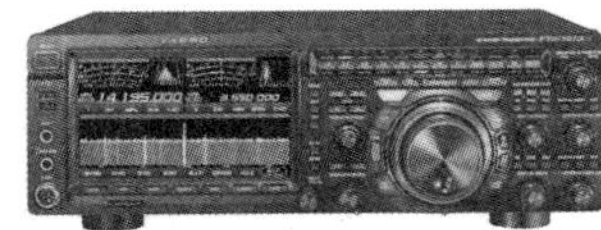

FTDX101D | *HF + 6M Transceiver*

• Narrow Band SDR & Direct Sampling SDR • Crystal Roofing Filters Phenomenal Multi-Signal Receiving Characteristics • Unparalleled - 70dB Maximum Attenuation VC-Tune • 15 Separate (HAM 10 + GEN 5) Powerful Band Pass Filters • New Generation Scope Displays 3-Dimensional Spectrum Stream

FT-710 Aess | *HF/50MHz 100W SDR Transceiver*

• Unmatched SDR Receiving Performance • Band Pass Filters Dedicated for the Amateur Bands • High Res 4.3-inch TFT Color Touch Display • AESS: Acoustic Enhanced Speaker System with SP-40 For High-Fidelity Audio • Built-in High Speed Auto Antenna Tuner

FT-891 | *HF+50 MHz All Mode Mobile Transceiver*

Stable 100 Watt Output • 32-Bit IF DSP • Large Dot Matrix LCD Display with Quick Spectrum Scope • USB Port Allows Connection to a PC with a Single Cable • CAT Control, PTT/RTTY Control

FTM-300DR | *C4FM/FM 144/430MHz Dual Band*

• 50W Output Power • Real Dual Band Operation • Full Color TFT Display • Band Scope • Built-in Bluetooth • WiRES-X Portable Digital Node/Fixed Node with HRI-200

FTM-500DR | *2M/440 Mobile*

• FM, APRS and Digital Voice (C4FM) Operation • Built-in GPS Receiver with 66 Channels • Large Easy-to-Read LCD Display • Front speaker with AESS

FTM-200DR | *C4FM/FM 144/430MHz Dual Band*

• 1200/9600bps APRS® Data Communications • 2" High-Res Full-Color TFT Display • High-Speed Band Scope • Advanced C4FM Digital Mode • Voice Recording Function for TX/RX

FTM-3100R | *Rugged 65W 2M FM Transceiver*

• Rugged & Compact • Crystal Clear Front Panel Audio • 220 Memory Channels • Weather Broadcast Reception • Severe Weather Alert Feature

FT-70DR *C4FM/FM 144/430MHz Xcvr*

• System Fusion Compatible • Large Front Speaker delivers 700 mW of Loud Audio Output • Automatic Mode Select detects C4FM or Fm Analog and Switches Accordingly • Huge 1,105 Channel Memory Capacity • External DC Jack for DC Supply and Battery Charging

FT-5DR *C4FM/FM 144/430 MHz Dual Band*

• High-Res Full-Color Touch Screen TFT LCD Display • Easy Hands-Free Operation w/Built-In Bluetooth© Unit • Built-In High Precision GPS Antenna • 1200/9600bps APRS Data Communications • Supports Simultaneous C4FM Digital • Micro SD Card Slot

FT-65R | *144/430 MHz Transceiver*

Compact Commercial Grade Rugged Design • Large Front Speaker Delivers 1W of Powerful Clear Audio • 5 Watts of Reliable RF Power Within a compact Body • 3.5-Hour Rapid Charger Included • Large White LED Flashlight, Alarm and Quick Home Channel Access

FTM-6000R | *50W VHF/UHF Mobile Transceiver*

• All New User Operating Interface-E2O-III (Easy to Operate-III) • Robust Speaker Delivers 3W of Clear, Crisp Receive Audio • Detachable Front Panel Can Be Mounted in Multiple Positions • Supports Optional Bluetooth® Wireless Operation Using the SSM-BT10 or a Commercially Available Bluetooth® Headset

• RETAIL LOCATIONS – Store hours 10:00AM - 5:30PM - Closed Sunday
• PHONE – Toll-free phone hours 9:30AM - 5:30PM
• ONLINE – WWW.HAMRADIO.COM
• FAX – All store locations
• MAIL – All store locations

YAESU
The radio

ANAHEIM, CA (800) 854-6046	**PORTLAND, OR** (800) 765-4267	**PHOENIX, AZ** (800) 559-7388
MILWAUKEE, WI (800) 558-0411	**WOODBRIDGE, VA** (800) 444-4799	**WINTER SPRINGS, FL** (800) 327-1917
SACRAMENTO, CA (877) 892-1745	**DENVER, CO** (800) 444-9476	**PLANO, TX** (877) 455-8750
NEW CASTLE, DE (800) 644-4476	**SALEM, NH** (800) 444-0047	**ATLANTA, GA** (800) 444-7927

SOTA, POTA, or Shack

Icom has the HF lineup you want

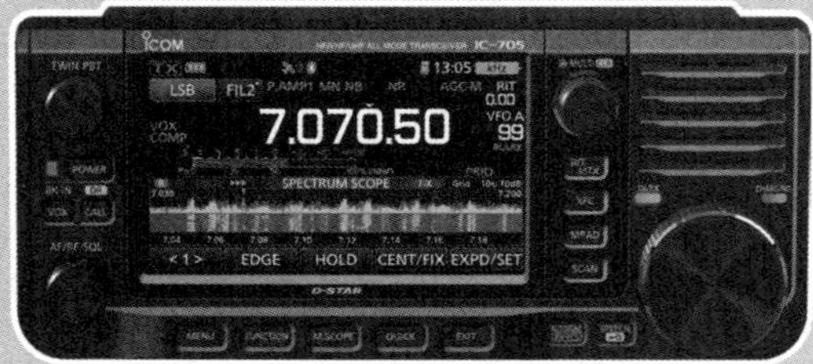

IC-705
HF / 6M / 2M / 70CM Transceiver

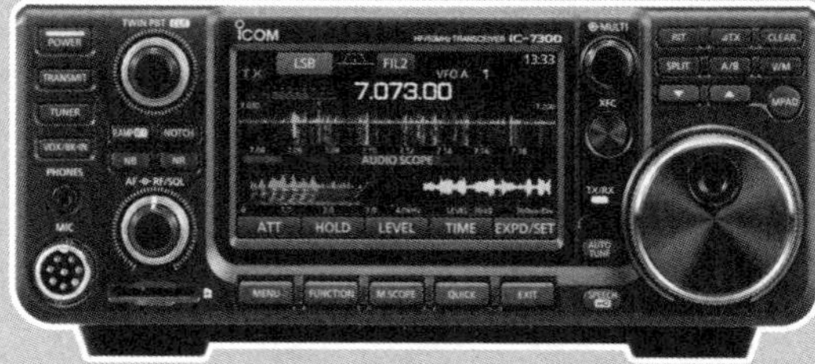

IC-7300
HF / 6M SDR Transceiver

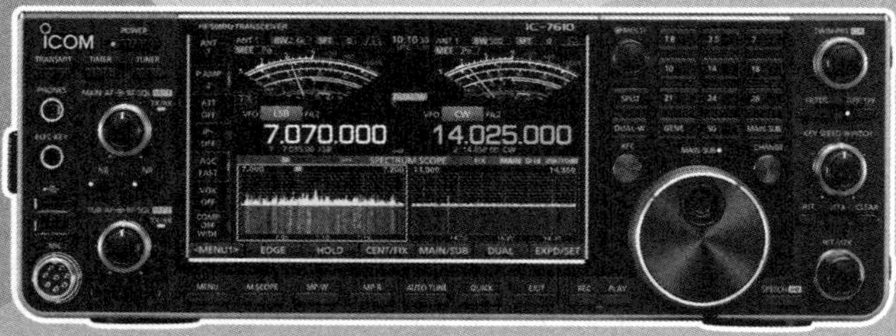

IC-7610
HF / 6M SDR Transceiver

IC-7851
HF / 6M Transceiver

For the love of **ham radio**.

www.icomamerica.com/amateur
insidesales@icomamerica.com

ICOM

CABLE X-PERTS INC. IS A MANUFACTURER OF HIGH-QUALITY CABLE ASSEMBLIES.

We are proud to be a part of Seminole Wire & Cable family of brands which includes JSC brand coaxial cables. We achieve fastest in the industry order delivery by consolidating stock of cables and assembly materials. All raw materials are carefully sourced, and cable is manufactured in Pennsauken, NJ.

OUR PL-259 CONNECTOR IS SPECIFICALLY DESIGNED AND MADE FOR CABLE X-PERTS

RG-8X COAXIAL ASSEMBLY-15YR GUARANTEE

ATTENUATION		KEY FEATURES
MHz	db/100ft	HF applications 1-30 MHz
1	0.3	Maximum 875 Watts
10	0.9	Lightweight and portable
30	2	Direct Burial with waterproof shrink tubing
50	2.3	Standard lengths (ft): 1.5, 3, 6, 9, 12, 18, 25, 50, 75, 100, 150.

RG-213 COAXIAL ASSEMBLY-15YR GUARANTEE

ATTENUATION		KEY FEATURES
MHz	db/100ft	MIL-C-17
10	0.55	Non-Migrating PVC Jacket
50	1.3	LOW LOSS HF COAX
100	1.9	Direct Burial with waterproof shrink tubing
200	2.7	Standard lengths (ft): 1.5, 3, 6, 9, 12, 18, 25, 50, 75, 100, 150.

RG-8/U COAXIAL ASSEMBLY-15YR GUARANTEE

ATTENUATION		KEY FEATURES
MHz	db/100ft	LOW LOSS
10	0.47	Durable UV Resistant, PVC Jacket
50	1.2	1 – 50 MHz or 6 METERS
100	1.8	Direct Burial with waterproof shrink tubing
200	2.7	Standard lengths (ft): 1.5, 3, 6, 9, 12, 18, 25, 50, 75, 100, 150.

400UF COAXIAL ASSEMBLY-15YR GUARANTEE (9913 Type)

ATTENUATION		KEY FEATURES
MHz	db/100ft	LMR-400-UF (BELDEN 9913) TYPE
30	0.8	Non-Migrating PVC Jacket
50	1.1	LOW LOSS UHF/VHF
150	1.8	Direct Burial with waterproof shrink tubing
450	3.3	Standard lengths (ft): 1.5, 3, 6, 9, 12, 18, 25, 50, 75, 100, 150.

DBFLEX400 COAXIAL ASSEMBLY-20YR GUARANTEE

ATTENUATION		KEY FEATURES
MHz	db/100ft	FLEXIBLE LOW LOSS 400
30	0.8	UV and Weather Resistant PE Jacket
50	1.1	LOW LOSS UHF/VHF
150	1.8	Direct Burial with waterproof shrink tubing
450	3.3	Standard lengths (ft): 1.5, 3, 6, 9, 12, 18, 25, 50, 75, 100, 150.

LMR400 TYPE COAXIAL ASSEMBLY-20YR GUARANTEE

ATTENUATION		KEY FEATURES
MHz	db/100ft	LMR-400 TYPE, SOLID CONDUCTOR
30	0.7	UV and Weather Resistant PE Jacket
50	0.9	LOW LOSS UHF/VHF
150	1.5	Direct Burial with waterproof shrink tubing
450	2.7	Standard lengths (ft): 1.5, 3, 6, 9, 12, 18, 25, 50, 75, 100, 150.

SALES AND CUSTOM ASSEMBLIES
1(800)828-3340
WWW.CABLEXPERTS.COM
Look for 'Cable Experts' on Amazon

EVERYWHERE MEANS EVERYWHERE.

As the pioneers of software-defined radios, we didn't set out to change the course of the entire amateur radio industry, but it kind of turned out that way. When you're looking to connect with people and places that may or may not even be on the map, you better have the best technology partner on the planet. We revolutionize for the love of amateur radio and the community that goes along with it. We aim higher and look farther in hopes of creating tools and solutions for things we can't even see just yet. We are your best partner to Find Everywhere. **FlexRadio.com**

THROW A DART AT A MAP. THEN HAVE A MEANINGFUL CONVERSATION WITH THE DART.

6400 | 6400M | 6600 | 6600M | 6700 | MAESTRO